A Dream Come True

A Dream Come True

The Collaboration of David Lynch and Angelo Badalamenti

Stephan Eicke

BLOOMSBURY ACADEMIC
NEW YORK · LONDON · OXFORD · NEW DELHI · SYDNEY

BLOOMSBURY ACADEMIC
Bloomsbury Publishing Inc, 1359 Broadway, New York, NY 10018, USA
Bloomsbury Publishing Plc, 50 Bedford Square, London, WC1B 3DP, UK
Bloomsbury Publishing Ireland, 29 Earlsfort Terrace, Dublin 2, D02 AY28, Ireland

BLOOMSBURY, BLOOMSBURY ACADEMIC and the Diana logo are
trademarks of Bloomsbury Publishing Plc

First published in the United States of America 2025

Copyright © Stephan Eicke, 2025

For legal purposes the Acknowledgments on pp. xii–xiii constitute an
extension of this copyright page.

Cover design: Eleanor Rose
Cover image: Angelo Badalamenti and David Lynch. Photo taken at the 2011 ASCAP
Film & Television Music Awards © Frank Micelotta. By kind permission of the artist

All rights reserved. No part of this publication may be: i) reproduced or transmitted in
any form, electronic or mechanical, including photocopying, recording or by means of
any information storage or retrieval system without prior permission in writing from
the publishers; or ii) used or reproduced in any way for the training, development or
operation of artificial intelligence (AI) technologies, including generative AI technologies.
The rights holders expressly reserve this publication from the text and data mining
exception as per Article 4(3) of the Digital Single Market Directive (EU) 2019/790.

Bloomsbury Publishing Inc does not have any control over, or responsibility for, any
third-party websites referred to or in this book. All internet addresses given in this
book were correct at the time of going to press. The author and publisher regret
any inconvenience caused if addresses have changed or sites have ceased
to exist, but can accept no responsibility for any such changes.

Library of Congress Control Number: 2025932175.

ISBN: HB: 979-8-7651-2905-0
PB: 979-8-7651-2904-3
ePDF: 979-8-7651-2907-4
eBook: 979-8-7651-2908-1

Typeset by Integra Software Services Pvt. Ltd.
Printed and bound in the United States of America

For product safety related questions contact productsafety@bloomsbury.com.

To find out more about our authors and books visit www.bloomsbury.com
and sign up for our newsletters.

Trigger Warning: This is a warning to readers that this book contains sensitive, perhaps
triggering, content, including references to and mentions of abuse, rape, depression,
violence, nuclear explosion, and other potentially disturbing material.

Dedicated to David Lynch, Angelo Badalamenti, John Neff, and Ann Kroeber, who passed away during my work on this book.

CONTENTS

List of Figures ix
List of Tables xi
Acknowledgments xii

Introduction 1

Part I: David. Angelo

1 Sound and Picture Moving Together in Time 5
2 Beautiful but Never Saccharine 19

Part II: David & Angelo

3 I Heard a Few Things About the Ear: *Blue Velvet* 31
4 Fallen Angel: *Twin Peaks* 53
5 Weird on Top: *Wild at Heart* and *Industrial Symphony No. 1* 92
6 Angel Falling: *Twin Peaks: Fire Walk with Me* 121
7 He's Deranged: *Lost Highway* 146
8 Meditation: *The Straight Story* 172
9 Questions in a World of Blue: *Mulholland Drive* 190

Part III: Angelo. David

10 The Most Wonderful Collaborator 219

11 The Logical Continuation of a Trajectory 235

Conclusion 256

Bibliography 259
Index 260

FIGURES

1. Elephant Man Theme (from *The Elephant Man*, 1980) 15
2. Adagio for Strings (1938) 16
3. I Hold No Grudge (1967) 22
4. Face It Girl, It's Over (1968) 23
5. Face It Girl, It's Over—Bar 10 (1968) 24
6. Falling (from *Twin Peaks*, 1990) 25
7. Twin Peaks Theme (from *Twin Peaks*, 1990) 25
8. Danielle of Amsterdam (1969) 27
9. Law and Disorder (from *Law and Disorder*, 1974) 27
10. Nashville Beer Garden (1979) 28
11. Mysteries of Love (from *Blue Velvet*, 1986) 41
12. Sandy and Jeffrey (from *Blue Velvet*, 1986) 43
13. Falling (from *Twin Peaks*, 1990) 56
14. Dark Introduction (from *Twin Peaks*, 1990) 60
15. Love Theme (from *Twin Peaks*, 1990) 62
16. Dance of the Dream Man (from *Twin Peaks*, 1990) 67
17. Audrey's Dance (from *Twin Peaks*, 1990) 69
18. Im Abendrot (from *Vier letzte Lieder*, 1948) 96
19. Dark Spanish Symphony (Edited String Version) (from *Wild at Heart*, 1990) 98

20　Dark Spanish Symphony 50's Version (from *Wild at Heart*, 1990)　99

21　Dark Lolita (from *Wild at Heart*, 1990)　103

22　Theme from Fire Walk with Me (from *Twin Peaks: Fire Walk with Me*, 1992)　129

23　The Voice of Love (from *Twin Peaks: Fire Walk with Me*, 1992)　130

24　Mr. Eddy's Theme II (from *Lost Highway*, 1997)　150

25　Rose's Theme (from *The Straight Story*, 1999)　176

26　Alvin's Theme (from *The Straight Story*, 1999)　178

27　Laurens Walking (from *The Straight Story*, 1999)　179

28　Take Five (1959)　203

29　Mulholland Drive Theme (from *Mulholland Drive*, 2001)　204

30　Diane and Camilla (from *Mulholland Drive*, 2001)　209

31　Heartbreaking (from *Twin Peaks: The Return*, 2017)　249

TABLES

1   Cue Card for the *Twin Peaks* Pilot   78
2   Music Cues in the TV Pilot and the Feature Film   196

ACKNOWLEDGMENTS

Over approximately three years, I assumed the role of researcher and chronicler by investigating the work of artists that poured their talent and soul into films, television shows, and albums. I could do little but marvel at their achievements.

My thanks go to those who took precious time out of their busy schedules in order to speak with me: Barry Adamson, Bob Gosse, Chuck Russell, David Grieco, David Slusser, Dominique Deruddere, Jeremiah Chechik, John Hancock, John Wentworth, Jon Huck, Ken Harrison, Lori Eschler, Mark Pellington, and Randy Thom. You were wonderful, kind, and indulgent.

I was shocked to learn that John Neff passed away not long after I interviewed him. John was about to retire. After some years of hardship, he appeared to have recovered himself and was back where he wanted to be. I wish he could have enjoyed several more years of contentment. He was a kind soul who shared all with me, and I learned a great deal from him about David, engineering, and sound design. May he rest in peace.

I learned of Ann Kroeber's passing shortly before I submitted the final manuscript to my publisher. Ann was a gentle sweetheart, who took me with her to the world of sound and shared countless wonderful memories. Thank you, dear Ann.

Angelo Badalamenti also passed away while I was working on this book. We communicated for a while via e-mail, and I'm deeply grateful for every little nugget he could share. This book is for him, the talented composer who could do it all and touched so many hearts.

David Lynch passed away in January of 2025, after I had submitted my manuscript to Bloomsbury. Fittingly, I had a dream the night before he died: my friends Gary, Matthew, and I were attending an Oscar ceremony with David. We were early, and the auditorium was nearly empty. I took the opportunity to excuse myself. When I returned from the bathroom, David's seat was empty. Gary, who had been sitting next to him, looked at me and held out his hand. "David left, but he asked me to give this to you." Gary handed me a handcrafted bracelet, a skull made out of bones attached to a row of beads. I searched the room. David was gone. I closed my hands around his gift and woke up.

I extend my gratitude to all those whom I did not quote in this book but who enabled me to deliver the work that now lies before you. Etan

Rosenbloom from ASCAP dug out a previously unpublished interview with Angelo which was invaluable since it answered many questions I had wanted to ask Angelo shortly before his passing.

On a more personal note, the years I spent working on this book were turbulent, and my dream would never have come true had it not been for the invaluable help and encouragement of close friends: Matt Townend, who provided company as my fantastic flatmate while we were locked in during the early months of Covid; Achim Esser-Mamat, who gave me food and shelter when I moved back to Germany from the UK; Gary Yershon, who was always curious to hear the latest updates from my research and inspired me; Isabel Grand, the best friend anybody could ask for; Melissa Goodwin, my then-partner, who spurred me on and celebrated with me when Bloomsbury agreed to publish my work.

Andy Morley was indispensable as a friend and colleague. He transcribed the music examples included in this book. He is not only a gifted conductor and beloved teacher but also a valuable support, a kind and warmhearted person whom I'm lucky enough to know.

I have worked with Gary Dalkin as my proofreader and editor for all of my books (English is, after all, my second language), and I cannot imagine ever working without him. He is a tireless fact-checker and a valued sounding board. He made my book leaner, more focused, and overall better.

Thank you Katie Gallof-Houck and Stephanie Grace-Petinos from Bloomsbury, for accepting my book proposal and guiding me through the process warmly and professionally. I always felt I was in the best hands, and I couldn't be happier that we finally had the chance to work together. Katie, do you remember I sent you the proposal for my first book seven years ago, and you rejected it? I'm glad you did. I wasn't ready then.

I'll let the reader judge if I'm ready now.

Introduction

"[David] has that artist mind," says John Wentworth. "His roots are in painting and abstraction and association. He can make associations that you can put on a piece of paper and that make sense. But it's intuitive. You simply have to trust it."[1] Having made his point, he leans back in his chair. Wentworth worked with David Lynch on several projects, starting with *Blue Velvet* as the filmmaker's assistant. He was sound effects recordist for *Wild at Heart*, associate producer and post-production supervisor on *Twin Peaks*, and co-producer on *Twin Peaks: Fire Walk with Me* and on *Mulholland Drive*.

Our interview has led us, inadvertently, to Lynch's *werdegang*, his progression and development as an artist, his mindset and philosophy. Ever since *Eraserhead* premiered, scholars and fans have tried to make sense of his work, to decode it. Reading academic papers and internet forums, my impression has always been that disparate factions have established themselves—individuals or groups that claim to be the holders of the only valid interpretation of Lynch's works. For their analysis it is, of course, irrelevant that Lynch operated from the subconscious and was often not able to explain the meaning behind his images. It is essential to point out this fact when ascribing a "definitive" meaning to his films, shows, songs, and paintings. The subconscious is an essential part of David Lynch the artist. He was fishing in the dark, experimenting until the final cut was locked. In the process, everything could change, long after shooting had wrapped. New possibilities opened up that Lynch reacted to intuitively. Nothing is definitive, nothing is set in stone.

Wentworth nods.

"It's very sad to engage with people who want to approach this kind of work with that kind of mindset. You are right, it's about intuition and association. That's a whole other conversation and it's very particular

---

[1]Author interview with John Wentworth, January 30, 2021.

to David's era and the connection between art, the twentieth-century modernism, film, media," Wentworth explains. After a brief pause, he continues: "He is right in this bridge that is just so interesting. It's about using the tools of abstraction combined with a whole series of technical innovations that make it possible for him to maximize his talents with the tools he is using. It's just phenomenal to watch it."[2]

There are various ways to investigate Lynch's creative approach. One is by examining music and its use in his films. This subject was the starting point of the conversation between John Wentworth and myself. Although David Lynch and Angelo Badalamenti's collaboration lasted close to forty years and brought us popular themes such as "Falling" from *Twin Peaks*, no book had been written about their work and their approach to it. It's especially curious since Lynch became an active, performing musician himself, and is one of the most-discussed American filmmakers of the twentieth and twenty-first centuries. I felt eager to explore the works of Angelo Badalamenti and David Lynch, who in interviews often called themselves brothers.

David Lynch was always wary of talking about his work. Although the Covid-19 pandemic was raging while I was writing this book, and Lynch stayed indoors for several months, he was not available for an interview. Instead, I included excerpts from an interview I conducted with him in 2011 (previously published only in German), and drew on secondary sources. Similarly, I used a previous interview of mine with Angelo Badalamenti in certain parts of this book.

Thanks to several friends and colleagues of both Lynch's and Badalamenti's, I have been able to examine how the duo has approached their music together, and how Lynch continually grew as both musician and sound designer. Thus, *A Dream Come True* is a portrayal of Lynch the filmmaker through an analysis of his use of sound, of music in particular. The book will show how the scores by Angelo Badalamenti came to be, how they were recorded, inserted into the individual films, and mixed. Via analyses and exclusive interviews, I will examine not only how music and sound design set the required mood and enhance emotion, but also how they serve as aspects of storytelling that often give valuable clues to the unlocking of a drama's possible mysteries.

On the way, quintessential questions need to be answered: How does Lynch treat Badalamenti's recordings in the post-production process? How does he capture and manipulate sounds? How does he insert both instrumental compositions and sound design elements to convey a particular atmosphere? To what extent does he pick pre-existing compositions and songs for his films, and to what end? What do these decisions say about both Lynch and Badalamenti as people and artists?

Together, we shall find out.

---

[2] Ibid.

PART ONE

David. Angelo

1

Sound and Picture Moving Together in Time

Every scholar and aficionado of Lynch's work can say with certainty that the inspiration for much of his work lies in his childhood and adolescence. The artist admits as much. *Blue Velvet* especially takes inspiration from the tranquility of the small-town suburbias Lynch grew up in. Of such there were several: born on January 20, 1946, in Missoula, Montana, as the oldest of three children (David, John, Martha), Lynch found it difficult to develop strong roots—his father was a research scientist for the US Department of Agriculture and the family moved a lot. Only two months after Lynch's birth, the family found themselves in Sandpoint, Idaho, albeit briefly. In 1949, they moved to Spokane, Washington; in 1954 to Durham, North Carolina; in 1955 to Boise, Idaho. There they remained for five years. Both Spokane and Boise inspired the young David enormously, even if he was not aware of it at the time. The look of Lumberton in *Blue Velvet*, for example, is inspired by Spokane, by the neighborhood in which the Lynchs lived.[1] In Boise, the would-be-filmmaker had an experience that would haunt him for years and lead to one of the quintessential, most controversial and therefore most discussed moments in *Blue Velvet,* when young David and his brother witnessed a naked woman appearing out of the shadows: "Something was bad wrong with her, and I don't know what happened, but I think she sat down at the curb, crying. It was very mysterious, like we were seeing something otherworldly."[2]

Still, David loved his time in Spokane and Boise. Leaving the tranquility of Middle America outright terrified him. Visiting his grandparents in Brooklyn

---

[1] Rodley, Chris, ed., *Lynch on Lynch* [Revised edition] (Faber and Faber, 2005), p. 139.
[2] *David Lynch: The Art Life*, Dir. Rick Barnes & Olivia Neergaard-Holm & Jon Nguyen, USA: Absurda & Duck Diver Films & Hideout Films & Kong Gulerod Film, 2016 [Film].

instilled pure terror in the young boy. Going down into the subway, young David felt like entering the ninth circle of hell. The "fear of the unknown"[3] held him tightly in its grip.

Although he had a happy childhood and adored his parents, he became increasingly anxious and rebellious. In Alexandria, Virginia, where he spent some of his teenage years, he suffered considerably. He developed spasms of the intestines, started smoking, drinking, and sneaking out of the house at night: "My mother's main saying to me a lot was, 'I'm very disappointed in you.' I was real busy not doing what she wanted, especially when I was in the ninth grade. I got in with a bad bunch and got into a lot of trouble, but I was really living in hell. I had lived two different lives."[4]

The topic of duality is, of course, frequently explored in his films.

Lynch found refuge from his fears in art. In school in Alexandria, he met Toby Keeler whose father was Bushnell Keeler, a professional painter. Bushnell became a second father to Lynch who, in order to paint, spent more and more time at the Keelers' place.

Although Lynch describes his parents as caring and warm,[5] they did not understand his creative endeavors and had little patience for what was most important to their son. It was a conflict for Lynch, who found himself torn.

It was Bushnell Keeler as David's mentor and guardian angel who tried to repair the damage. Keeler took it upon himself to call Lynch's father. The painter informed him that David was a most disciplined student when it came to painting, that he was not goofing around but had found something that he burned for with passion. This phone call created a big impression on Lynch's father who, as a result, gave his son his consent to paint for as long as he wished. David knew this was something he wanted to do in his life and that he would never stop.

Enthralled with painting, in 1964 Lynch had decided to enroll at the School of the Museum of Fine Arts in Boston and, for the young man from Alexandria, the most restless and unfocused time of his life began. The big black dog started following him.

His father helped with the move into a Boston apartment: "Then I went back in my apartment and I never left. It was two weeks before school. I had a transistor radio. So sometimes I listened to music, but I ended up sitting in a chair. The only time I got out of the chair was to pee or eat."[6]

Lynch gathered the little strength he had in him to go to school. The painter found it an uninspiring place and not nearly as creatively nourishing as he had hoped. After a few months in Boston, he left.

---

[3]Breskin, David, "David Lynch," *Rolling Stone* via David Breskin, September 6, 1990, https://davidbreskin.com/magazines/1-interviews/david-lynch-2/ (accessed December 17, 2024).
[4]*David Lynch: The Art Life.*
[5]Lynch, David & McKenna, Kristine, *Room to Dream* (Canongate, 2018), p. 19.
[6]*David Lynch: The Art Life.*

With his friend Toby Keeler, Lynch decided to travel to Europe. He had learned nothing in Boston and felt now was as good a time as any to pay a visit to the painter Oskar Kokoschka, who lived in Switzerland but occasionally taught in Austria. Keeler and Lynch had planned to stay in Europe for three years. However, they were quickly turned off by Salzburg and returned to the United States after only two weeks.

In 1966, he made the fateful decision to move to Philadelphia. The city inspired him endlessly. One of his neighbors was racist and reeked of urine. Another neighbor would walk on her hands and pretend to be a chicken, as Lynch remembered: "She came up to me one day on the street and she said, 'Oh, my nipples hurt,' and she was squeezing her breasts and standing in front of me squeezing and shaking." This wasn't all: "There is a very nice lady with her little boy, a little baby on her lap, out on the stoop. I'm walking by and I said, 'How are you doing?' 'How are you doing, how are you doing?' She turned to her little baby and said, 'You grow up like that and I'm gonna fucking kill ya!'"[7]

The woman imitating a chicken evokes Freddie Jones in his small but memorable cameo in *Wild at Heart*. Similarly, there are many instances in Lynch's films in which a person makes an out-of-the-blue, inappropriate, and therefore absurd statement not unlike the ones he had heard in his neighborhood.

Lynch recognized Philadelphia as his biggest inspiration, although he despised living there and was filled with fear day in and day out. Art remained his refuge. Lynch, by then living with his girlfriend, Peggy Reavey, found great joy in assembling installations. These could consist of mounds of dirt placed inside the house, or of meat slabs on which he poured honey, eager to observe how the food changed its structure after insects had discovered and crawled all over it. His parents grew even more concerned when his father visited him. After seeing what his son created in his basement, Donald Lynch unsuccessfully tried to hide his worry and confusion, the pained expression on his face.[8]

At their parting, he advised his son never to have children. Unbeknownst to both of them, Peggy was already pregnant at the time, and Lynch's first child, Jennifer, was born in April 1968.

Lynch's first short film had been created one year previously. It was entitled *Six Men Getting Sick*. For Lynch, developing a film was only the next natural step as a painter, for he saw film as a moving painting. He would later explain, "Cinema to me is sound and picture moving together in time, and for me it was born out of painting."[9]

---

[7]Ibid.
[8]Ibid.
[9]Friday Arts [PBS WHYY], "Unedited David Lynch Interview," *PBS*, September 10, 2014, https://video.whyy.org/video/friday-arts-unedited-david-lynch-interview/.

In *Six Men Getting Sick*, developed at the Pennsylvania Academy of Fine Arts, six men get sick—six times. Lynch shows their heads and stomachs, the bile in bright red rising up until their stomachs contract and the men vomit. The scenario is underscored by a siren which Lynch used as a sound effect. Lynch—who at the time didn't like to talk and communicated more in grunts and gestures than in proper words, as his girlfriend at the time shared[10]—did not use language in this first short. Evidently, one is unable to talk while vomiting. The sound of the siren as an alarm signal was an obvious choice, not particularly subtle but certainly effective.

Language is essential to Lynch's next short film, *The Alphabet*. Inspired by Reavey's niece, who recited the alphabet in her tormented sleep, the 4-minute short presents itself as a mix of live action and animation. Lynch prepared several paintings and drawings which he then animated. He filmed his girlfriend writhing around in her bed, recorded his infant daughter Jennifer crying, and let a friend recite a nonsensical song. Thus, a new work about the fear of learning came to be, as Lynch himself explained later.[11]

For this new work, Lynch had rented an Uher tape recorder from the Calvin de Frenes-laboratory. After having recorded various sounds, the director noticed that the recorder was broken. The sounds were distorted. Lynch loved it. The mixing and syncing process at Calvin de Frenes was pure magic.[12]

Lynch achieved a distorted wind sound in *The Alphabet*, as well as a sustained, high-pitched buzz, which was a combination of a siren and his daughter's wailing.

His next film, *The Grandmother*, was more ambitious. Having written the script for the 35-minute short, the young father applied for a grant from the American Film Institute. He was successful, and the AFI wired him the proposed budget of $7,200.

The Grandmother is a film heavy with contrasts. Dealing with alienation and isolation, it follows a young boy who grows a grandmother in order to be comforted by her, to escape the violence and neglect in his own household. The contrasts are manifold: while the rooms in the film are painted pitch-black, the bodies of the protagonists are white as snow. The sound design often has nothing to do with what is seen on screen. Lynch uses, for example, a distorted choir when the mother scolds the boy. At other times, there are subtle references to cicadas when the action takes place indoors. In places the sound design explains what we do not see. For example, the boy peeing in his bed is represented acoustically by the rushing of water.

---

[10]Olson, Greg, *David Lynch: Beautiful Dark* (Scarecrow Press, 2011), p. 28.
[11]Rodley, *Lynch on Lynch*, p. 40.
[12]Lynch & McKenna, *Room to Dream*, p. 83.

It was his most mature work to that date. However, his keen ear for sound might never have developed as it did without the assistance and guidance of Alan Splet. Lynch had planned to create the sound for *The Grandmother* at Calvin de Frenes with his friend Bob Column, but Column was busy and suggested Lynch work with his new employee: Alan Splet. They spent sixty-three days, nine hours a day, creating new sounds.[13]

For the grandmother's whistle in Lynch's short, Splet decided to buy an air-conditioning duct three dozen feet long. After Splet had placed his recorder in one end, Lynch whistled into the other. This wasn't enough to receive the desired effect, though. The reverb wasn't sufficiently sustained. Consequently, Splet then played the recording through a speaker, with the sound traveling through the duct. That procedure was repeated several times over the course of several days until Lynch was satisfied. For him, it was important to use raw, organic sounds.

Unsurprisingly, George Stevens Jr., as head of the American Film Institute (AFI), was perplexed by what Lynch delivered. Nevertheless, he suggested to Lynch and Spiet that they apply to the AFI for a scholarship, so they could both work and study in Los Angeles. Both applications were successful.

Following his being awarded the scholarship, Lynch moved with his family to Los Angeles.

The first project David Lynch developed in Los Angeles was *Eraserhead*, like Lynch's previous (short) films, a study of alienation and loneliness. It also deals with the responsibility that comes with being a father, with the burden of having to care for someone with whom one does not feel a strong emotional bond.

Since Lynch's money kept running out on a regular basis, his feature-film debut took five years to complete. Although the director felt comfortable in Los Angeles, he was still in emotional pain, and lived through years of turmoil. At the suggestion of his sister, who recognized how unhappy her brother was, Lynch took up Transcendental Meditation (TM). He claimed it changed his life forever, and he quickly found himself rid of anxiety and pain.[14]

David Lynch, the innocent boy scout from Middle America, found himself afflicted by darkness, but eventually came out the other side—as do several characters in his films, most notably Jeffrey Beaumon in *Blue Velvet*.

Henry, as the main character in *Eraserhead*, also finds his way out of his depression. Lynch's debut feature shows a journey to freedom and therefore happiness. In his films, that journey of cleansing and self-growth

---

[13]Ibid., p. 89.
[14]Ramshaw, Emily, "David Lynch Thinks Transcendental Meditation Can Save Your Life," *Coveteur*, October 12, 2018, https://coveteur.com/2018/10/12/david-lynch-transcendental-meditation-benefits-can-save-life/ (accessed June 19, 2024).

can have a bittersweet end. At the end of that journey stands a death, after all.

Alan Splet's work here is yet more advanced than in *The Grandmother*. It is the sound design in *Eraserhead* that accompanies Henry's journey and acts as a commentator. More than that, it takes the place of music, in that it fulfills at least some of the functions usually ascribed to film music.

> STEPHAN EICKE: *How important would you say is music in your films?*
> DAVID LYNCH: Every element is a 10 so music is a 10. But music isn't a 10 and others are a 7. Every element has got to be as close to the original idea as possible.
> STEPHAN EICKE: *Do you sometimes use music to give the audience clues or is music supposed be neutral in that way?*
> DAVID LYNCH: Music is never completely neutral or you wouldn't put it in. The music fulfills beautiful functions. Many times music is mood and music is emotion.[15]

In *Eraserhead*, sound design is both mood and emotion. Furthermore, it helps to guide the viewer toward an interpretation. Its goal is not to represent reality as seen shot-by-shot, but to reach for a deeper truth.

This can be disorienting at first. Sometimes, the sound atmosphere doesn't change when the location does. Splet's work underlines the sameness of the various areas by creating a soundtrack for the dark hell Henry is walking through. There is a threatening presence looming over all of it, driving Henry down like a depression, like the big black dog that holds him tightly in his grip.

There are other times when the shots change but the sound design remains the same. In the middle of the film, Henry stares forlornly at the cupboard next to his bed. The cupboard has its own sound effect. It becomes a character trait. The whirring noise and the camera lock on said cupboard. Suddenly Lynch cuts to Henry's postbox in the hallway. A few days prior, Henry had taken a letter containing a worm out of the postbox and put it in the cupboard. As he had opened the cupboard, an acoustic presence filled the whole room. Now that acoustic presence returns. Thus, the viewer is reminded of Henry's earlier act. The whirring noise ties the postbox and the cupboard together. Sound design acts as a memory aid.

Throughout the film, the sound design helps create the atmosphere of each scene. Henry's awkward dinner at Mary's place serves as a striking case in point. When the main character arrives, the small house—more a cabin than anything else—is a mess. The furniture is damaged, the carpet

---

[15]Eicke, Stephan, "Silencio! Reise in den Abgrund," *Cinema Musica* 29, no. 3 (2012): pp. 20ff.

dirty, a dog is whining while it feeds its puppies. Equally, the sound design is overbearing and disturbing. The constant rumble represents the clutter Henry finds himself surrounded by.

A few moments later, the dining room is cleared up. Suddenly, a bright tablecloth is laid on the table, a flowerpot stands nearby. The clutter at least momentarily has been replaced by order. The sound design represents the change in arrangement and atmosphere, as all sounds vanish but for a quiet, high hiss from the oven which connects the dining and living rooms.

Shortly before and after the revelation that Mary recently gave birth to a premature infant, everything is in turmoil again, both visually and acoustically. Henry moves to a dark corner with Mary's mother, the walls dirty and dripping with grease. More and more sounds emerge onto the soundtrack. The cleanliness has again been replaced with clutter, both literally and metaphorically.

Henry finally leaves his torment behind him, the pressing, alienating depression that has accompanied him as represented by the overbearing rumble of his neighborhood and the noise of his partner and child. In order to find bliss, he must kill what torments him. This torment is represented by Mary's miscarriage, his own ugly, premature infant that has instilled terror in Henry from the first day he laid eyes on the child. As Henry takes the scissors to cut open the bandages and eventually murders the beast that is lying on his table, a volcano of sound erupts, beginning with a note played on an organ. A cornucopia of noises joins in, as if every sound utilized in the course of the film is now being stacked on top of each other. Henry is in terror as his world implodes, both visually and acoustically. With a Big Bang of sounds, Henry is finally set free. As the noises stack up and eventually explode, the main character of David Lynch's *Eraserhead* finds bliss and happiness. Aurally, the remaining scenes represent a world of quietude and calm. The overbearing rumble is gone.

Lynch and Splet worked in a garage studio with several tape recorders and a console through which every effect created was fed. Effects such as reverb were then added to peak frequencies or reverse sounds. Creating, distorting, and editing the various sounds took Splet and Lynch more than a year. As for *The Grandmother*, every element was supposed to be natural, organic. In order to create the high, hollow sound for the scene in which Henry makes love to his neighbor (with his baby acting as a disruptive force), Splet and Lynch utilized a Sparkletts bottle placed in a bathtub. In the bottle itself, they put a garden hose and a microphone. Lynch then blew air through the hose into the bottle. This created a hollow, high sound that lent the scene the dreamy, ethereal feel they were looking for.

Lynch also experimented with "room tone," something he was always fascinated with, and which he would later explore in all of his films. These tones are the "presence" in a room, the sound that is barely audible, nothing more than a subtle hum, hiss, or drone. The filmmaker uses these very subtle sounds to establish an atmosphere in which the characters live, and thereby builds their world and that of the film as a whole. Part of these room tones can be—and very often are—electricity, running very softly through the wires while the characters go about their daily lives.

The "pure" music in *Eraserhead* is carefully woven into the sound atmosphere even though the sound design itself serves as music by fulfilling its functions in providing mood and emotion. Here, sounds are played live and/or recorded as raw material before they are edited and often transformed by means of, for example, filters and reverb. Later, they are assembled in the form of a montage. Is it still noise or already music?

Part of that soundtrack is jazz by Fats Waller. It's the music Henry himself listens to, the soundtrack that is supposed to either reflect his mood or lift it. (When he enters his apartment and turns on the record player, he places the needle on different parts of the vinyl until he has found the passage he likes to listen to.) Waller's music is like a counterpoint to the threatening rumble of the sound design that hovers over everything. It's tranquil and harmonious, often resonating in the air, when, for example, Henry's focus shifts from the terror of his daily routine to the Lady in the Radiator. She represents everything Henry is seeking: peace, love, and bliss.

For Lynch, there was not a psychological or intellectual reason for placing Fats Waller's music in the film. Like most of his decisions, it was a spontaneous, even subconscious one. Alan Splet had listened to Waller's music, and as soon as Lynch heard it, he knew it had to be in his film as an integral part of its soundtrack. Similarly, the invention of the Lady in the Radiator was entirely accidental, as Lynch admitted:

> I did a drawing of this little woman. I was looking at this little woman and she was a woman that made me feel good. There was a warmth to her. I suddenly got the idea that she lived inside the radiator. […] I went running into Henry's room and looked at the radiator. There was a place in the radiator. […] Probably less than 1 percent of the radiators have a place where someone could live like that.[16]

For the Lady in the Radiator, the imaginary creature living in Henry's mind and dreams, Lynch wrote a simple song, "In Heaven," not dissimilar to later compositions such as "Mysteries of Love," written for *Blue Velvet*, or "Up in Flames" from *Wild at Heart*. ("In heaven / everything is fine / You got your good things / and I've got mine.")

Compared to "Mysteries of Love," "In Heaven" is a more traditional song in that it has a strict meter and its lyrics rhyme. David Lynch's friend Peter Ivers wrote the musical accompaniment and also sang it.

---

[16] *L'image originelle: David Lynch*, Dir. Pierre-Henri Gibert, France: Télérama, 2019 [Film].

David Lynch had hoped to show *Eraserhead* at the Cannes Film Festival. However, it was not selected. The New York Film Festival also rejected it, and when it was finally shown at the Los Angeles Film Festival it became clear why others had been reluctant. It certainly was controversial. The reviewers' reactions ranged from disgusted terror to mild interest to careful praise. Especially conservative reviewers objected to the graphic nature of the film, and quite a few of those who were repulsed by what they understood as the story had their critical judgment clouded by the horror of their instantaneous gut reaction. But *Eraserhead* started to attract a cult following, not least thanks to director John Waters, who had seen the film and urged everybody to seek it out. It became part of the midnight movie circuit and went on to inspire artists and their fans alike.

The year 1977 was an important year for Lynch, an exciting period in which he celebrated both his feature film debut and his wedding. His first wife Peggy and he had separated amicably during the production of *Eraserhead*. The filmmaker had fallen in love with Mary Fisk, the sister of his production designer Jack Fisk, who would become one of Lynch's closest friends and collaborators. For several years, Lynch tried to film his script *Ronnie Rocket* about "a man who's three and a half feet tall, with a red pompadour, who runs on sixty-cycle alternating-current electricity."[17]

Nobody was willing to finance it. Then producer Stuart Cornfeld suggested a script called *The Elephant Man*. Cornfeld handed the screenplay by Christopher De Vore and Eric Bergren to his friend. Lynch fell in love with it on first reading. Based on a true story, *The Elephant Man* examines the relationship between Dr. Frederick Treves and John (Joseph in real life) Merrick, a heavily deformed young man who has been exploited at carnivals for the amusement of others in Victorian England.

Mel Brooks agreed to produce Chris De Vore and Eric Bergren's script with Lynch as director. Since Merrick's was a British story, Brooksfilms set up production in London. They cast Anne Bancroft—an American and Mel Brooks' wife—along with such lauded British stars of screen and stage as John Gielgud and Wendy Hiller. Anthony Hopkins was cast as Dr. Treves.

The Elephant Man is a typical Lynch film insofar that the story is a study of alienation and loneliness. No sound is more important in all of *The Elephant Man* than John Merrick's breathing. It is the sound that introduces Dr. Treves' staff to him. As sound designers, Alan Splet and David Lynch had to show great sensitivity. The breathing is the film's sonic center, not the hiss of gas lamps, the soft pounding of the elevator, the distant rumble of the factories outside the hospital.

Splet's sound design for *The Elephant Man* is less abstract than for *Eraserhead*. It can truly shine when Lynch leaves his characters and captures

---

[17] Lynch & McKenna, *Room to Dream*, p. 161.

a heavily industrialized London, letting the camera glide along heavy tubes and smokestacks. Lynch's fascination for factories, and particularly their noise, was undiminished.

Acoustically, there is never any doubt about which time and place the story is set in. Inside the isolation ward there is a constant, albeit soft, clanging. Outside, the factory noises are ever-present and overbearing. Splet uses these sounds to create a hyper-reality. Instead of simply making audible what can be seen on screen, he adds a layer on top of it. What the viewer sees and hears often defies logic and reason. For example, as Treves walks through dirty neighborhoods to meet John Merrick for the first time, the creaking, rumbling, and clanging of building work accompany him on his journey. It never changes. As he moves further and further away from the camera, it doesn't noticeably decrease in volume. As he moves toward it, it doesn't increase. It's a constant. In *Eraserhead*, as Henry is walking around his neighborhood, it constitutes a similarly overbearing presence. It is a suffocating companion from which there is no escape.

Splet's sound design carefully creates an atmosphere, often evoking an emotion such as dread and so generating suspense. This is particularly evident in the opening scene, which as a metaphorical dream sequence allows Splet and Lynch more creative freedom in their sound design. John Morris's music is slowly replaced by a low rumble and a rhythmic, metallic pounding. However, nothing is visible that would ordinarily make these sounds. The effect is disorienting and emphasizes the surrealism of the images.

While Alan Splet designed both the hard (the rumble of the elevator) and abstract sound effects (the rhythmic pounding during the opening sequence), John Morris wrote the original score. The composer enjoyed an especially close relationship with Mel Brooks, their first collaboration having taken place in the 1950s when they worked on a short-lived Broadway musical entitled *Shinbone Alley*. It would take ten years for them to have their big breakthrough on the screen: in 1967, *The Producers* celebrated its debut. Though barely profitable, it won Brooks and Morris (who wrote the legendary showstopper "Springtime for Hitler" together) much praise and many accolades.

Since *The Elephant Man* was the first motion picture financed by Brooksfilms, Morris was his friend's trusted choice to provide the music. Although David Lynch had no say in the matter, the director would be richly rewarded for the trust he put in the composer's hands.

STEPHAN EICKE: *How did you work with John Morris on The Elephant Man?*

DAVID LYNCH: I love John Morris. I worked with John in a talking way and he did a beautiful, beautiful job.

STEPHAN EICKE: *You never got to work with him again.*
DAVID LYNCH: I never worked with him again but not because I didn't like him or what he did. I just started working with Angelo and that simply took over.[18]

On *The Elephant Man*, Lynch described scenes and moods to Morris who subsequently developed the appropriate thematic material, though the director would later refine his approach of working with a composer. Morris crafted an elaborate concept for the story of John Merrick and Frederik Treves, building his score around two themes. Introduced first, in the opening credits, is a melody in ¾ time: an off-kilter, macabre waltz with a simple melody. Orchestrated like a carnival number with glockenspiel, percussion, and a barrel organ, it shares similarities with the laconic, wry music Nino Rota wrote for Federico Fellini, Lynch's favorite director. The parallels can be found partly in the orchestration, partly in a chromatic slide drawn downwards—a trademark of Rota's.

FIGURE 1 *Elephant Man Theme (from* The Elephant Man, *1980). Transcribed by Stephan Eicke.*

Morris's theme describes, as the title suggests, the "Elephant Man," the "creature" that is put on display by its ruthless master and stared at by paying spectators, who are fascinated and repulsed at the same time. Fittingly, it's a theme that displays an all-pervading sadness, a deep melancholy that not only conveys the atmosphere at the carnival, but also harks back to Merrick's childhood through the use of the glockenspiel, an instrument often used in lullabies and called upon in film music to portray or underscore a child-like innocence.

In contrast to the theme for the "Elephant Man," Morris devised a theme for John Merrick as the refined gentleman who can recite poetry and is respected and welcomed by the people in his immediate environment. In music, the "Elephant Man" becomes a different person. He is transformed from a "creature" to a human being with a beating heart and blood pumping through his veins. Fittingly, the theme is first used as John Merrick recites the psalm that wins over the heart of Gielgud's character, Carr Gomm, and makes him reconsider his initial harsh judgment toward him. Played exclusively by strings without any references to Merrick's background at

---

[18]Eicke, "Silencio! Reise in den Abgrund," pp. 20ff.

the carnival, John Merrick's theme is closer to the gentle lyricism of Gustav Mahler or Ralph Vaughn Williams than to the off-center playfulness of Nino Rota, Carl Orff, or Kurt Weill.

Morris treats the "Elephant Man" and John Merrick as separate entities. In the music and therefore the film, they are different beings.

John Morris had planned to use John Merrick's theme in its most lyrical variation as he decides to lie down and finally sleep like every other human being. The consequence, he knows, will be his death. On the soundtrack album the theme is entitled "Recapitulation." However, Morris wouldn't get the satisfaction of hearing this music in the final cut of the film. David Lynch decided to use Samuel Barber's "Adagio for Strings" instead, a piece he had fallen in love with during the production.

As with most of Lynch's artistic decisions, his insistence on using "Adagio for Strings" stemmed from a gut feeling, an instant emotional reaction. As such, the artist himself cannot justify it with an intellectual explanation. Lynch *felt* it was right. As musicologist Conrado Xalabarder notes in his book, *The Music Script in Film*, Lynch's spontaneous reaction to Barber's piece and his firm decision to use it in his film on emotive grounds only completely dismantle John Morris's concept.[19]

Just as Merrick felt he had found his place in the world, his newly found freedom (appropriately accompanied by Morris's elegant "John Merrick Theme") is about to be destroyed by a gang of abusers. Thus, the composer deconstructs his "Elephant Man" theme: Merrick's construction of his church model is harshly interrupted by the intruding guard and his visitors. He is now no longer John Merrick but again the "Elephant Man." Correspondingly, Morris uses the theme by distorting it heavily to

FIGURE 2 *Adagio for Strings (1938).*
Transcribed by Stephan Eicke.

---

[19]Xalabarder, Conrado, *The Music Script in Film* (Self-published, 2013), p. 25f.

craft a wild, off-kilter ballet. The initially melancholic and somber piece heard in the opening credits is now ruthless and dissonant.

The incident turns out to only be a precursor to an even more alarming sequence: as John Merrick shuffles through Victoria Station, he is attacked by a vicious mob. Underscoring this most brutal scene in the film, Morris presents only brief fragments of his "Elephant Man" theme. Heavily distorted by now, it is barely recognizable. It is the worst experience Merrick has had to go through.

Back home, John Merrick is again John Merrick. Marked by his recent encounters, he is graciously accepted back into the community, one which is larger than ever, as becomes clear when he attends a pantomime. Sitting next to Alexandra, Princess of Wales, and addressed by one of the most celebrated actresses of the time, John Merrick is who he always wanted to be. Having put the finishing touches on his church model, and sensing that his end is near, he decides to go out with dignity. Here, John Merrick's theme would have played, had not Lynch decided against using Morris's musically logical conclusion. The director found Barber's "Adagio for Strings" more powerful emotionally.

John Morris was miffed, as he admitted a few years later.[20] Since the last piece heard before "Adagio for Strings" was the theme for the Elephant Man, John Merrick is denied his dignity in music. The John Merrick theme does not return. The main character dies as the Elephant Man, not as John Merrick.

In his book, Conrado Xalabarder writes: "Lynch saw no other solution than to end the film with a muted version of the 'Elephant Man' theme. In other words, the process of dignifying and humanizing Merrick had not served for anything. He ended up again an animal."[21]

Nevertheless, John Morris was rewarded with an Oscar nomination for his efforts, one of eight the film received.

Following the premiere of *The Elephant Man*, Lynch was inundated with offers. George Lucas discussed producing *The Empire Strikes Back* with Lynch. Eric Bergren and Christopher De Vore wrote *Frances*, a biopic about the actor Frances Farmer, which Lynch briefly pondered directing. Lynch turned down an offer to adapt Robert Harris' *Red Dragon*. *Ronnie Rocket* was still close to his heart, but the financing could still not be attained. He met with producer Dino De Laurentiis, who was planning an adaptation of Frank Herbert's science fiction classic *Dune*.

The exploration of enlightenment in Herbert's *Dune* interested Lynch. Dino De Laurentiis, on the other hand, wanted action. Relying on some

---

[20]Howard, Jeffrey K., "John Morris Interview. Part One," *Film Score Monthly*, The Lost Issue, August 21, 2001, https://www.filmscoremonthly.com/daily/article.cfm?articleID=3502 (accessed June 19, 2024).

[21]Xalabarder, *The Music Script in Film*, p. 26.

rather clunky exposition, Lynch managed to fit in the most obvious and basic plot points of the book into his version. When De Laurentiis cut the film down to 137 minutes (from around three hours), he added a narration to explain the more obvious plot holes.

The shoot quickly became a challenge for Lynch. It was a massively budgeted project, and its producer tried to assert control wherever possible. *Dune* was a commercial and critical failure. As a result, two planned *Dune* sequels were scrapped.

TOTO devised their score with the help of Marty Paich and Allyn Ferguson. Since the members of the group had no experience in orchestration, they had their instrumental rock music transformed into orchestral music by keyboardist David Paich's father Marty, an experienced composer, arranger, and record producer who worked closely with Lynch. Paich was assisted by Ferguson, a successful composer for the large and small screen.

David Lynch also had the chance to work again with his close friend Alan Splet as sound designer. Ironically, *Dune*—Lynch's only straight science fiction venture—didn't allow Splet much creative freedom. Much space on the soundtrack was taken up by hard, diegetic effects due to the busy spectacle on screen. Hence, *Dune* is lacking in abstract effects and soundscapes. With a huge production such as *Dune*, there was no opportunity for sounds to tell the story. Every single sound was entirely bound to the movement on screen. There was no opportunity for sounds to inspire images.

Indubitably, the most positive thing that came out of *Dune* was *Blue Velvet*. Although the former had bombed miserably when it was shown in cinemas, Dino De Laurentiis agreed to finance a passion project of Lynch's, a script he had already written and kept perfecting. The producer would even give the young filmmaker full creative control—in exchange for a meager budget of only $4 million.

Blue Velvet was made on a shoestring budget, and yet it would change David Lynch's life forever. His, and Angelo Badalamenti's.

2

Beautiful but Never Saccharine

Angelo Badalamenti had, by all accounts, a happy childhood. Unlike David Lynch, whose parents initially disapproved of his creative work, Badalamenti's parents, despite their modest income, supported his passion for music by paying for piano lessons.

Badalamenti's grandparents on his mother's side were born just outside Matera in Italy, but emigrated to the United States. Here, they welcomed the birth of their daughter. Badalamenti's father was born in Cinisi, a small town in Sicily. He was five years old when his parents relocated to the United States with him. Several decades later, with the rise of Gaetano Badalamenti, a powerful member of the Sicilian mafia who had his hometown of Cinisi strictly under his thumb, the surname would become infamous in and around Sicily. Angelo once remarked that he and Gaetano may have been fourth or fifth cousins.[1]

Two decades after emigrating the two families became one: Angelo Badalamenti's parents met, fell in love, married, and started a family in Bensonhurst, Brooklyn. Despite modest means, they bought a small house on West 7th Street, then a Jewish neighborhood with its own synagogue.

Angelo Badalamenti was born on March 22, 1937, and from his infancy music played a pivotal role in his life. To him, the most important part of the furniture was the seductive upright player piano which could play music on its own without requiring somebody to touch the keys. It was pure magic.

Could Angelo make a living from music? Since he was constantly surrounded by music, it was difficult for him to imagine doing anything else. His cousin was Vince Badale, a successful trumpet player who blew his horn in Benny Goodman's band, who performed with Harry James and Tony Pastor, as well as on film soundtracks.

---

[1] Unpublished interview with ASCAP, 2012. Used with friendly permission by the American Society of Composers, Authors and Publishers.

Angelo's older brother, Steve—whom the composer credits as his biggest influence—did not make a living as a musician but played jazz trumpet with gusto and encouraged Angelo to stick with music. It was Steve who regularly filled the house in Bensonhurst with music from the bebop era, and who brought home musicians such as flautist Herbie Mann for jam sessions.

Angelo started taking piano lessons at the age of eight. Steve could be merciless, pushing him on. He was successful, as Badalamenti admitted: "When I was eight my piano teacher told my parents, 'This boy has some talent.' I had to practice after school, and I'd look out the window in Bensonhurst at my friends playing stickball, punchball, stoop ball, Johnny on a pony, laughing and having fun—and I'm going 'do re mi … '"[2]

Following his stint at Public School 177, the local elementary school in Bensonhurst, Angelo attended Seth Low Junior High School at the same time as Dan Hedaya. Coincidentally, the latter would become a well-known actor and—half a century later—share the screen with his schoolmate in David Lynch's *Mulholland Drive* as Vincenzo Castigliane. Already in elementary school, Angelo's teachers called on him to perform at special functions in the school's auditorium—a request which he didn't dream of turning down, and fulfilled to the great satisfaction of the audience. The piano would soon be joined by another instrument and, although he hadn't chosen it himself, it didn't take long for him to fall in love with it: "Once I got into junior high school I had a teacher named David Astraf. […] He said, '[…] I know you play piano and I want you to be in the music department. There's an instrument here that requires a very good ear to play. I think this could be good for you.' 'What is it?' 'A French horn.'"[3]

By that time, Angelo had already started composing small pieces on the piano. Inspired by the show tunes he admired, his adolescent pieces foreshadowed his later work in pop, soul, and film. When he grew tired of writing one instrumental piece after another, the young composer went to the high school library and researched poems he could use. Abstract poetry attracted him especially. It delighted him as a reader and suited his musical style.

His teachers pushed him on and supported his composing, albeit not for entirely altruistic reasons. When they needed a processional march for the upcoming graduation, they called on Angelo, who was happy to provide one. His commissioned work was performed in both the years preceding and following his own graduation.

---

[2]Deyneko, Yelena, "Angelo Badalamenti," *Spirit and Flesh Magazine*, March 30, 2015, https://spiritandfleshmag.com/interviews/interview-with-angelo-badalamenti/ (accessed June 19, 2024).
[3]Unpublished interview with ASCAP, 2012. Used with friendly permission by the American Society of Composers, Authors and Publishers.

Badalamenti graduated from Lafayette High School in Brooklyn and subsequently majored in the French horn at Eastman School of Music in Rochester, New York. After two years he enrolled at the Manhattan School of Music from which he received his bachelor's and master's degree.[4]

Angelo Badalamenti made more of his talent as a pianist than as a horn player. In his summer holidays from Eastman he used to drive to the Catskills, where popular resorts played host to entertainers such as Sid Caesar and Louis Armstrong. Badalamenti accompanied various comedians, dancers, and singers on the piano, which required him to learn a wide variety of songs quickly. Efficiency was not the only quality from which he would benefit later in life as songwriter and film composer. Since the entertainers in the Catskills delivered shows often vastly different from each other's, the young Badalamenti, barely out of puberty, had to master a colorful repertoire. Whether it was jazz, pop, classical, or show tunes, he was required to know it all. Even more importantly, Badalamenti learned how to negotiate with both businessmen and artists. Decades later, whenever he had to serve several masters on a film production, he would often remember the tactics he learnt in the Catskills.

Following his graduation from Eastman, Angelo Badalamenti took on a teaching position at the Dyker Heights High School in Brooklyn. Teaching alone would never have satisfied him, though. The young educator was twenty-two years old, had a master's degree in his pocket, and wanted to continue composing.

While he taught at Dyker Heights, Badalamenti kept traveling into Manhattan to play ideas for pop compositions to music publishers. Inspired by his cousin Vincent, he assumed the stage name Andy Badale, thus anglicizing his surname as many artists, especially those with Italian or Jewish names, did at the time. "You didn't want to sound too ethnic," Badalamenti mused.[5]

Since he didn't feel comfortable penning his own lyrics, "Andy Badale" decided to pay for newspaper ads in which he asked for original song texts. The best lyrics he received were written by a man named John Clifford, and the two soon struck up a productive creative relationship by post. When, in 1961, Angelo Badalamenti needed to stage a Christmas play with his sixth and seventh-graders at Dyker Heights, he decided not to use pre-existing material, but write a brand new operetta based on Charles Dickens' *A Christmas Carol*. The lyrics were written by Clifford, who the teacher

---

[4]Badalamenti, Frances, "An Interview with Angelo Badalamenti," *Believer Mag*, August 1, 2019, https://believermag.com/an-interview-with-angelo-badalamenti/ (accessed June 19, 2024).
[5]Marcone, Stephan & Philp, David, "Interview with Angelo Badalamenti," *MusicBiz101*, 2017, https://musicbiz101wp.com/twin-peaks-is-back-our-interview-with-soundtrack-composer-angelo-badalamenti/ (accessed June 19, 2024).

still hadn't yet met in person. The operetta was such a success that shortly thereafter it was performed for the Parent-Teacher-Association at Charles DeWolf Middle School in New Jersey.

By 1966, Angelo Badalamenti had already left his teaching position to follow his dreams. His departure from the school had been made possible by his work on *A Christmas Carol*: following the first television airing of the program, a children's music publisher from New York City asked Angelo Badalamenti for his services. The name of the independent publisher, who would change the educator's life forever, was Frank Stanton.

In his first meeting with Badalamenti, Stanton expressed his wish to publish *A Christmas Carol*, and additionally asked his guest to pen some compositions in the style of Kurt Weill. Badalamenti went home, obliged, and shortly thereafter presented the pieces to his new business partner. Content with what he heard, Stanton agreed to publish these as well. Furthermore, he offered Badalamenti a full-time position as a partner in his company.

Angelo Badalamenti was nothing if not determined, aggressive even when it came to promoting his music. In 1960, Badalamenti had driven down to Broadway to watch *Bye, Bye, Birdie*, the new hit musical with Dick Van Dyke. In the intermission, Badalamenti noticed that Nat King Cole was in the men's room. Without any hesitation, the then-teacher introduced himself to the famous singer as a potential new musical partner. Politely and yet decisively, King Cole informed him that this was neither the time nor the place to conduct business.

Badalamenti didn't change his forward approach, though. Sometimes it proved successful. A few years later, in the mid-1960s, Badalamenti and Clifford wrote two songs they were especially proud of: "I Hold No Grudge," and "He Ain't Coming Home No More." Fumbling through the *Yellow Pages*, Badalamenti stumbled across a listing for Nina Simone Enterprises and decided to pay the High Priestess of Soul a visit. He remembered: "I sing 'Hold No Grudge' and [...] 'He Ain't Comin' Home No More.' She says, 'Okay, give me that lead sheet too—bye, nice meeting you.' On my way out the husband says, 'Come to A&R Studios next Wednesday and you're gonna hear Nina and the piano with forty violins and orchestra, and these two songs.'"[6]

FIGURE 3 *I Hold No Grudge (1967)*.
Transcribed by Stephan Eicke.

---

[6]Deyneko, "Angelo Badalamenti."

As Angelo Badalamenti was walking down to the recording studio in New York City that day in 1967, he could already hear the soulstress intoning "I Hold No Grudge." She accompanied herself on the piano, recording the song in one take.

Badalamenti's style of writing—all the unrestrained emotion he had always been attracted to in Italian operas, and the jazz influences he had picked up by hearing his brother jamming with his friends—naturally attracted Black singers and other artists inspired by them.

He didn't restrict himself to penning soul music, though. In the mid-1960s he partnered with Jean-Jacques Perrey, a pioneer of electronic music. Together, they wrote various instrumental pieces, some of which they used as jingles. One of their compositions was commercially released on Perrey and Kingsley's 1966 LP *The In Sound From Way Out!* Titled "Visa to the Stars," Badalamenti's track features an Ondioline, an electronic keyboard invented in the early 1940s.

In 1967, Badalamenti could even be heard singing in the movies, when *Mondo Balordo (A Fool's World)* was released theatrically in the United States. The American distributor hired Boris Karloff as narrator and let Angelo Badalamenti croon the opening pop song.

A year later, in 1968, the composer celebrated his biggest commercial success so far: "Face It Girl, It's Over," with lyrics penned by music publisher Frank Stanton. The creative duo took the song to Phil Kahl, owner of Diamond Records, for whom Badalamenti had already written "I Want to Love You For What You Are." Kahl didn't understand the lyrics and refused to buy the song, but in one of his many strokes of luck, Badalamenti found the successful music publisher Clyde Otis lounging in the office. He listened to the song and convinced Kahl to pay Stanton and Badalamenti a $250 advance. The demo then found its way to singer Nancy Wilson's producer: "Dave puts on the song, listens to eight bars, takes it off, doesn't say a word, picks up the phone and says, 'Nancy, we found what we have been looking for.'"[7]

FIGURE 4 *Face It Girl, It's Over (1968).*
Transcribed by Stephan Eicke.

---

[7]Unpublished interview with ASCAP, 2012. Used with friendly permission by the American Society of Composers, Authors and Publishers.

"Face It Girl, It's Over" made the pop charts, though it especially delighted Badalamenti and Wilson to land in the Top 5 of the soul chart.

By 1968 Badalamenti had perfected his approach to pop and soul, and "Face It Girl, It's Over" presents itself as a best-of Badalamenti's work up to that time. Its big band jazz provides the song with an energy that constantly drives it forward, while the soaring strings present a soulful, melancholic counterpoint. The main melodic line, laconically sung by Nancy Wilson as a woman who has accepted the situation she finds herself in, has the same bittersweet quality that reviewers would later ascribe to Badalamenti's compositions for David Lynch's work. Already, the composer had fallen in love with the suspensions that make it "distinctly Angelo Badalamenti."[8] When later talking about *Twin Peaks*, Badalamenti explained: "There are a lot of off-center things going on. Like any composer I have the melody on top and the bass on the bottom—but what it [sic] makes it distinctively Angelo Badalamenti is the *middle* stuff, beautiful dissonant things that kind of rub you wrong. Sometimes they resolve, sometimes they don't. It's beautiful but never saccharine."[9]

Suspensions occur frequently in his work: when a note does not fit into a harmonic structure, it creates a dissonance. Said dissonance evokes a tension until it is resolved. Badalamenti finds great joy in delaying the resolution (or, in other words, sustaining the dissonance), and this sustaining of the dissonant note is called suspension. In "Face It Girl, It's Over," it occurs, for example, at the end of the first verse.

In the famous *Twin Peaks* theme ("Falling"), the suspension is particularly obvious, making the piece memorable for its haunting uneasiness. It occurs already in the first bar.

FIGURE 5 *Face It Girl, It's Over—Bar 10 (1968). Transcribed by Stephan Eicke.*

---

[8]Soghomonian, Talia, "Angelo Badalamenti Interview—'Twin Peaks Just Will Not Die'," *NME*, August 20, 2011, https://www.nme.com/blogs/the-movies-blog/angelo-badalamenti-interview-twin-peaks-just-will-not-die-773313 (accessed June 19, 2024).
[9]Ibid.

FIGURE 6 *Falling (from* Twin Peaks, *1990)*.
Transcribed by Stephan Eicke.

FIGURE 7 *Twin Peaks Theme (from* Twin Peaks, *1990)*.
Transcribed by Stephan Eicke.

Badalamenti swiftly continues with his heavy use of suspensions following the famous twangy opening on the Fender Rhodes.

The success of "Face It Girl, It's Over" opened more doors for Angelo Badalamenti and would keep him afloat financially for the next few years. By 1969, he had worked with Nancy Wilson, Ruby Winters, Ronnie Dove, and Nina Simone.

In mid-1973, Angelo Badalamenti and Frank Stanton started work on a show they wanted to take to Broadway. *The Boy Who Made Magic* was based on *The Prince With Many Castles*, a book of fables for children, conceived and written by Sarah Churchill, Baroness Audley, the daughter of the former British prime minister. Churchill was supposed to star in the show, and the team even took the musical on a short tour in 1974. Unfortunately, they could not attain enough financing to set up their production on a big stage for a season. Instead, *The Boy Who Made Magic* saw only a couple of performances within the next few years, among them one in the Haycroft Theater in Washington, DC, in 1977.

In 1973 Badalamenti's good friend Al Elias started work on what would become an animated television series called *It's a Brand New World*. This would eventually air in 1977 to great critical acclaim. Elias conceived the episodes and co-wrote the music for the show. One afternoon, he called on his friend Andy Badale to contribute to the songs. The prolific tunesmith didn't hesitate to accept. Thus, he started to work for the moving image.

Angelo Badalamenti and Al Elias were writing songs in the offices of Palomar Pictures, where at the same time Ossie Davis was directing a film titled *Gordon's War*, a work of blaxploitation. Two years prior, in 1971, *Shaft* had made blaxploitation popular, a hard-hitting sub-genre of exploitation films in which the main characters were Black.

On his own initiative, Badalamenti developed a few themes for the film plus a title song, co-written by Al Elias. When Badalamenti saw Ossie Davis on the lot, he approached him as self-confidently as he had Nina Simone a few years prior. Davis was in a hurry, but agreed to spend a little time listening to the young Italo-American at the piano. It would be worth his while, Badalamenti promised.

Ossie Davis was sold as soon as he heard what would become the song "Child of Tomorrow." But Badalamenti had more in mind. He was well-prepared. Describing a dark night on the streets of Harlem, with drug pushers on the prowl, the composer played a theme he imagined accompanying these images: "Ossie loved it and said, 'You know, this is an all-black film, and I'm thinking about using a brother to score it. Maybe Barry White. But I love what you're playing for me.' And I said, 'Ossie, you know I'm Sicilian. I may not be your brother, but I certainly am your cousin!'"[10]

Ossie Davis laughed and a deal was struck. Angelo Badalamenti would score *Gordon's War* as Andy Badale and write the songs with Al Elias.

While Angelo Badalamenti was working on television shows for Palomar, he also managed to get his hands on a film script called *Law and Disorder* (1974). It was being directed by Ivan Passer, a celebrated Czechoslovakian director who had moved to the United States in the late 1960s. The filmmaker listened to the proposed themes for the main characters. Badalamenti got the job.

What Badalamenti didn't tell Passer was that he had written the theme in 1969. The piece, composed in collaboration with Jean-Jean Perrey, was originally called "Danielle of Amsterdam."

His compositions for the film are a mix of jazz and light symphonic music, with the influence of Kurt Weill clearly audible. Since Badalamenti adored the composer's work and had delighted Frank Stanton with his Weill pastiche in the 1960s, he had found his feet and was on safe ground. The shadow of the German musician, most famous for his collaborations with Bertolt Brecht, looms large in Badalamenti's heavy use of brass and percussion. While neither Weill's nor Badalamenti's music is atonal, it plays deliciously

---

[10]Schweiger, Daniel, "The Madman and His Muse," *Film Score Monthly* 6, no. 8 (2001): p. 25.

FIGURE 8 *Danielle of Amsterdam (1969)*.
Transcribed by Stephan Eicke.

FIGURE 9 *Law and Disorder (from* Law and Disorder, *1974)*.
Transcribed by Stephan Eicke.

with sneaky dissonances, and thus creates an off-kilter atmosphere while it always remains melodious.

Badalamenti's main theme is catchy yet, due to the subtle dissonances that rub against the melodic line, melancholic and sorrowful. Rather than emphasize the comedic elements in the film, the music plays it straight and creates a contrast—an approach Badalamenti would use frequently from then on, both in his work with David Lynch and in comedy films such as *National Lampoon's Christmas Vacation*. It is this sharp contrast—the decision to treat a comedy as a drama—that adds to the humor.

One of the hits Angelo Badalamenti celebrated following his brief stint in movies was "Nashville Beer Garden," a country instrumental that he recorded with a band in 1979. The single sold well. Enthused by its success, in 1981 Badalamenti and Frank Stanton decided to release an LP of compositions in the folk/country mold. The album, put out by Sunbird Records, featured standards such as Jerome Kern's "Look for the Silver Lining" in a new arrangement, as well as "Badale" and Stanton's own compositions ("Annalisa's Dance," "Opryland in Paris," "Silver Sombrero," "Madame Stella Theme," among others).

Despite hits with stars such as Nancy Wilson and Nina Simone, Angelo Badalamenti entered a difficult period in the mid-1980s. At the time, it appeared to him that his biggest successes already lay behind him. He had married his wife Lonny, an artist, in 1968. They had two children who needed to be provided for. Badalamenti's income was declining, and as a freelancer

FIGURE 10 *Nashville Beer Garden (1979).*
Transcribed by Stephan Eicke.

there was never any guarantee he would have another commercial success. Then one afternoon, he received a fateful phone call.

PART TWO

David & Angelo

3

I Heard a Few Things About the Ear

Blue Velvet

Jeffrey Beaumont finds an ear. At first he doesn't know what to do with it. The ear repulses and fascinates him at the same time. Why would an ear simply lie around in a grassy field in this peaceful little town with its white picket fences, clean lawns, and beaming citizens? Is it a real, severed ear, or just a silly, irritating prank? Is it a body part fabricated with silicon and sold in a shop to young boys, who giggle with delight at the thought of giving their granny a fright? Jeffrey decides it must be real, and that it has been there for quite a while indeed: there are small specks of moss on it. Who would have thought a severed ear would ever be found in a town as peaceful as Lumberton?

On that afternoon, Jeffrey Beaumont's journey begins. It is as much a physical journey as it is one of psychological transformation, as in the course of a few hours, the pale-faced boy becomes a man.

Blue Velvet is a film about many things. Hovering above all is the idea of transformation, which Lynch approaches similarly to his earlier exploration of it in his feature debut, *Eraserhead*. Here, in *Blue Velvet*, the main character lives in quiet suburbia, a tranquil place where on the surface everything is calm and everybody is happy. Lumberton is a town untouched by evil. Or so it seems.

It doesn't take a lot of poking for the misery to reveal itself. As long as Lumberton's citizens don't pry, their happiness is not threatened, and they can continue to lead a perfectly content yet superficial existence. Is such a superficial existence worth living? Jeffrey is confronted with his own demons, and those of other people. He grows as he faces them in the course of his journey. He comes out the other side enriched. He meets his love, appreciates the beauty of nature to its fullest, and copes with whatever life throws at him. He has jumped into the deep end, just as David Lynch did some ten years prior to writing *Blue Velvet* when he took up Transcendental Meditation. Meditation is, after all, a practice that allows the individual to dive into their subconscious in order to "transcend," to find clarity and eventually, a happier, calmer existence.

> *It ended up having to be an ear. I never thought about anything else, really. It was so beautiful to find as a ticket to another world and it served also to pull you in and it led to a mind which is kind of interesting. It was a mysterious ticket. I like the shape of the ear. I like the shape of a lot of things. The shape of an ear in a grassy field with ants crawling on it, there's hardly anything better than that. In order to go [to] other dimensions I think you have to pass through something. Maybe there's many different holes that we can go through. This is just one of them.*[1]
>
> DAVID LYNCH

Blue Velvet also deals with incest, with Dorothy Vallens and Frank Booth as stand-ins for Jeffrey's parents, who are notably absent for most of the film. Jeffrey is fascinated when he spies on Dorothy and Frank having sex. They treat Jeffrey as their son. Dorothy takes Jeffrey into her arms like a mother does with her infant before she gives him her breast ("Take my breast and feel it"). Frank, meanwhile, declares his love to Jeffrey by giving him a smack on the lips after having forbidden Jeffrey (as the son) to touch Dorothy (the mother). *Blue Velvet* is ripe with symbolism. Sometimes Lynch spells out what he aims to convey. Frank Booth does not say to Dorothy, "Frank wants to fuck." He says, "Daddy wants to fuck." The incestuous implication is clear. Both Dorothy's father and her son want to sleep with her.

Lynch infused his *Blue Velvet* script with references to one of his favorite films, *The Wizard of Oz*. According to Isabella Rossellini, Lynch named her character Dorothy because of the 1939 classic, in which Judy Garland played a young girl of that same name who is transported into a country far away from Kansas.[2] Much like *The Wizard of Oz*, *Blue Velvet* shows the hero's journey to a different, dangerous place that follows its own logic—a dream logic as opposed to a realistic one. There are multiple events taking place in *Blue Velvet* that cannot be explained rationally (e.g., the dead man in the yellow blazer standing up). *Blue Velvet* is a nightmare that explores depression, violence, and incest while working toward a transformation for

---

[1] *David Lynch: Décembre 88*, Dir. Janine Bazin & André Labarthe & Alain Plagne, France: La sept-art productions, 1989 [Film].
[2] Lynch, & McKenna, *Room to Dream*, p. 218.

its characters into an idyllic world. This ideal realm is a carefree existence in a close-knit community, a harmonic link to nature, a place of pure love where people enjoy a warm relationship to their parents. Ultimately, *Blue Velvet* is a conservative film. The inspiration, Lynch claims, does not stem from his own childhood but from the song by Bobby Vinton chosen by Lynch. It gives the film its title.

> *Sometimes when we listen to music ideas come out of the music. You never know what's going to happen, and it doesn't mean it's the first time you hear the music. On* Blue Velvet *I never liked Bobby Vinton's version of* Blue Velvet, *and then one time I heard it but ideas started coming out of that song. So, music is so fantastic and it's abstract and if you are in a certain place, in a certain mood, and a thing comes on, it can jump so much emotionally and mentally. It's a magical medium.*[3]
>
> DAVID LYNCH

For Lynch, there was no question that he had to play "Blue Velvet" in *Blue Velvet*. Indeed, he used the music in different ways. While Vinton's original recording makes its appearance, Isabella Rossellini's interpretation of the classic crooner's standard provides one of the film's key scenes. Initially, though, her rendition didn't promise to provide the highlight it eventually became. Although Lynch adored Rossellini both as a person (he was dating her at the time) and as a performer, he was aware that her qualities as a singer were lacking. That much became clear to the director as he shot his film in Wilmington. Although Rossellini had already secured the services of a vocal coach, her lessons didn't yield the expected results. Then, producer Fred Caruso had an idea. Ten years previously he had worked as associate producer on *Law and Disorder* and *Gordon's War*. The music had been provided by Angelo Badalamenti, a well-versed composer and lyricist who had worked with internationally renowned singers in the 1960s and 1970s.

By 1985, Badalamenti was worried his peak creative years were behind him. He was living mainly off his royalties, the music scene having changed notably over the past few years, and work as a lyricist and composer was hard to come by. His two children would soon become teenagers and life was getting difficult financially. To make matters worse, his car had just broken down and he couldn't afford to buy a new one. Instead, he decided to spend the $1,000 in his bank account on a used car at an auction. As he was about to leave the house and try his luck as a bidder, his phone rang.

---

[3] International Music Summit, "IMS Engage 2014: David Lynch in Conversation with Moby," *YouTube*, April 24, 2014, https://www.youtube.com/watch?v=IueKCZjOAc8 (accessed June 19, 2024).

STEPHAN EICKE: *How did you get involved in* Blue Velvet?

ANGELO BADALAMENTI: It all started with two producer friends of mine, the line producers Fred Caruso and Peter Runfolo, who worked with Dino De Laurentiis on *Blue Velvet*. I had previously worked with them, composing the music for two feature films very early on. They asked me if I would go to Wilmington, North Carolina, the next day to work with the actress Isabella Rossellini and coach her to sing the title song for the club scene. It was quite urgent. At first I said I couldn't go because I had other obligations. Besides, I told them, "What do you need me for? There are so many piano vocal coaches out there. It's not a big deal!" They said that they had been hiring people to work with her but both David and Isabella were not satisfied with how she was feeling about it. I thought about it for a moment and I said to myself, "There should absolutely be no problem getting a good vocal because Isabella is half Italian. And the whole world knows that all Italians can sing!" I changed my mind and flew down the next day.

STEPHAN EICKE: *Were you familiar with David Lynch's work when you flew down to Wilmington?*

ANGELO BADALAMENTI: The only piece of material that he did and that I was familiar with was *Eraserhead*. I saw it right before I met David. I didn't know his work previous to that. Before we decided to team up—even before starting to work with Isabella Rossellini—the line producer, who is a friend of mine, was talking about various directors and he said, "I am going to work with David Lynch! Have you seen *Eraserhead*?" "No, I haven't. Send it to me!" He did, and I watched it. It was quite overwhelming. I was in my house, it was a dark, dark night full of thunder and lightning. It was full of noise and the house was shaking. I put the video cassette in and there was no one in the home. I turn this movie on and I see this strange infant and all these weird kinds of things. It was a little freaky. But, of course, I appreciated the creativity and saw how unique this man's talent is. At that time I didn't even know I was going to have a relationship with him. I saw *The Elephant Man* after I met David. We already had a relationship. I wanted to know more about David and got the cassette.

STEPHAN EICKE: *What did you make of John Morris's music?*

ANGELO BADALAMENTI: Let me first say that the score of John Morris is so beautiful and sensitive! He was a brilliant composer. Would I have approached the film differently? It is safe to say that no two souls, no two musical souls on this planet, are identical. Considering the fact that David and I have had this experience of working so closely, it would be obvious that some of the writing would turn out to be conceptually different, simply because we are two different people and our style of writing is different. When I came into the picture with David, it was something totally different. But let me repeat myself: Morris's score is much to be admired.

STEPHAN EICKE: *How did you work with Isabella when you came down to the set?*

ANGELO BADALAMENTI: I met with Isabella and sat down at the piano with her. We worked for a couple of hours. I put a little cassette recorder atop of the piano and we recorded the vocal. David Lynch was shooting the last scene of the film when we walked over to the set. We were introduced to each other.[4]

ANGELO BADALAMENTI: David put on his earphones and, as he was listening to our demo, his smile really became broader and broader. And when the tape was finished, he took off his headphones and he said, "That's the ticket. This is peachy keen." And I said to Fred, "What does that mean?" You know, I'm from Bensonhurst—we don't use those words. And then Fred responded, "He adores it."[5]

DAVID LYNCH: Angelo did come down. In the lobby of this little rooming house was a piano. Angelo in one morning got Isabella in sync with the thing. [...] And I looked at Angelo and said, "This is so good we could cut this into the film right now." I thought, "Geez, he's got something."[6]

Indeed, Badalamenti knew how to achieve his desired result, even though he had to play a few tricks in order to get it. After Rossellini had described her character Dorothy to him as somebody who is "transported over the rainbow"[7] when she sings, they started working diligently on the vocal. Still, her performance was not good enough to be played in the film. Taking matters into his own hands, the composer edited the various vocal

---

[4] Eicke, Stephan, "Mein Bruder David," *Cinema Musica* 29, no. 3 (2012): pp. 21ff.
[5] Grow, Kory, "Dream Team: The Semi-Mysterious Story behind the Music of 'Twin Peaks'," *Rolling Stone*, July 25, 2014, https://www.rollingstone.com/music/music-news/dream-team-the-semi-mysterious-story-behind-the-music-of-twin-peaks-78506/ (accessed June 19, 2024).
[6] *Le son de David Lynch*, Dir. Michel Souhaité & Elio Lucantonio, France: Nomad Films, 2007 [Film].
[7] Lynch & McKenna, *Room to Dream*, p. 218.

recordings he and Rossellini had taped by taking the best phrases from each version and cutting them together. Lynch—unaware of how that recording had come about—was delighted. Cinema audiences were stunned by the actress as a singer so much so that for years she would receive invitations to perform at galas.[8] She politely refused.

Since Rossellini's new vocal coach was already present on the film set and able to play the piano, Lynch decided to use him in a cameo. He made his acting debut by accompanying the actress.

> STEPHAN EICKE: *How did it feel being on set?*
>
> ANGELO BADALAMENTI: Everybody wants to be on camera. They say, "I would kill just to be able to walk across the screen—I don't have to say anything!" When you watch *Blue Velvet*, I play piano while Isabella is singing on stage. We have a little trio and you see her. She is right in front of me. I see where the camera is and I notice that she is blocking me out. I say, "My God, the camera is just there!" So I start leaning over to my right and then she is singing and she leans over more. I lean over to my right, so I am really tilted to the right and my hands are all the way to the left on the keyboard. I don't even know how I got to play the notes. David says, "Cut, Cut!" Isabella says, "What is it, David? Am I doing okay, David?" And David says, "You are doing wonderful Isabella, but stay to the left because Angelo is going to fall off!"
>
> STEPHAN EICKE: *Did you make a habit of going on sets?*
>
> ANGELO BADALAMENTI: Sometimes I visit sets, depending on the location of the shoots. I don't go out of my way to go visit sets. I have enough work to do. I live on the East Coast. They could be shooting in LA or in the mountains and I don't need to go there. It doesn't do much for me. Show me what you shot and I will look at it a hundred times.[9]

David Lynch had other uses for Angelo Badalamenti, since the director needed another specific piece of music for his film. After the composer had coached Isabella Rossellini and played his part as on-screen pianist, he received the opportunity to write an original song. Lynch was desperate to use a pre-existing recording by This Mortal Coil titled "Song to the Siren." The piece, written by Tim Buckley and Larry Beckett in 1969 and made famous by Elizabeth Fraser and Robin Guthrie in 1983, was supposed to accompany the pivotal love scene between Sandy and Jeffrey as they slowly dance before they embrace for their first kiss. In their lyrics, Buckley and Beckett refer to Homer's *Odyssey*, the hero sailing through the seas, his ears wide open despite the dire warning that the sirens will seduce and ultimately destroy him.

---

[8]Ibid.
[9]Eicke, "Mein Bruder David," pp. 21ff.

Lynch had heard the ethereal song with its metaphorical lyrics and fallen in love with it. The subject of unrequited love spoke to him. The imagery of sailing into an unknown future, of wanting to embrace someone who is calling out, but who represents something dark and potentially dangerous, would perfectly describe the relationship between Sandy and Jeffrey. By the time the song was to be played in the film, Jeffrey would have walked through the darkness, explored his demons, and come to terms with them.

Just like with Fats Waller's recordings for *Eraserhead* and Barber's *Adagio for Strings* for *The Elephant Man*, Lynch had heard a pre-existing piece and experienced a gut reaction. It just felt right, and no alternative would do, or so Lynch thought when he insisted on using "Song to the Siren" in *Blue Velvet*. There was one problem: the production company was not willing to spend $50,000 on licensing the song, the amount music producer Ivo Watts-Russell demanded. It seemed that this time David Lynch wouldn't get his wish, much to his and "Song to the Siren" co-writer Robin Guthrie's dismay. As Guthrie later explained, he would have loved to be part of *Blue Velvet*: "It all got blown up because Ivo at 4AD, I guess he was in control of the This Mortal Coil project, and he just asked for way too much money ... I regret that because that would have been really cool to be in a David Lynch film, wouldn't it!"[10] Now, the filmmaker needed to consider an alternative. At first Lynch was hesitant to approach Badalamenti. He had proven talented as vocal coach, but there was no guarantee he could write and produce a song that would satisfy the director.

> STEPHAN EICKE: *By the time you were asked to write a new song you still weren't firmly attached as composer of the score, were you?*
> ANGELO BADALAMENTI: No. It makes sense that I was given a trial period because there were multiple tasks that I was asked to do that David needed. I guess I did them to his satisfaction and he was impressed that I came through for him. The first task was my initial work with Isabella Rossellini when no one could be satisfied with how her vocal sounded. Then David asked me—I was in New York, he was in Los Angeles—to record the title song with Isabella singing in New York. I put a band together and I got her to sing the song. The next task, which is probably the most important that happened, was writing that somewhat unusual music to David's somewhat abstract song poem, "Mysteries of Love." The next task was my finding a singer for that song. I was lucky to know Julee Cruise. David asked me for an angelic voice. I worked with Julee so that she would sound like an angel.

---

[10]Staff, "The Music of Twin Peaks," *Post-Punk*, October 6, 2014, https://post-punk.com/the-music-of-twin-peaks/amp/ (accessed June 19, 2024).

STEPHAN EICKE: *Didn't David want to use "Song to the Siren"?*

ANGELO BADALAMENTI: Yes. David took very little money from Dino De Laurenttiis for *Blue Velvet* because he wanted total creative control. He traded that for money. I don't know if he took any money at all or if they just paid his expenses. David also had the right to use any songs he wanted. He was in love with "Song to the Siren" but that cost $50,000 for the sync rights. The line producer—Freddy Caruso—asked me if I could write an original song to replace "Song to the Siren." I said I could, but since I only write music I want the director David write a title and a few lines because if he just gives me a title and a few lines it sets a mood for me and I can do my own music. I remember Freddy took the shot and went to David.

STEPHAN EICKE: *What did David think?*

ANGELO BADALAMENTI: David thought this whole idea was preposterous. He had a song he loved so much—one of his favorite songs of all time—and here the line producer says, "Get this composer and you write some words to replace it!" It made no sense to David. But on the other hand he figured, "Let me sound like I am cooperative. Then I can say I don't like it and they have to pay $50,000 for 'Song to the Siren.'" I told Freddy, "Look, I don't write lyrics and David has been working on this movie for a long time. Why doesn't he write some lines?" Before getting involved with movies, I was also in the business as a songwriter. I had the good sense to say, "Instead of my getting a lyricist to give it a shot, let the director do it." I tell young composers it's not a bad idea to make the director your partner. The director is then predisposed to liking that song better than something else.[11]

STEPHAN EICKE: *Obviously, David eventually gave in.*

ANGELO BADALAMENTI: David was reluctant to agree. Anyway, I am working with Isabella Rossellini in New York and we are recording the *Blue Velvet* song. She comes into the studio and hands me this little piece of yellow paper—which I have framed in my house—that had David's lyrics on it. On top of it, it said "Mysteries of Love." I am looking at it

DAVID LYNCH: I wanted this "Song to the Siren" by This Mortal Coil to be in *Blue Velvet*. And Fred Caruso, bless his heart, looked into it and they wanted a whole lot of money and Fred said, "David, you are always writing these things on pieces of paper. Why don't you write something and send it to Angelo and he'll write

---

[11]Eicke, "Mein Bruder David," pp. 21ff.

and I am saying, "What the heck is that? There is no rhymes, there is nothing. It has no form. It's prose. Maybe it's some kind of an art poem." I was sorry that I said, "Ask this director to write the lyrics," because I am used to writing songs that have hooks in them, things where you can latch on to something. There was nothing to latch on to. It was just words without any lines or form, no structure. I called David and said, "David I got your lyric. Let me tell you something David, it's really something. It's really something!" I don't remember if I said it was a great lyric but I said it was really something. I said, "What kind of music do you want?" He just said, "Just make it like you are on the sea of time and you are floating, soft and warm like the wind." I hear this kind of description and I had no idea what he was talking about. I sat down at the keyboard and out came the music. The bottom line— which is a credit to what David wrote—is that I never changed a single word. I used exactly that and made the music work with it all. He absolutely loved it and met Julee.[12]

a song for this?" I said, "Fred there are 25 trillion songs in the world. I want 'Song to the Siren' by This Mortal Coil. What makes you think I can write these little things on a piece of paper, send it to Angelo and he'll write something that will top that? There is no other song that I want." One thing led to another and eventually I send these little scribbles up to Angelo, these lyrics. Angelo laughed at them. He said, "They don't rhyme, they are not traditional lyrics!" He tried one thing that didn't work, and he said, "What's the problem?" I said, "It's gotta sound angelic, it's gotta float. It's got to have that angelic floating thing." So he got Julee Cruise, and Julee Cruise and Angelo worked on it and then it had this very beautiful feel. I still loved, and always will love, This Mortal Coil's version of "Song to the Siren," but I got to use it in *Lost Highway* after this. But "Mysteries of Love" does have a good feel for this and it's turned out to be in my book a good song.[13]

---

[12]Ibid., p. 22.
[13]Lynch, David, "David Lynch Teaches Creativity and Film," (11 video lessons), *MasterClass*, March 18, 2019, https://www.masterclass.com/classes/david-lynch-teaches-creativity-and-film#details (accessed June 19, 2024).

Born in Creston, Iowa, near Des Moines, Julee Cruise knew from a young age that she wanted to become a musician. At Drake University she studied French horn, just as Angelo Badalamenti had done at Eastman years prior. She was multi-faceted as an instrumentalist. She picked up drums, piano, electric bass, trumpet, and showed a versatility that enabled her to find jobs with the Des Moines Symphony and the Minneapolis Chamber Orchestra. In Minneapolis she joined the Children's Theater Company as an actress. In New York she won a part in Badalamenti's musical *The Boys in the Live Country Band*, although her success was short-lived. At the end of 1983, the musical was staged by the New Theater Works, a developing company, in Greenwich Village. For Badalamenti and his team, it seemed a way to attract investors for a bigger, official staging, as the composer explained: "It's one thing to sit in your office and write your songs or read your book. [...] It's another to see it on its feet, develop it, make the changes. It would've cost us $50,000 to do a showcase and most writers can't afford that. So Musical Theater Works was a fantastic opportunity for us."[14]

Although a producer showed interest in picking up the production, negotiations eventually failed and the show folded. Having admired his sheer talent, the singer gave the composer her phone number after the show's closing, hoping to work with him again. Badalamenti then got in touch with her when he was looking for singers who would be right to record "Mysteries of Love." Badalamenti auditioned quite a few musicians. None of them convinced him. "[Julee] sent a couple of girls to me, and they sang but they simply didn't cut the mustard," Badalamenti admitted.[15] Exasperated, he eventually asked Cruise to demo herself. She got it immediately.

> *Still, I hesitated because I wanted "Song to the Siren," so nothing was going to come up to that, even though I really liked "Mysteries of Love." "Song to the Siren" is sung by Elizabeth Fraser. I hear she's a recluse and is super private, but she has got the stuff. I think it was her boyfriend playing guitar on the song, washed in reverb like crazy, and they conjured magic. It goes into a cosmic kind of thing, while "Mysteries of Love" is warmer and it's for two people. It's got some cosmic thing that opens up, too, but it's warmer.*[16]
>
> DAVID LYNCH

"Mysteries of Love" is indeed warmer than "Song to the Siren," thanks to the heavy, thick chords Badalamenti played on his Fender Rhodes. This

---

[14] Freedman, S. G., "Musical Theater Nurtures Aspiring Students," *The Cincinnati Enquirer* [Cincinnati], January 23, 1984, p. 13.
[15] Grow, "Dream Team."
[16] Lynch & McKenna, *Room to Dream*, p. 234.

Mortal Coil's arrangement is more sparse. There are, however, similarities between the two pieces. Both have abstract lyrics that don't rhyme. In "Mysteries of Love," Lynch shows his affinity for the spiritual, for a cosmic lyricism. The wind, Lynch's favorite sound, also plays an important role in the lyrics. Here, two people who love each other "float in darkness," unable to explain their love until "a wind blows" which resolves everything and enables them to see the light. Love is something mysterious that lights a flame in both parties, in Sandy and Jeffrey who finally admit to themselves that they cannot live without each other.

> SANDY: I had a dream. In fact, it was the night I met you. In the dream there was our world, and the world was dark because there weren't any robins, and the robins represented love. And for the longest time there was just this darkness, and all of a sudden thousands of robins were set free, and they flew down and brought this blinding light of love and it seemed like that love would be the only thing that would make any difference. And it did. So I guess it means there is trouble until the robins come.

FIGURE 11 *Mysteries of Love (from* Blue Velvet, *1986)*. Transcribed by Stephan Eicke.

Pleased with Angelo Badalamenti's composition and arrangement, David Lynch entrusted him with the scoring of *Blue Velvet*. Their song would play a pivotal part in the score. Moreover, Lynch's direction for Badalamenti was to consider Shostakovich's catalog. The Russian composer had inspired Lynch during the writing process. Already in 1984, having finished his third draft, Lynch had noted on the cover of his script to use Shostakovich's *Symphony No. 15* in the film, the composer's last. Badalamenti, who had scored his previous film more than ten years previously, accepted the job gladly, though he admitted to Lynch that he was not even 10 percent as good as Shostakovich. Similarities between Badalamenti's score and Shostakovich's are scarce, except for a fugue and the fact that both the concert work and the main title to *Blue Velvet* are written in a minor key.

Lynch's and Badalamenti's approach to the *Blue Velvet* score was remarkably different from how they would eventually collaborate from *Twin*

Peaks onward. Their working process would develop gradually. On their first film together, their approach to the score was, of all their projects together, the most traditional. As opposed to sitting next to each other at a keyboard—with Lynch conjuring up worlds with his words that Badalamenti would then try and capture in music—the composer simply received a script along with a rough cut of the film. The music was developed based on the latter.

> STEPHAN EICKE: *Do you usually develop ideas based on the individual script?*
> ANGELO BADALAMENTI: On *Blue Velvet* I had a script. I do receive most of the scripts because the producers send it. I simply scan through them without analyzing them. With David, what you are visualizing when reading might be totally different than what ultimately winds up on the screen. You read a story and then what you see is not what you read or how you perceived it would be. That would get me on the wrong track musically.
> STEPHAN EICKE: *Does David tell you anything about a project before you start developing the music together?*
> ANGELO BADALAMENTI: What David would do is give me an idea of a project he is working on. A lot of times David would be telling me, "I got this idea for *Lost Highway*. I got this idea for *Mulholland Drive*," or whatever it is. He will give me an idea. Through his words I gain the insight and the inspiration to compose.[17]

> *Most composers request a script first. But I prefer to see some footage. I'm a more visual person. Seeing how a project is shot, how the actors perform, sensing openings for musical opportunities tells me all I need to know about the feel of a project. In most cases, I would watch a film with the director and then we'd exchange ideas and musical concepts to complement the project. I would then begin writing and we go from there.*[18]
>
> ANGELO BADALAMENTI

Sometimes screenplays proved valuable for Badalamenti. In the case of *Cousins*, a film directed by Joel Schumacher and released in 1989, Badalamenti went through the script and sketched out several musical ideas. The film had not been shot yet, hence the script was his only source of inspiration at the time. Badalamenti developed a demo on synthesizers which Schumacher took with him to the shoot.[19] The actors could then move to a

---

[17]Eicke, "Mein Bruder David," p. 23.
[18]Fensom, Michael, "Angelo Badalamenti: Boonton Composer Makes Music for Movies," *Inside Jersey*, November 18, 2014, https://www.nj.com/inside-jersey/2014/11/angelo_badalamenti_boonton_composer_makes_music_for_movies.htm (accessed June 19, 2024).
[19]Müthing, Thomas, "Ich schreibe in vielen unterschiedlichen Stilen," *FM—Der deutsche Filmmusik-Dienst* Nr. 30, April 1995, Germany. Translation by Stephan Eickel.

specific rhythm, as could the director of photography. The music helped to put the cast and crew in the mood the director wanted to convey on screen. Two years prior to the release of *Cousins*, Badalamenti had already taken that approach with Norman Mailer's *Tough Guys Don't Dance*. Both Schumacher and Mailer not only played their composer's music on set, but then edited their film to that music.

Despite Lynch's deep-rooted admiration for Shostakovich and especially his *Symphony No. 15* (which he had played on set for the actors), Angelo Badalamenti refused to plagiarize the great composer's work. Only a brief fugue in Angelo Badalamenti's score for *Blue Velvet* is vaguely reminiscent of Shostakovich's style, with its low strings in a minor key and the development of a macabre, off-kilter atmosphere. It can be heard as Jeffrey walks down the street at night following his introduction to Sandy. The atmosphere is jolly as they slowly roam the neighborhood. As they tell jokes to each other, Jeffrey's anxiety seems to vanish; the fear he felt as he entered Sandy's house only a few minutes before, is gone.

A variation is used later, in the film's third act, as Jeffrey picks up Sandy at her parents' house. The movie's main theme, which makes its appearance several times, is in its lushness and sweeping gestures (though also in a minor key), close to the sound of Hollywood movies of the 1940s and 1950s, an era Lynch especially appreciates in cinema. Skillfully, Badalamenti combines the symphonic elements of his score with jazz to pay tribute to the aspect of the story concerned with the detective procedural. It foreshadows his work on the *Twin Peaks* show and its cinema prequel, *Fire Walk with Me*, which both lean heavily on layered smokey late night jazz peppered with dissonance.

The whole score is written—or, rather, played—from Jeffrey Beaumont's perspective, accurately capturing the emotions he is experiencing at any given moment. Acoustically, the viewer is put in Jeffrey's shoes. When the hero meets Sandy for the first time, Badalamenti's score is dark and ominous. After all, Jeffrey doesn't see Sandy at first. All he hears is an unfamiliar voice that could possibly belong to a person who presents a threat. Only as Sandy walks out of the shadows of the night does the music open up and blossom. The person who has been speaking has revealed herself as a beautiful young woman. She is Detective Williams' daughter. Similarly, dissonant, brassy chords accompany Jeffrey as he is taken to a joyride by Frank Booth and his gang. What is joyous for them is a threatening excursion for Jeffrey, who sits pressed into the backseat, silent with horror.

In one of the score's highlights, Badalamenti combines diegetic music (music coming from a source in the film, i.e., a live singer or a radio) with

FIGURE 12 *Sandy and Jeffrey (from* Blue Velvet, *1986).*
Transcribed by Andrew Morley.

non-diegetic music (music coming from outside the film itself) by blending the former with the latter. As Dorothy Vallens finishes her rendition of "Blue Velvet," Badalamenti uses the final chords of the song (as played by himself) so that his fingers come crashing down on the keyboard to segue into a non-diegetic piece composed specifically for the film. The transition happens as Sandy and Jeffrey are about to go up to Dorothy's apartment. Although Angelo Badalamenti had only worked on two films previously, his work on *Blue Velvet* shows a composer well-versed in the traditions of and approaches to music for the moving image.

"Mysteries of Love" becomes a crucial part of his instrumental score. Badalamenti uses the composition as a leitmotif for Jeffrey and Sandy's relationship. Accordingly, the first rendition of the song plays as Jeffrey and Sandy sit in a car outside a church. While Sandy speaks, an organ performs an instrumental version of the melody—now, as Sandy describes a dream of robins who represent love, Jeffrey is falling in love with the blonde schoolgirl. The second version of "Mysteries of Love" plays as Sandy and Jeffrey kiss for the first time. The full song, as interpreted by Julee Cruise, is then heard during one of the film's pivotal moments—as the couple dance slowly and happily, embracing warmly and sharing a kiss that cements their romance. Following a rupture in their relationship at the hands of Dorothy Vallens, Sandy quickly assures Jeffrey she forgives him as she sobs into the phone. An instrumental version of the song delivers the appropriate comment. "Mysteries of Love" makes its final appearance as the nightmare ends, as following the death of Frank Booth, Sandy and Jeffrey embrace each other in the hallway. Lynch then cuts to a close-up of Jeffrey's ear. In the next scene, the hero is relaxing in a sun-lounger, attentively observing a robin—the symbol of love—before Sandy calls him inside. Their love has endured. Life is perfect again.

Other songs are used to directly aid the storytelling. The most obvious example is "In Dreams" by Roy Orbison, one of David Lynch's favorite singers, and one of the greatest pop stars of the 1950s.

> *It started that I was riding in a cab with Kyle MacLachlan through Central Park and on the cab radio came "Crying" by Roy Orbison. I thought, wait, that could go in* Blue Velvet, *and as soon as I got down to Wilmington, North Carolina, I got Roy's* Greatest Hits. *I listened to "Crying," and I listened to some more cuts, and then I heard "In Dreams" and everything stopped and I said, If ever there was a song that fit into this film it's this one, "In Dreams," and that started a whole thing going that grew out of this song. Strangely enough, "Crying" came back again in* Mulholland Drive.[20]
>
> DAVID LYNCH

---

[20]FRAME INTO FOCUS, "David Lynch on Roy Orbison's in Dreams," *YouTube*, April 27, 2021, https://www.youtube.com/watch?v=R7zukRlfzh8 (accessed June 19, 2024).

Like most, if not all, of David Lynch's creative decisions, the one to use "In Dreams" in *Blue Velvet* was a spontaneous and intuitive one. The song felt right for the story and atmosphere that Lynch had set out to build. Like most songs used in his works, "In Dreams" does not have one but multiple meanings. Its message changes as the story progresses.

The song appears for the first time as Frank Booth takes Jeffrey for a joyride and visits Ben, the heavily made-up pimp who seems to have known the local gangster for many years. After a brief conversation with Ben, Frank takes out a music cassette and asks Ben to play "In Dreams." The conversation that follows is brief but crucial, not for the story but as a prelude to the song that is about to play: Frank tells Ben about Gordon, a highly skilled confidante of Frank's, who "went right up to them" and "took all those drugs away." Frank emphasizes: "Candy-colored clown they call the sandman. That's me." Candy is used as a slang for drugs, and Frank is in the mood to celebrate his drug-running business. Thus, he puts on Roy Orbison's "In Dreams" with its first line about a "candy-colored clown they call the sandman." In this way "In Dreams" becomes an ode to drug-taking: the dealer tiptoes to his client, careful not to be seen by law-enforcement. After he has supplied the client with drugs, he walks away again, his duties fulfilled, his stardust sprinkled. His promise will come true: the drugs will make his client feel better, smooth over the edges. His client floats away, his pain disappears. He is now "in dreams."

Roy Orbison's original lyrics are more literal: the sandman is the imaginary figure introduced to children by their parents. He is the one who makes boys and girls fall asleep gently. In the song, a man evokes the Sandman. He is desperate to sleep, to dream about his lost love who he can only be with when he is unconscious. In real life, she left him some time ago.

Dreams are a constant topic in David Lynch's work, and *Blue Velvet* is no exception. By the time Jeffrey is taken for a joyride with Frank and his friends, Sandy has already shared her dream of robins with Jeffrey in front of the church. Later, after the encounter with the badly bruised Dorothy Vallens, and following Jeffrey's reassurance to Sandy that he really does love her, Sandy breaks down crying, as she asks herself, "Where is my dream?" She is longing for the Sandman as she is afraid of losing the love of her young life. Sandy knows Jeffrey is about to visit Dorothy Vallens' apartment again. Although the singer won't be there, Sandy knows her boyfriend will put himself in great danger. But he can't help himself. He has unfinished business to resolve. Pure love is the sweetest dream of all—the straightforward journey of two hearts. Sometimes the dream threatens to collapse, to turn into a nightmare.

"In Dreams" plays again after Frank's visit to Ben. In one of the most bizarre, absurd exaggerations of a father-son conflict, Jeffrey punches Frank in the face during their joy ride. The latter doesn't hesitate to drag the young rebel out into the night. As Frank commences threatening Jeffrey, he once again asks for "Candy-colored Clown" to be played. It is not the song's real title. (Dean Hurley, who started work as David Lynch's studio engineer in 2005, later shared that his employer never called songs by their title but by a particularly memorable line. Lynch considered this "emotional pinnacle of the song" its actual title.)[21] After some cursing and screaming, Frank starts quoting the song thereby changing its meaning from when it was first heard a few scenes earlier: Frank makes clear that Jeffrey cannot escape him. Frank will follow him in his dreams. Now, a dream is no longer a metaphor for a heavenly drug experience. Dreams are not an escape either, as Roy Orbison claims as he is crooning in the background. Quite the opposite: Frank will walk with Jeffrey in his sleep and never leave him in peace.

> *Music is going along and it makes pictures form in your mind. If you can build those pictures and put them up and play the music with ... if it gave you a feeling inside your head it might do the same thing to others. You kind of go this way. To make an interpretation or to understand them intellectually is not what it's about.*[22]
>
> DAVID LYNCH

In an earlier monologue, Frank referred to yet another song that will make its appearance a short while later: "Love Letters" as sung by Ketty Lester, an innocuous standard about a lovelorn woman who yearns to be close to her lover as she reads his missives sent from a great distance. Again, Lynch through Frank Booth transforms the song: the gangster—thinking Jeffrey lives next door to Dorothy—forbids the young man to be a "good neighbor." In a speech delivered with great emotional force, the father denies the mother to the son. But what if the son just can't help himself? In that case, Frank as the father will send Jeffrey as the son a love letter straight from his heart—a deadly bullet.

Only in the film's third act does it become apparent that Frank referred to Ketty Lester's "Love Letters." While Jeffrey is in Dorothy's apartment—he has not left her alone as Frank had demanded—the gangster is caught in a shootout with the local police. As the bullets fly, Lynch uses the song on the soundtrack, and thus refers back to Frank Booth's earlier speech. A love letter from his gun was what he meant—it was the father who sent love letters to his son from the heart that is his gun. The appearance of the song in that scene is disorienting at first—not because of its contrast with the violent images but because initially it sounds as if Lester's voice is coming from a radio. Did a radio go on in Dorothy Vallens' apartment after the man in the

---

[21]Lynch & McKenna, *Room to Dream*, p. 420.
[22]*A Conversation with David Lynch, Angelo Badalamenti & Julee Cruise on Industrial Symphony No. 1*, Prod. Warner Reprise, USA: Warner Reprise Home Video, 1990 [VHS].

yellow blazer had hit the lamp to his left side? Lester's voice accompanies the shootout, and the song stops suddenly as Jeffrey leaves the apartment and closes the door behind him. No echo can be heard. The song doesn't fade out or becomes quieter as one would expect when Jeffrey shuts the door. Instead, it stops immediately as if the apartment was sound-proofed. For a diegetic piece, a decrease in volume upon the door closing would have been appropriate. For a non-diegetic piece, a continuation until the end of the scene would have been expected. Lynch does neither. "Love Letters" sits between these two conventions. A hyper-realism is established and dream logic applied. It adds to the surreality of Jeffrey's observations and the situations he finds himself in. *Blue Velvet*, like *The Wizard of Oz*, follows its own road.

Since Dino De Laurentii's budget for *Blue Velvet* was not sufficient to cover the expense of a score recording in Los Angeles or New York, Lynch and Badalamenti decided to go to Prague instead. While the musicians were just as talented behind the Iron Curtain, the costs were considerably lower, which allowed Lynch and Badalamenti to fully execute their creative vision for the music. It was a trip they would never forget. Lynch found it so inspiring that he and his composer would return to the city to record both *Lost Highway* and *Mulholland Drive* there.

ANGELO BADALAMENTI:
The country was still under communist control then, and it was winter when we arrived. [...] The people on the street, the musicians, the house engineers—everyone you met was afraid to speak, and there wasn't a smile on anyone's face. It was so strange. Our hotel rooms were bugged, we were videotaped in the dining room, and there were men in black coats trailing us. We'd walk on icy streets to the studio, and there would be garbage cans in the doorway, then we'd enter a dark hallway with low, flickering lights and

DAVID LYNCH: Angelo and I went to Prague to do the score for *Blue Velvet*, and it was incredible there. There are rooms that have certain kinds of wood and acoustics, and they produce what I call Eastern European air, and it comes into the microphone. It's a sound and a feel, and it's not sad but it's old and it's so beautiful. When Angelo and I went to Prague the communists were still running things, and you're walking down the street and you look into a clothing store and see beautiful dark wood shelves and there would be maybe three sweaters on them. Empty. And bleak. No one talks.

climb a long staircase into an even darker studio room. The mood of the people, the buildings, and the deep quiet were the perfect environment to record music for *Blue Velvet*, and David loved it.[23]	You go into a hotel, there are prostitutes all lined up in the lobby; it was fantastic. And you figure there are cameras and microphones everywhere, you just get this feeling. I'd lie in my bed and listen to see if I could hear high tones. I loved it there.[24]

During the final mix, Lynch fused Alan Splet's sound design with Angelo Badalamenti's music. Oftentimes they are indistinguishable. Shortly before the score recording commenced, Lynch had an idea.

David said, "Angelo, I need some firewood." I said, "What do you mean, firewood?" He said, "I just need you to make long tracks, very slow with very low instruments." I said, "You mean the celli, the basses, the bassoon and the contra-bassoon and contrabass clarinet, all down to hell?" "Yeah, just those instruments. No violins, no piccolos. Record me ten minutes of music, very slow, and use a click track." So I wrote those very long notes, tied all over the place. He said, "That's good, Angelo." Later he said to the engineer, "Play this back half-speed." Now, you are going to play what's already down there at half speed suddenly from the bottom you are way below bottom. "Duuuuuuuum." Then he said to the engineer, "That really sounds cool, but now can you make it quarter speed?" Now, David from that ten minutes has a fifteen- to twenty- minute track of these slow, rumbling sounds. It may work in so many places.[25]

ANGELO BADALAMENTI

Lynch and Badalamenti would make a habit of capturing "firewood" when recording a new score. Sometimes Lynch would play these recordings backwards, slow them down, add reverb. The advance of new, digital technology later allowed Lynch to load the firewood recordings into ProTools, a digital audio workstation, and interlace the orchestral parts with these elements to create a complex collage that capture the required mood for an individual scene.

Blue Velvet was—up to that point—the most challenging project for Lynch and his sound designer Alan Splet regarding the combination of sound

---

[23]Lynch & McKenna, *Room to Dream*, p. 219.
[24]Ibid., p. 234.
[25]*Interview from 2017 with Composer Angelo Badalamenti* in Blue Velvet, Dir. Angie Bucknell, USA: Criterion Collection, 2018 [Blu-ray].

effects and music. Both provide atmosphere and emotion, and Badalamenti's firewood often acts as sound design. Just as in *Eraserhead*, Splet did not simply capture literal, necessary sound effects. In the abstract effects, his talent shines brightly. As Jeffrey walks to Dorothy Vallens's apartment for a second time, a low rumble is clearly audible on the soundtrack. Part of it appears to be low-pitched air being blown into an empty bottle, plus dark, altered basses grinding beneath it. The acoustic atmosphere doesn't change—as one would expect—with the location or shot. As Jeffrey walks up to the apartment, as he enters it, and as Sandy watches the street from outside, Splet's sound design in addition to Badalamenti's firewood remains the same. As a constant, it ignores conventions. The sounds from an unknown source add to the tension on screen. They stop abruptly as the phone rings. Then following Dorothy's brief conversation with Frank Booth, she puts the phone back on its hook and the sounds emerge again, suddenly, almost violently. They stop as she finally discovers Jeffrey in her closet. Here, Badalamenti's original score takes over before fading out. Immediately, Splet's sound effects are injected again as Dorothy walks Jeffrey to her couch. The low rumble on the soundtrack is just as unnerving as Badalamenti's score was with its dense clusters. Music and sound work arm in arm.

Yet another example for how interchangeably sound design and music are used to create mood and emotion can be taken from one of the early scenes in the film: as the camera glides into the grass and joins the crawling ants, it is not dark, frightening music that is playing, but dark, frightening sound effects—a whoosh and a rumble, as terrifying as any avant-garde composition. Similarly, an ominous sound effect drone sets in as Jeffrey walks along the hallway in the local police station and sees the "Yellow Man." Here, it is Splet's sound design that signals danger. Badalamenti's music is absent.

Similarly to Badalamenti's instrumental score, Splet's sound design follows a clear conception: for instance, as Jeffrey walks up the steps to Dorothy Vallens' floor for the first time, the noise of the ventilation system is barely audible. However, it is constant. As the film continues the place—and therefore its sound—becomes progressively more threatening to Jeffrey. The next time he walks up the fire ladder, the sound has increased in volume, though it is still coming from the same source. Even later, the noise of the ventilation system erupts into a dense soundscape that accompanies Jeffrey's nightmare. It creates a violent and disturbing acoustic backdrop to the main character's frightening visions. The next time Jeffrey walks up the ladder, everything has calmed down. The noise of the ventilation system is drowned out by the title song. Although it is still the same building, the area outside Vallens' apartment building has lost a lot of its threat to Jeffrey who has already started to mature and develop a much-needed self-confidence. Like the music, the sound design was designed from Jeffrey Beaumont's perspective.

It does more than raise and sustain tension. The sound design gleefully disorientates the audience: following his beating on the hands of Frank Both, Jeffrey Beaumont wakes up the next morning with his face in the dirt. As he slowly opens his eyes, a strange noise off-screen can be heard. Jeffrey and therefore the audience only find out where they are several moments later. At first, there is confusion. What is this sound? Instead of giving a clue about Jeffrey's location, Splet's sound effect further alienates. It makes it impossible to identify the scenery. Is Jeffery lying in the yard of somebody's house, his face in the gravel of a driveway? The noise as it turns out is from a sprinkler, and yet Jeffrey is not in a house's yard, the sort of place where sprinklers are often used. Accompanied by the repetitive sound, Jeffrey stands up and finally realizes he is in a timber logging yard where the sprinkler keeps stacks of wood wet. Due to Alan Splet and David Lynch's decision to focus on a sprinkler acoustically, the viewer was just as stumped as Jeffrey. Using sounds from the near-by mill would have been too direct, focusing on birds too obtuse.

As intricate and lauded as his work was, Alan Splet had a tough time working on *Blue Velvet*. He, as his wife Ann Kroeber remembers, eventually left the production and instructed his team to finish the work. Kroeber worked as a sound mixer on the film.

STEPHAN EICKE: *Somebody told me that Alan was disturbed by* Blue Velvet.

ANN KROEBER: He was by that movie. That got to him. The sexual violence got to him. It really bothered him. They hadn't a falling out, but it distanced Alan from David a bit. He didn't like that movie. They differed on it.

STEPHAN EICKE: *Did you and Alan talk about it?*

ANN KROEBER: I'm sure we talked about it. You couldn't change what he was feeling. It was his thing. He felt it very strongly.

STEPHAN EICKE: *How did you react to the film, especially to Frank Booth?*

ANN KROEBER: Frank Booth didn't bother me. The violence didn't feel real to me. David was able to communicate it. I got it. I did sense where he was coming from. I liked him as a person. He is a really nice person. There was something really kind about him.

STEPHAN EICKE: *Did you work a lot with Angelo Badalamenti's "firewood," as David calls it?*

ANN KROEBER: I do remember that, yes, exactly. David would come in here and we would play around with it. That was fun. Alan and I had some input when he and David were playing with the recordings.

STEPHAN EICKE: *David would often say how inspired he was by Alan and his approach to sound—*

ANN KROEBER: The way Alan would create sounds was new to David, how he designed things and how we could slow things down, pitch them up. "Low and lower" was the motto often.

STEPHAN EICKE: *You captured some sounds with a Frap microphone, which David loves. What is a Frap and why is it so special?*

ANN KROEBER: The Frap is the size of the first digit of your small finger. It's rectangular. The trick is the beeswax you put on it. The army had developed it. It was a combination of beeswax and something else that you put on the microphone to have it stick to things. The microphone would pick up the vibrations inside of a particular object. You put it on the refrigerator and you hear the inside of the refrigerator. The amount of wax you put on would change the sound.

Someone had told me about the Frap. I was about to work on *Dune*, and I found out that the guy who invented it lived in San Francisco. I went to him and he designed a special Frap microphone just for me. I would go up to listen and say, "That's great but if you can get a little more of this or that." I took it back and it was a total experiment. When I got the microphone I came back to the studio and told Alan about it. He was curious. We just went around with it. We were standing under an air conditioning ventilator overhead. I said, "Maybe we should stick it on that." If you put the Frap on something with metal around it, it would have a metallic sound. It would pick up the metal, the vibrations going through the metal. I put it on this ventilator. What you heard when you were standing there was the normal air-conditioning sound. When we put the Frap on the ventilator, you hear the sound going through the air ducts and the building. It was just incredible. It was symphony going on inside there. Alan thought it was great.

I went around experimenting and trying different things. I put it on heaters, refrigerators, seeing what we could get. […] I got a lot of amazing sounds. Sometimes we mixed the sound of the Frap and the actual sound together to ground it. That was cool to have both. It was a whole new world of creativity and magic going on with that little microphone. I eventually ran out of the beeswax. The inventor passed away and I couldn't get it. People said, use whatever, but it's not the same. It really isn't. It was so transparent. It didn't sound waxy at all. The vibrations were amazing. The beeswax lasted for a long time, though. It lasted years and years. It ran out after Alan died.

STEPHAN EICKE: Blue Velvet *was the last film of David's that Alan worked on …*

ANN KROEBER: He was struggling for a number of years before he died. We all stayed in touch, and I stayed in touch with David after Alan died. David came to the memorial. We were close. It was nice. David would call me up now and again for other films. I was hurt when he didn't ask me to work on his films. It's a male thing. I had a lot of input that could really help, but I'm a girl.[26]

As it would turn out, many critics and members of the audience shared Splet's sensitivity and *Blue Velvet* divided people when it came out in 1986. It took a while for the film to find its audience following its premiere at Telluride Film Festival. Still, it turned an impressive profit for Dino De Laurentiis, grossing nearly $7 million worldwide[27] and receiving mostly favorable reviews.

Following his frustrating time on *Dune* and its disappointing reception, *Blue Velvet* served as Lynch's comeback. He even netted a Best Director nomination at the Oscars, but lost out to Oliver Stone, who took home the award for *Platoon*. With *Blue Velvet* it felt Lynch had finally arrived. *Eraserhead* had been a low-budget independent film popular among a small but devoted crowd, while *The Elephant Man* had been brought to but not developed by him. *Dune* had been a creative disaster for Lynch, a failure which the producer had wrestled away from the director. *Blue Velvet* was pure Lynch. It marked a departure for the former boy scout from Missoula, Montana.

---

[26]Author interview with Ann Kroeber, September 11, 2020.
[27]https://www.imdb.com/title/tt0090756/?ref_=nv_sr_srsg_0 (accessed June 19, 2024).

4

Fallen Angel

Twin Peaks

Although ABC advertised *Twin Peaks* with the question, "Who Killed Laura Palmer?," printed in big letters on posters and other promo materials, the series is not about who killed Laura Palmer. The murder of the beauty queen, wrapped in plastic, swept ashore, was never more than a Hitchcockian McGuffin, something to draw the audience in and let the actual stories unfold. The network had made an inverted soap opera, a *Peyton Place* for a younger generation—filled with shrill, shrewd, and scheming characters.

As many reviews have pointed out since *Twin Peaks* first aired, the mostly absent Laura Palmer was the link that connected everybody in the sleepy titular town. They had nothing in common but their grief for this young dead woman who seemed almost a saint to them. In reality, Laura Palmer was more complex than that.

As Lynch would later depict in *Twin Peaks: Fire Walk with Me*, Laura Palmer was not an untouchable virgin, the beauty queen with a pure heart, but a fallen angel who brought suffering to many people, and who herself had to suffer most of all before and during her tragic demise. *Twin Peaks* is another *Blue Velvet*, in that it looks beneath a glossy surface and shines a bright light into the dark corners of people's perceptions. Under closer investigation, those perceptions change. A glowing smile becomes a deformed grimace, something so terrifying one wants to immediately avert their face. Lynch, of course, forces the viewer to look. You need to see the darkness and fully embrace it in order to make it through alive and sane, to come out the other side.

Yet there is also a lot of light in *Twin Peaks*, in the series and in the town, just as there was a lot of light in Laura Palmer. Lynch's show is a unique mix of suspenseful mystery, absurdist comedy, nightmarish surrealism, and gut-wrenching tragedy. The inhabitants of the seemingly peaceful town of Twin Peaks are united in their grief for the latest homecoming queen. The stories unfold from this starting point like a kaleidoscope of bright colors and patterns.

> *In the case of* Twin Peaks, *Mark Frost and I never intended to solve the murder of Laura Palmer, it may recede into the background but it needed to be there because that was the mystery that enabled everything to happen. And once it was gone, it was over, and the show just drifted. So human beings love mysteries. I love a mystery, that at the end of the mystery, allows you room to dream. Continue the dream.*[1]
>
> DAVID LYNCH

While everybody plots and schemes—behind the fences, in their own homes, between the sheets—FBI Special Agent Dale Cooper and his team of trusted investigators try to solve the mystery of who killed Laura Palmer. The crime investigation and the overtly soap operatic elements of the story involving the town's inhabitants are closely interlinked, creating an intricate spider's web.

The inception of *Twin Peaks* was difficult. It began in 1986, when David Lynch was introduced to writer Mark Frost. They clicked and committed to develop a screenplay together. For United Artists, Lynch and Frost penned *Goddess*, a film about the life and death of Marilyn Monroe. However, nobody was willing to finance their version of the story, not least because the writers had implicated the Kennedys in Monroe's death.[2] After having abandoned *Goddess*, Lynch and Frost started work on an absurdist comedy to be produced by Dino De Laurentiis called *One Saliva Bubble*. Shortly before shooting was slated to begin, with Steve Martin and Martin Short in the leading roles, De Laurentiis announced he had run out of money and could not finance the movie as promised. Next, Lynch and Frost pondered writing a series called *The Lemurians*, about evil creatures who reside on the continent of Lemuria and are being hunted by FBI agents. Although there was interest in the property as a feature film, nobody was willing to bankroll a series. At the end of 1988, they secured financing for another project, with ABC giving the green light for a series called *Northwest Passage*. Conceived as a mix of mystery and soap opera, it was to tell the stories of people in a small town called Twin Peaks.

---

[1] Douridas, Chris, "Interview," *Morning Becomes Eclectic* radio show, broadcast by KCRW on February 19, 1997, https://www.kcrw.com/music/shows/morning-becomes-eclectic/david-lynch-3/ (accessed December 18, 2024).

[2] Breskin, David, "David Lynch," *David Breskin*, June/July 1990, https://davidbreskin.com/books/inner-views/david-lynch-3/ (accessed December 17, 2024).

Buoyed by their collaboration on *Blue Velvet*, David Lynch was eager to continue working with Angelo Badalamenti. *Twin Peaks* would be their biggest commercial and critical success. Its main theme—"Falling"—was an instant hit and became a cult classic. However, "Falling" had not been written originally for *Twin Peaks*. In 1987, the director had taken a meeting with a music agent about producing an album with Julee Cruise and Angelo Badalamenti. Inspired by their experience with "Mysteries of Love," Lynch sought to cowrite further songs for Cruise, and signed a deal at Warner Bros. Records. Two years later the album *Floating into the Night* was released. The second track was titled: "Falling."

> *Once we created "Mysteries of Love," which [Julee] sang, we started putting an album together for her. One of the songs was "Falling." David wrote the lyric called "Falling," and I wrote the melody. I would always ask David to give me a title and a couple of lines. I don't need more than that. "From there I'll create a whole melody and then you play with the lyrics and we go back and forth and collaborate." David gave me a whole bunch of different lyrics, and I wrote eight to twelve songs. They were all right for Julee. We did the* Floating into the Night *album with Julee. "Falling" became the pop song out of that, it was number one in eight countries around the world as a vocal.*[3]
>
> Angelo Badalamenti

In the course of their work on *Floating into the Night*, David Lynch and Angelo Badalamenti refined their approach. When they had developed "Mysteries of Love" for *Blue Velvet*, Isabella Rossellini had simply handed Badalamenti a piece of paper with Lynch's lyrics, from which the composer subsequently developed a song. This time, David Lynch took a more involved approach. He sat down with Badalamenti in his studio in New York City. The latter had his hands on the keyboard as Lynch gave him a word or two—night, or falling, for example. Badalamenti was then instructed to "just noodle around"[4] until Lynch heard a few notes, a motif, or a theme that particularly struck him. The director latched on to a particular phrase and then encouraged his composer to develop it. Bit by bit—by experimenting—a melody emerged that would become the accompaniment for Julee Cruise's vocal.

---

[3]Marcone & Philp, "Interview with Angelo Badalamenti."
[4]*A Conversation with David Lynch, Angelo Badalamenti & Julee Cruise on Industrial Symphony No. 1.*

FIGURE 13 *Falling (from* Twin Peaks, *1990).*
Transcribed by Stephan Eicke.

Lynch liked the evolving mood to be "dreamy."[5] His words influenced Badalamenti's music and vice versa. The music coming out of the composer's keyboard inspired Lynch to daydream and come up with new words based on the images he was seeing in his mind. Badalamenti then fleshed out his sketches, transforming them into arrangements for musicians to play.

By the time *Floating into the Night* was recorded, the composer had become infatuated with the sound of Excalibur Studios, located at 46th Street and 8th Avenue in New York and owned by Artie Polhemus. Here, Badalamenti and Lynch would later also record the music for *Twin Peaks*. The director especially loved the unpretentious venue. It looked slightly run down and was sparsely furnished—the opposite of a corporate recording studio in which the pop stars of the day would feel at home.[6]

David Lynch was present during the recording of *Floating into the Night*, and gave instructions when necessary, though it was important for both him and Badalamenti to leave the musicians creative space, freedom to improvise. Thus, Badalamenti devised a method: first, he played a particular piece in order to convey the mood required. Then he handed over the lead sheets. Sometimes Lynch chimed in. For example, before saxophonist Al Regni even touched the instrument, the filmmaker informed him it needed to sound like "big chunks of plastic."[7] Lynch didn't communicate his ideas in musical terms but via imagery, metaphors, and symbols.

Keyboarder Kinny Landrum was part of the ensemble for the *Floating into the Night* recording sessions. He had been recommended to Badalamenti by Polhemus. It was in fact Landrum who came up with the signature sound of *Falling*, the three opening notes that became synonymous with *Twin Peaks*

---

[5]Ibid.
[6]Stone, Russell Dean, "We Talk to the Man behind the Twin Peaks Soundtracks," *I-D UK*, September 25, 2017, https://i-d.vice.com/en_uk/article/a3k7w4/we-talk-to-the-man-behind-the-twin-peaks-soundtracks (accessed June 19, 2024).
[7]Dellamorte, H., "Twin Peaks Series Retrospective Week 7: Part 1," *YouTube*, April 15, 2013, https://www.youtube.com/watch?v=ltZtyYI-9Uc (accessed June 19, 2024).

and, due to its success, more generally with mystery and intrigue in film and television. As the musician explained:

> I remembered this sort of Duane Eddy twangy guitar sample I had on my Emulator 2. [...] While there were low notes from strings, piano, etc., there wasn't a real bass part on the record. So I said to David, "I have this sort of guitar sound I could play in the bass register." [...] I think I did one take and that was it.[8]

The sound of *Twin Peaks* emerged through the creative freedom Lynch and Badalamenti gave to the musicians. However, "Falling" was not intended, when it was written and recorded, to be put over the opening credits of the television show. The pilot hadn't even been filmed yet. Lynch surprised Badalamenti a year later when he invited him to watch the pilot before its official premiere. By that time, the duo had already developed all the other themes for the series. "Falling" had never been mentioned in their conversations.

> *I don't think there was any thought about* Twin Peaks *[when we worked on* Floating into the Night*] because "Falling" was recorded about a year prior. We were just working with Julee and writing songs. When we recorded, in some cases I actually put an instrumental melody on top of the track. With the vocal, you don't ever play the melody with the singer. So we just happened to have that particular melody. About a year later, much to my surprise, David started to edit* Twin Peaks *and he showed me one of the very first cuts of the show. It was the titles, and what do you know, there's the instrumental of "Falling." Oh my god! He used my instrumentals as the main title theme! I had no earthly idea. He thought that the song should be there. I had nothing to do with it. He heard it and said, "Angelo, this is the title. This is the identity of* Twin Peaks*." It was a dream come true.*[9]
>
> ANGELO BADALAMENTI

The chorus as sung by Julee Cruise in the vocal version was replaced, without Badalamenti's involvement, by a French horn sample played by Kinny Landrum. Music editor David Slusser had suggested it: "They got the titles back for *Twin Peaks*. You are panning across the little town. I was there for every track. They would bring in Kinny Landrum. He was

---

[8] https://www.reddit.com/r/Music/comments/391bfa/i_am_the_twin_peaks_synthesizer_player_and_more/.
[9] Ivie, Devon, "Angelo Badalamenti Tells the Stories behind 5 Twin Peaks Songs," *Vulture*, September 15, 2016, https://www.vulture.com/2016/09/twin-peaks-songs-stories-angelo-badalamenti.html (accessed June 19, 2024).

a keyboardist who, back in those days, the late 80s, had a sample library. Those strings are all sampled in that opening montage." For the pan over the waterfall, Landrum had initially planned to use a cello pad. Slusser had an idea, as he remembered that Badalamenti had played the French horn: "When I saw the waterfall I was thinking of this background watery sound of a French horn, also because I knew that on those primitive libraries you can tell it's a sample when they are playing the cello pads. The French horn was one of the few things where it was hard to tell that it was a sample."[10] David Slusser rarely spoke up during the mix, but this time he had made an exception. The sound of the French horn coming in during the pan across the waterfall was his idea.

Angelo Badalamenti was not surprised the *Twin Peaks* theme caught on. He knew the short motif at the beginning had "that magic"[11] that viewers immediately respond to.

When Badalamenti and Lynch started working on the music for the show, it was still called *Northwest Passage*, and the director had already shot the pilot. Most of the themes were developed away from the picture. Badalamenti relied on his director to sit next to him at the piano and conjure up moods, describe the characters and action.

> STEPHAN EICKE: *How did your working-relationship change from* Blue Velvet *to* Twin Peaks?
>
> ANGELO BADALAMENTI: For our very first collaboration, *Blue Velvet*, the process was very traditional because it was the first time I met him and I didn't know him. I was a babe in the woods anyway because I had only done a couple of scores before. When it came to *Blue Velvet*, I then found it's more traditional where you sit down with the director. You spot the film and David would say, "Let the music start here." He would give me an idea about it. I would then go home, write the music and record it. That was the only traditional one. Since then our working process has been David would sit next to me at the keyboard and to this day just talk to me very slowly and very softly—usually in my right ear as I am sitting at the keyboard because he sits to the right of me. What he does is he paints a verbal picture that would suggest a mood. He plants ideas in my head and that radiates back to my fingers. His words go through my head and my fingers go down on the keyboard. I just keep playing, playing and playing based on

---

[10] Author interview with David Slusser, February 23, 2021.
[11] Ivie, "Angelo Badalamenti Tells the Stories behind 5 Twin Peaks Songs."

what he says. Then, even as I am playing, he will paint me some more pictures. I'll be on to something for five or ten minutes and then he wants me to break the mood a little and go to a different place. Then he starts painting other pictures with his words. At the same time we record every note I play, either at the computer or in the early days with a little recording device on the keyboard. Sometimes if I don't capture what he envisions right away he will find a new set of words.

STEPHAN EICKE: *It appears that you found your voice as a composer of instrumental music through your work with David—the low, brooding sounds, the off-kilter harmonies, suspensions, the use of synthesizers ...*

ANGELO BADALAMENTI: Luckily for me and David, what is captured is a style of composing that marries and compliments his vision and has its own musical identity. That was lucky for both me and David because our projects complimented his vision. It worked for him and his movies and I was lucky because it also created a musical identity that a lot of people associate with me, even though I can write in almost every style. But with the David projects that identity is what I guess people appreciate, especially the fact of how we collaborate and work as a team.[12]

The first theme that Badalamenti wrote for what would become *Twin Peaks* was "Laura Palmer's Theme." On the official soundtrack album, it appears twice—as "Laura Palmer's Theme," and, in a different arrangement, as "Love Theme from Twin Peaks." Both start with a dark introduction which then segues into a version of Laura's theme.

Frequently in the show, "Dark Introduction" (as the part is called in the cue sheets for the series) and "Laura Palmer's Theme" are used separately. "Dark Introduction" is used when foreboding, anguish, fear, or danger needs to be conveyed to the viewer, and *Twin Peaks* is ripe with opportunities for its appliance. In the pilot alone it can be heard eighteen times, for example, when Pete Martell finds a body washed on the beach; the police investigates the body; Sarah Palmer calls her husband to inquire about their daughter's whereabouts; Bobby Briggs understands that he is seen as a suspect for the murder of his girlfriend, and when Ronnette is walking on the railway tracks, battered and bruised, barely conscious. Later, in season 2, "Dark Introduction" is used when, for example, Donna and Audrey secretly watch Benjamin Horne and Eileen Hayward discuss a brief affair they once enjoyed. It dawns on Donna she might be Benjamin's daughter. What she

---

[12]Eicke, "Mein Bruder David," pp. 22ff.

believed to be true for nearly two decades starts to fall apart in that moment, and Badalamenti makes her anguish palpable through his music. Though "Dark Introduction" serves as the intro to "Laura Palmer's Theme" on the soundtrack album, the homecoming queen herself is absent from the scene and this particular story line. "Dark Introduction" has ceased to function as a leitmotif and become mood music.

> EILEEN: Donna, please, listen.
> DONNA: I heard enough.
> EILEEN: Please just let me explain.
> BEN: Donna.
> DONNA: Leave me alone!
> BEN: It isn't your parents' fault. It is mine.
> DONNA: My parents? Who are my parents anyway?
> BEN: I only wanted to do good. I wanted the peak-hood, and it felt so good to tell the truth. After all these years.

FIGURE 14 *Dark Introduction (from* Twin Peaks, *1990).*
Transcribed by Stephan Eicke.

"Laura Palmer's Theme" was written solely for the seventeen-year-old homecoming queen, now lying on the beach, dead, wrapped in plastic. The theme was intended to portray her serene beauty, but also her inner turmoil, the darkness, and despair that raged within her breast. In the pilot, Lynch uses her theme whenever people mourn her passing. The memory of Laura evokes Badalamenti's bittersweet music which tells the viewer how her friends, family, and acquaintances saw her—fragile, troubled, ravishingly beautiful. Correspondingly, Laura's melody can be heard as the police recognize Laura as the body on the beach and Andy starts sobbing; when Leland Palmer is informed of his daughter's demise; when the school principal breaks down in tears as he announces Laura Palmer's passing; and when Donna watches video footage of herself and Laura while being interrogated by Special Agent Dale Cooper. Badalamenti managed to capture in music both Laura Palmer as a character and the grief her death has caused in the small community. For him and Lynch, the development of Laura Palmer's theme marked the starting point for their work on *Twin Peaks*, though both remember their initial music session slightly differently.

David would say that the music should be very dark and slow. He said, "Imagine you are alone in the woods at night and you hear only the sound of wind and possibly the soft cry of an animal." I'd start playing and David would say, "That's it, that's it! Now keep playing for a minute, but get ready for a change because now you see a beautiful girl. She's coming out from behind a tree, she's all alone and troubled, so now go into a beautiful melody that climbs ever so slowly until it reaches a climax. Let it tear your heart out."[13] David looked at me and said, "Angelo, don't change a note, you've captured 75 percent of the mood of Twin Peaks." *I said, "David, I was just ad-libbing. I have to work on it." "Please don't change a note."*[14]

ANGELO BADALAMENTI

We'd already written "Falling" so, for "Laura's Theme," I went into Angelo's office/studio and he said, "Can you tell me what it is you want?" And I told him, "I'm not sure." And I'm talking to him and he starts, you know, writing and playing. The pilot episode had already been shot, so we were working to the picture. [Angelo Badalamenti and Kinny Landrum dispute they were working to picture for the pilot.] I can't remember the exact sequence, but I remember saying, "It's got to build!" And Angelo was building this thing, and it was so beautiful to me, I'm starting to cry![15]

DAVID LYNCH

Contrary to popular belief fueled by Badalamenti's and Lynch's anecdotes quoted above, the theme heard in the show was not fully formed when the musicians arrived at the recording studio to lay down their tracks. "Laura Palmer's Theme" evolved in the process, in the studio, as keyboard player Kinny Landrum remembered: "We only had a lead sheet for it. I never even asked about how it went. The vamp, the minor key at the beginning of the song, had been written as two half-notes. With the whole-note that was tied—where you hold the note but you don't replay it."[16] Landrum suggested adding a low piano note, which Badalamenti promptly agreed to. A year later, the estate of Sergei Rachmaninoff threatened ABC with a

---

[13]Rodley, Chris, "The Icon Profile: David Lynch," *Icon*, April 1997. Reprinted in *David Lynch Interviews*, ed. Richard Barney (University Press of Mississippi, 2009), p. 192.
[14]*Literatti: Angelo Badalamenti*, PBS, 1990 [TV programme].
[15]Rodley, *Lynch on Lynch*, p. 170f.
[16]Ivie, Devon, "The *Twin Peaks* Song That Was Threatened with a Rachmaninoff Lawsuit," *Vulture*, December 16, 2022, https://www.vulture.com/2022/12/twin-peaks-laura-palmer-theme-angelo-badalamenti-backstory.html (accessed June 19, 2024).

lawsuit since they deemed the theme plagiarized the composer's "Prelude in C-Sharp Minor" with its three opening notes. The suit was never filed.

As the show progressed, the "Love Theme" was used as such—as a love theme. It was not ascribed to specific characters, but to the concept of love as a whole. Viewers hear the tune whenever characters in the series feel a deep romantic attachment to somebody or speak about true love, suggesting that this love must be genuine. For example, the love theme is used as James and Donna take each other's hands over Donna's dinner table, having fallen in love with each other; Cooper remembers someone who once taught him the pain of a broken heart; James tells Donna about his family secrets; Doc Hayward assures his daughter of his paternal love for her. The employment of the love theme also informs the viewer how characters really felt about Laura Palmer—Bobby is distraught when Jacoby forces him to examine his relationship with Laura; Jacoby himself breaks down in tears as he listens to the last tape Laura ever recorded; and Benjamin Horne eventually confesses to his daughter he had an affair with Laura. Visibly uncomfortable, he strokes the photograph of Laura's on his desk. Her familiar theme spills out in a warped, de-tuned variation.

> AUDREY: How long have you owned One Eyed Jacks?
> BEN: Five years.
> AUDREY: Did you know Laura worked there?
> BEN: She was only there for a brief time.
> AUDREY: Did you know?
> BEN: Yes.
> AUDREY: Did you in any way encourage here to work there?
> BEN: No. I had no idea. She asked if she could work in the department store. Battis sent her without my knowing.
> AUDREY: Did you sleep with her?
> BEN: [*pause*]
> AUDREY: Did you?
> BEN: Yes.
> AUDREY: Did you kill her?
> BEN: I loved her.

FIGURE 15 *Love Theme (from* Twin Peaks, *1990).* Transcribed by Stephan Eicke.

When characters either talk about or show love that is not of a genuine romantic or paternal kind, the love theme is notable for its absence.

Accordingly, Lynch used "Falling," as opposed to the love theme, as Cooper discovers Audrey in his bed, nude and crying. He assures her he likes her very much, but they vow to remain friends and not give in to their desires. "Falling" is also employed as Albert gives a rousing speech only to then confess his love to Sheriff Truman. The piece explains that the misanthropic Albert is by no means talking about romantic love, as could otherwise be assumed.

In these ways, the love theme serves as a guide. Even though, at Kinny Landrum's suggestion, a note was added, the melody itself wasn't changed since Badalamenti had improvised it on his old Fender Rhodes with Lynch sitting by his side. The composer would learn in the process that it was useless to try and play a trick on his collaborator: "One thing about David is that when he says, 'that's it,' that is it. If I try to change a chord or a note three weeks later without telling him and then play it for him, he'll say, 'That wasn't what you played for me.' He's really in tune."[17] Badalamenti, though, was never as taken with the theme as Lynch was, possibly because he would never get the chance to refine it.[18]

The three aforementioned themes are guideposts: "Falling" indicates platonic love, "Dark Introduction" emphasizes danger and anguish, and "Laura Palmer's Theme" (the love theme) signals genuine romantic feelings. Few leitmotifs are employed in *Twin Peaks*: "Wheeler's Theme" for Billy Zane's character; "Earle's Theme" for Wyndham Earle; "Hank's Theme" for Norma's husband; "Jean Renault's Theme" for the oldest of the Renault brothers; and "Harold's Theme" for the shy recluse who eventually kills himself over the loss of his carer, Laura Palmer. The melody for the latter theme, played on a Fender Rhodes, is in tempo, mood, and color reminiscent of the love theme, thus treating Harold as an equally tragic figure as Laura.

Other themes—even if they refer to specific characters in their title—do not serve as leitmotifs. (Those that are not available on the official soundtrack can be heard on the *Twin Peaks Archive*, which Lynch released himself in 2011.) Their primary function is to evoke a specific mood, as opposed to following pre-established rules. "Leo's Theme," for example, mostly plays when Shelly's husband is seen or spoken about. However, it can also be heard as Leland Palmer sneaks into the hospital and kills Jacques Renault. Badalamenti's piece had not been written for the latter scene—it had been composed for Leo—but it conveyed the right mood for the moment and was therefore employed by Lynch. If leitmotifs are used inconsistently, they cease

---

[17]Staff, "FEATURE: The Sound of Twin Peaks," *RockandRollJunkie*, October 7, 2015, http://web.archive.org/web/20190222151751/https://rockandrolljunkie.com/2015/10/07/13043/ (accessed June 19, 2024).
[18]Rodley, *Lynch on Lynch*, p. 171.

to be leitmotifs. For Lynch, the music simply felt right. "Music is a feeling thing," as he is fond of saying.[19] Whatever works.

There are other inconsistencies: (Benjamin) "Horne's Theme" is simply a short variation on "Audrey's Dance" and therefore not an original theme for the scheming businessman as the title implies. A theme originally conceived for James (and which the cue sheet for the pilot refers to as "James's Theme") is used for various purposes in the course of the show. However, in the pilot it solely accompanies Laura Palmer's (secret) boyfriend. When Donna and James meet at school, its placement is particularly memorable. For the first time in the show, Lynch employed a trick that he would grow fond of in the course of *Twin Peaks*, and which contributed to the disorienting effect some scenes continue to have on members of the audience: shortly before Donna and James meet in the hallway, a schoolmate can be seen moving to the cue's rhythm and snapping his fingers. Shortly thereafter, the impression of the composition as a diegetic piece of music is shaken. Does the kid hear the same music as the audience? If so, how? The music must be coming from the loudspeakers in the hallway, though the quality of the sound quickly belies that impression. The music is not processed but clean like the non-diegetic pieces in the show. In this way Lynch tears down the invisible wall between the characters and the audience. What is really happening? What is reality, what only a dream? Are the images to be trusted?

There are other, more audacious examples of the trickery that Lynch uses throughout: in episode two Audrey slowly dances to "her" dance—"Audrey's Dance"—in her father's office. The sound quality, as with the music in the school hallway referred to above, implies it plays as a non-diegetic piece of music. It is not being filtered through speakers in the room—yet Audrey can clearly hear it. As her father comes in, he brusquely turns off the "racket." Consequentially, the music stops immediately. It slowly fades in again following Audrey's tense conversation with Benjamin. Nobody had turned on the record player, though.

The placement of music in *Twin Peaks* challenges our perceptions. Music editor Lori Eschler remembers the scene in question: "That was such a good moment and so stylized. It set the convention that we were breaking. 'It is okay to try this.' That was great to be able to do that because essentially it's Audrey. It's in her head."[20] This doesn't explain the music not being filtered to create the impression that it is being played from a record, or how Benjamin could hear it, too. As in the example given previously, the use of music in this scene eludes a logical explanation. There is no pattern that is being followed throughout the show.

---

[19] *Le son de David Lynch*.
[20] Author interview with Lori Eschler, January 19, 2021.

As noted above, "James's Theme" is, contrary to what the title suggests, not a leitmotif for James. In the course of the first few episodes, James's melody (as can be heard in "The Bookhouse Boys") accompanies various characters, notably Bobby when in episode 4, for example, he poses as Jesus Christ in front of his parents' crucifix, or as he and Shelly have breakfast in episode 6. Bobby, however, is not part of the Bookhouse Boys. Hence, the theme should not apply to him. Lynch used it anyway since its mood, its chilling yet cool off-kilter quality, fit the images. (Note that "The Bookhouse Boys" on the original album release is a suite of various themes from the show, while on the *Twin Peaks Archive* the piece can be heard in its pure form.)

Although jazzy pieces such as "The Bookhouse Boys" and "Audrey's Dance" are different in approach to the electronic neo-romanticism of "Laura Palmer's Theme" and "Falling," both styles share a dreamy, off-center quality with dark undertones. Sweet on the surface, bitter at the core, Angelo Badalamenti's compositions became the musical identity of *Twin Peaks*.

> *I knew that* Twin Peaks *had to have a sound and its own musical identity. The show is so unique. It was really very natural to come up with the musical sound and the style of the writing. I just knew that it had to be somewhat traditional, but on the other hand, underneath the surface—as what goes on with some of these characters—I went along with that vein in the music so that it's slightly twisted or off-center. But not off-center in a stereotyped way. It's got its own sound. Through all seven episodes, I've stayed with that and developed it in that area.*[21] *The thing about Twin Peaks music is it runs the gamut of styles. [...] It also incorporates pop, blues, some country, soft rock, film noir—no question about that—nightmarish stuff.*[22]
>
> ANGELO BADALAMENTI

It is indeed a rich mix of styles Badalamenti employs. Some of the influences for the show's jazz pieces are more obvious than others. Badalamenti pays tribute to the smooth, seemingly effortless piano cascades by Oscar Peterson and Bud Powell; the elegant bass plucks of Ray Brown and Charles Mingus; the wild, extroverted brass solos by Miles Davis and Charlie Parker; and particularly the groundbreaking vibraphone spiel by Milt Jackson and Terry

---

[21] Staff, "FEATURE: The Sound of Twin Peaks."
[22] Grow, "Dream Team."

Gibbs. All these musicians influenced Badalamenti as a young man.[23] As an adult composer working on a groundbreaking show, he drew from a rich palette while infusing everything with his own character, his unique style of writing, and specific compositional trademarks. The suspensions and dark organ points—the low notes as harbingers of evil—are ever-present, even in the show's cool jazz pieces. At the same time, they display a wry, effortless humor and verve, particularly in the casual finger snapping as employed, for example, in "Dance of the Dream Man." This particular ingredient, though, was not an original idea of Badalamenti's. Instead, Kinny Landrum had suggested it to David Lynch as a tribute to "Cool" from *West Side Story*. Richard Beymer, who played Benjamin Horne in *Twin Peaks*, had made a name for himself as an actor in the original 1961 film adaptation of the musical. As a tribute to the film and Beymer's performance in it, Landrum convinced David Lynch to let him add finger snaps "on the back beat. If you don't like them, you can wipe them ... "[24] Lynch liked them.

Badalamenti's jazz pieces are commonly associated with the younger characters in the show, of which Agent Cooper is one. "Audrey's Dance," "The Bookhouse Boys," "Freshly Squeezed," and "Dance of the Dream Man" accompany James, Bobby, Donna, and the FBI agent when either quirkiness or a lascivious sensuality is called for. Before "Dance of the Dream Man" becomes associated with the Dream Man as he performs his dance routine in the Red Room, it serves as a descriptive accompaniment for Agent Cooper by underscoring his eccentricities. Accordingly, the piece is used as he speaks to a colleague through a tape recorder on his drive into Twin Peaks, and as he hangs upside down in his room at the Great Northern Hotel as part of his morning routine.

> DALE COOPER: Diane, 11:30 a.m., February 24th. Entering the town of Twin Peaks. It's five miles South of the Canadian border, 12 miles west of the state line. I've never seen so many trees in my life. As W. C. Fields would say, "I'd rather be here than Philadelphia." 54 degrees on a slightly overcast day. Weatherman said rain. If you get paid that kind of money for being wrong 60 percent of the time, it would beat working. My mileage is 79,345, gauge is on reserve. I'm riding on fumes here, I gotta tank up when I get into town. Remind me to tell you how much that is. Lunch was $6.31 at the Lamplighter Inn. That's on Highway 2 near Lewis Fork. That was a tuna fish sandwich on whole wheat, slice of cherry pie and a cup of coffee. Damn good food. Diane, if you ever get up this way, that cherry pie is worth a stop.

---

[23]Ibid.
[24]Combs, Jim, "Wrapped in Plastic: Would You Believe Midi Cables?" *Keyboard*, November 1990, p. 72.

Okay. Looks like I'll be meeting up with a Sheriff Harry S. Truman. Shouldn't be too hard to remember that. He'll be at the Calhoun Memorial Hospital. Guess we're gonna go to intensive care and take a look at that girl that crawled down the railroad tracks off the mountain. When finished, I'll be checking into a motel. The sheriff will be able to recommend a clean place and reasonably priced. That's what I need. A clean place, reasonably priced.
Oh. Diane, I almost forgot. I've got to find out what kind of trees these are. They're really something.

FIGURE 16 *Dance of the Dream Man (from* Twin Peaks, *1990).* *Transcribed by Stephan Eicke.*

The piece had come about—like several others—through composition and improvisation. Most of the time, the musicians were recorded separately. Tenor saxophonist Al Regni had arrived at the studio early to put down his part, and spent the time playing over Ron Carter's bass line that the engineers were mixing. The sax player wanted to warm up for his own session. Regni remembered: "After playing through the chorus nearly twenty times, David Lynch rushed into the studio very excited. He was so thrilled and said he would use the recording he had just made, unbeknownst to me. I didn't think I was any good at the time and was really just warming up in the style that I thought would be needed."[25] That secretly recorded version was used in the series.

While "Freshly Squeezed" in its multiple variations is first associated with Audrey's flirtatious behavior toward Cooper—as she sits down with him in the breakfast room, and as Cooper smells an envelope she had slipped under his door—it is subsequently used more broadly when a subtle quirkiness is called for that also provides a sense of mystery. For example, it is used as Cooper announces to Diane he wishes to invest in property, and as the Bookhouse Boys meet with Cooper to entrust him with their secret. (It is not the cue for the Bookhouse Boys that is used in this scene as the title would suggest.) Out of all of *Twin Peaks'* jazzy cues, the aforementioned "Audrey's Dance" deserves special consideration.

---

[25]Dukes, Brad, *Reflections: An Oral History of Twin Peaks* (Short/Tall Press, 2014), p. 128

> *I like to do off-centered things, for the little man, for example. You do a little snap thing, a jazz thing; or for Audrey, the sexy girl in* Twin Peaks, *you do something very sensuous and yet very dark underneath it. That's the key, these abstract, dissonant things, and yet you have something sexy going on on top and on bottom. I do like to go with that. In film scoring I like to do things that go against what you are watching. It gives you an uncomfortable feeling, but that works for me. Not the cartoon stuff.*[26]
>
> ANGELO BADALAMENTI

"Audrey's Dance" had an unusual origin. Although it was written with Audrey Horne in mind, in the first few episodes of the show it is used nearly exclusively in association with Bobby Briggs. Even in the cue sheet for the pilot episode the melody is referred to as "Bobby's Theme." Lynch employs it as Bobby leaves Norma's diner with his love interest Shelly; as he arrives at school only to be ordered into the "office" immediately; when he is subsequently being interrogated; as he drives up to Norma's house with Mike; and as they arrive at the roadhouse at night and intimidate James. For this reason, scholars have assumed that "Audrey's Dance" was originally written for Bobby. (In her book *Angelo Badalamenti's Soundtrack from Twin Peaks*, Clare Nina Norelli writes that associating the [jazz] music with Audrey seems to have been an afterthought.)[27] It was, though, the other way around: David Lynch had given his composer instructions to capture the young, rebellious Audrey Horne in music.[28] He wanted something dreamy. ("Isn't it too dreamy," Audrey sighs before she starts dancing to "her" melody in Norma's diner.) With its chords rubbing against the melody, Badalamenti created what Lynch desired for Audrey specifically: a piece full of tension, though upbeat and sensuous at the same time. It was a perfect description of Audrey Horne as a character. Badalamenti's composition is full of quirks and unexpected twists. The signature opening triad (which also appears in "Dance of the Dream Man") already is an indication of the weirdness to come: an F-sharp, G, and C follow an F natural (as opposed to F-sharp). With heavy reverb added, the music creates tensions that at the same time evoke a dreamy atmosphere. That feeling is only accentuated by abstract sound layers in the background. Clarinets sliding downwards are delayed in time in relation to each other, creating an additional dissonance.

---

[26]Marcone & Philp, "Interview with Angelo Badalamenti."
[27]Norelli, Clare Nina, *Angelo Badalamenti's Soundtrack from Twin Peaks* (Bloomsbury, 2017) p. 59.
[28]Ivie, "Angelo Badalamenti Tells the Stories behind 5 Twin Peaks Songs."

The heavy accents put on the notes for the synthesizer make the instrument sound like the siren of a fire engine. The finger snapping and the walking bass meanwhile, by providing a clear rhythm, are the only steady element that holds everything together.

"Audrey's Dance" captures Audrey's character, creating a sharp contrast to the image of her moving her body to the piece's rhythm. Its use is nothing if not ironic. After all, an abstract jazz piece with dissonant clarinets, finger snapping, and crashing synthesizers is not something ordinarily offered by a jukebox in a small town's unsophisticated diner. Expectations are subverted throughout, however, and are one aspect of *Twin Peaks*' originality and genre-bending success. Julee Cruise whispering "The Nightingale" serves as another example: the song transcends established genres and is far removed from the country ballads one might expect to hear in such a venue. Said contrasts contribute greatly to a sense of disorientation. There is more to it, as Badalamenti pointed out: "The songs with Julee serve a two-fold purpose: they contrast the visuals and they set the tone for the show. Often, the thing that works best is a song or piece of music that goes against the visuals, something that functions as a contrast or a counterpoint."[29] Lynch's gleeful experimentation, transforming non-diegetic music into diegetic music and vice versa, makes the viewers question their assumptions about what is transpiring on screen in the show's reality. The placement of "Audrey's Dance" in particular opens a rift between music and image. What kind of place is this town?

> *Well,* Twin Peaks *characters are so outrageous. But Audrey, [chuckling] she was just so sexy. God almighty! It was marvelous to see her dancing to this abstract jazzy music. [...] That music is dreamy but sensuous and sexy. She played with all this innocence, a little teenage girl from junior high school with a short skirt, it was incredible, this other side of her. But underneath it she was also a pretty dark character.*[30]
>
> Angelo Badalamenti

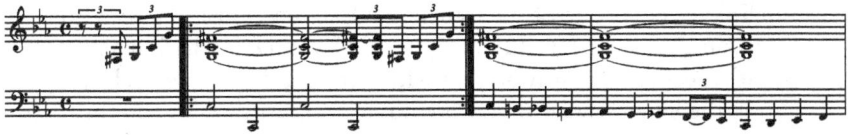

FIGURE 17 *Audrey's Dance (from* Twin Peaks, *1990).*
Transcribed by Stephan Eicke.

---

[29]Halskov, Andreas, "A Marriage Made in Heaven: The Music of Twin Peaks according to Composer Angelo Badalamenti and Music Editor Lori Eschler Frystak," *International Journal of TV Serial Narratives* 2, no. 2 (Winter 2016): p. 69.
[30]Deyneko, "Angelo Badalamenti."

Yet another essential part of Angelo Badalamenti's contribution to *Twin Peaks* is his "firewood"—long, rumbling sequences performed entirely by low-pitched instruments in their deepest register. Lynch enjoyed toying with these pieces that were entirely devoid of melody or even motifs. One of those pieces Badalamenti called "The Lowest Circle in Hell." The title already suggests its sound. It consists of sustained notes for low instruments, nearly fifteen minutes in length. Badalamenti himself found his maelstrom of sadness and despair "transcending" and "beautiful."[31] The director then took these "firewood" recordings, just as he had for *Blue Velvet,* and instructed his music editor, Lori Eschler, to slow them down on the mixing board.

David Lynch had already interviewed various music editors for the show. For the pilot, he had hired David Slusser, who was working for George Lucas and Francis Ford Coppola at Skywalker Sound, the sound effects, sound editing, sound design, sound mixing, and music recording division of Lucasfilm in Northern California. In order to work on the regular episodes Slusser would have needed to move to Hollywood, which he refused to do. A replacement was needed. However, none of the interviewees were deemed suitable by Lynch, as they proved to be by-the-book, conventional music editors whose rigid approach clashed with his own experimental method. He was in luck when sound recordist Jon Huck recommended the director speak with Lori Eschler, a friend from Montana who was creative, unconventional, and a musician herself. Lynch took a meeting with Eschler and chose her for the job immediately.

> STEPHAN EICKE: *What did you do with the drones you mentioned— the "firewood," as Angelo calls it?*
> LORI ESCHLER: I would sometimes reverse some of the themes or slow them down and record them backwards at half speed, then slow them down again and get a completely different piece of music. That was fun. It never had been done before. I knew of a lot of electronic composers that were experimenting with things like that, like my friend Carl Stone, who is a composer and lives in Tokyo. He is one of the fathers of electronic music. He is quite amazing, makes beautiful music. Angelo and David had invented that wheel and I just took that wheel and made more wheels. I took the vibe of what they were doing and just developed it in various directions.
> STEPHAN EICKE: *Did David give you very clear directions as to what he wanted to have slowed down?*

---

[31]Willman, Chris, "Setting Lynch's Muse to Music," *The Los Angeles Times* [Los Angeles], September 29, 1990, p. 87f.

Lori Eschler: Yes. Not on every episode, but he is the one that got me started on that track, in that mode of working. When I first started I had no idea how they had created stuff. He had me get a tape recorder that was variable speed and start slowing everything down. It was crazy. On the second season I changed from working on film with magnetic tape to a digital audio system that was one of the first ones, made by SSL, a company that made mixing boards. That was a completely different way of working but it was so much faster and so much less physical work.[32]

In the series, the slowed-down "firewood" is used to evoke dread and anguish. In the pilot, Lynch puts one example—titled "Half-Speed Orchestra 1 (Stair Music/Danger Theme)"—under an aggressive Nadine calling out to her husband, Ed. Lynch uses another version—"Slower Speed Orchestra"—to underscore a different scene of marital discomfort: the low rumbling basses accompany Leo's confrontation with Shelly as he finds cigarette stumps in his ashtray. Other moments in the show are more dangerous: "Half-Speed Orchestra 1" is used as Sarah Palmer wakes up from a brief, shallow nap and envisions a person scrambling through the dark woods and picking up the necklace Donna and James had hidden there. In the second episode, Sarah Palmer receives Laura's friend Donna, only to see her dead daughter in her guest: "Slow Speed Orchestra 1 (24 Hours)" accompanies Sarah Palmer's chilling cries.

Angelo Badalamenti's compositions were altered under the director's instructions without the composer's involvement. Badalamenti commented: "That's the kind of music that David has always heard in his mind before he met me. He always said to me, 'Angelo what you play for me is the music that I have always heard.'"[33]

David's descriptions have brought out another side of my musical composition which I guess I have. [...] [The music is] spare. I guess it's just doing things that are very slow and sustained and to try and write the most beautiful kinds of melodies that you can play with one finger, to make them stand on their own and reach people. Underneath all of that, on a lot of the music in Twin Peaks, *there are many elements, lots of dissonant things and harmonies that rub up against each other. There are dissonant, low clarinets and things which bring both of these worlds together. I think that's what we were striving for.*[34]

Angelo Badalamenti

---

[32] Author interview with Lori Eschler, January 19, 2021.
[33] *Le son de David Lynch.*
[34] *Literatti: Angelo Badalamenti.*

Apart from writing and recording the main themes for the show, and as well as providing the "firewood," Angelo Badalamenti also wrote most of the source music—music played on radios, jukeboxes or sung by characters in the show. While ordinarily television shows license pre-existing hits to include them as source cues, Lynch and Badalamenti decided to develop diegetic pieces themselves. They needed to be part of the overall *Twin Peaks* fabric. For the source cues, the composer could flex his muscles in many genres. No other collaboration with David Lynch (and no other singular project Badalamenti ever worked on) showcases his versatility better than *Twin Peaks*. The off-kilter, extroverted prog-rock/jazz-mélange "I'm Hurt Bad" is a standout, a piece which plays in the pilot episode on the jukebox in Norma's diner as Bobby leaves the establishment with Shelly in tow. Badalamenti and Lynch would later use that piece in their stage show *Industrial Symphony No. 1*.

"The Nightingale" and "Into the Night" had already been written for Julee Cruise's album *Floating into the Night*, and respectively feature in the show as Cruise performs at the roadhouse and as Cooper and his team enter the cabin in which Laura Palmer was held hostage. "One Eyed Jack's Country" is a straightforward country instrumental that evokes memories of Badalamenti's "Nashville Beer Garden" which had been released by GP Records in 1979. "South Sea Dreams" and "Hula Hoppin'" are tributes to traditional Hawaiian folk music, so cliched they would pass as parodies if they didn't feature out-of-place country elements ("Hula Hoppin'") and, curiously, a jazzy vibraphone ("South Sea Dreams"). Both cues are used as source pieces when Donna and James steal into Dr. Jacoby's office and Donna accidentally switches on the radio. Here, Lynch plays yet another trick on the audience: he slowed down "Hula Hoppin'" to half-speed and put it beneath "Dark Introduction" as the camera pans over Jacoby's eccentric wallpaper featuring images of palm trees. With the use of the Hawaiian folk music, Lynch at first suggests the scene is taking place on a remote island as opposed to in Twin Peaks. Truth is then gradually revealed.

Only few standards were used, but to remarkable effect. Glenn Miller's hit "Pennsylvania 6–5000," for example, plays as a diegetic piece in episode 3. A hurt and traumatized Leland Palmer stands alone in his living room. He puts on a record. Glenn Miller's recording, a swing jazz standard of the 1940s, is a piece of music that epitomizes nostalgia. In the scene in which it is used the vibrant associations of the music clash violently with the dour images on screen. As music editor Lori Eschler explains, the source cues—including "Pennsylvania 6–5000"—were carefully chosen by Lynch himself:

> Whenever Leland had a scene like that, the producers were like, "Oh God, we can't afford that song," and David said, "We absolutely are getting that song." He even had a lot of music on the set that he would play to

set a mood. Some of the standards that played in those Leland moments were pre-decided by David. Then the producers had to make it happen.

Badalamenti adds: "You are going against what's happening. Laura has died, and [Leland] is doing this crazy, Benny Goodman-like dance. David loves that kind of thing, like in *Blue Velvet* where Ben is singing 'In Dreams'." These choices tell something specific about a character's state of mind, as he continued: "But then, in the end of the scene, the mood changes, as we hear 'Laura Palmer's Theme', as if we're back to reality. By the way, Ray Wise has told me that when they were shooting that scene, Ray actually cut his hand on the glass, and they kind of improvised the rest of the scene."[35]

A vital ingredient of *Twin Peaks* is *Invitation to Love*, the soap opera within the soap opera, and apparently the most beloved show in town, since nearly every character at one point or another stares at a television screen showing it, as if hypnotized by the spectacle unfolding in front of their eyes. Badalamenti wrote a few cues for Lynch's particular version of *Days of Our Lives*—sophisticated parodies of succulent, overstrung soap opera music.

The series presented a heavy workload for the composer who had to come up with all the show's main themes, variations, "firewood," and source music. In order to keep up with the requirements and deliver the necessary music on time, Badalamenti and Lynch devised an efficient approach early on: they built a music library.

> *["Laura Palmer's Theme" is] kind of disguised and altered in orchestration and in the selection of instruments playing the theme. It varies. It could be a synth sound or it could be a solo clarinet or it could be an alto flute. These are very delicately selected. It's not the kind of score where I used hundreds of musicians. I'm not afraid of using a single instrument playing for a minute and a half. For some reason, it works very well. I might use a snare drum with brushes.*[36]
>
> ANGELO BADALAMENTI

The various separate music tracks were combined according to the needs of a specific scene by the show's music editor. After his positive experience mixing *Blue Velvet* in Northern California, Lynch returned there for work on the *Twin Peaks* pilot and, as already mentioned, hired David Slusser, one of the few music editors at the time living and working in the region. Slusser was a musician by night and a reluctant music editor by day—yet he had made it his career path. As an engineer, mixer, and sound designer at George Lucas's Skywalker facility, he had worked as an audio technician

---

[35]Halskov, "A Marriage Made in Heaven," p. 71.
[36]Staff, "FEATURE: The Sound of Twin Peaks."

on the ill-fated *Howard the Duck*, sound editor on Mel Brooks' *Spaceballs*, and assistant music editor on *Cocoon II*. When working for Lynch, Slusser served as the "director's music editor" as opposed to a "composer's music editor." The difference is essential, as he explains: "You have a music editor that works for a composer and his job is to make sure that everything he wrote on paper was executed according to his timeline and score. That's one type of music editor." While working in the Bay Area, Slusser put down temp tracks for films and cut music from a library. He continues: "That is a different kind of music editor who actually edits music, takes it apart. A composer's music editor would never do that."[37] As music editor for the pilot, Slusser had played a crucial role already during the recording of the music. Going in, he knew it would be his responsibility to give the musicians a tempo when they recorded to picture, to have music and images match to a split second. Unfortunately for him, Slusser had only limited experience in this respect. To his relief, Badalamenti and Lynch did not score to picture—with one exception.

> STEPHAN EICKE: *Were there instances when they recorded to picture?*
> DAVID SLUSSER: I showed up at the session in New York and I had a bible of all the click times for footages. It was *this* thick. Doing the calculations I was just learning that craft. You had to take tempo and click based on frame per second, so there's a whole cross-section of things. I only had to use that bible one time in the pilot, when Audrey is walking to the car. That was done to tempo. They said, "Figure this out, give me a tempo." I was looking into my book, scratching my head and sweating bullets that I gave them the right tempo because I was not used to calculating that way. But it came off perfectly. That was the only time they did it.
> STEPHAN EICKE: *I'm surprised of all the scenes in the pilot this was the one that was scored according to the tempo of the scene—scored to picture, so to speak.*
> DAVID SLUSSER: Basically, the question was, "How many bars should we make it?" They had the tempo down. It was [Audrey's] gait. I had to give the exact timing for the musicians. I had watched the scene once. That was one of the few pieces of film that I saw at all in the recording session. The other one was the title.
> STEPHAN EICKE: *But that must mean that Lynch and Badalamenti had conceived that piece for a specific scene in the pilot, which is rather unusual for them.*
> DAVID SLUSSER: You are giving it too much credit as a piece as opposed to a bit of movement. It was just a segue type of thing,

---

[37] Author interview with David Slusser, February 23, 2021.

an improvisation for which they needed to know the timing and give it to the drummer, Grady Tate. We might have recorded Kinny [Landrum] doing a bass patch and a vibes patch before we recorded Grady. I had to get the due diligence on the beats per minute for that little thing. Angelo put it in a key. It was 'traveling music' as we say in American show business. We might have even called it that at the session. It was just Audrey getting into the car and everyone dropping their jaws about how sexy she was.[38]

For (nearly) every theme, such as "Bobby's Theme/Audrey's Dance," "James's Theme/The Bookhouse Boys," "Laura Palmer's Theme," "Hank's Theme," and "Freshly Squeezed," Badalamenti prepared several versions. The melody always remained the same but would be performed on different instruments and in different tempos. In the cue "Caroline," for example, Badalamenti has the "Dark Introduction" performed using a different keyboard sample than in the original version. In "Letter from Harold #2," it is played using yet another sample while the arrangement remains otherwise the same. That approach meant Badalamenti didn't have to rewrite cues—he simply had to re-record parts of what he had already composed. In several versions of "Dark Introduction," a piano takes over for the Fender Rhodes, playing either solo or accompanied by synthesized strings. There also exists a variation for vibraphone only.

For "Freshly Squeezed" the musicians recorded a variation for clarinet as opposed to vibraphone, and a variation for flute as well as one for bass clarinet. They played the original version, a mid-tempo and fast version. It helped David Slusser, as music editor for the pilot, that the various parts had been recorded on separate tracks. That way, he could easily mix and match. Slusser remembers the recording sessions as fluid: "There would be a morning session and afternoon session. We would have Grady [Tate] come by this afternoon and have Al Regni come by with his clarinet by 2 p.m. We were tracking. It was very rarely a group of musicians." The session would last all day with musicians coming in and leaving through a revolving door, as Slusser says: "It's building up tracks. They loved working that way. Of course David was very much into the whole creative process and Angelo was in his element like he was doing production for TV or commercials but with license to play."[39]

After the individual parts had been recorded separately, David Slusser too was given a license to play. He could combine various parts of some pieces with parts of others. Slusser was reveling in his freedom as music editor, creating entirely new cues from already existing material. It was his

---

[38]Ibid.
[39]Ibid.

responsibility to take every single track from the 24-track tape and transfer every solo individually to magnetic film and mix the parts down in every imaginable combination. "David and Artie [Polhemus] and Angelo would mix down the master takes and do four or five songs they knew they were going to use in the movie, like the *Twin Peaks* theme," says Slusser, who took all the other pieces with him to Berklee to work with them.[40] That way, he could create a piece with only vibes playing, or vibes in combination with bass, or bass in combination with a string pad. Everything was separate. Working on a flatbed editor (which allowed the music editor to run four tracks at a time), Slusser created different combinations for different moods. He explains: "When I created what we call elements—when a scene would go up to be mixed—I would have a combo ready. I would also have some of those other individual mono tracks hung on the big dubbers back in the machine room."[41]

David Lynch would then decide at the mixing console which combinations he wanted to use for a specific scene. If Slusser presented him with a mixdown he had prepared, the director would either approve it right away or suggest a different combination of the individual elements. All these discussions took place in the editing room. Lynch participated actively, as Slusser continues: "The hard part is making sure you have sync marks on each of these elements as they are hanging in the mix. They can't slide. That's the combination you are striving to achieve." According to Slusser, Eschler, and Lynch, *Twin Peaks* was always treated like a feature film production.

Since Slusser was unavailable to serve as music editor on the series, he sent the various tapes with the individual music tracks to his colleague in Southern California, Lori Eschler. It was crucial to explain the working procedure to her and go over the pieces that had been recorded. Many compositions had been conceived for specific characters, and Slusser's successor needed to familiarize herself with them in depth. Occasionally, Eschler would call Slusser (who was then busy mixing *Wild at Heart* at Skywalker Sound in Northern California) and pick his brains when searching for certain track combinations.

> STEPHAN EICKE: *How involved were David and Angelo when it came to choosing the individual pieces for the individual scenes?*
> LORI ESCHLER: We had conversations all the time. We would sit down and spot each episode together, talk about what each scene needed or wanted. In the first few episodes, David was really involved because he had directed them. He also picked people he trusted and he got everybody started. Then he let people get

---

[40]Ibid.
[41]Ibid.

creative. Duwayne Dunham directed one of the early episodes and he already knew the language David was starting to develop in his films because he had worked on *Blue Velvet*. That's a way to look at it. It's all so integral as a part of his film language, which he developed up to *Mulholland Drive*. I think that that was a masterpiece as an example of his film language. This was what he was doing in the early days of *Twin Peaks*. He was developing this style of "This is how I make films and I know this is TV but we are going to do it this way." Most of the people he had hired were film people, not television people. That's what distinguished me from some of the music editors at TV at the time.

STEPHAN EICKE: Twin Peaks *was never considered a television product, then?*

LORI ESCHLER: Right. After the first episode aired on television, it was really eye-opening to us because they ran the audio through a compressor and all this beautiful stuff we had created was compressed to this tinny sound. Everybody was very, very upset. That's when negotiations started with ABC. David had the producer on the phone with these people, the tech people who were using this compressor, and he said, "We are mixing for surround here and we check everything with a mono speaker as well but you can't compress it." Pretty quickly they adjusted what they were doing so it sounded better.

STEPHAN EICKE: *How did you spot the episodes when nothing had been or would be written to picture?*

LORI ESCHLER: We would start out by getting Angelo on the phone. It was a big deal, the first few spotting sessions. It was super fun and everybody was very excited. We would go scene by scene and take notes. The sound editor would be there as well and we would spot it together. That was helpful because we could say what the music is going to be doing in a scene so they were informed and you didn't have that big surprise when you got to the dub. It was really inspirational.

David also uses metaphor in his direction a lot and there was no telling what he was going to say next. It was entertaining. Inspirational. It was really fun. I keep thinking of examples. He would talk about painting the music in the branches of the bushes and around the bushes, things like that. It made total sense to me for some reason. We would talk also about instrumentation in the spotting session: "This time we use the theme with the tenor sax," or "This is just going to be drums and then we will get to this point in the scene and let's start introducing the 'Dark Woods' theme." We talked about that. That kind of established how we did the rest of the series, even when David and Angelo weren't there. They had established this mode of working and we just kept going with it. It was really fun. Most of the directors loved it. They used to come in and say, "What, this is not scored to picture?" "No, we have this whole library of stuff to work with." Some of them were intimidated but most of them were just thrilled because it was so fun and creative. One director was so upset that he made Angelo score a scene to picture in his episode. Angelo had to overnight it because it was last minute. It was the late 80s. It was not easy to get things done that quickly. It was not what we were doing, scoring to picture. It's that technique, so TV and on-the-nose. [The director] threw a little bit of a tantrum and I said, "You know what, we are starting the final dub tomorrow, I think you should take a walk, come down and get back when you feel ready to work." I was so intimidated because he was the director but he took a walk, came back after about an hour and sat down and we finished. The next day he sent me flowers. He was super sweet, he was a great guy. All the directors they hired were wonderful to work with. We had so much talent, it was incredible.[42]

With his library music approach, Badalamenti gave David Lynch and other directors the opportunity to pick and choose what they deemed appropriate for individual scenes. It also made Badalamenti's job easier by allowing him to write all the music—diegetic and non-diegetic—for the show without having to rely on ghostwriters or ask for more time than the schedule allowed.

A cue card for the pilot alone conveys an impression of how the library was used, which versions were picked for which purpose and to what effect. Brief musical sound effects such as bumpers are not included in this overview. (The *Twin Peaks Archive* describes the digital album released by David Lynch on his homepage in 2011.)

TABLE 1 *Cue Card for the* Twin Peaks *Pilot*

Title on cue sheet	Length	Description	On album	In TP archive
Falling	02:40:00	Opening Credits	Twin Peaks Theme	
Dark Introduction	01:50:00	Pete finds a body on the beach	Laura Palmer's Theme	
Dark Introduction	01:20:00	Police investigates the body—segues into:	Laura Palmer's Theme	

---

[42] Author interview with Lori Eschler, January 19, 2021.

Title on cue sheet	Length	Description	On album	In TP archive
Love Theme from *Twin Peaks*	01:51:00	Police recognize it's Laura Palmer when they turn over the body. Laura's mother starts looking for her daughter. "Dark Introduction" is included and starts as she goes up the stairs into Laura's room	Laura Palmer's Theme	
Grady Solo	01:20:00	Drum solo as Audrey exits the Great Northern and gets into a car		Solo Percussion 1
Dark Introduction	01:14:00	Leland receives a call from Sarah inquiring about Laura shortly before Harry Truman arrives to bring the news of Laura's passing—segues into:	Laura Palmer's Theme	
Love Theme from *Twin Peaks*	01:14:00	Leland is still holding the phone in his hand. The Love Theme aka "Laura Palmer's Theme" starts playing as Leland realizes what must have happened	Laura Palmer's Theme	
Don't Do Anything I Wouldn't Do (Visual Instrumental, Juke Box)	00:30:00	Bobby flirts with Norma as he leaves the diner with Shelly, having put on this cue on the jukebox		I'm Hurt Bad (Industrial Symphony No. 1 Version)

Title on cue sheet	Length	Description	On album	In TP archive
Cool Cool Kyle	00:53:00	Bobby and Shelley drive away from the diner in Bobby's car		Audrey's Dance (Fast) (Clean)
Sting	00:27:00	Bobby sees a truck in front of Leo's place and smells danger. Low rumble		Dark Vibrato (with Noise)
James's Theme	00:51:00	James and Donna meet in school		The Bookhouse Boys
Bobby's Theme	00:51:00	Bobby arrives in school and is called away from class—segues into:		Audrey's Dance (Clean)
Bobby's Theme	00:32:00	Bobby is interrogated by police as Sheriff Truman arrives		Audrey's Dance (Clean)
Dark Introduction	01:16:00	Bobby flies into a rage as he understands that Truman views him as a suspect. The school's principal makes an announcement concerning Laura's death—segues into:	Laura Palmer's Theme	
Love Theme from *Twin Peaks*	00:57:00	The principal breaks down in tears and requests a moment of silence. Donna is comforted by her friends	Laura Palmer's Theme	

FALLEN ANGEL

Title on cue sheet	Length	Description	On album	In TP archive
Dark Introduction	00:28:00	Ronnette appears for the first time, walking on the railtracks like in trance—segues into:	Laura Palmer's Theme	
James's Theme	01:05:00	James drives up to Big Ed's Gas Farm and speaks with Ed about Laura		The Bookhouse Boys
Slow Orchestra	00:30:00	Nadine calls out to her husband, Ed		Half Speed Orchestra 1 (Stair Music/ Danger Theme)
Cool Cool Kyle	01:32:00	Agent Cooper appears, driving toward Twin Peaks while speaking into his dicta-phone	Dance of the Dream Man*	Dance of the Dream Man (Original)
Echo Cool Sax	00:12:00	Cooper and Truman meet at the hospital, accompanied by a distant saxophone in the background		Dance of the Dream Man (Solo Sax)
Dark Introduction	00:22:00	Ronnette suddenly says something while in hospital during Cooper's visit. The one-armed man appears	Laura Palmer's Theme	
Grady Solo	02:07:00	Cooper and Truman sit down at the Sheriff's station to examine Laura's diary		Solo Percussion 1

Title on cue sheet	Length	Description	On album	In TP archive
Dark Introduction	01:03:00	The police have found where Laura was killed. Andy is on the phone with Lucy, sobbing	Laura Palmer's Theme	
Norwegians	01:15:00	Audrey decides to irritate her father's potential business partners by barging into a meeting of theirs and telling them about her dead friend		Norwegians
Love Theme from *Twin Peaks*	01:56:00	Donna is interrogated by agent Cooper. He wants to know who took the video of her and Laura		Love Theme (Solo Rhodes)
Dark Introduction	00:22:00	Cooper enlarges a frame of Laura's video and discovers the wanted person drives a bike. A connection to James is established	Laura Palmer's Theme	
Norwegians	00:30:00	The Norwegians leave the Great Northern prematurely and in distress, much to Audrey's delight		Norwegians
Dark Introduction	01:23:00	The police investigate the scene of the crime and find Laura's necklace	Laura Palmer's Theme	

Title on cue sheet	Length	Description	On album	In TP archive
Swells	00:18:00	Cooper and Truman discover a photograph of Ronnette in a copy of *Flesh Magazine* owned by Laura		
Slow Orchestra	00:53:00	Leo confronts Shelly about cigarette stubs he found in the ashtray		Slow Speed Orchestra 1
Grady Solo	0:15	Nadine aggressively demonstrates her curtains to Big Ed		Solo Percussion 1
Dark Introduction	02:50:00	Doc Hayward tells his wife what he knows about the investigation into Laura's death while Donna secretly listens	Laura Palmer's Theme	
Bobby's Theme	02:20:00	Bobby and Mike drive over to Donna's house and Doc Hayward realizes his daughter is not in		Audrey's Dance (Clean)
Night Clarinets	00:49:00	Cooper and Truman sit in the police car at night and are told Donna has vanished		Audrey's Dance (Percussion & Clarinets)
Falling (Visual Vocal, Featured Performance)	01:37:00	Julee Cruise performs at the roadhouse	Falling	

Title on cue sheet	Length	Description	On album	In TP archive
Night Clarinets	00:19:00	Cooper and Truman watch the roadhouse, see Bobby and Mike arrive		Audrey's Dance (Percussion & Clarinets)
The Nightingale (Visual Vocal, Featured Performance)	02:28:00	Julee Cruise performs at the roadhouse	The Nightingale	
The Nightingale (Vocal Background)	00:12:00	While Julee Cruise is still singing, the big brawl continues	The Nightingale	
Dark Introduction	02:41:00	Cooper and Truman are looking for Donna in the dark of night. Donna meets with James—segues into:	Laura Palmer's Theme	
Love Theme from *Twin Peaks*	02:55:00	James starts to cry. He and Donna kiss	Laura Palmer's Theme	
James's Theme	01:27:00	Cooper and Truman spot James and Donna driving past on a motorcycle—segues into:		The Bookhouse Boys
Bobby's Theme	00:46:00	James enters the prison inside the Sheriff's station and meets Bobby and James there		Audrey's Dance (Clean)
Love Theme from *Twin Peaks*	01:00:00	Donna and her father sit in the car, the latter assuring the former he is not mad at her but loves her very much		Laura Palmer's Theme (Piano A)

Title on cue sheet	Length	Description	On album	In TP archive
Bobby's Theme	00:38:00	James is in prison, being threatened and intimidated by Bobby and Mike		Audrey's Dance (Clean)
Love Theme from *Twin Peaks*	00:34:00	Sheriff Truman walks up to Jocelyn as it becomes clear they are having an affair—segues into:	The Swan—Instrumental**	- (taken from album *Floating in the Night*)
Dark Introduction	00:34:00	Catherine Martell is on the phone, plotting against the couple she is spying upon—segues into:	Laura Palmer's Theme	
Slow Orchestra	00:35:00	Sarah lying on her couch at home, screaming as she envisions somebody walking through the woods, picking up something		Half Speed Orchestra 1
Love Theme from *Twin Peaks*	00:44:00	End credits over a photograph of Laura Palmer's face	Laura Palmer's Theme	

*"Cool Cool Kyle" in its previous use (cue 9) was "Audrey's Dance (Fast) (Clean)." The fact that here "Cool Cool Kyle" is in fact "Dance of the Dream Man" indicates the insertion of "Dance of the Dream Man" might have been a last-minute change and that the cue sheet is incorrect.

**Again, this must have been a last-minute change since the "Love Theme" is not used here though the cue sheet indicates such.

The cue card for the pilot shows how minimalist the musical approach to *Twin Peaks* was. "Dark Introduction," for example, the first part of "Laura Palmer's Theme," is used eighteen times in ninety minutes. Whenever the situation was called for and a feeling of dread needed to be evoked or emphasized, Lynch inserted Badalamenti's moody suspense cue. Sometimes he shortened it to just a few seconds, sometimes he looped it to extend its running time. The second part of "Laura Palmer's Theme," the romantic melody the viewer has come to associate with Laura and the love her friends feel for her, is used eight times, as is "Audrey's Dance" in various versions and disguises. Throughout the whole of *Twin Peaks*, in both its first and the second seasons, most episodes feature wall-to-wall music. The two-hour pilot is comparatively sparsely scored. It features "only" fifty-four minutes of music. In episode 3, the cues used total forty-six minutes of music. The episode is only forty-six minutes long. Several cues, though, overlap, and some are placed on top of each other.

David Lynch and his colleagues could layer different compositions as required, since most of Badalamenti's main themes were written in C minor and in the 4/4 time signature. These significant similarities made it comparatively easy to place several cues on top of each other. The most advantageous use of this technique can be observed in episode 3, as Bobby and Mike meet with Leo in the woods. Here, several musical cues play at once. Some start at the same time, some are slightly delayed, some are sped up, some are looped: "Dark Introduction" from "Laura Palmer's Theme," "Half Speed Orchestra 1," "Half Speed Orchestra 5 (Leo's Theme)," "Horne's Theme," "Audrey's Dance (Solo Rhodes)," and various sound effects at one point all play at the same time to evoke a dense atmosphere of disorienting dread. By mixing several cues that had already been recorded, the director and his team didn't need to call on the composer to write a new cue specifically for a scene. Instead, David Lynch sat down at the mixing board and experimented with the various existing recordings until he had found what he needed. This approach worked well for everybody involved.

> STEPHAN EICKE: *Did Angelo give you separate tracks for every cue he had recorded in New York?*
> LORI ESCHLER: Yes. […] They gave me a few drones as well. I took those and ran with them. I created other kinds of bizarre musical sound effects essentially. When you watch *Twin Peaks*, it's hard to discern music from sound. We all worked together. The final mix for each episode was a creative dream with the mixers and sound editors and the director and music editor. It was incredibly fun.
> STEPHAN EICKE: *Did you have detailed discussions with the sound designers on the show as well?*
> LORI ESCHLER: On the first season, it was more difficult because we hadn't quite established that synergy and understanding. In the second season they moved me over to the building where the sound editors were. I was right across the hall from Richard Davis, one of the sound editors. We all had many conversations. I would go down the hall to one of the editor rooms when he wanted to show me something and ask about the music. It was a very interactive process with these sound editors because when

you bring all of these guns to a scene you can't hear any of it. We would have to carve out little moments which said, "Okay, the music is going to swell here and we'll let the rain go away." For pretty much every scene we would do that either before we went to the final dub or when we were mixing. Everybody got onboard and they were mixing the way that David would have it. Sometimes he wasn't there and it was just a big mess. The head mixer, Gary, would just say, "Wait, let me just do a few things," and he would fix it himself. He knew how to carve those moments out. It was also great because I was very young and they listened to me. There weren't many women back then so it was nice to have a crew that respected what I was saying and trying out my suggestions. It was great.

STEPHAN EICKE: *Was David always present at the spotting sessions?*

LORI ESCHLER: Oftentimes if he wasn't the director he wasn't there. He would come for every episode and screen the final mix. Sometimes he would just change a couple of things and other times he would take a scene, take everything out, and put one thing in at a time, be it a sound effect or music. He would have us rework the scene if it wasn't working. That happened pretty often. He was very hands-on at the end of the day.

STEPHAN EICKE: *Overall, it sounds like working on* Twin Peaks *was a very playful experience for you.*

LORI ESCHLER: Right. There were never rules. A lot of the things that were being done were being done to save time. There were assumptions made. We would say, "This is how we did it in episode 3 and it worked, so let's try it here." If it didn't work, it didn't work. [...] That is how David lives his life. It's about the meditation and coming to this free place. He resets every day. At that time it was at four o'clock and he would reset. I had a really nice editing room with a brick wall and he decided that that was his meditation room. Every day I would have to leave for thirty minutes while he was meditating, which was fine with me. With him, he was always super curious and fascinated by so many different things. He would point things out that seemed like mundane, everyday things but suddenly you could see the beauty he was seeing because he showed it to people. That's why I said I was spoiled by *Twin Peaks*. [...] It was fun because it brought that element of play and kind of a communal effort. That was a thing that was really magical about it. We worked super hard and it was super fun and stressful at the same time. When we finished the last episode of the first season, I remember everybody looking at each other. David turned around and said, "I don't know if anybody is going to like this but I do." We had no idea what the response was going to be, but I believe that that approach he uses—that approach in all of his work—is one I am constantly striving for in my own life. It is a freedom to let my voice speak out and be Lori, be authentically me in everything I do. I was lucky in so many ways.[43]

Working with David Lynch had been, of course, equally playful for Angelo Badalamenti.

> *Almost everything in* Twin Peaks *was based on [David] coming to my office. He would then talk to be able to capture all the themes, which is an incredible way to work. With every project we have done in thirty-one years it's been where he has talked to me. In most cases I didn't even read a script. I didn't have to. I didn't have to see anything. He just talked to me, and then he would hear the music and he would know where it fits and where it belongs. It's a dream, an incredible collaboration.*[44] *We work in my office, and we go across to the same deli, every time. We never change or waiver. We walk in. The food is practically on the table by the time we get to the table. The same waitress brings over two turkey sandwiches, side order of fries, one—we split it—and a side order of bacon, cremated. And a couple of hot cups of darn good coffee.*[45]
>
> ANGELO BADALAMENTI

Badalamenti extended his music library for the show's second season by writing new pieces. Prior to that he was rarely called upon to deliver an additional cue. The burning of the Packard sawmill—in which Catherine Martell cuts Shelly's ties before a plank falls down dangerously close to them—was composed and recorded to picture, as was Benjamin Horne's miniature Battle of Gettysburg on his ping pong table.[46] Another scene for which Badalamenti wrote specific music was Leland Palmer's grotesque dance with Madeleine, a pivotal moment which occurs shortly before Leland is revealed as Laura Palmer's killer. Kinny Landrum had suggested developing a macabre waltz for the scene—a variation on "Laura Palmer's Theme" in ¾ time. Although David Lynch had imagined the scene to play in silence, Badalamenti liked Landrum's idea and wrote a cue to picture. In the end, he couldn't convince Lynch to use it, though. The director clung to his original idea and let the scene play without music. It ends simply with a needle scratching on the turntable. For Lynch, it was more haunting that way.[47]

---

[43]Ibid.
[44]*Angelo Badalamenti and the Music of Twin Peaks: Fire Walk with Me*, Prod. Susan Arosteguy, USA: Criterion Collection, 2017 [Blu-ray].
[45]*Literatti: Angelo Badalamenti.*
[46]https://www.reddit.com/r/Music/comments/391bfa/i_am_the_twin_peaks_synthesizer_player_and_more/.
[47]Ibid.

Lynch's longtime friend and associate Alan Splet was only peripherally involved in the sound design: his wife Ann Kroeber delivered a few dark wind sounds to the director following his requests.[48] Still, without Splet, *Twin Peaks* would have been a different show. The backwards-and-reverse talk in the Red Room scenes was inspired by Lynch's early days with Splet. Already in 1971, Lynch had started thinking about the sonic approach to his feature film debut, *Eraserhead*. Working with Alan Splet that year, Lynch recorded himself saying "I want pencils," and then asked his friend to reverse the sentence. The director listened carefully and learned to say what he was hearing, to say "I want pencils" backwards. After Splet had recorded it, he again played it to Lynch. Backwards. The director loved what he was hearing—a strange pattern and rhythm of speech, eerie and fascinating, backwards but forwards at the same time. Lynch didn't use the effect in *Eraserhead*, but remembered it as he was plotting *Twin Peaks*. When he shot the first scene in the Red Room, he used the technique and made his actors speak backwards.[49] Lynch was like a big kid on a playground. He had the time of his life.

The show would become a smash hit on television. Viewers worldwide were gripped by the mystery of who killed Laura Palmer and obsessed by the quirky, irresistible characters, curious to see in which direction this show would go—a show that was anything but predictable, refusing to bow to cliches long established in crime shows and soap operas. Although Angelo Badalamenti was proud of his work on *Blue Velvet*, which had proved a surprising success at film festivals, it was *Twin Peaks* which firmly put him on the map as a composer for film and television. In just a few months following the premier of the pilot, Angelo Badalamenti would become one of the industry's most sought-after musicians.

I never thought that Twin Peaks *would catch on like this, to be perfectly honest with you. It was just so outrageous and so quirky in a way. I was just thinking of all of America and saying, "Oh my goodness, what's going to happen in Iowa somewhere?" Or even in the major cities, it was just so unusual and innovative and so different that I thought there was not much of a chance, but I'm very happy I was incorrect about this.[50] I think it's the funniest show I have ever seen. [...] I have seen all the writing and all the critics and all the people calling saying, "Well, the music is just setting up so many of these moods, and it's like the music*

---

[48] Author interview with Ann Kroeber, September 11, 2020.
[49] Rodley, *Lynch on Lynch*, p. 165f.
[50] *Literatti: Angelo Badalamenti*.

makes you kind of wanna watch," and stuff like that. I don't know. I don't take the credit for that. It's totally by accident.[51]

ANGELO BADALAMENTI

Thirty-three percent of American households tuned to the channel broadcasting the pilot.[52] The premiere of the first regular episode brought ABC their best ratings in four years for the time slot (Thursday at 9 p.m.).[53] Its debut was a colossal success. The reviews for the pilot were nearly unanimously positive.

But ABC soon got restless. When the second season was commissioned, David Lynch found himself pressured by executives to reveal Laura Palmer's killer. He did so with great reluctance. He was by then busy with his next project, *Wild at Heart,* and the execution of the second season was mostly left in the hands of colleagues. The ratings plummeted and *Twin Peaks* died a quick death in its second season. Badalamenti's music, though, would live on, though nobody had thought about producing a soundtrack album as the pilot was shown and the first few episodes rolled out. Nevertheless, the instantly recognizable music turned out to be so beloved that people were clamoring to hear it away from the images. That became clear to Badalamenti as radio stations taped the show's main theme off the television to play it on the air. Only then did Warner Bros. decide to release a CD.

A single was quickly rushed out containing "Falling" with Julee Cruise, the *Twin Peaks* title theme, and "Floating." It peaked at number 11 on the Billboard Alternative songs chart. The album followed shortly thereafter, entering the Billboard 200 at number 72. It eventually peaked at number 22, two months after its release in September 1990. For the "Twin Peaks Theme," Angelo Badalamenti won a Grammy for Best Pop Instrumental Performance, beating Kenny G, Phil Collins, and Quincy Jones.

I asked David Lynch this question: why did we sell three million CDs with music for a television show world-wide? We made history. People all over the planet fell in love with the music. I really don't understand why they were so attracted to it. David, on the other hand, explained it very simply: the music was incredibly beautiful and it spoke to people. Maybe that's the answer. Although we would write exactly that kind of music every day if we really knew the answer to that question. Everybody who

---

[51]*A Conversation with David Lynch, Angelo Badalamenti & Julee Cruise on Industrial Symphony No. 1.*
[52]Bickelhaupt, Susan, "Twin Peaks vs. Cheers," *Boston Globe,* April 12, 1990.
[53]Carter, Bill, "Twin Peaks May Provide a Ratings Edge for ABC," *The New York Times,* April 16, 1990.

doesn't say so is a liar.[54] *[People] just thought there was a certain mood to the score. It captured David's visionary concept of the show.*[55]

ANGELO BADALAMENTI

Twin Peaks has a rich legacy. Even its harshest critics admit that it was highly influential. However, the legacy of *Twin Peaks* is tainted by the lackluster second half of its second season. After Leland Palmer, aka Bob, had been disclosed as Laura Palmer's killer, the show became a straightforward soap opera, and after thirty episodes, it was taken off air. A third season was not commissioned by ABC. Even David Lynch disliked the turn the show took in its second season. By then, he had already started to develop other projects.

---

[54]Müthing, "Ich schreibe in vielen unterschiedlichen Stilen."
[55]Schweiger, "The Madman and His Muse," p. 26.

5

Weird on Top

Wild at Heart and *Industrial Symphony No. 1*

The world is bad. Lula and Sailor know this from first-hand experience: as a teenager, Lula was raped by a friend of her father's and then forced to have an abortion. Later, she saw her father burn to death. Sailor grew up an orphan after his mother's passing from lung cancer. In desperate need for money, he became the driver for a ruthless criminal, the contract killer responsible for the death of Lula's father, Clive.

Sailor and Lula take refuge in each other's arms. Their love is their castle in which they can weather all storms. Together they are strong. Individually, they have found ways to deal with their traumas. Lula suppresses particularly horrifying details of her life (she remembers events quite differently from how they are presented on screen), while Sailor—donning a snakeskin jacket that expresses his "freedom and individuality"—imagines himself living in the 1950s, a much more innocent time. He croons Elvis songs and purports a coolness that echoes Marlon Brando in his early films. Anything that threatens Sailor and Lula's relationship must be destroyed.

Herein lies the film's big irony: Sailor wants to protect Lula and yet frequently puts her, himself, and their union in harm's way. For example, at the very beginning of the film he erupts when a male friend of Lula's mother, Marietta, confronts him in a hotel lobby. For Sailor, protecting his relationship with Lula means destroying the intruder. He does so swiftly and is separated from Lula shortly thereafter, condemned to nearly two years in a correctional institution. Here, David Lynch's *Wild at Heart* starts.

Sailor's and Lula's love for each other is strong enough to survive their separation. Both are aware, though, that they cannot stay in their familiar environment. Marietta is out for blood. They go on an odyssey that is likened by Lula to Dorothy's journey on the yellow brick road in *The Wizard of Oz*.

Although the heroes of *Wild at Heart* are hardened by their experiences, they live in a fantasy world. The constant references to one of Lynch's favorite films emphasize this, even though Sailor and Lula's journey is very different to that of Dorothy. Their journey is one of disenchantment. They find out what they always knew, that the world is a bad place full of crazy people. No decent character crosses their path. Compared to the people they are surrounded by, Sailor and Lula seem like citizens so ordinary they are almost boring. All they want is to be left in peace, to enjoy themselves.

Lynch was looking for a new project to take on when he met with his friend Monty Montgomery, who was eager to adapt Barry Gifford's novel *Wild at Heart: The Story of Sailor and Lula*. Montgomery passed a copy of the book to Lynch, who asked if he could direct the film if he happened to fall in love with the source material. His friend agreed.[1]

After having read it, Lynch informed Montgomery he would have to take him at his word: Lynch had fallen in love with the novel and wanted to adapt and direct it himself. Although he changed the source material considerably (by adding several references to *The Wizard of Oz*, making up characters, and changing the ending), Gifford was pleased with Lynch's work. Production was able to begin swiftly.

> Fire is the predominant symbol in *Wild at Heart*.
> The opening credits appear over a big wall of fire.
> Lula's father burns to death.
> The striking of matches is shown in radiant close-ups.

Fire has for centuries stood for passion. Sex and death are both often represented by flames—and Lynch gleefully combines the two. The director cuts to a match striking in the exact moment Lula reaches an orgasm. He shows Lula's father stumbling through his house as he realizes he is about to burn to death. His death by fire eventually unites Sailor with Lula, since the former witnessed the death of her father and partly blames himself. Thus, a death leads to love and sex. When Sailor finally confesses to Lula his role in the death of her father, he describes how he sat in the car, "until that whole place went up in flames."

Sex and death are also connected through the metal song "Slaughterhouse" by Powermad which plays several times in the film. It is used for the first time as Sailor smashes in the head of Marietta's friend who had threatened to kill him. The second time it can be heard as Sailor and Lula passionately make love. Lynch continues to use "Slaughterhouse" in moments of pure

---

[1] Rodley, *Lynch on Lynch*, p. 193.

passion, whether it is a moment of violence or love. Just a few notes of the track erupt as Sailor loses his cool. He is barely able to control himself when Marietta confronts him in a toilet cubicle. He suddenly punches the door. It is a brief moment of violence, a reflex, underscored by not even a bar of music from "Slaughterhouse." The song makes its appearance again later as Marietta remembers Sailor pointing at her, cigarette in his mouth, his hands bloody from the murder he just committed in the hotel lobby. Then, again, it can be heard as Sailor and Lula make love.

Wild at Heart is chock-full of songs, of pre-existing music of every genre: classical romanticism ("Im Abendrot"), metal ("Slaughterhouse"), jazz ("In the Mood"), rock ("Love Me Tender"), ethnic/world music ("Far Away Chant"), and avant-garde ("Kosmogonia"). It is the richest, most vibrant musical tapestry in any of David Lynch's films. The employment of different musical genres, of pieces from different periods, contributes greatly to a feeling of displacement. When does *Wild at Heart* take place? Sailor and Lula have clearly taken refuge in nostalgia, in the 1950s, while Marietta's home and Mr. Reindeer's mansion look unmistakably modern. The latter especially seems to have been constructed by an architect far ahead of their time. Sailor and Lula live in their own space, in the castle they have built for themselves as a couple. Although Sailor croons Elvis songs, they also listen to modern hard rock. It's the genre. For them, that genre represents freedom.

> *There's a lot of rock 'n' roll in* Wild at Heart. *Rock 'n' Roll is a rhythm and it's love and sex and dreams all swimming together. You don't have to be young to appreciate rock 'n' roll, but it is kind of a youthful dream about reveling in freedom.*[2]
>
> DAVID LYNCH

Sailor's immediate reaction to Lula's announcement of her pregnancy is to light two cigarettes instead of one. Unsurprisingly, Lula has doubts about keeping the baby. As an addition to their union, a baby is a threat to their freedom. For the entirety of their relationship, they have sought pleasure, diversions from their traumas. If they keep the baby, they will have to take responsibility. This constant pleasure-seeking is reflected in the soundtrack. Lula and Sailor cannot bear silence, cannot stand to be alone with their thoughts without the comfort of a benign presence humming and strumming in the background. Lynch plays a cruel joke on Lula when he has her driving the car and makes her listen to horrifying news of mutations, murders, and other catastrophes on every single channel on the radio. Lula cannot stand to hear more than one sentence from any

---

[2]Lynch & McKenna, *Room to Dream*, p. 299.

broadcast before she frantically turns the knob. She is a pleasure-seeker, and music gives her a respite.

Sadly, when she tells the story of Dell, she herself is not even aware of the irony: Lula explains to Sailor that she has a cousin named Dell who wanted to celebrate Christmas every day. Making Christmas an everyday occurrence of course robbed it of being something special. Lula knows this, and she calls it a bad idea. But she herself has the same attitude as Dell: she never wants her journey on the Yellow Brick Road to end, for it means unlimited, never-ending freedom. But refusing to take responsibility will eventually rob her of her liberty. She falls pregnant. When one celebrates freedom every day of the year, it eventually ceases to be freedom. It becomes its very own prison.

Throughout, it is Sailor's role to protect Lula from the badness and madness of the world, from her own traumas which threaten to resurface. When she is unable to find a channel on the radio that does not transmit news of utter horror, she eventually jumps out of the car and—as if about to cry hysterically—begs her partner to find a comforting piece of music for her. He does. Rock music starts playing, and their world is whole again as they start embracing in the sunset's orange glow. The rock song is quickly replaced by "Im Abendrot," by Richard Strauss, a vastly more romantic piece that also plays under the opening credits. It is part of Strauss' cycle *Four Last Songs*, and the composition is one of unbridled passion and longing. Strauss wrote it shortly before his death, in 1948, when romanticism had long been deemed passe and the concert hall celebrated the abstract serialism of Arnold Schoenberg and his followers.

Lynch uses Strauss' composition for its raw emotional power. It is pure passion captured in music, old-fashioned and therefore particularly fitting for Sailor and Lula. After the opening credits and the couple's sensual kiss in the sunset, the piece plays again as Lula lies on the bed in her motel room, wide awake, worried about Sailor, who has just gone off to rob a store. It is an endeavor that could, and does, rip them apart. Sailor does not die, as the sorrowful music might suggest, but he is caught by the police and put in prison for six years. Lynch cuts all other sound to let the music speak, to give room to its emotional power. Despite the intense feeling of longing "Im Abendrot" conveys, it is much more ambiguous in its mood than, for example, Samuel Barber's *Adagio for Strings* which David Lynch used in *The Elephant Man*. Strauss's music is not a funereal piece (solely) applicable to heighten scenes of tragedy and loss. Lynch also places it at the end of the film, when Sailor and Lula reunite in arguably the film's most uplifting moment. Like *Eraserhead* and *The Straight Story*, *Wild at Heart*'s ending is a happy one, while the denouements of *The Elephant Man*, *Lost Highway*, and *Mulholland Drive* are by comparison more ambiguous. Lula has learned to take responsibility by caring for her child. She has become what society deems a proper member. At the same time, the flame of passion

FIGURE 18 *Im Abendrot (from* Vier letzte Lieder, *1948).* Transcribed by Stephan Eicke.

between Sailor and Lula has not been extinguished. Their love is as strong as ever, having endured a grueling odyssey on the Yellow Brick Road and six years of separation.

Lynch uses Badalamenti's "Dark Spanish Symphony," a forceful and passionate piece for strings, in a similar manner. Its origin explains in a nutshell the intuitive working of Lynch and his composer.

> STEPHAN EICKE: *How did "Dark Spanish Symphony" come about? The film is not set in Spain and it doesn't feature any Spanish characters ...*
>
> ANGELO BADALAMENTI: This is a great story: David told me he was working on a movie called *Wild at Heart*. David comes in and says, "Angelo, let's have a writing session." He was staying in a hotel and I had another office, a very small one, across the street from Carnegie Hall on 57th Street. All I had in that office was this old Fender Rhodes. I still have that. David wants to put it in a museum, but I am not going to let him have it. David comes running in and says, "Angelo, can you write something Spanish for this film? Just sit down and play me something Spanish." I sat down and in no time at all I wrote the whole melody of "Dark Spanish Symphony." David was stunned. He said, "Angelo, you are not going to believe what I am going to tell you! You are not going to believe it!" "What, David?" He said, "I heard this music in my ears, the whole theme you just played, while I was riding in the train coming up to your office." "What?" "Angelo, I am not lying to you. What you just played I heard in my head as I was on the train coming up to your office!"
>
> STEPHAN EICKE: *Was he serious?*
>
> ANGELO BADALAMENTI: He was dead serious. Dead serious! That was it! He said it with a straight face, no smile, no laugh. I don't know. I mean, I am not one to deny that. He is very perceptive, very spiritual, very psychic or whatever. But he swears he heard what I played.
>
> STEPHAN EICKE: *It is a beautiful melody, romantic and yet with a dark undercurrent.*

Angelo Badalamenti: "Dark Spanish Symphony" was very important to me, in addition to it being in *Wild at Heart*. The Olympic committee in Barcelona was thinking about which composer to get for the music in the opening ceremony of the Olympic ceremony in 1992. They had a lot of composers, including Morricone and John Williams. They called me and said, "We are from the board of the Olympic committee and we would like you to be the composer for the opening ceremony in Barcelona." It stunned me. I said, "This is a great honor." Then I was thinking, why were they calling me? I am sure they knew *Twin Peaks* and all of that, but there had to be more to it. After I got to know the director he said, "Angelo, we were all in a room and we all heard 'Dark Spanish Symphony.' Once we heard it, we knew we had to get this guy." It's wonderful how a piece of material can get you these opportunities. What happened was they said, "Angelo, when you compose the music, give us a piece between five and seven minutes. Make a demo for us because we have to time the ceremony."

That ceremony was the one with the flaming arrow. They shot the arrow over the cauldron and the flaming arrow lit the cauldron. It was one of the best openings of the Summer Olympics. You can look it up on the internet. It's a great moment. I said I'd be happy to do it. They said, "You have three months to do it." "Great!"

I knew it had to be something special. I kept working on some things but I wasn't happy. They kept writing to me: "Dear Angelo, is it possible to get us this demo because we have to time when the man who comes into the arena has to hand over the torch? We have to deal with precise timings, so we need your music." I said, "I am working on it." I didn't have it. I wasn't happy.

Maybe three weeks before the Olympics, they stopped calling me "Dear Angelo." They were sending me a fax saying, "Dear Mr. Badalamenti." I knew I was in trouble. When you change from "Dear Angelo" to "Dear Mr. Badalamenti" you know you are in trouble. "We need to have that music!" That Saturday I was taking a shower at home. My wife and I were about to go out to a wedding of a friend of ours. I am taking a shower and I start to sing. I said, "What the hell am I singing? Holy God! That's the torch theme!" I run out of the shower, put a towel over myself, my wife says, "Angelo, would you drop the garbage?" I said, "Shut up! Be quiet!" I run downstairs to the piano and in twenty minutes I write the whole piece and get it out to them. I take a lot of showers now.[3]

---

[3]Eicke, "Mein Bruder David," pp. 23ff.

"Dark Spanish Symphony" is heard in *Wild at Heart* twice in its original version and twice as a variation. In its bittersweet nature, it is a theme typical for Badalamenti, and it aptly describes the relationship between Sailor and Lula—it is romantic, expressive, soaring while at the same time full of sorrow, longing, and darkness. Correspondingly, it is used in scenes of great intimacy, watershed moments in the main characters' romance: it makes its first appearance as Sailor and Lula have arrived in Big Tuna and are lying in their cheap motel room. Lula just "barfed," as she calls it. It is the first sign of her pregnancy. By that point, though, both think she might simply be carsick. The music plays in its original version for strings in the background.

> LULA: Do you think we could stay and rest here a couple of days?
> SAILOR: Are you carsick, sweetheart?
> LULA: A little, I guess. Sail, honey ... I hope seeing that girl die didn't jinx us.
> SAILOR: I got this for you. [*Hands her a candy necklace.*] It has forty different flavors. One for every reason I love you.
> LULA: Sail, I'm gonna save this. But if I ever eat it, I'll be thinking of you.

FIGURE 19 *Dark Spanish Symphony (Edited String Version) (from* Wild at Heart, 1990).
Transcribed by Andrew Morley.

The piece comes back a little while later as Lula writes to Sailor that she is pregnant. This time, "Dark Spanish Symphony" plays in a variation for guitar, piano, and drums as an homage to the 1950s. Following the failed robbery, Sailor sits in prison and reads a letter from his sweetheart shortly before he is to be released. The string version of "Dark Spanish Symphony" is barely noticeable in the background. The 1950s version comes back as Sailor and Lula see each other again out in the streets following his release from prison. Outside the facility, in the blistering sun, he meets his child for the first time.

> SAILOR: Lula.
> LULA: Sailor.
> SAILOR: You must be my son.
> LULA: Shake hands with your daddy, Pace.

SAILOR: It's a pleasure to meet you, Pace. I've read a lot about you.
LULA: You hungry?
SAILOR: Lead the way.

FIGURE 20 *Dark Spanish Symphony 50's Version (from* Wild at Heart, *1990)*. Transcribed by Andrew Morley.

"Dark Spanish Symphony" is Lula and Sailor's theme, a piece of intimacy and longing. Krzysztof Penderecki's "Kosmogonia" is its antidote. The director has been an admirer of the Polish composer's work for a long time. When Penderecki passed away in March 2020, Lynch grieved publicly on Twitter, writing: "Dear Twitter Friends, So sad to hear of the passing of Krzysztof Penderecki. Krzysztof Penderecki was one of the greatest composers of all time!!!"

Penderecki's work can be heard in *Twin Peaks: The Return* and *Inland Empire*. The composer's abstract sound collages appealed to the director for their unbridled power, but licensing "Kosmogonia" was a challenging undertaking, as David Slusser, the music editor on *Wild at Heart*, remembers: "We had to be prepared not to get the licensing because Penderecki said, 'You may use my music but not in a violent scene.' When Diane Ladd's character has ordered a hit on Sailor and you see her from behind, she is talking on the phone. Then she faces the camera and her whole face is red from lipstick."[4] Here, Penderecki's composition makes its appearance. Alas, the composer deemed the scene too violent. Slusser continues: "There is no violence in the scene, it's just this image of this agonized mother in red face crying and screaming with a face of pain in the camera."

Following some back and forth with the Polish maestro, Lynch received permission to use the piece. It also plays briefly as Sailor arrives at Perdita Durango's house in the middle of nowhere. In this way, Lynch draws a connection between Marietta and Perdita. What they have in common (apart from their strikingly blonde hair) will become clear only much later in the film. As Perdita appears for the first time, she is presented as Sailor's close ally. But the threatening, discordant music by Penderecki that accompanies Sailor's walk to her front door signals that his feelings about the woman are misguided: Sailor sees her as an old

---

[4]Author interview with David Slusser, February 23, 2021.

friend, but in fact—as Lynch later reveals—she is double-crossing him. Like Marietta, she wants to see him killed. Like Marietta, Perdita played a significant part in the death of Lula's father. Even before Perdita enters the stage, Lynch makes a musical connection to Marietta. Both women share a goal.

Lynch uses another song as a clear signal, a sardonic wink: as Johnny Farragut drives down to New Orleans out of love for Marietta, "Baby please don't go, down to New Orleans" can be heard on his car radio, a line from "Baby Please Don't Go" by Big Joe Williams, as performed by Them. As Johnny sees the sign welcoming him to New Orleans, he can only sigh "The Big N-O." He knows he is committing a grave error, but it is too late to abandon his fatal odyssey. He was a fool for love. He should have listened to Them.

The dark blues tune, "Up in Flames," was written by David Lynch and Angelo Badalamenti before shooting commenced (along with the instrumental pieces that Badalamenti contributed). Stylistically, it is unmistakably a Lynch/Badalamenti song: with its laid-back brushes, abstract electronic effects, downwards sliding saxophones, and minimalist lyrics it could have been part of the jukebox selection in Norma's diner. The song, about a love lost, and the pain that comes with a relationship going "up in flames," does not get much room to shine in *Wild at Heart*, though. Still, Lynch loved the piece for it evokes a whole story with just a few words. (Another piece he had written with Badalamenti was not used in the final cut.)[5] Koko Taylor's raspy voice intones only one verse before the camera cuts to Sailor and Lula sitting in a bar and the song continues quietly in the background as an instrumental. Sound mixer and music consultant Jon Huck remembers shooting the scene: "We had a live scene of Koko Taylor in a club with a band playing and she is singing a song. Besides Koko Taylor they had some really cool jazz and blues musicians. [...] They had earpieces in. When there is dialogue you can't have people playing music or you can't cut. So you can't have people playing music."[6] The musicians had to act as mimes. Huck was embarrassed: "For me to be this stupid kid going up to these incredible musicians who had worked with famous people to be like, 'Can you please not touch the cymbals? Don't strum the guitar.'" By that point, the piece had already been recorded.

For a different scene Huck also worked with Red Holloway, a celebrated saxophonist, though he is out of focus and silent: during a dinner scene at Mr. Reindeer's place, Holloway plays the saxophone, along with Dave MacKay at the piano, Kenny Wild on bass, and Joe Porcaro on drums.

---

[5]Ciment, Michel & Niogret, Hubert, "Interview with David Lynch," *Positif*, October 1990. Reprinted in *David Lynch Interviews*, ed. Richard Barney (University Press of Mississippi, 2009), p. 109.
[6]Author interview with Jon Huck, January 26, 2021.

Music supervisor Mark Roswell had heard Holloway play in a club in Los Angeles and approached the sax-player for *Wild at Heart*. The group happily accepted and played a tune Kenny Wild had written, "Blues Cake Jazz Icing." Following the recording of the first take, music coordinator Cheryl Churchill requested Holloway improvise a different opening, which he swiftly did.[7] Churchill was pleased. Yet, Holloway and his colleagues can be seen but not heard in the film. Instead, a duet for piano and violin plays, a light classical piece that could have been performed in European coffee houses toward the end of the nineteenth century. That discrepancy between sound and image gives the scene an eerie feel, which is supported and enhanced by the grotesque characters on screen. It is not the only mismatch between image and sound in *Wild at Heart*.

Red Holloway's appearance is an example of the absurd in the film. As Albert Camus observed, "The absurd is lucid reason noting its limit." Here, the audience cannot trust their eyes and ears. What can be seen or heard does not necessarily reflect reality. Lynch plays with the audience from the very beginning: as Sailor starts crooning his Elvis song in the dance club, enthusiastically screaming women can be heard cheering him on. However, nobody can be seen screaming despite the fact that Lynch shows several dozen club guests. They clearly enjoy Sailor's performance and adore his expression of true love for Lula, but their screaming seems to take place solely in either Lula's or Sailor's head. To make the moment of absurdity perfect, the club guests do clap their hands on the screen as the applause is heard from the soundtrack.

The most obvious examples for a mismatch between images and sound are Lula's memories of her father's death and the rape she experienced at the hands of his friend. As Lula and Sailor sit in bed, naked, she tells her boyfriend how she thinks Clive died. The camera stays on the couple as Lula explains what she was told by Marietta: her father poured kerosene all over himself and lit a match. Lynch then cuts to a flashback of a burning Clive stumbling through his living room in a blind panic—not the image of a man who did this to himself willingly. Unbeknownst to Lula, Sailor was present and knows how her father really died. Through the flashback—which differs from Lula's telling of the story—the audience learns what really happened. Lula's memory is not to be trusted. She has become an unreliable narrator.

When she recounts the aftermath of her rape, Lynch employs the same approach. Although Lula says her mother never knew anything about what happened between her and "Uncle Pooch," the flashback shows Marietta coming into the room shortly after the incident. She understands

---

[7] Zan, Stewart, "An Encyclopedic Review of the Idiom; Brunch to Aid Black Music Foundation," *Los Angeles Times*, September 13, 1989, https://webcache.googleusercontent.com/sea rch?q=ca che:OJ15gi3Vp4gJ:https://www.latimes.com/archives/la-xpm-1989-09-13-ca-2070- story.html +&cd=17&hl=de&ct=clnk&gl=de&client=firefox-b-d (accessed June 19, 2024).

immediately what transpired and starts attacking the rapist. Lula has suppressed that particular part of her trauma. In another instance, Lynch makes clear that what Lula is hearing does not reflect reality. She and Sailor lie next to each other in their hotel room as she asks him if he sometimes hears the wind and sees the Wicked Witch of the West fly by. He does not, as he ensures her. The wind is audible on the soundtrack, though only to Lula (and the audience). There is no chill in their hotel room. Lynch then cuts to an image of Marietta as the Wicked Witch of the West—an image Lula is seeing as a fantasy.

Sailor's confession to Lula that he was present when her father died marks a turning point, in that it signals the start of Lula's awakening: she realizes that Sailor knows about her father's death. The memory she has suppressed resurfaces as she understands that the version of events she was told by Marietta is highly unlikely to have been what transpired—her father did not set fire to himself. Suddenly, she has to face truths she never wanted to accept. Truths are being revealed—a painful process that disturbs Lula. The car crash the couple come across shortly thereafter is one of Lynch's less subtle symbols for his character's inner life.

> *I intended to include an accident where all the suitcases broke open so that clothes were strewn all over the road. I visualized that scene happening at night, and that image remained in my mind. Driving at night, and seeing, little by little, some pieces of clothing appear … It's one of my favorite scenes in the film, and it took shape in stages, and the last was the music. You come across different sorts of emotions—fear, mystery, horror—then this girl comes out of nowhere; there's humor in the dialogue, a horrible humor, and a sadness that saturates everything. And the music lifts the scene to another dimension. It's very simple music, like the kind children love. It's a very good scene for Sailor and Lula, because it defines their relationship better, how they become closer.*[8]
>
> DAVID LYNCH

After seeing pieces of clothing on the road, Sailor and Lula slow down their car. On the side of the road, they find a vehicle, overturned. They discover two corpses. A few moments later, a young woman appears (an unnamed character played by Sherilyn Fenn), out of the dark of night. Several things become clear to Sailor and Lula immediately: the girl is in shock, highly disturbed, not aware of what has just happened to her. They also understand that she is severely injured. There are pieces of her brain sticking in her hair. She picks at it. As she keeps searching for her items on the ground, she still hasn't grasped her situation.

---

[8] Ciment & Niogret, "Interview with David Lynch," p. 109.

Throughout the scene, Lula is helpless. She relies on Sailor to approach the woman and interact with her. Their plan is to get her in their car and drive her to the nearest hospital. The woman will never even make it to their car. She dies in front of them, and so Lula is confronted with death yet again, only briefly after having accepted the painful truth of her father's death. Her eyes are now fully open to the cruelty of the world, its horror and absurdity. The scene shows not just one death but two—the literal death of a young woman in the desert, and that of Lula's child-like innocence and naivety. Throughout the whole episode, a serene, minimalist piece by Angelo Badalamenti plays, "Dark Lolita."

> GIRL: This bobby pin ... I can't find it. My mother's gonna kill me ... it's got all my cards in it ... It was in my pocket. Now my pocket's gone. Gotta help me find it ... My mother's gonna kill me. It's got all my cards in it. And it was in my pocket. It was in my pocket. My purse is gone. My purse is gone! Now she tells me! Now she fucking tells me!
> SAILOR: Let's get a hold of her quick!
> LULA: Do you think she is going to make it?
> SAILOR: Don't know, but she's gonna bleed all over our car, I'll tell you that!
> Hey ... hello! Girl! Come with us, honey!
> GIRL: Leave me alone! Robert? Robert! Shit. Got this damned sticky stuff in my hair ... got sticky stuff in my hair.
> SAILOR: You better come with us, honey. Come on!
> GIRL: I gotta find my wallet ... Don't say one word of this to my mother, please. God, she's gonna kill me!
> SAILOR: Can't worry about that ...
> GIRL: Where's my hairbrush?
> LULA: God, she's dying right in front of us, Sailor.
> GIRL: Get my lipstick ... It's in my purse.

FIGURE 21 *Dark Lolita (from* Wild at Heart, *1990).* Transcribed by Andrew Morley.

Badalamenti chose not to underline the scene's horror with an avant-garde composition à la Penderecki, not with dissonant glissandi or dark synth pads that evoke dread and danger. Instead, he and Lynch devised a piece so simple and innocent it sounds like a lullaby. Played by Kinny Landrum with one finger on his keyboard, the piece exudes harmony and bliss. At first glance, it stands in direct contrast to the images, which are highly disturbing. But a piece as naive and tranquil as "Dark Lolita" brings an emotional depth to this scene of a person dying. Their circle of life is closed. Moreover, it is an apt score for the scene's symbolism, a contrast only on a superficial level. After all, it also accompanies the death of Lula's childlike innocence. What better piece to use than a quasi-lullaby? Judging from interviews with and statements by Lynch and Badalamenti, they did not analyze and interpret the scene and its music that way. "Dark Lolita" was devised and played solely for its raw emotional impact.

> *There's a beautiful scene in* Wild at Heart, *when Sailor and Lula come across a tragic car crash on the side of the highway. It's a traumatic event; it's horrible and tragic. A couple people have evidently died and they spot a bloodied girl wandering around confused. She's in shock, and not making sense. They want to help her but they can't—she's dying—and this simple music, a tune on the piano, plays over the scene. And the reactions of Sailor and Lula are wonderfully acted—it feels so real. Somehow David captured it.*[9]
>
> ANGELO BADALAMENTI

Establishing a contrast between music and images was, of course, Badalamenti's daily bread and butter when it came to Lynch's films. As the composer explained: "Sometimes the best kind of music goes against the images. A certain magic can come from that. In the whole of the *Twin Peaks* show—and in David Lynch's other films—I was going against the images intuitively as a composer. [...] It can be very effective."[10]

As already described, in *Twin Peaks* (and Lynch's other films) there are countless examples of music serving as a counterpoint to the images and overall story. This counterpoint can take many forms: Julee Cruise performing abstract alternative rock in a dingy roadhouse on the outskirts of a small town is one kind of contrast. Another is the placement of the skat/blues piece, "A Real Indication," over images of Bobby walking gleefully backwards in *Fire Walk with Me*, or the use of a partly dissonant blues number in the Pink Room. Lynch's world is full of such contrasts. However, "Dark Lolita" is an unusually direct composition for the reasons mentioned above.

Angelo Badalamenti's role as a composer for *Wild at Heart* was limited by the heavy use of pre-existing songs, some of which Lynch had fallen in

---

[9]Hundley, Jessica, "Pop Reinterpreted," in *Beyond the Beyond*, eds. J. C. Gabel & Jessica Hundley (Hat & Beard Press, 2016), p. 71
[10]Müthing, "Ich schreibe in vielen unterschiedlichen Stilen."

love with before shooting commenced. "Wicked Game" by Chris Isaak was one of them. Isaak, who would later play Chester Desmond in *Fire Walk with Me*, had released the song as a single in 1989, but it only became the success he had hoped it would be after the premiere of *Wild at Heart*. In early 1991 it reached number 6 on Billboard Hot 100, and it rose to number 1 in Belgium.

Lynch was always open to ideas for songs and other musical suggestions. He remained so throughout the production of *Wild at Heart*. Sometimes he asked music consultant Jon Huck for songs to use during the shoot, as the latter remembers:

> He would just ask me for a kind of music and say, "This is what's happening in the scene. It's a strip club, so find something sleazy." At the end of the film Nicolas Cage gets into a fistfight on purpose. David asked me to bring the Joe Morello drum solo from "Take Five." He wanted something like *West Side Story*.[11]

Not all pieces Lynch played on set were used in the movie. Sometimes, an alternative had to be found for financial reasons. At other times, Lynch came across a piece during editing that proved superior. Regardless, there were clear advantages to Lynch using music on set, as he had done previously. Although it was unusual for an American production to use music for the shoot, an initially taken aback Jon Huck quickly realized how beneficial this approach was: "[Playing music on set is] a step to get you closer to the complete picture or to have a help to get you more connected to what you are trying to do. Anything that helps is great."[12] Huck did not listen to the music since he had to pay close attention to any background noise. He continues: "The music was just for David and usually the script supervisor and a producer."

> STEPHAN EICKE: *Are you involved in choosing songs for David's films?*
>
> ANGELO BADALAMENTI: The answer to that is no. Directors like David—and Martin Scorsese, Woody Allen, etc.—choose the perfect memorable source songs for their films that they know will evoke these various emotions of a very special period in time. You can't write something new. You can't try to emulate something. It's not memorable because it's not in the memory of the people. It doesn't bring you back to the special period in time. David chooses the songs. He chooses what to include in the movie.

---

[11]Author interview with Jon Huck, January 26, 2021.
[12]Ibid.

He chooses the source songs and the songs we write together. You have to understand that he lives with these projects for such a long time. That's why he knows what works best for him.

STEPHAN EICKE: *Do you—or does he—make a difference between what an original composition of yours and a pre-existing song can achieve in a film?*

ANGELO BADALAMENTI: Both source material and score can evoke mood. That original score can be really tailored and at the same time hopefully be unique. It can have a strong force, an impact without the need for words. That's the strength of the score as opposed to the source. The bottom line is it really just depends on the scene.[13]

With *Wild at Heart*, Lynch knew early on that due to the nature of the story Badalamenti's instrumental pieces would take a backseat in favor of pre-existing rock pieces. *Wild at Heart* was neither *Blue Velvet* nor *Twin Peaks*, in which hardly a minute was left un-scored. The composer summarized it thus: "David Lynch always knows beforehand which material he wants to use for certain scenes. On that basis we discuss the original score. Those decisions are mostly taken by directors."[14]

As mentioned previously, Badalamenti started developing material sometimes long before Lynch commenced shooting. There are clear advantages to working that way. There are also disadvantages. Lynch treats his screenplays as a blueprint. They are therefore subject to severe changes throughout production. Sometimes, the film maker discovers late in post-production that he needs more instrumental underscore than originally anticipated. In that case, he has to call on his composer to provide additional pieces at short notice. In the cases of *Wild at Heart* and *Twin Peaks: Fire Walk with Me*, Badalamenti was not available at that late stage.

In both instances, Lynch turned to David Slusser, who had already worked on the *Twin Peaks* pilot. Slusser was still employed at Skywalker Sound when Lynch hired him as music editor on *Wild at Heart*. Luckily for Lynch, Badalamenti was able to send a 24-track recording of a string arrangement of his "Dark Spanish Symphony." Slusser recalls that the composer, then busy in Europe, had recorded the cue at the end of a session for an altogether different film. Recording it on a 24-track tape allowed Slusser and Lynch to extract individual parts—such as the lower strings—and use them as a bed for other music or sound effect elements. Moreover, it allowed them to transfer single notes from these individual parts onto a Synclavier, an early digital sampling system. When David Slusser pushed a key on the keyboard,

---

[13]Eicke, "Mein Bruder David," p. 23.
[14]Müthing, "Ich schreibe in vielen unterschiedlichen Stilen."

the Synclavier would play back one note as recorded by the strings in Badalamenti's session. That way, Slusser could use Badalamenti's original string sound but electronically modulate it according to the needs of a particular scene.

The moment between Marietta and Johnny Farragut as they sit in a hotel restaurant in New Orleans serves as an example: here, late in post-production, Lynch needed a musical filler. Since Badalamenti was unavailable, Slusser sampled Badalamenti's European string recording by transferring the notes onto his Synclavier. He then pressed a key for as long as Lynch wanted the note to last. Slusser played the Synclavier live to picture, during the film mix take. His playing went on the master file. It was an improvisation that didn't allow for a single mistake, says Slusser: "I'm actually playing an orchestra pad that was sampled from one track of Angelo's 24-track. I needed to get the same string sound. I said, 'Let's do this cello note and I will spread it across the keyboard.' You can do that on a Synclavier."[15] This was the way it worked:

> Take one sample and play it at several pitches so that the top notes are shorter than the bottom notes if you hold down the keys. You are actually playing samples of music. You have to play it a little differently in the right hand than in the left hand because you are going to run out of real estate in the right hand.

Thus, Slusser had created an undercurrent live to picture.

> STEPHAN EICKE: *What was the instruction David gave you then?*
> DAVID SLUSSER: "Go back there and play something low underneath." I was up to my own devices harmonically. The important part is it was a dialogue scene, so I had to play in a range that is not going to get in the way of the dialogue. Sometimes there would be some crazy business in the background track, guys fighting in the kitchen of the restaurant, for example. Finding when there is a little hole in the fabric of both the dialogue and the effects was my chance to make a change. I would feel my way through that like a fly on the wall, but playing live at the same time.
> STEPHAN EICKE: *It sounds as if it was an extraordinarily rich and even stressful mixing session ...*
> DAVID SLUSSER: Every day we had this creative stew. It was like Miles Davis directing some of his funky deep funk bands. [David] would just point at people with little motions. That was it, every single

---

[15] Author interview with David Slusser, February 23, 2021.

day. I had prepared material, I had Angelo's material, we had the sound effect things, we had the Synclavier plucked into the console and Angelo's 24-track tape, but that wasn't enough. It's the picture editing process and David would say, "I know it when I get it." We came to a dead end on a couple of scenes because of the way he felt about the characters. He was out riding at night during the mix for inspiration, to think, and he heard a song on the radio, and suddenly it made "Bing." "I know what to do with the scene." He comes in the next day and says, "Slusser, can you get a band together?" They were there the next day to do a knockoff of that tune that David heard on the radio. It's called "Perdita" on the album. I don't want to tell you what I was copying. This is what every music editor has to do, if they can't get the licensing: have your people do a knockoff. While we did the knockoff, we also did knockoffs of Angelo's piece, the "Dark Spanish Symphony," played by a bar band, my group. It had that 50s feeling, that nostalgic, sentimental thing that is underneath a lot of his more tense and violent things. It fit the formula perfectly.

STEPHAN EICKE: *"Perdita" and the 50s version of "Dark Spanish Symphony" are credited to Rubber City. That was you, then.*

DAVID SLUSSER: Yes. We did two pieces. One was Angelo's theme. I remember when we were tracking the original at Excalibur [Studios]. I had that arrangement in my head and we just did our own version of it. The knockoff is not related so much musically but in mood. "Perdita" and "Dark Spanish Symphony" really aren't of the same makeup but they do have that mood, and the mood is reinforced by having one band do both pieces in the same style. I was feeding David's love of that style.

STEPHAN EICKE: *"Perdita" plays as Sailor goes to visit Perdita Durango in her hut. Were the two pieces written to picture?*

DAVID SLUSSER: No, not at all. The knockoff we started—due diligence on my part—exactly in the same tempo and the same key. I think it was D sharp minor. I'm not a real piano player. I'm doing this 8th note thing, and after about ten takes my hands were rubber. That was done as an exact knockoff. As we were doing it David would come in to talk to the musicians and say, "Let's do it a little slower." It went from being an exact knockoff to what it became through David's direction. That's why he is the co-composer of that piece.[16]

---

[16]Ibid.

For Slusser, it was the most extraordinary mixing session he had ever been part of. His purview during post-production was manifold. For his adaptations and recordings of "Dark Spanish Symphony" and "Perdita," he hired musicians from Northern California, friends he had already worked with. The musicians stayed true to the idiom of the original pieces to deliver what Lynch envisioned. With "Perdita," Slusser allowed his musicians room for improvisation.

As music editor, it was also David Slusser's job to supply so-called "patches" using his Synclavier. These could be musical patches—as in the restaurant scene between Marietta and Johnny Farragut—or sound design patches. The difference between the two, though, became increasingly murky. For Lynch, it was all sound, as is exemplified by an idea he had for the film's penultimate scene. On the last day of mixing, the director requested yet another arrangement of Badalamenti's "Dark Spanish Symphony"—as Sailor jumps over the hoods of cars to take Lula in his arms, and indirectly propose to her, Lynch wanted car horns to play the melody of Badalamenti's original composition. The string version would then take over as Sailor and Lula embrace.

Slusser struggled with Lynch's request. At that point in the mix, he was exhausted, as he confesses: "I knew what I was going up against because the klaxon is usually two pitches, maybe at an augmented fourth. European car horns are different. These would be American horns but I tried to sneak a couple of European cars in there because their horns might have been a more simpler harmonic tone."[17] The American car horn is a tritone, which proved the biggest challenge for Slusser: "I was trying to play 'Dark Spanish Symphony' on a Synclavier using car horns. I tried it a million ways. I used every horn I could find in the Lucasfilm sound library. This is the last day of the mix and I'm sampling all these things and I'm playing it live." It didn't work, as he had to admit to himself: "I could not play 'Dark Spanish Symphony' on the car horns. [...] The movie would have been much better with car horns playing Angelo's theme. That's what we needed there."

Lynch's idea, so Slusser thought, was a good one: the car horns would slowly fade out and blossom into Badalamenti's yearning theme for strings, emphasizing the dream-like quality of the scene in which Sheryl Lee makes her appearance as the Good Witch. Thinking back, Slusser laughs: "You are asked to do that a couple of times a day on this mix. Do the impossible and let's see what happens."[18] For once, Lynch's idea did not work.

Wild at Heart showcases a wide range of audio, in terms of both music and sound design. Some effects nearly make the audience jump out of their seats. Already the appearance of the title *Wild at Heart* in the opening credits

---

[17]Ibid.
[18]Ibid.

is an assault on the senses, accompanied by extreme blasts of sound. Every match strike is amplified, nearly bursts the audience's eardrums. David Lynch always liked extremes.

Mixing in Dolby Stereo—the first of Lynch's films to use that system—allowed the film maker to expand the sound field exponentially. Some pieces of music are barely audible. Lynch also employed some of his favorite tricks: Chris Isaak's "Wicked Game" plays on the car radio as Lula and Sailor drive through the night. The sound is muffled, as if recorded in a bucket under water. Lynch had filtered the singer's voice. Prior to shooting, Chris Isaak had given the director both the vocal and instrumental recordings of the song.[19] Subsequently, Lynch did with both versions what he had grown to love during his working-relationship with Alan Splet: with Isaak's permission he slowed them down to half-speed.[20] Lynch loved the eerie sound he created using this technique.

As music editor, David Slusser worked closely with sound designer Randy Thom during the final mix at Skywalker Sound. It was Thom's responsibility to take the production sound and ambient recordings, manipulate, and insert them into the film according to Lynch's instructions. Ambiences had already been recorded during the shooting of the film—an unusual approach, as sound mixer Jon Huck remembers, since such materials are normally only created in post-production. Lynch, though, was insistent to ambiences recorded on and around the sets. He called on his former assistant John Wentworth who had already captured field recordings for the *Twin Peaks* pilot.

> STEPHAN EICKE: *After* Twin Peaks *you worked on* Wild at Heart ...
> JOHN WENTWORTH: It was super interesting to work during that time because the transition from analog technology over to digital platforms was in full swing. You had to be able to say, "Okay, look, this analog stuff is junk, how do we do digital?"
> STEPHAN EICKE: *Did David give you any instructions as to what kind of sounds and ambiences he wanted you to record?*
> JOHN WENTWORTH: Honestly, no. I went through the scripts with *Wild at Heart* and the *Twin Peaks* pilot. I would just highlight specific needs for sounds and then I would record the specific sounds. I would just get ambient sounds at all the different places we went.
> STEPHAN EICKE: *Do you remember specific places you went to for* Wild at Heart?

---

[19] Marcone & Philp, "Interview with Angelo Badalamenti."
[20] Grow, Kory, "David Lynch and Angelo Badalamenti on Their Wild Jazz Experiment," *Rolling Stone*, October 31, 2018, https://www.rollingstone.com/music/music-features/david-lynch-angelo-badalamenti-talk-experimental-album-thought-gang-749688/ (accessed June 19, 2024).

JOHN WENTWORTH: I have one very distinct memory. I had a stereo digital audio recorder with a nice Sennheiser microphone. I went out to try and find desert ambient sound. I went out to this town called Trona which is north of Mojave, way out in the desert. It's a desert version of a David Lynch hellscape. It's different than Philadelphia but it's a hellscape. There was a large, long train sitting in a siding. I think it was probably Coleman's. I think they mine borax there. The atmosphere was really still, super quiet, hot. Clear. I was recording and I was getting great little sounds coming out of the industrial plant, the sounds of the idling locomotives. It was so beautiful, and to be listening to it in stereo in digital was like, "This is the coolest shit ever." While I was recording it, unbeknownst to me, a locomotive about half a mile away backed up into the cars. It was completely unexpected. I could hear in stereo each one of these cars bumping one into the next into the next into the next one. The whole thing took like a minute and went all the way through right in front of me and went on off to the right. It was just the most mind-blowing thing. In that desert setting, it was so quiet it sounded crystal clear.

STEPHAN EICKE: *Do you know where this particular sound was used in the finished film?*

JOHN WENTWORTH: I have no idea. Again, at the end of the day I was an employee for the production. Sometimes they would say, "What is a sound recordist?" "Fine, man, maybe you don't get the kind of aesthetic you are dealing with." I would deliver all my material to the production. I didn't give it to David. I would tell David about it and I made sure that when it came to the post-production and mixing that the sound designer knew about it and knew how to read my logs. I made sure it made its way through to the production. What they did with it I don't know. I was not a sound designer. A lot of the sound designers would record their own effects and then they would know what they had. I wasn't a sound editor. [...] I would walk them through all the stuff I recorded and then they would start to build their tracks. They might use a sound from one scene in a completely different place.

STEPHAN EICKE: *Fire plays a pivotal role in* Wild at Heart ...

JOHN WENTWORTH: Yeah, and I recorded a lot of fire. David likes fire a lot. Fire is pretty tricky. It doesn't sound like a whole lot. If it's wood fire it does some popping. If it's a gas jet fire that sounds like something but typically when the mix comes into it, it could be anything.

STEPHAN EICKE: *David loves room tone. Did you record any of that?*

JOHN WENTWORTH: No. As part of the production process, the sound recordist takes room tone. They record the ambient noise of the room that they are shooting in. You got to have it for when you are cutting dialogue. I was never worried about getting that kind of audio. That was the on-set sound recordist's responsibility. I was looking for crazy stuff, for stuff of which I figured 90 percent would never get used. I went out to find the most extreme types of things, as full a variety of different textures that David and the sound designers could work with. By the time I started doing this I was making my own short film and I was getting a lot more experience with audio mixing, so I understood what David was talking about when he said "firewood." I said to him, "I am going to give you as wide a variety of things as possible that I can find and I appreciate that 90 percent of it probably no one is going to listen to anyway." It's important that my logging, my description, was clear because I knew that the first set of eyes was going to be the sound designer or the sound effects editor saying, "I need this." At the time you started to see digital libraries on CDs. They could just pull a foghorn off the CD. I was collecting "firewood," unique things. I wanted to make sure I collected things that were not going to be in those sound effects libraries they had on these CDs.

STEPHAN EICKE: *Did David use libraries?*

JOHN WENTWORTH: Yes. The sound effects editors would just use it. It was interesting because during this period a lot of analogue recordings were digitized and burned onto CDs. Typically you get on the mixing stage, they preview the scene and start bringing everything together. David would say, "I need something over here. I need this or that." A lot of times the obvious effects like a car horn were fine but you would never know what he would start obsessing over. Then it was a question of "Do we have it in the tracks?" The sound effects editors and designers were very aware David would ask for these things on the mixing stage. They would have tracks built. If David said, "I need something," they would say, "Look at track 26." "Mixer, play that, see if that will work." They wanted to be prepared.[21]

The final mixing sessions of *Wild at Heart* were, according to both David Slusser and Randy Thom, highly creative and utterly exhausting. Lynch set out to manipulate a plethora of various songs, insert and filter ambient sounds, and fill musical gaps live to picture. He was much more directly involved and hands-on than other directors Slusser and Thom had worked with.

Like any other area of his craft, the editing process was for Lynch not an intellectual one. He edited with cue cards, as David Slusser shared. It was a

---

[21] Author interview with John Wentworth, January 30, 2021.

highly unusual procedure, especially for an American filmmaker operating within the studio system.

On each square card Lynch had sometimes handwritten, sometimes typed the name of a scene. He then pinned the cards on the bulletin board in the editing room. Sometimes he shuffled them around, as Slusser recalls when remembering how musician John Zorn applied the same approach to music: "John would record an A roll and a B roll. That's how you get all these quick cuts in his music. You would have eight players and they would each be assigned to an A set of tracks and a B set of tracks on a 24-track machine."[22] It was an intricate system that was highly successful, as Slusser continues: "When, for example, cue card 6 ends, the next time you roll tape you punch in on the bottom set of tracks with cue card number 12. That's how you get these really quick cuts. David worked the same way, especially with *Wild at Heart*."

Lynch's particular approach to editing meant Randy Thom and David Slusser had to remix several reels of the film. A scene which had previously been at the beginning of the movie suddenly moved toward the end. Since sounds bleed in and out of any scene, prepared elements had to be re-synced. As Thom and Slusser were constantly "improvising," as both call it, they had to work quickly, keeping several balls in the air at the same time. Luckily, David Lynch had found the right partner in Randy Thom, a sound mixer and sound designer who had previously worked on *Raiders of the Lost Ark*, *Return of the Jedi*, and *Apocalypse Now*. For neither man, the line between sound and music was not thin—it was imaginary. When Thom previewed some of his initial ideas to Lynch, it became immediately clear that they were on the same wavelength.

> STEPHAN EICKE: *How did you get involved in* Wild at Heart?
> RANDY THOM: Alan Splet, a genius and a very gentle soul, was having a hard time dealing with the violence in *Wild At Heart*, and he decided he couldn't work on it. Duwayne Dunham, the film's editor, and I had met on *The Empire Strikes Back*, and he recommended me to Lynch as someone to replace Alan. I had a meeting with David, and he liked me enough to hire me on Duwayne's recommendation. Nobody could ever have filled Alan's shoes. He was a unique talent, and his collaboration with Lynch was also one of a kind.
> STEPHAN EICKE: *Were you familiar with some of David's previous work?*
> RANDY THOM: I was very familiar with David's work, and I had actually met him before. A girlfriend of mine had worked at the Pacific Film Archive in Berkeley, CA. When *Eraserhead* came out

---

[22]Author interview with David Slusser, February 26, 2021.

David did a Q&A at a screening there, and we were tasked with taking David out to dinner. We were told that David did not like fancy restaurants, so we took him to a Denny's, I think.

STEPHAN EICKE: *I heard unconfirmed rumors that the scene with Nicolas Cage beating Bob Ray Lemon to death was originally taking place much later but was moved to the beginning of the film in the course of the edit ...*

RANDY THOM: By the time I began working on the film, the beating scene was at the beginning. That's the first scene I worked on. I wanted to quickly do it as a sound design sketch to see if I was approaching the movie aesthetically in the way David wanted me to. I made the scene as violent as I could, sonically, and played it for him in a screening room. He and I sat together in the front row, with nobody else in the room except a technician in the back. I had made the scene extremely loud ... the punches, the guy's head being pulverized on the stair railing, etc. To say I was nervous about how David would react to it would be a gross understatement. When the projector stopped David turned to me and said, "Randy, you have no idea what sound like that does to me." The technician in the back said "That'll never go to optical," meaning that it was so loud that it would be impossible for it to be reproduced by the analog audio track most common in those days on film prints played in movie theaters. I didn't care. We would worry about that later. I had passed the audition.

STEPHAN EICKE: *How did working on* Wild at Heart *differ from other projects?*

RANDY THOM: *Wild at Heart* might have been the most intense working experience I ever had. I was supervising the sound, creating almost all of the sound design, and supervising the mix. It's rare for one person to be doing all of those things simultaneously on a high-profile film with a famous director. And it was still very early in my career. I was extremely nervous about attempting to fill Alan's shoes and working with David, this icon of the art film. The mix was especially stressful because we were constantly improvising, and of course we didn't have an unlimited time to complete it. The movie had to show at the Cannes Festival. That was our deadline. I almost had a nervous breakdown. David demands a tremendous amount of you, but he is a kind person with a wonderful sense of humor. That's what kept me from going over the edge.[23]

---

[23] Author interview with Randy Thom, December 14, 2020.

David Lynch kept himself protected from a nervous breakdown by meditating twice daily for twenty minutes. Then, it meant back to work, and since Lynch always enjoyed layering various sound effects and musical pieces, "firewood" and ambient soundscapes, every single one of the eighty inputs on the mixing console at Skywalker would be in use. Lynch participated actively, and quickly Randy Thom assigned the director his own fader on the console. With this fader, Lynch was now able to mix sound and music himself. Briefly, Lynch and Thom considered sharing the credit for sound designer. Eventually, though, Lynch decided against it. The sound design for *Wild at Heart* is credited as Randy Thom's work alone.

As Thom and Slusser noticed early on, nothing about their work on the film was orthodox. Nothing they had learned and observed on previous projects could be applied to Lynch's approach. Unlike any other director, David Lynch refused to pre-mix. For him, this meant enjoying greater freedom in experimenting with sound. It was all about improvisation. David Slusser explains: "[David Lynch] would bring in a sound if he wanted it to follow whatever his trail of images were. Randy was doing it at the same time, so things would weave in and out. Film mixes are always fluid that way."[24] At this stage, everything is constantly changing. However, things were still changing during the final mix. Says Slusser: "Laying down an effects pre-mix is like playing music. The final mix where everything should be, 'Faders straight line, we've got all the pre-mixes done … ' no, not on this film. It was recorded live to the film."

Randy Thom quickly understood that sound and music for Lynch were purely "about emotion," as was every other element in his storytelling.[25] The sounds had to reach under the audience's skin. And so they did. The sound effects are as violent and extreme as the images seen on screen. They grab viewers by the throat and shake them, refusing to let go. The quickly rolling thunder that accompanies the title card—*Wild at Heart*—prepares the audience for what they will hear throughout the film. To communicate his ideas, Lynch spoke to Thom as he did with Angelo Badalamenti: he described individual scenes with dream imagery.

Despite the heavy workload, Lynch and his team managed to finish the picture in time for the premiere at the Cannes Film Festival in 1990. It won the Palme d'Or. The pilot for *Twin Peaks* had just premiered a few weeks before to rapturous reviews. Although the critics' reaction to *Wild at Heart* in the United States was mixed, there was no question that David Lynch was then at the peak of his career. He was the rare American film maker who could triumph at Cannes and simultaneously engross the masses at home in an altogether different medium.

---

[24] Author interview with David Slusser, February 26, 2021.
[25] Author interview with Randy Thom, December 14, 2020.

Although *Wild at Heart* may seem at first an unusual, surprisingly literal film by the abstract artist, it is upon closer inspection undeniably a creation by Lynch. Much like *Eraserhead*, *Twin Peaks*, and later *Lost Highway* and *Mulholland Drive*, it depicts the individual's journey to freedom. To find inner peace, in *Eraserhead* Henry eventually rids himself of the monster that is his child. In *Blue Velvet*, Jeffrey Beaumont over the course of just a few nights grows up to become a man able to face the darkness of the world. In *Twin Peaks*, Bob is the evil spirit that possesses people and makes them commit horrible crimes—only then does he leave their body and search for another host. But in *Fire Walk with Me*, Laura refuses to be host to Bob. Her death presents itself as an odyssey into another dimension, where she, resting in the arms of angels, experiences contentment and, finally, bliss. In *Lost Highway*, Fred Madison murders his wife and escapes into a dream world. He is unable to cope with his feelings of guilt until he is forced to face up to his crime. In its depiction of guilt, *Lost Highway* is a close cousin to *Mulholland Drive*. Lula in *Wild at Heart* has not committed a crime, but has suppressed her traumas. She has constantly sought pleasures in order to not have to face and deal with her life's cruel truths. Already before she and Sailor arrive in New Orleans, the facade that she has built to shield herself has begun to crack. In its sonic texture, in music and sound design, *Wild at Heart* is undeniably and unmistakably a pure David Lynch film. Considering the mixed reviews for *Wild at Heart* and *Lost Highway*, and the outright hostile ones which *Fire Walk with Me* would receive, it seemed that the world, and particularly the United States, was not yet ready to consider Lynch's themes of trauma and the spiritual road to bliss.

Yet Sailor and Lula's love for each other was not destined to last. They split up shortly after Sailor has crooned "Love Me Tender." It is he who makes the decision to uncouple and move on. For Lynch, their painful separation over the telephone is the starting point for his *Industrial Symphony No. 1: The Dream of the Brokenhearted*.

> LULA: Where are you? You sound far away.
> SAILOR: Yeah. Well ...
> LULA: What's wrong?
> SAILOR: Listen, I ...
> LULA: What is it?
> SAILOR: I am taking off, baby. I can't do it no more.
> LULA: Can't do what? What?
> SAILOR: I guess I'm saying goodbye is what I'm doing.
> LULA: Goodbye? You saying you don't love me anymore?
> SAILOR: I can't ... I mean, I gotta go.
> LULA: You are joking me, aren't ya, baby?
> SAILOR: No, I ain't sugar. Ain't nothing wrong with you. It's just us I can't handle. I'm saying goodbye.

LULA: Don't say that. Please don't go.
SAILOR: I can't do it no more. I gotta go.
LULA: Please. Please.

And so to *Industrial Symphony No. 1: The Dream of the Brokenhearted*. The Brooklyn Academy of Music was organizing a New Wave musical festival and was keen to commission a work by Lynch. In a meeting, the director mentioned half-heartedly he and Badalamenti were working on a project entitled *Industrial Symphony No. 1*. Much to Lynch's surprise, the Brooklyn Academy seized on the opportunity and hired Lynch and Badalamenti to develop the project for the stage. The duo briefly looked at each other and rolled up their sleeves.

The truth was, they had no idea what they wanted to do. The name *Industrial Symphony No. 1* had come to Lynch spontaneously, subconsciously as often happened.[26] There was no specific concept behind the title and *Industrial Symphony No. 1: The Dream of the Brokenhearted* was prepared to be staged in the span of a few days.

The forty-five-minute show was performed at the Brooklyn Academy of Music in November of 1989, and it illustrates Lula's inner turmoil following Sailor's traumatic breakup with her. Lula's inner world is not a pleasant one: most of the stage is pitch-black, only certain spots are illuminated, dimly, by a handful of overhead lights. The abandoned wreck of an old car sits in the middle of the stage. Pipes run everywhere. A small drilling tower looms over the characters. It is an industrial hellscape. One of the characters is a grizzly, tall monster—a disfigured deer, blood-red as if all its skin had just been pulled away. Ballet dancers swirl around in homage to Lynch's beloved 1950s swing music. Michael J. Anderson, the arm from *Twin Peaks*, saws a log on stage. *Industrial Symphony No. 1* showcases several of Lynch's works in one one-hour performance: *Wild at Heart* had not premiered yet, but still Sailor and Lula open the production before Julee Cruise enters to sing "Up in Flames" from the film. Later, she sings "I Float Alone", the first of several pieces from her album *Floating into the Night,* a record that had just been released a few weeks earlier. *Twin Peaks* would be the talk of the town in just a few months, when the pilot would be shown on ABC.

During the course of the ambitious stage show, Cruise, hanging from a rope, floats in the sky like an angel. She is locked into the trunk of the abandoned car, then watches on as semi-naked dancers swirl around to the ever-present noise of a dark wind that permeates everything. Michael J. Anderson then enters the stage again—accompanied by the sounds of the composer's son, André Badalamenti, playing the clarinet. Anderson repeats

---

[26]*A Conversation with David Lynch, Angelo Badalamenti & Julee Cruise on Industrial Symphony No. 1.*

Sailor and Lula's last conversation. It is a dialogue that Lula simply can't get out of her head. It is her torture.

Badalamenti wrote a few musical bridges which served as a showcase for Julee Cruise and helped promote her then-recent album. There was hardly any time for Badalamenti to do more. *Industrial Symphony No. 1: The Dream of the Brokenhearted* was quickly put together, and preparing for the two performances on November 10th was a hair-raising experience.

> STEPHAN EICKE: *Do you remember anything in particular about* Industrial Symphony No. 1?
>
> ANGELO BADALAMENTI: It's not a big deal. The *Industrial Symphony* was put together so fast, you cannot believe it. I almost felt like doing it over night because David and I already had the music done on tracks that he incorporated into it. There is not much to say on it. It all worked out and it was fun project. He would let a man walk on stilts and put Julee Cruise in a car coming out of a trunk on cable wires. But as far as the music was concerned, we had most of that. I had my son André play clarinet and then Laura Dern would tell the story. That's really what was done under David's direction.[27]

The endeavor was complicated since elements for the production—such as Sailor and Lula's conversation at the beginning—had to be pre-recorded and then inserted into the live show. Then there were more practical issues that needed to be solved such as developing a costume for the deer and making actor John Bell walk on stilts without having him topple over mid-performance. Lynch and Badalamenti had two days to put up the set and rehearse. Due to the technical specifications, it proved a nightmare for everybody involved. Having cameras swirl around the stage to capture the action from different angles complicated the preparations even further. The elaborate sound design and musical bridges had to be carefully synced with the action on stage. For example, baby dolls would fall down and hit the boards before a pre-recorded song was to play. There would be no more performances of the show afterwards. That much was clear even at the time.

Jon Huck was responsible for making sure that the sound worked. It was one of the tensest experiences he has ever had on any job, as he remembers: "That was one thing where we triggered sounds live. The soundtrack for the show was played back on a DAT. That was nerve-wrecking because during the rehearsal there is a climactic scene: everybody is on stage, there is a guy on stilts, and Julee Cruise is on the trapeze. There is this cacophony going on. It was new technology."[28] Suddenly, everybody's worst nightmare became

---

[27] Unpublished quote for Eicke, "Mein Bruder David," pp. 20–5.
[28] Author interview with Jon Huck, January 26, 2021.

a reality: the digital tape machine just stopped working during rehearsal. Dead silence. Every actor froze in their position. Huck was positioned in the booth, Lynch stood in the front of the theater. The former drew a breath: "We were all on headphones. There was this big silence and nobody knew what to do. We were all just looking at each other. There were three guys working with me. I hear David's voice on the headphones after a long pause: 'This can never happen.'"

The show itself went fine, which was a surprise to everybody who had been present and actively involved in the rehearsal, during which an accident had occurred: John Bell had fallen from his stilts and bruised himself. The video recording of *Industrial Symphony No. 1* shows him moving only tentatively and slowly, holding on to the rig to his left. His movement was supposed to be more fluid and confident, though Bell was by then reluctant to put himself in any danger again.

As wild as the sound collage of *Industrial Symphony No. 1* is, with its constant wind sounds, instrumental bridges, songs and noises from, for example, screaming animals, its original concept was even more outrageous. Huck elaborates: "The whole piece was mapped out on this piece of tape. It was almost like a music video. [...] David had a lot of input about the samples and during rehearsal. [He would say,] 'Don't play too many of these screaming animals.' We cut some of the sounds down. We had a huge library of stuff that was pulled out."[29]

The show was a success in that *Industrial Symphony No. 1* didn't suffer any unforeseen mishaps—a miracle considering the technical challenges and the short time everybody involved had had for preparation. Lynch enjoyed the experience greatly. As a result, in the mid-1990s he and Badalamenti pondered staging a Broadway musical based on the life of Nikola Tesla. It was an idea they discussed regularly through the next few years before eventually abandoning it.[30] Emerging feature film director Eli Roth worked as a research assistant for Lynch and Badalamenti.[31] Lynch's then-studio manager John Neff details: "[Eli] was researching everything he could get on Tesla. He did it as an intern so he wasn't being paid for it."[32]

A short while later, Roth planned to shoot his feature debut, *Cabin Fever*, a horror film about a group of high school students who are attacked by a deadly virus in a remote cabin. Roth managed to secure financing for his project after he had convinced his then-employer, David Lynch, to

---

[29] Ibid.
[30] De la Vina, Mark, "A Composer Hitting His 'Peak'," *Philadelphia Daily News* [Philadelphia], October 18, 1990, p. 56.
[31] Roth, Eli, "Cabin Fever Liner Notes," *Cabin Fever*, Prod. Ford A. Thaxton, Nathan Barr, La-La Land Records, 2003 [CD].
[32] Author interview with John Neff, June 18, 2021.

serve as producer. However, there are no traces of Lynch's early involvement in the finished film. Neff continues:

> When David saw a rough cut of it, he took his name off it and he said, "This isn't my cup of tea," but Eli already had the money and the movie was already shot. Eli wanted to mix it in David's theater but David wouldn't allow it. Eli had to mix it elsewhere. [...] Angelo volunteered some cues for free. It was sort of a payback [for Eli's research work on *Tesla*].

John Wentworth, who worked as producer on *Industrial Symphony No. 1*, is not surprised plans for a Broadway show never went anywhere, saying: "*Industrial Symphony* was very interesting because the script for that was the album, the Julee Cruise record. There was a script which was the album. There was no narrative associated with it. It was very abstract. [...] With the idea of David and Angelo doing a Broadway show I'm sure they ran into, 'Who's going to write the book?'"[33] After all, when it comes to financing an expensive Broadway show, producers are reluctant to invest without seeing a book first that maps out the concept and individual scenes. Considering Lynch's reluctance to be wedded to a precise script, it is not altogether surprising that producers were not willing to back a project based on vague descriptions alone, even by a renowned director. However, David Lynch had enough ideas to keep himself busy over the next few years.

---

[33] Author interview with John Wentworth, January 30, 2021.

6

Angel Falling

Twin Peaks: Fire Walk with Me

Within the first three minutes, it is clear that *Twin Peaks: Fire Walk with Me* will be very different from the TV show on which it is based. At the end of the title credits stands a smashed television set. It is one of David Lynch's less subtle images. Large swaths of critics and the audience were sorely disappointed by—and even angry at—the film. The show had set up certain expectations that were not met. Arguably, the film's first act is misleading, being in tone both as quirky and haunting as *Twin Peaks* was as a television show. It is only after Chester Desmond's disappearance that the film shifts gears, and not just in tone but also in setting.

The reaction to *Fire Walk with Me* was not divisive at the time. It was unanimous. While critics and members of the audience shared multiple reasons for their hatred, a decisive factor for the film's poor reception was how confidently it strayed from the popular series. Freed from the leash that had been held by producers at ABC, David Lynch and co-writer Robert Engels created something that was unashamedly violent, dark, gory, and abstract. They were simply not interested in rehashing old themes and repeating tried jokes. *Fire Walk with Me* was a different animal, a wild beast that refused to be tamed.

One year prior to Laura Palmer's death, the evil spirit that is Bob claimed the life of a seventeen-year-old waitress and part-time prostitute called Teresa Banks. Following the discovery of her body floating on the water, wrapped in plastic, the FBI starts to investigate the circumstances of her passing. It is up to Special Agent Dale Cooper to pick up the pieces. He finds that Bob's helpers—an old lady and a young boy who will taunt Laura Palmer shortly before her death—had set up shop in the trailer park, but left abruptly following Teresa Banks's death. Cooper senses that something strange is going on, and he fears that the prostitute will not be the last victim of the killer.

At this point, *Fire Walk with Me* undergoes a sudden change. Lynch fasts forward one year: Laura Palmer is walking down a leafy street in her hometown of Twin Peaks. Slowly, the director unveils the darkness hidden behind shallow facades: Laura Palmer might be smiling as she is heading to school, but turmoil is raging inside her. She is becoming aware of the fact that her time on earth is running out. The ghosts chasing her will not rest until she is in her grave.

Fire Walk with Me is a relentless portrayal of teenage angst and depression. It is the study of a breakdown. Laura has been raped by her father since she was twelve years old. Heavily traumatized, she slips into madness. She experiences visions, behaves erratically, and is increasingly cruel toward her best friend, Donna. *Fire Walk with Me* is also a film about Donna's pain, which she expresses in quiet, long glances. Overwhelmed, she is silent as she witnesses how Laura transforms into a stranger before her eyes. It is shocking and painful. Donna tries to save her friend but is unsure how to go about it, while Laura keeps hurting her out of malevolence, as Donna perceives it. It's a pain familiar to anyone who ever was a teenager, who ever experienced the end of a friendship, or saw their object of desire hook up with a nemesis. Helplessly, Donna keeps trying to impress Laura, to get back in her good books. Every attempt is in vain. Laura's pain is Donna's pain, James's pain, even Bobby's pain. It is a pain that is endless. It runs in circles.

Audiences at the time did not expect to see a committed, confident, and unforgiving study of pain and suffering. They had hoped to see more *Twin Peaks*, a show that dealt with the same subjects with a different focus and in a slightly lighter way. While the show left much of its horror to the viewer's imagination, *Fire Walk with Me* put the camera right in front of it, where it hurt. The camera does not look away as a topless, drugged Laura Palmer receives oral sex in a secluded party room with ear-splitting music drilling through the speakers. Here, look, Lynch says, this is who Laura Palmer was, the person you perceived as an angel as you saw her lifeless body on the pebble beach. But although the director doesn't spare Laura Palmer from trauma, it was a film born out of love for her—as paradoxical as it may seem.

> *I happened to be in love with the world of* Twin Peaks *and the characters that exist there. I wanted to go back into the world before it started on the series and to see what was there, to actually see things that we had [only] heard about. There is a danger, of course, that the more you know about anything, the more depth of appreciation you can get from it. [sic] But I think, although I have been wrong many times in the past, that*

someone could get very much from [the film] not having seen anything of the series.[1]

DAVID LYNCH

Following Lynch's winning the Palme d'Or at Cannes and the initial huge ratings received by *Twin Peaks* on TV, everyone wanted to work with him. Producers, actors, and writers aimed to catch some of the light that Lynch now radiated with the popularity he had achieved.

Lynch initially saw this success as a chance to finally realize his passion project, *Ronnie Rocket*. When the French production company Ciby 2000 courted the director—by, among other things, promising him to finance *Ronnie Rocket*—Lynch decided to sign a three-picture deal with them. The first film in this new creative partnership would not be *Ronnie Rocket*, though, but *Fire Walk with Me*. Everything seemed to be going well. Although several actors from the show refused to participate in the movie, and despite the script being heavily revised several times, less than a year went by from putting finishing touches to the screenplay to the film's screening in Cannes.[2]

In that time David Lynch also worked on the music with Angelo Badalamenti. Following their successful collaborations on *Blue Velvet*, *Twin Peaks*, and *Wild at Heart*, Lynch was eager to resume the creative partnership with his "long-lost brother" as he called him.[3] Their method of devising and recording music prior to filming had proved effective. Although the feature is more abstract and experimental than the series, Lynch and Badalamenti didn't simply invert the musical landscape they had developed for the show. Instead, they expanded it by including abstract and experimental pieces: "The Black Dog Runs at Night" and "A Real Indication" are two examples. Familiar themes and musical moods from the show make their appearance, albeit briefly. Appropriately, "Falling" is only used once, as the town sign of Twin Peaks appears on screen for the first time, seven days prior to Laura Palmer's murder and one year after Teresa Banks' death. As a signature tune, the instrumental puts the audience among the Douglas Firs, in the leafy green streets of a small town that initially appears just as innocent and clean as Lumberton did in *Blue Velvet*. But whereas "Laura Palmer's Theme" was used more than a dozen times in the show's pilot alone, Lynch and Badalamenti insert it only briefly in the film—thrice, sometimes barely audible and distorted, as if they were ashamed of it. Still, it fulfills the same

---

[1]Murray, Scott, "Twin Peaks: Fire Walk with Me. The Press Conference at Cannes 1992," *Cinema Papers* 89 (August 1992): p. 28.
[2]Chion, Michel, *David Lynch* [2nd edition] (BFI Publishing, 2006), p. 134.
[3]Eicke, "Silencio! Reise in den Abgrund," p. 13.

function as in the show in that it signifies pure love. As Leland confesses his love to his daughter, it is the fatherly affection he feels for his child. Free of Bob for the time being, Leland's feelings are pure, even if his daughter doubts their authenticity. It is a scene that illustrates how guided Lynch is by intuition, how he places mood over intellectual concepts: although the scene is seen from Laura's point of view—the camera looks up at Leland as Laura sits in front of him—the music reflects his feelings, not hers. It is *his* love he is sharing. Laura does not respond in kind. By this point she knows that none other than her father is her rapist. Nonetheless, a theme expressing pure love is playing on the soundtrack.

Following being raped by her father, "Laura Palmer's Theme" is the only comfort afforded to her as she sits in her classroom, barely conscious, her face puffy, swollen from crying. Nobody else is available to help or even hug the damaged wreck that is Laura Palmer, the girl under the influence, radiant on the outside, dying on the inside. Tellingly, the love theme is absent as Laura meets her various boyfriends. Although both James and Harold appear genuinely besotted by the seventeen-year-old (whereas Bobby seems to view her as little more than his plaything), Lynch refuses to approve their feelings as he had in the show. The theme acknowledging pure love is not used. These scenes are told from Laura's point of view, both visually and acoustically. After having been raped repeatedly by her father for five years, she has no love to give to anybody. Just her desperate, passionate goodbye to James—her goodbye to the world as a whole, shortly before her murder—is accompanied by the Laura Palmer theme. It was preceded by "Dark Introduction," the danger motif that indicates what the viewer already knows: Laura's end is near. Even so, she has to expect more intense suffering before she is released into the arms of the angels. (Although the "Dark Introduction" opens the movie, it is used solely as an accompaniment to a yearning trumpet solo, a new theme devised for the film. Here, old and new are combined, joining forces.) Later, "Dark Introduction" is used in a variation, played on a synthesizer using high-pitched chords as Laura's body, wrapped in plastic, is dumped in the river by her father. He is again possessed by Bob.

> *I think the scoring is more darkness than horror. We imply power through the darkness of the music. At least, that is what the intention was. [...] Musically speaking, it might be a shade broader and just a little larger than the approach on the television series. But very similar to the characters and the style.*[4]
>
> ANGELO BADALAMENTI

There are a few other musical quotes from the series, used briefly and fleetingly. For example, the saxophone solo from "Dance of the Dream

---

[4]Murray, "Twin Peaks: Fire Walk with Me. The Press Conference at Cannes 1992," p. 28.

Man" plays as Special Agent Dale Cooper enters the story. In the show, audiences were introduced to the theme as they saw Cooper for the first time, driving toward Twin Peaks, speaking into his Dictaphone to Diane. Fittingly, "The Bookhouse Boys" is played as Laura meets James at the school and they start making out—unbeknownst to Bobby who is entering the hallway while his girlfriend is being caressed. Later, Lynch uses "Dark Mood Woods" and "Night Bells," two pieces originally written for the series as dark, abstract ambient collages that underscore the dread and danger which lie in the misty woods around the titular town.

There are other similarities to the series. Most notably, *Fire Walk with Me* is scored wall-to-wall. Hardly a minute is left without music. Badalamenti's and Lynch's pieces accompany Laura at all times—as she is going to school, lying on her bed, sleeping with Bobby, confessing her fears to Harold, chatting innocuously with Donna. *Fire Walk with Me* is an overwhelming sound collage, in terms of both music and sound design. As in the series, the two elements are often indistinguishable. In his book on David Lynch, scholar Michel Chion observes: "*Fire Walk with Me* contains a whirligig of stressed sound effects [...]. This constant sound activity, the source and nature of which often remain obscure, is one of the film's most original aspects. It creates a sense of the screen as a fragile membrane with a multitude of currents pressing on it from behind."[5]

In one of the film's pivotal scenes—Leland's confrontation with Gerard at a crossroads—Lynch uses one of Badalamenti's pieces as "firewood" to startling effect: "It's Your Father" is slowed down to half speed and played in reverse, a technique Lynch had already applied with great proficiency in *Blue Velvet* and *Twin Peaks* the show. Sometimes, Badalamenti's "firewood" is layered with other elements: a theme for Laura and Harold (used when Laura unburdens herself to the young man who is unable to leave his house) is put underneath the so-called "Unease" motif that had previously been used in the series under the title "Slow-Speed Orchestra 2."

Julee Cruise continued her musical partnership with Lynch and Badalamenti, making an appearance in the roadhouse singing their composition, "Questions in A World of Blue." They would later put the song on Cruise's second album *The Voice of Love*, released in 1993. Although the record was less enthusiastically received than *Floating into the Night*, it still earned favorable reviews. For example, the *Chicago Tribune* noted that, "it has a fuller sound than its predecessor, Cruise's voice is richer and the last album's gimmicky mid-song shifts have been replaced by less jarring stabs at playfulness, such as the finger-snapping 'Kool Kat Walk'."[6]

---

[5]Chion, *David Lynch*, p. 142.
[6]Caro, Mark, "Julee Cruise—The Voice of Love," *Chicago Tribune* [Chicago], November 25, 1993, p. 104.

> *Sometimes you want the music to go along with what's happening on screen. Other times I love the idea of the music going* against *what's happening—that's often a cooler way to do things. Like Julee Cruise, with her ethereal, angelic voice ... to have her singing in a rough redneck bar, as she does in* Fire Walk with Me. *I mean, there's no way in hell that would really happen. It's the contrast that makes it work. So I always have one major question for a director when I compose a soundtrack: what do you want your audience to feel? Do you want to scare the shit out of them? Squirm in their seat? Feel beautiful? And how they answer that question gives me cues to work on. I translate their words into music.*[7]
>
> ANGELO BADALAMENTI

Both "A Real Indication" and "The Black Dog Runs at Night" serve as examples of the more audacious musical nature of *Fire Walk with Me* when compared to the TV show. The latter cue combines sound design with dreamy wind sounds and jazz featuring a walking bass figure. It includes an avant-garde poem that Badalamenti himself recites and that consists solely of its title, repeated over and over and over again. In the film, it is used twice, as a leitmotif for the elderly lady—Mrs. Chalfont—and a young boy. The audience is introduced to the piece as Laura sees the two figures in a photograph: Mrs. Chalfont and the boy stand in the barely furnished room above the convenience store, in Bob's lair. The piece appears again briefly as Leland—in a flashback—gets cold feet about his rendezvous with Teresa Banks and runs away from the motel where they were supposed to meet. The small boy appears behind his back, apparently upset about Leland's decision. Mrs. Chalfont and the boy are watchmen, servants of Bob, eager to see Teresa and Laura killed by Leland Palmer. They are impatient to have the girls possessed by Bob. When both Teresa and Laura refuse to let the evil spirit enter their bodies, they have to die. "The Black Dog Runs at Night" is Mrs. Chalfont's and the boy's leitmotif.

Lynch has declined to comment on the title's meaning. Famously, the English writer Samuel Johnson had coined the expression "black dog" to describe his periods of depression. It was later used by Winston Churchill, who suffered from prolonged feelings of desperation and dread. He was often unable to leave his bed for days at a time. When speaking about his fragile mental health, he repeatedly referred to his depressive episodes as the "black dog." For some people suffering from depression and anxiety, the symptoms are especially severe during the middle of the night, when they are unable to sleep, gripped, and haunted by the darkness that surrounds them. Then, the black dog runs rampant.

---

[7] Soghomonian, "Angelo Badalamenti Interview—'Twin Peaks Just Will Not Die'."

Laura has every reason to be depressed and anxious. Her nights are especially grim; as she breaks down when she is assaulted by Bob, as she tearfully says goodbye to James, as she goes wild in the Pink Room. Mrs. Chalfont and the boy are harbingers of evil who literally contribute to Laura's nightmares: they hand her a photograph that will serve as a portal to her worst dreams.

> STEPHAN EICKE: *Did David Lynch ask you specifically to reuse some themes from* Twin Peaks *the show in the feature film?*
> ANGELO BADALAMENTI: Of course, with something like that David and I would get together and think about it and discuss it. We were fortunate because we already had developed that musical identity from the television series that had its own unique sound that had stuck in the collective psyche. It was just a matter of developing that and working in new ideas that suited the longer form of a feature film.
> STEPHAN EICKE: *Can you elaborate on how one of the new pieces—"The Black Dog Runs at Night"—came about?*
> ANGELO BADALAMENTI: We were in my office in New York. I had an office in the early days in the hotel McAlpin, West 34th Street. My keyboard was there and David would come up when he wanted to talk about a project. I had a microphone there. He opened up a window—it was on the 12th floor—and I had this cross ventilation going. David jumped up and said, "Listen to that sound, listen to that sound!" "What sound, David?" "Listen to that sound of the wind! It's only two windows open and air is coming through. But it's beautiful!" So, he said, "Put this microphone here, start recording this sound and I got this thing 'The Black Dog Runs at Night.' I want you on the microphone to just say 'The Black Dog Runs at Night.' Just keep repeating it." It was off the cuff and what I did was I spoke it in my deepest and most basso profundo voice. That's what we used. He loved it. It was just a fun thing.[8]

Angelo Badalamenti's voice can be heard in another cue: "A Real Indication," a quasi-rap piece with jazz playing under its abstract lyrics. It is used in *Fire Walk with Me* as Laura shares a brief conversation with Bobby in the front of her school. Smug and arrogant, her boyfriend starts dancing backwards following their encounter. Whereas in the series, similar scenes displaying Bobby's carefree suaveness were usually accompanied by Badalamenti's instrumental cool jazz—"Audrey's Dance" in the pilot, for example—here

---

[8] Eicke, "Mein Bruder David," p. 23.

Bobby's confident gait is heightened by the music, even to the point where it is ridiculed. Lynch does this by having him walk backwards, like in a carefully choreographed musical, and by underscoring his gait with a piece so abstract in itself that it appears to have been conceived for a different scene.

> During Twin Peaks: Fire Walk with Me, *we were in the studio, working on a track, "A Real Indication." David came up with a lyric and he kept asking, "Who can we get to sing (and speak it)?" I told him I was going to sing it. This made David nervous. So, I went into the studio and we started to record this outrageous thing. David laughed so hard in the studio that night he was crying and eventually doubled over. He actually had a hernia. He had to go to the hospital the next day.*[9]
>
> Angelo Badalamenti

A doctor advised Lynch to undergo surgery immediately. Concerned, the filmmaker informed her that he had to go out and shoot a movie. Hesitating briefly, the doctor allowed him to finish work first. Although Lynch enjoyed shooting *Fire Walk with Me* and being reunited with many old friends both in front of and behind the camera, he forever remembered the pain he was in throughout the shoot.[10] Lynch did not let his pain show. Quite on the contrary, his meticulousness impressed and occasionally frustrated some members of the crew, as sound mixer Jon Huck describes: "During *Fire Walk with Me* up in Washington State there was a dead body [of Teresa Banks] that is in one scene, in a cabin. They were doing an autopsy. The woman who was the dead body was not right. David ended up working with the make-up artist."[11] Lynch would not budge, much to the initial frustration of some crew members, as Huck recalls: "It was not decayed enough to his specification, to what he had in his head. He was like, 'Everybody go drink coffee, we are gonna fix this.' They spent a lot of time on that which would not happen in a normal shoot."

Devising other new themes and arrangements was less painful than recording "A Real Indication" had turned out to be. One of these new pieces was the opening, a mournful blues piece for muted trumpet (played by Jim Hynes) that signals how different the film is going to be from the series. While Lynch and Badalamenti had used jazz in the show and even though their cool jazz pieces had included abstract effects, *Fire Walk with Me* is, with the exception of brief passages that were either lifted from the

---

[9] Gabel, J. C. & Hundley, Jessica, "Interview with Angelo Badalamenti," in *Beyond the Beyond*, eds. J. C. Gabel & Jessica Hundley (Hat & Beard Press, 2016), p. 35.
[10] Lynch & McKenna, *Room to Dream*, p. 325.
[11] Author interview with Jon Huck, January 26, 2021.

series ("Dance of the Dream Man") or written in post-production by David Slusser ("Deer Meadow Shuffle"), devoid of that specific musical sub-genre. Instead, Badalamenti's jazz is darker, similarly abstract, but more dissonant and unsettling. It offers none of the loftiness that pieces such as "Freshly Squeezed" displayed. The "Theme from Fire Walk with Me" is haunting, bathed in dissonant minor chords.

"Dark Introduction" is used, placed unmistakably in the background, indicating that danger is lurking around the corner. Nothing good is going to happen to any of these characters in the next two hours. As if "Dark Introduction" was not enough to imply as much, a muted trumpet dances forlornly in the foreground. It yearns and mourns while the upright-up bass seems strangely disconnected both to "Dark Introduction" and the new theme. It doesn't so much react to their rhythm and phrases as it performs its own solo dance, seemingly oblivious to its musical surroundings. This has a disorienting effect, especially since the piece is placed over images of a dead television. On the soundtrack, though, several elements play at the same time.

> *The opening, the main title, was just this rhythm section—piano, bass, drums—and it's the only time I've used a muted trumpet. Then in the middle part it became very dark, but it segued in a certain way: it's got dark chords, but it still felt cool but melodically. I'm planting a seed and say, "Hey, it's gotta be cool but watch out!" That opening title was important because it did set a little bit of a jazz feel. Using the instrumentation was great, the sound of the vibraphone, special guitars and of course the synth and a stand-up bass as opposed to an electric base so the player could so some very special picking and bowing, [to create something] dissonant and eerie. There was a lot of that in* Twin Peaks: Fire Walk with Me.[12]
>
> ANGELO BADALAMENTI

Another noteworthy piece in *Fire Walk with Me* is an original composition by Badalamenti, entitled "The Voice of Love." In its full version, it appears at the end of the film, when Laura is already dead and has finally found

FIGURE 22 *Theme from Fire Walk with Me (from* Twin Peaks: Fire Walk with Me, *1992).*
Transcribed by Andrew Morley.

---

[12] *Angelo Badalamenti and the Music of Twin Peaks.*

her peace. She encounters a bright, radiant angel in the Red Room. Laura is relieved of her anxiety and depression, of the torment she had to endure while she was alive. Heavily made up, wearing expensive-looking jewelry, her hair glamorously styled, she cries tears of joy after years of going through hell. Here, in *Fire Walk with Me*, death is a happy ending. It is a scene accompanied by the most uplifting piece on Angelo Badalamenti's soundtrack, a serene composition of dense synthesizer chords. The music also serves as a reminder to the audience. It is a throwback to an earlier scene that foreshadowed the film's finale: as Donna and Laura are lying in the living room of the Palmer house, innocently chatting about James's sweetness, the conversation suddenly swerves into darker territory, becoming an existential discussion about death and the afterlife. Donna doesn't realize it, but when Laura answers her friend's initial question, she is talking about herself. Laura, sensing the end is near, shares her vision of herself shortly before her ascent into heaven.

> DONNA: Do you think that if you were falling in space that you would slow down after a while or you go faster and faster?
> LAURA: Faster and faster, and for a long time you wouldn't feel anything. And then you would burst into fire. Forever. And the angels wouldn't help you because they have all gone away.

FIGURE 23 *The Voice of Love (from* Twin Peaks: Fire Walk with Me, *1992)*. *Transcribed by Andrew Morley.*

While Laura is sharing her thoughts with Donna, gentle synthesizer chords carefully hint at Badalamenti's "The Voice of Love." The music foreshadows Laura's death as it will be shown just before the end credits start rolling. The end—death itself—is the release after Laura's long and vertiginous fall. By the time she is sharing her thoughts with her best friend, Laura is not yet burning, but her clothes have already caught fire. She is dead inside—mocking Donna and James, sticking her tongue into old men's mouths in the Pink Room, prostituting herself. Eventually, she bursts into fire. Laura realizes she is soon to die when one night the angel in a painting disappears. The angel afforded her serenity. Now her time has come, and nobody is there to help her. The angel is the first figure whose love Laura can fully accept, in the alternate dimension that is the Red Room.

> *When David was describing it to me, [he said], "This is the end of her life, right, right up to the day before." He told me there is going to be a picture on the wall and Laura is going to be looking at this. She now knows what's in store for her, and her father also knows that she knows what's really been going down. She sees this picture, and there is this angel. She is looking at it and the angel kind of disappears. David said, "Angelo, she is gone already but there is going to be an angel that's going to be on top of her, doing all of this, and there's going to be tears coming out of her eyes, even with a smile as she's crying, I want everyone that sees this to cry with her and feel for her, because they love her so much and know what she's gone through. It's gotta be so beautiful." These were my instructions.*[13]
>
> ANGELO BADALAMENTI

"The Voice of Love" is immediately preceded by Badalamenti's "Sycamore Trees." As Leland Palmer enters the Red Room and starts floating in front of Gerard and the Man From Another Place, Lynch introduces the instrumental version of a song he had developed with Badalamenti prior to shooting. The vocal version is included on the soundtrack album. The lyrics, penned by Lynch, had been developed more than a decade prior, in the years following the director's success with *Eraserhead*. They appear—though in slightly different form—in Lynch's still unproduced script for *Ronnie Rocket*. There the text is not sung but spoken when a young woman addresses a tattooed man in a hotel room. She is being overheard by a detective as she asks the man to take her for a walk among the sycamore trees at night. Under the branches they will be able to "see each other." The man threatens her, rejects her suggestion. In the early 1990s, Lynch pulled the piece of dialogue out of his drawer and encouraged Badalamenti to write an accompaniment. Despite the lyrics not having been written for *Fire Walk with Me*, the piece forms an appropriate, integral part of the album (as a song) and of the film (as an instrumental). It features a similar bluesy flavor to the mournful opening credits, and shares the dark synthesizer chords with both "Dark Introduction" and "The Voice of Love."

Unsure about who to book as vocal artist, Lynch and Badalamenti received a suggestion from Warner Bros., the label that had released *Floating into the Night* and that would also release the soundtrack for *Fire Walk with Me*. The company suggested a voice talent they had under contract called Jimmy Scott, a jazz singer with a high contralto voice. Scott had scored several hits in the 1940s and 1950s before his career started to slump in the 1960s and Scott saw himself forced to work menial jobs. By the time he was suggested for the recording of "Sycamore Trees," Scott had just experienced a small comeback

---

[13]Ibid.

that would be cemented with the release of his album *All the Way* in June 1992. Lynch was open to the idea of using Scott and suggested Lynch and Badalamenti audition him. After the vocalist had listened to the composer play his accompaniment and after he had read the lyrics, he started to sing, and—according to Badalamenti—"nailed it" immediately.[14] Scott proved the perfect choice for the song. With his gentle, yet slightly raspy voice, he gave the composition exactly the kind of desperate yet hopeful yearning that it required. Badalamenti was transported right back to his childhood, to the songs of the jazz artists he had so admired in the 1940s and 1950s.

> *I was brought up on jazz as a youngster. My older brother Steve was a jazz trumpet player in the bebop era of Charlie Parker and Miles Davis. He'd bring these jazz musicians to the house every Sunday. My mother would be making macaroni and meatballs for them! I'd hear all of this stuff, and I ended up playing it. As far as the film noir feel goes, David loves movies from the 1950s. He's into Roy Orbison. So on projects like Twin Peaks: Fire Walk with Me, I'd work on the jazz end. I used trumpets a lot in the style of Miles, who influenced me. So I fall naturally into that somewhat dark, bluesy music that has that off-center feel about it. Yet I try to keep my own identity when I use that style.*[15]
>
> ANGELO BADALAMENTI

Lynch and Badalamenti had written a wide variety of instrumentals and songs. For the first time in his film-making career, the director did not license pre-existing pop songs by other artists. Only one piece of music that had not been devised under the supervision of Lynch was included in *Fire Walk with Me*: The *Requiem in C minor* by Luigi Cherubini, written in the early nineteenth century. In the film, excerpts from the composition are used twice; as Leland—possessed by Bob—finally stabs his own daughter to death while Gerard and the Man From Another Place look gleefully on, and as the end credits roll.

Again, Lynch found it useful to play music on set during the shoot. Badalamenti's compositions had already been recorded. By listening to the music on his headphones, the director knew how characters were supposed to move, how the music would impact the mood of the scene, and how he could later edit the corresponding footage. Jon Huck found Lynch's approach to play music during the shoot highly unusual. It wasn't ordinarily done in film: "Everybody had headphones, the director and the script supervisors. We only played the music through the headphones with the dialogue. David could hear the music mixed in the headphones just for the vibe. The actors

---

[14]Ibid.
[15]Schweiger, "The Madman and His Muse," p. 26.

didn't hear anything. It was just for him to see how it was playing with the music."[16]

The advantages for Lynch became immediately clear to Huck: "I think he is so attuned to sound and music and knowing the mood he had already worked out with Angelo that it's easier for him to have all the pieces of the puzzle in place. [...] For David it was probably just helpful to see if the scene was really working with the mood he was going for."[17]

However, as rich as the tapestry was that Lynch had developed with Badalamenti during pre-production, the director later noticed he needed more material still. As Lynch discovered during the editing, several scenes did not work either without music or with any of the compositions that had already been recorded. *Fire Walk with Me* was developed, shot, and edited quickly, and both Lori Eschler and John Wentworth (who served as co-producer on the film) remember the post-production process as stressful, even troubled. Lynch initially feared that the project was not coming together as he had envisioned. Eschler says,

> Everybody was all in in terms of no life. We were cloistered nuns and monks and all we did was go to the dub stage and work day and night. Because it was a much more complex piece of storytelling [than *Twin Peaks*], we would get to these points where nothing was working because there were so many new side stories and subtexts.[18]

Composer David Slusser saw another reason why Lynch felt increasingly uncomfortable during the post-production on *Fire Walk with Me*: unlike *Blue Velvet*, *Twin Peaks*, and *Wild at Heart*, the prequel to the television show was not assembled and edited in Northern California, but in Los Angeles. It was a much more controlled environment, with less creative freedom for Lynch and his crew. The director resented the restrictions imposed upon him by the various unions, as Slusser recalls: "They are much more union conscious down there. In Northern California nobody gave me crap for being a music editor cutting sound effects into David Lynch's music tracks. In LA they say, 'Get your music out of my sound effects tracks,' and 'Get your sound effects out of my music tracks.'"[19] That was not the way David Lynch wanted to work. It felt restrictive and small-minded. Slusser continues: "To him it's all sound. They might not have given him a fader [like he was given during post-production on *Wild at Heart*]. That's the difference."

---

[16] Author interview with Jon Huck, January 26, 2021.
[17] Ibid.
[18] Author interview with Lori Eschler, January 19, 2021.
[19] Author interview with David Slusser, February 23, 2021.

According to Lori Eschler, editing was a challenge not solely for bureaucratic or logistical reasons: "He was creating this alternative, above-the-convenience-store mystery. The original music for *Twin Peaks* didn't quite cut it and neither did the stuff they [recorded] in New York. We used a lot of that but there were moments when he needed something different."[20] Since Angelo Badalamenti was by then busy with other projects, Lynch called on David Slusser.

> STEPHAN EICKE: *How did you get involved in* Fire Walk with Me?
>
> DAVID SLUSSER: Angelo and David had written their songs that they would do in different incarnations. Then David is on the West Coast, Angelo is writing for other films. Come time to mix, I am the guy that already worked with David, that knows how to imitate Angelo. What would Angelo do? That was my job. [...] I knew my job was to step up and fill the Angelo seat for a couple of cues that Angelo was not able to write. Logistically that ship had sailed. It was late in post-production and that would mean that maybe the picture was close to being locked. I got the call to get a band together to do a couple of cues.
>
> STEPHAN EICKE: *This time you were not involved in the sound design or sound editing process at all?*
>
> DAVID SLUSSER: No. The division of labor down south made it cut and dry. That was all I was going to do. I would like to recall the phone call I received. David is a very charming man. Can I get a band together and record a couple of cues? "You bet I can! When do you need it?" Fortunately, I was still sound designing commercials at the time so I could skip an assignment and say, "Don't give me the next one." By that time we were freelancers, so if David called I wouldn't take any more mixing gigs and work with him for that week instead. He must have called, I must have called up my calendar and made frantic calls to my musicians.
>
> STEPHAN EICKE: *How did you choose the musicians?*
>
> DAVID SLUSSER: I had some improvising musicians. We have a very strong improvised music community in the Bay Area that I have been part of. There are some that do non-idiomatic improvisation and some that do idiomatic improvisation. I take the idiomatic improvisers because they can improvise any idiom. That's who I brought to the studio to be flexible to do just about anything.
>
> STEPHAN EICKE: *The cues you recorded and that were used in the movie were "RR Swing," "Deer Meadow Shuffle" and "Best Friends." Did you record everything in the same session?*

---

[20] Author interview with Lori Eschler, January 19, 2021.

DAVID SLUSSER: Yes. David is sitting next to me and I am trying to channel Angelo. What would Angelo do? I keep doing this simple cadence thing and he kept saying, "Simpler. No, no, simpler." It was like breathing. I am just using a one chord and a two chord, G to A minor seventh, then some peddle D, 5 to 1. I'm just trying to keep my hands off the keyboard so he doesn't say "simpler" again. But he drew that out of the band, too. One of the greatest drummers in the world was just doing ding ding ding. David was in the room and giving instructions. "Louder, lower, higher." All these descriptions, but he is good at it and he is so into it. When he has something he is close to then he gets excited and you know you are focusing in with him. He sounds like Jimmy Stewart, it's almost funny. He is very involved.

Then the "Deer Meadow Shuffle" was a throwaway at the end of the session. [...] We still had time on the clock. We didn't see the tape. He described it. We are all sitting around in the studio with David and he says, "You keep going through these doors. There's a security camera, you keep going down these hallways. You see something in the distance and when you get there it's not there. It's like a dream. We are going through these doors. It's light and quiet." While he is doing all that we got the idea, "Okay, this is Grady-Tate-with-the-brushes time." Donald [Bailey] laid that down. He got a beat that David liked. He wanted it to be jazzy, and I instructed my bass player to leave some holes. Let's say we are in C. It wasn't in D sharp like "Perdita" [in *Wild at Heart*] but the bass was just coming in in sections and I was trying to be Angelo. Just a little piano. I was really channeling Gil Evans. When Gil plays, it's called arranger's piano. He doesn't solo. He just plays chords. I took a part, self-studied Gil Evans's music and how he voiced chords. I was channeling Angelo channeling Gil Evans. C minor 9th. David was digging it and when it was over, I thought, "Oh, that'll never be used," and it probably almost wasn't. But that was the genesis. David would be in the studio, directing. "Louder, put a lid on it!" He was very much involved. That's why he is the co-composer. He would improve the tempo.

STEPHAN EICKE: *Interestingly enough, the "Deer Meadow Shuffle" was not used for the scene David was describing. It was then used to accompany Chester Desmond's adventure in Deer Meadow.*

DAVID SLUSSER: I am not sure where it fit in with David's plans because it was definitely conceived for Agent Cooper walking down the corridors. It's David Bowie appearing. That's the scene it was conceived for. I have no idea how it was used in Deer

Meadow. Our instructions were for the scene of Kyle going down [the hallway], looking at the security camera.[21]

Following the recording of the cue that would later be titled "Deer Meadow Shuffle," Lynch decided to use it as an accompaniment for Chester Desmond and Sam Stanley's investigation into Teresa Banks' murder. The scene Lynch had described to Slusser was eventually underscored by "Mysterioso," a "firewood" track conceived by Badalamenti and played at a greatly reduced speed. By replacing "Deer Meadow Shuffle" with "Mysterioso," the scene becomes altogether different: the latter cue gives the scene an uneasy feel of dread and mystery—indicating that something potentially dangerous is about to happen as a confused Cooper walks through hallways and checks security cameras. "Deer Meadow Shuffle" is a relaxed, smooth easy listening cue that would have emphasized Cooper's quirkiness much like "Dance of the Dream Man" had in the series. The scene would have been slightly comedic and amusing, creating the stark contrast between music and image that Lynch was so fond of: Cooper is irritated by what the security camera is showing, walks around helplessly like an exaggerated version of Columbo. And yet something significant is about to happen as Phillip Jeffries appears and refuses, with a disconcerting manner, to speak about Judy, the source of all evil.

"Deer Meadow Shuffle" is not the only cue Lynch replaced in post-production. While substituting one already existing cue with another was a quick and painless procedure, underscoring the infamous scene in the Pink Room was decidedly more challenging: one night, Laura Palmer decides to visit the roadhouse. She is secretly followed by Donna, whose feelings she had just upset. After a few drinks, Laura goes into a secret backroom and makes out with several men at once, takes drugs, and lets a stranger go down on her—all the while abstract avant-garde jazz plays relentlessly. The music feels as out of place in the venue as Julee Cruise does singing in a remote small-town setting. The music is so loud that Lynch decided—after much evaluation and late during the editing process—to add subtitles to the scene.

Filming Laura losing herself in the Pink Room proved a challenge: a four-walled set had to be built since Lynch decided to capture the increasing delirium in the room with 360-degree-camera pans as a wild carnival ride. Only a few crew members were allowed on the set. Since Lynch had music playing through speakers during the shoot, the dialogue recorded was not usable for the finished film and had to be recorded as ADR in post-production. Jon Huck worked as backwards ADR-recordist: "I was on the outside. I could not see inside which is extremely unusual. [...] The

---

[21] Author interview with David Slusser, February 23, 2021.

music was blasting. They wouldn't have been able to use the dialogue. The only thing you can do in production is to record a scratch track where maybe you hear something for [the actors] to mime along to."[22] It was clear to everybody that the production sound recording could not be used in the final edit. Still, the actors were recorded, which was helpful, as Huck points out:

> The actors can listen to it in ADR and mime along to the timing. It's helpful for them to get the timing to match. My assistant, the boom man, was inside that room. It was so intense and they had closed up this small box. Usually you have one wall up when you are shooting on a stage. That was pretty unusual.

The music cue Lynch played on set for that scene was not used in the final film. Neither was a new improvisation by a jazz group conducted by David Slusser. The director's idea for the (unused) piece had been even more idiosyncratic than "The Pink Room" that was used eventually.

> STEPHAN EICKE: *Among the few pieces you recorded for* Fire Walk with Me *was an unused cue for the roadhouse scene, wasn't it?*
> DAVID SLUSSER: Yes. David specifically asked me to have a harmonica player. I was asked to record a blues number for the roadhouse. [...] He had mentioned a couple of things he needed to do. One was the roadhouse cue that somebody else ended up doing and another was "Best Friends" which were the two girls talking intimately. It was a very quiet cue, and then I had to be prepared to make up some other stuff on the fly. [...] A harmonica player? I thought, "I'm going to get X amount of money for the session. How cheap can I do this?" I found a fantastic drummer named Donald Bailey who I knew. He also played harmonica. I hired him for the session. He was Jimmy Smith's drummer. He is since deceased but he is one of the unsung heroes of jazz. Then I had my guitar guys and a vibes player and my dear friend playing acoustic bass. They didn't use my cue with harmonica. I always wonder about David's sometimes anachronistic use of earlier music. [...] For some reason ["The Pink Room"] was David's vision, his little tableau that he was trying to set for that scene. And whatever we did he didn't like as much as the music that was eventually used. It was totally an atmospheric question and probably we sounded too clean in the studio. We could have been a lot more raucous but we also tried to play that other theme, the "Best Friends" cue, in

---

[22] Author interview with Jon Huck, January 26, 2021.

the same session. You are lucky if you get one in the movie. I was doing this without picture so I had no idea what the roadhouse thing was but we all knew how to kick ass. We call it bonehead music, not very intellectual. Maybe that was the point of the music.

STEPHAN EICKE: *David is credited as the sole composer for the "Pink Room" cue that was eventually used. He is credited as co-composer on "your" pieces—"Best Friends," "Deer Meadow Shuffle," "RR Swing." You mentioned that he is credited as co-composer because he would direct the musicians, give them instructions ...*

DAVID SLUSSER: Yes. It was just my job as a musical contractor to provide David with a canvas. He put a band together so that I can co-write with him. [...] The stuff that's credited to me means that he was happy enough to give me a credit. On the other one ["The Pink Room"] he was able to take full credit. It's just a business thing. David has been very generous to me. [...] In the mid-2010s they did a repackaging of extra scenes from *Twin Peaks*, and David paid me a lump sum and said, "We want to use some more of your music for that thing. Let me buy you out." He didn't have to do that. I got a nice fat check from David because he spread it around. It was pretty cool. Personally I was not making my living as a musician. I was working for such an outstanding creative director. I would have given him the shirt off my back just to see him finish the damn movie successfully. That's the type of loyalty that pays dividends in future years.

STEPHAN EICKE: *For which piece of music did David want to buy out?*

DAVID SLUSSER: "Deer Meadow Shuffle." "Deer Meadow Shuffle" was the unexpected thing at the end of the session, and that whole track is the genius of Donald Bailey and his brushes. The only guy that could do that similarly is Grady Tate. I hired the right guy for that cue. They did an extended version of that cue later for the re-release.

STEPHAN EICKE: *Did you ever speak with Angelo Badalamenti as you were "replacing" him on* Wild at Heart *and* Fire Walk with Me?

DAVID SLUSSER: Only in the context of supporting his work in the production. [...] I was just happy to be a fly on the wall in the creative conversation that Angelo and David had. That's where I got my orientation and instruction. I didn't call up Angelo later. [...] I really want to give Angelo the credit he is due because a lot of what I was doing was trying to stay within the parameters, the identity of the score that he had started. That makes it easier as a musician when you write for hire. You know what you are supposed to be doing. It's not, "This is David [Slusser]'s concerto." How do I integrate Angelo's score, which is the bulk of things, in the best possible way with what I'm contributing? I was following that guy's lead. The music that I would play would be more crazy, more contemporary, maybe more electronic. But here I was definitely trying to channel this little relationship that they had, the sentimentality and musicality. Angelo's Italian, his music has a bel canto quality that runs through his pieces. It's something you have to respect because obviously it gave so much flavor to an extended collaboration between these guys. As a craftsman I'm there to do what I'm being paid for.[23]

Lori Eschler remembers the recording of Slusser's music and the "Pink Room" cue: "The band was recorded away from the picture. The band was directed by David in his metaphors. They were jazz musicians so they got it. They made some pretty music. There was enough input from David. He had this deal with Angelo that they would share publishing and composing on certain things that they collaborated on."[24]

Drummer Steve Hodges, guitarist Dave Alvin, and bassist Don Falzone had been contacted by Lynch years prior to provide music for *Ronnie Rocket*. The musicians recorded some pieces Lynch thought would accurately describe the atmosphere he wanted to evoke in his next film. Years later, in 1992, he approached Hodges, Alvin, Falzone, and pianist Andy Armer to record the "Pink Room" and "Blue Frank" cues (both of which play during the club scene) for *Twin Peaks: Fire Walk with Me*. Since Alvin refused to drive down to Los Angeles on short notice, he was replaced with Dave Jaurequi. The ensemble recorded their cue at Capitol Records, guided by Lynch, who remembered the recording of the "Pink Room" piece: "I was standing in the hallway and I heard this bass thing in my head so I wrote down the kind of thing that reminded me of the steps, so when the three guys were there I went up to Don Falzone and I said, 'This is the bass line.' I hummed it to him and he said, 'Okay. Great.'"[25] Falzone started playing and then suggested he double up every other note. Lynch agreed: "Then Steve started going on the drums and then Andy started going and it got this thing going and they laid down this long track of this thing. It was solid." The magic happened when Dave Jaurequi finally showed up. He was twenty minutes late, as Lynch remembered: "I said, 'Okay, this is a kind of 50s thing, and just float these chords over this thing and just go with this feel.' [...] What he did was kick

---

[23] Author interview with David Slusser, February 23, 2021.
[24] Author interview with Lori Eschler, January 19, 2021.
[25] Hodges, Steve, MonosonicJukeJoint, "Daivd [sic] Lynch Fox Bat Strategy behind The Music," *YouTube*, February 1, 2018, https://www.youtube.com/watch?v=ya9GozeYUjs (accessed June 19, 2024).

that fucking thing, man. It was so cool because he would do these builds and brought it to life like crazy. It was magic." Falzone played the three-note bass line with his bow. Jaurequi took an amplifier off his guitar and had Falzone record his bass with it. Lynch recorded them all with heavy reverb. The result was a strange, abstract instrumental piece, minimalist and relentless.

With Angelo Badalamenti's pieces from the *Twin Peaks* show, the cues written for *Fire Walk with Me*, David Slusser's contributions, Lynch's own "Pink Room" recording, and Cherubini's *Requiem*, the director finally had enough material to finish post-production. For the first time, David Lynch was his own sound designer.

During his work on *Wild at Heart*, he had asked Randy Thom to continue working with him. Unfortunately, the sound designer was based in Northern California, and Lynch needed somebody locally in Hollywood, somebody close-by who would always be at his beck and call. Having learned greatly from Alan Splet, Lynch decided to act as his own sound designer. In doing so he created a deeply disturbing, rich tapestry of abstract musical sound effects that add to the uneasy atmosphere in the town of Twin Peaks days before Laura Palmer's murder. In *Fire Walk with Me*, there is not a second of silence. More is more, and Lynch went over the top like a child in a sweetshop who has been told they can help themselves to as much as they can carry. Lynch designed a rich, garish wallpaper of music, effects, ambiences, and everything between the three. As he did in the series, pieces were slowed down, played backwards, layered with expressive sound effects, and musical cues written by Angelo Badalamenti.

The most extreme example of *Fire Walk with Me*'s outrageous sound collages accompanies the intense encounter between Gerard and Leland as they meet in their cars at a street crossing. Lynch cuts back and forth between Gerard, Leland, and Laura. He inserts revving car engines and a cacophony of horns. He has the One-Armed Man shout at Leland without repose, which quickly leads to Laura crying violently. But that is not enough. Lynch also puts in dark wind sounds and a composition by Badalamenti, "It's Your Father." Everything is extreme both visually and acoustically, turned up to 11: Laura's unbearable crying fit; Leland's clenched hands and jaw, his sweat running down his face while he tries not to explode; the cars' honking and revving; and of course Badalamenti's music, which in itself is a wild mélange of low-electronic drones and abstract effects that sound like defamiliarized human screams, abandoned souls in captivity shouting in wild crescendos for their freedom.

As is usual for a Lynch film, sound design and music are often difficult to distinguish. For the director, they are all one element. They are sound, and Lynch loves to layer all forms of it. The scene in which Chester Desmond and Sam Stanley inspect Teresa Banks' trailer serves as another example of the director's carefully layered soundscaping: an elderly woman enters.

As she does so—the camera shows her point of view—fragments of a jazz piece are audible, brushes slowly striking the cymbal. Dark wind sounds and slowed down "firewood" as recorded by Badalamenti are heard. Sounds of electricity then join the mix. There is more of "Mysterioso," Badalamenti's piece of "firewood." Elements join each other and separate again.

Arguably the most memorable sound both in the *Twin Peaks* show and its theatrical prequel is the buzzing, humming, and droning of the fan on the second floor in the Palmer house. In *Fire Walk with Me*, it is used to great effect, both as a literal and an abstract sound. Lynch took the original fan recording from the show and placed it in the film. John Wentworth, who worked as co-producer on *Fire Walk with Me*, muses: "Once David gets a sound he likes he wants that sound again. 'That was perfect, I want that!' [...] Once he gets a sound it's in his mind. 'Go back into the mixes and find that sound because I want it again.'"[26]

Of course the fan does not sound like an ordinary fan. Its whirring is exaggerated. Lynch's manipulation makes it sound more like a helicopter preparing to take off, its propellers rotating. Still, when the fan is first heard in the Palmer house in the film, it is presented as a literal sound effect. The sound's source is plain. The fan can be seen. Later, it is used as Laura walks around downstairs, carefully inspecting her home following her frightful encounter with Bob. The source of the sound is still clear. Although the fan cannot be seen, its sound is recalled from its previous appearance. Still, its sound now seems unreal. It is too far away from Laura and her environment to justify its volume. In that sense, it is both an abstract and literal sound effect. It becomes wholly abstract at the end of the film: the fan's incessant whirring is clearly audible as Laura and Ronette are being tortured. It is audible under the cacophonous sound collage as Leland/Bob strikes in the empty train carriage. This time, there is no fan. Although it is present acoustically, it is absent visually. It is no longer a literal sound effect. It has morphed from being literal to being both literal and abstract to being purely abstract. By the time the fan is heard for the last time, its sound has become a symbol of evil, a harbinger of danger—it whirred as Laura found Bob, it whirred as Leland came to rape his daughter, it whirred as Laura was being tortured.

> Twin Peaks: Fire Walk with Me. *It came out and got knocked. It's one of my favorites that David did. Very underrated and only now being recognized. Like Stravinsky and* The Rite of Spring—*at the premiere they were throwing tomatoes at him, booing and walking out on this great masterpiece. They didn't understand it.*[27]
>
> ANGELO BADALAMENTI

---

[26] Author interview with John Wentworth, January 30, 2021.
[27] Deyneko, "Angelo Badalamenti."

David Lynch was as involved in *Fire Walk with Me* as he had been in any of his previous films. He had devised the story, co-written the screenplay, acted, composed music, developed the sound design, and directed it. He loved the universe of *Twin Peaks* and its characters deeply, and it was an especially grueling shock to realize that hardly anybody else outside the *Twin Peaks* cast and crew enjoyed *Fire Walk with Me* as much as he did. While audiences had at first reacted positively to the show, they did not appreciate watching their angel, Laura Palmer, being put through the wringer.

The reaction at the film's premiere in Cannes prepared Lynch for the reviews that were to come. *Fire Walk with Me* was panned for various reasons, as press clippings show from that time. According to Lori Eschler, the backlash also was related to the cultural landscape, societal changes, and political headlines in the United States:

> [David] had been on the cover of *Time* magazine just a year before. People just couldn't digest the themes in that film. He was so aware of it that he was being shunned. It was petty stuff, but it really affected what he was doing and what he wanted to do. It affected his motivation to continue in this mainstream world.[28]

Many people turned on Lynch. Eschler felt some of the blowback herself: "Even some of my friends were in on that with me, saying, 'I can't believe you worked on that! How could you?' Okay. It was this political Hollywood pettiness. Also, contextually it was at this time in our country where Anita Hill had essentially been ignored by the senate judiciary committee and *Thelma and Louise* came out." In Eschler's view, the audiences were unable to accept a father raping his daughter as a work of art, all the while a new wave of feminism was sweeping the country: "People couldn't deal with it. Contextually it was at a time when nobody had the palette for it." Few reviews were kind to Lynch and his then most recent movie.

David Lynch was deeply hurt and upset by the reaction his work received. It was painful to read statements such as this one by Vincent Canby, renowned film critic at the *New York Times*: "Everything about David Lynch's *Twin Peaks: Fire Walk with Me* is a deception. It's not the worst movie ever made; it just seems to be. Its 134 minutes induce a state of simulated brain death, an effect as easily attained in half the time by staring at the blinking lights on a Christmas tree."[29]

But Lynch was not about to retreat simply because he had received a critical drubbing. His star was falling in the eyes of many, but the director

---

[28] Author interview with Lori Eschler, January 19, 2021.
[29] Canby, Vincent, "Review/Film: One Long Last Gasp for Laura Palmer," *The New York Times*, August 29, 1992, https://www.nytimes.com/1992/08/29/movies/review-film-one-long-last-gasp-for-laura-palmer.html (accessed June 19, 2024).

kept busy with various projects. He was steadily working on paintings, and he developed a project for HBO entitled *Hotel Room* with Barry Gifford. Three episodes, taking place over several decades, depict the lives of various people who stay in the same hotel room in New York City. While it was a chance for actors such as Lynch regulars Harry Dean Stanton and Freddie Jones to shine, HBO did not like the episodes, airing them strung together as a pilot in January 1993. Without the support of the channel and strong reviews, *Hotel Room* was a failure, much as an earlier project, *On the Air*, had been the year before.

Co-developed, co-written, and directed by Lynch, *On the Air* depicts the humor found during the preparation and broadcast of a live television show in 1957. The director and his co-writer Mark Frost reveled in the absurd gags they were able to place in the show, but *On the Air* was far from the television milestone that *Twin Peaks* had initially been. Shot in 1991, ABC shelved the show for a year, before they eventually aired three of the seven completed episodes in 1992. Asked about *On the Air* and *Hotel Room*, associate producer John Wentworth shrugs his shoulders: "Those were opportunistic endeavors. David was hot. People just said, 'Let's make deals, let's make money and make shows.' *On the Air* was a pretty funny show. Mark Frost was involved in that. It was more a Mark Frost sensibility than a David sensibility. They were finely produced but they weren't hits."[30] HBO had hoped to make money with *Hotel Room*. Alas, it didn't. Wentworth continues: "These are endeavors that had David's name on it and they had pieces, a feel and a look that was David's, but they weren't things that were pushing the envelope."

Despite the disappointing feedback both *On the Air* and *Hotel Room* received, Lynch had loved working with the crew, people he trusted. Among them was Angelo Badalamenti as composer. The music for *On the Air* was every bit as idiosyncratic as viewers had by then come to expect from the duo. One of Lynch's ideas was to incorporate jazz—recorded away from the picture—performed by musicians who had previously never come in close proximity to that genre, as Lori Eschler points out: "I remember this session with a bunch of really great classical players that they had pulled in to play swing, loose music. They were so uptight, it wasn't swinging at all. So David said to these guys, 'Okay, it's technically perfect, I just want you to do it again but play like there is a Sunday School on fire.'"[31] Lynch had planned all this: the resulting culture clash led to the wonky performance he had sought.

Despite the fun he still had working on his projects, Lynch was disappointed, saddened, and upset that his more recent work had been torn

---

[30] Author interview with John Wentworth, January 30, 2021.
[31] Author interview with Lori Eschler, January 19, 2021.

to shreds—the second season of *Twin Peaks*, *Fire Walk with Me*, *On the Air*, *Hotel Room*. He was no longer the poster boy of American independent cinema, not still viewed as a true genius of film, as *Time* magazine had declared him not so long ago. His star had fallen.

> With *Dune*, *I sold out on that early on, because I didn't have final cut, and it was a commercial failure, so I died two times with that. With* Fire Walk with Me, *it didn't go over well at the time, but I loved it so I only died once, for the commercial failure and the reviews and things. But, over time, it's changed. So now, people have revisited that film, and they feel differently about it. When a thing comes out, the feeling in the world—you could call it the collective consciousness—is a certain way, and so it dictates how the thing's going to go. Then the collective consciousness changes and people come around.*[32]
>
> DAVID LYNCH

It had an afterlife: in 2014, David Lynch released *Twin Peaks: The Missing Pieces*, a selection of deleted scenes from *Fire Walk with Me*. In 2018, Sacred Bones Records put out an album entitled *Thought Gang*, featuring "A Real Indication" and "The Black Dog Runs at Night," two of the pieces Lynch and Badalamenti had devised and recorded for the film. In fact, all the pieces on the album were recorded by Lynch and Badalamenti (as a duo called Thought Gang) around the time they worked on *Fire Walk with Me*. Inspired by their collaboration on the show and the film, Lynch and Badalamenti called on a group of musicians. The director then described images to them. It was their task—much like it had been Badalamenti's ever since *Twin Peaks*—to improvise music according to the pictures Lynch was painting with words. The result was the kind of abstract free jazz mixed with ambient soundscapes that Lynch used in the *Twin Peaks* show and its prequel. In 2017, Lynch used excerpts from the fifteen-minute moody avant-garde improvisation "Frank 2000" in *Twin Peaks: The Return*. While the first pieces—"A Real Indication" and "The Black Dog Runs at Night"—were recorded in 1991, another group of musicians were assembled in the recording studio after Lynch had shot *Fire Walk with Me* in 1992. Thought Gang was a project Lynch and Badalamenti would return to whenever they had a quiet moment. While most of it was recorded in the early 1990s, Lynch added a few elements—such as a scratchy guitar and vocals—when he and

---

[32]Wise, Damon, "Encore: David Lynch Refuses to Explain 'Twin Peaks: The Return'—'Ideas Came, and This Is What They Presented'," *Deadline*, August 20, 2018, https://deadline.com/2018/08/twin-peaks-the-return-david-lynch-interview-showtime-emmys-news-1202407985/ (accessed December 18, 2024).

Badalamenti eventually decided to put out a record that had garnered dust for a quarter of a century.

"Thought Gang" is of course an ironic description considering the director's ideas about music being a feeling thing rather than intellectual. Equally ironic is that Lynch presented himself and his musical collaborator as the chained monkeys he painted for the front cover of the album.[33] Inspired by Pieter Bruegel's sixteenth-century work, *Two Chained Monkeys*, Lynch took the motif, put a black-and-white filter over it, and added a lightbulb over each of the monkey's heads. Lynch has roamed about as freely as a wild animal eager to catch the prey that was his idea.

> *It was energetic, inspiring, creative, exciting and a heck of a lot of experimental fun. [...] Working and collaborating with David through all these years has been warm and tied together with true, brotherly love. Regarding our Thought Gang project, we had some of the best studio musicians who eagerly shared this unusual musical experience. There were no arrangements or preset orchestrations. We simply gave a tempo and an initial key to get started and asked them to play what they felt, rhythmically and harmonically.*[34]
>
> ANGELO BADALAMENTI

Since its premiere, *Fire Walk with Me* has been re-evaluated, not least because of the release of *The Missing Pieces* that closed a few gaps, and the broadcast of *Twin Peaks: The Return* which answered a few remaining questions. Furthermore, Lynch went on to make *The Straight Story* and *Mulholland Drive*, two universally acclaimed works that in the eyes of many critics restored his image as a uniquely talented filmmaker and led to a re-appraisal of his earlier work.

---

[33]Grow, "David Lynch and Angelo Badalamenti on Their Wild Jazz Experiment."
[34]Ibid.

7

He's Deranged

Lost Highway

Fred Madison is not a well man. Signs of his poor condition become visible early on. When he first appears, he looks unkempt, unshaven, hungover. The doorbell is ringing. "Dick Laurent is dead," is the message relayed to him. But who is Dick Laurent? And who is the person who conveyed this information? Fred peeks through the windows. Police sirens are audible in the distance. However, no police car is visible. Has he reason to expect the police on his doorstep? As it will turn out, he does.

Fred is a saxophone player who performs in a hip venue in present-day Los Angeles. His house is sparsely furnished and yet oddly claustrophobic. Dark. He is married to a beautiful woman named Renee. They must have been happy once. Now, communication between the two has broken down. What brings them together, at least for fleeting moments, are the videotapes left on their doorstep. The first tape shows only the exterior of their property. The next one is more disturbing: a camera has captured the interior. When did somebody get in—and, even more importantly, how, why, and who were they?

Fred and Renee decide to call the police. They can only speculate and, stumped, give up on the case shortly after. The situation for the couple worsens. Fred is jealous, convinced his wife is cheating on him, and in a fit of rage, he murders Renee. Unable to deal with his feelings of guilt and remorse, Fred experiences a psychogenic fugue—or dissociative fugue, as it is now commonly referred to in psychiatry. In such a case, a traumatic event leads to an altered state of consciousness. The person flees from their environment sometimes both literally and metaphorically and loses their memory of themselves and their background, forgetting even their name and address.[1] Such cases are rare, and few have been researched in detail.

Lynch presents Fred's dissociative fugue as both a metaphorical and literal event—in prison, a severely disturbed Fred Madison turns into a person called Pete Dayton. Pete, a young and handsome mechanic, replaces Fred in his cell—an impossible act. And yet, in this dream-like scenario, Fred becomes Pete: suddenly, the former sax player is in an altogether different environment. Initially, it even appears like a different decade with its visual tributes to the cinema and the design of the 1950s. Fred now looks like Pete, has new friends, a new background, a new lover and new parents, as well as a new job as a skilled mechanic—the best in town, apparently. So brilliant he is at his job that ruthless gangster Mr. Eddy entrusts only Fred as Pete with the maintenance of his car.

At first, Fred's world as Pete seems perfect. The sun is always shining, his family is loving, his friends look up to him, and he has the support of a person who appears the perfect protector. But then Pete meets Alice, and things start to slide. Alice, a glamorous, ravishing blonde who, like Renee, is also played by Patricia Arquette, is Mr. Eddy's girl, but Pete is so enchanted he can't help fall for her. He knows that his life will be over when his protector learns of their entanglement. As they commence an affair, Fred is no longer able to control his fantasy. Suddenly his peaceful existence is threatened. Disturbing elements from his real life start to creep in—the life he wishes he had left behind. When his dream has collapsed, Fred must flee again, on the never-ending highway into a better life. It leads nowhere.

Reckoning is a familiar topic in Lynch's films. Jeffrey experiences it after he has slept with Dorothy in *Blue Velvet*; Leland Palmer eventually breaks down as he realizes it was he, possessed by Bob, who killed his own daughter Laura; Sailor and Lula breathlessly seek pleasure by running away from responsibility until the harshness of real life catches up with them in *Wild at Heart*. Naomi Watts' character in *Mulholland Drive* will later experience a reckoning similar to Fred's in *Lost Highway*. In this and other respects, the latter is a film typical for Lynch. Initially, though, it wasn't the project he wanted to tackle after *Twin Peaks: Fire Walk with Me*. Along with co-writer Robert Engels he had penned a script entitled *Dream of the Bovine*, an absurdist comedy about three people who once were cows and still behave like them.[2] After the commercial and critical failure of the *Twin Peaks* prequel, not even Ciby2000, with whom Lynch had a three-picture

---

[1]Loewenstein, R. J. & Putnam, F. W., "Dissociative Disorders," in *Kaplan and Sadock's Comprehensive Textbook of Psychiatry. 8th ed.*, Vol. II, eds. B. J. Sadock & V. A. Sadock (Lippincott Williams and Wilkins, 2009), pp. 1870–3.
[2]Staff, "Exploring David Lynch's Bizarre Abandoned Film 'Dream of the Bovine'," *Far Out*, June 8, 2020, https://faroutmagazine.co.uk/david-lynch-abandoned-film-dream-of-the-bovine-story/ (accessed June 19, 2024).

deal, wanted to finance it. The filmmaker then became enthused about *Lost Highway*, an idea sparked by one of Barry Gifford's novels. The two had already worked together on *Wild at Heart*.

> I read Barry Gifford's book Night People. *And in it two characters were talking about going down a lost highway, and just a feeling came over me based on those two words. And I said, "Barry, I love these two words, 'lost highway'." And he said, "Well, let's write something." So about a year or a year and a half later we got together.*[3]
>
> DAVID LYNCH

Musically, *Lost Highway* is closer to *Wild at Heart* and *Fire Walk with Me* than to any other of Lynch and Badalamenti's preceding collaborations. It offers a rich, colorful palette of different musical pieces and sound design. Something is always buzzing. The film features instrumental compositions by Angelo Badalamenti; pre-existing songs by David Bowie, Marilyn Manson, Rammstein, This Mortal Coil, Antonio Carlos Jobim, and others; instrumental pieces composed by Barry Adamson and Trent Reznor; pre-existing pieces from Adamson's catalogue; and various drones and "sound spheres" that express both mood and emotion.

The difference between *Lost Highway* and Lynch and Badalamenti's previous collaborations is the lack of irony, of contrast. Lynch's choice of songs and score for each scene fit the established mood, enhance it, and accurately capture the inner turmoil that Fred Madison aka Pete Dayton is experiencing at any given moment. The first half of the film—the Fred Madison section—is appropriately bleak, both visually and acoustically, free of the bittersweet contrasts between image and score as experienced in, for example, *Twin Peaks*. The saxophonist is wrecked by jealousy and feelings of inadequacy, particularly in bed but also more generally in his relationship with Renee as a whole. His joyless existence is underscored by the moody sounds that Lynch puts under the images, by the slowed-down "firewood" provided by Badalamenti and by his composers' atonal orchestral pieces written in homage to Krzysztof Penderecki. Even the diegetic music Fred plays himself—titled "Red Bats With Teeth" on the soundtrack album—is arhythmic and atonal. There is nothing soothing about the film's cold first half.

The change is abrupt: following Fred Madison's transformation in his prison cell, Pete Dayton is released. He uses his new freedom to lounge in his parents' sunny backyard, accompanied by Antonio Carlos Jobim's easy

---

[3]Schwartz, David, "A Pinewood Dialogue with David Lynch," *Museum of the Moving Image*, February 16, 1997, https://movingimage.org/wp-content/uploads/2020/12/64075_programs_transcript_pdf_202.pdf (accessed December 18, 2024).

listening number "Insensatez." It is a radical acoustic and visual change. The scene is flooded with light as Pete (aka Fred) now feels confident, secure, and at peace, and the music reflects that feeling. It doesn't provide another layer of meaning, but emphasizes a mood already established by Lynch and his cinematographer Peter Deming through their bright images. However, Fred's dream soon starts to crack, and this is reflected in Lynch's choice of music. No cue demonstrates this better than the recurrence of "Red Bats With Teeth" as a diegetic piece: as Pete is working in the garage, the instrumental for saxophone and ensemble that Fred had performed in his club earlier starts playing on the radio. Irritated and suddenly slightly anxious, Pete gets up and turns it off. His colleague—played by Lynch regular Jack Nance—is angry with him. He likes the music, he says. "I don't," Pete replies. This comes as no surprise. Of course, he does not appreciate being reminded of his real life—the one he sought to escape. The appearance of "Red Bats With Teeth" on the radio station's playlist pulls Fred as Pete back in, revealing that the blissful facade he has built is not as strong as he likes to believe.

> *So we're recording Fred's sax solo with this musician named Bob Sheppard in the recording studio at Capitol Records, and Bob does a take and I tell him, "I can barely hear you. It sounds like church music." So he'd play a little harder and I'd say, "It's a mosquito; there's no feeling there at all; you're not wild at all." I had to push him, but he finally got into this place, and once he got there he killed it.*[4]
>
> DAVID LYNCH

David Lynch eventually got what he wanted from Bob Sheppard—a frenzied performance that satisfied the director's love for extremes. By the time "Red Bats With Teeth" is playing on the radio, the music in *Lost Highway*'s second half—the Pete Dayton section—is already becoming progressively darker.

The weightless Jobim piece that had accompanied the mysterious young man as he was relaxing in the backyard was replaced by the Smashing Pumpkins' "Eye," the track accompanying Pete and his friends walking into a night club. It's a hip soft-rock piece with cool groves and smooth vocals to which Pete and his girlfriend Sheila dance in a close embrace. As she asks him where he was the previous night, subtle dark synths find their way onto the soundtrack. They are a disturbance, just as Sheila's question was a disturbance to Pete—after all, he does not wish to be reminded of anything that happened just a few hours prior. Or as Fred Madison himself put it when policemen examined his house: "I like to remember things my own way. [...] How I remembered them. Not necessarily the way they happened."

---

[4] Lynch & McKenna, *Room to Dream*, p. 355f.

When Sheila asks Pete the question that briefly throws his emotional world into turmoil, the roles are reversed: Fred had previously—in his true life—been the suspicious partner, filled with jealousy. In his delusion as Pete, his partner is the one who is jealous, anxious to be with him, and constantly on guard. She suspects—rightly—that he is a lady's man who has his eyes on other women and would not hesitate to cheat on her. These fears had previously been Fred's in regard to Renee—it feels much better to be the object of affection than the needy partner that ruminates on the other half's possible affairs. Similarly, Lynch later shows how Fred's relationship with Renee is inverted in Pete's fling with Alice, Mr. Eddy's girl.

As the gangster drives up in his car to the garage where Pete works, Barry Adamson's instrumental, "Mr. Eddy's Theme," makes its first appearance. It is a cool, jazzy piece, not dissimilar to the kind of jazz that was used in the Hollywood crime dramas of the 1950s and 1960s, most notably in *Crime in the Streets* (with music by Franz Waxman) and *Walk on the Wild Side* (composed by Elmer Bernstein). Although it is an appropriately aggressive piece for Mr. Eddy, it carries with it a sober coolness that captures the gangster's clear-cut business attitude. So far, Pete has nothing to fear. Mr. Eddy is still his friend. How quickly things can change becomes evident to Pete when he goes on a joyride with the gangster, where the aggression that emanates from Mr. Eddy is emphasized in the music. Barry Adamson incorporates sharp brass staccatos as the gangster leaps out of his car to scream at a man who was tailgating him, and Pete watches on from a distance. His queasiness is communicated through the music. Pete now knows that his friend can become very ugly indeed. He must be careful, though inevitably, his worst fears will later be confirmed.

> MR. EDDY: Wait a minute. [*He hands Pete money.*]
> PETE: Thanks, Mr. Eddy.
> MR. EDDY: No, thank you. I'm bringing the Caddy by tomorrow. You like pornos?
> PETE: Pornos?
> MR. EDDY: Give you a boner?
> PETE: No. No, thanks.
> MR. EDDY: Suit yourself.
> PETE: Well, I'll see you then.
> MR. EDDY: YOU WILL.

FIGURE 24 *Mr. Eddy's Theme II (from* Lost Highway, *1997).* Transcribed by Andrew Morley.

Although Angelo Badalamenti is the main composer credited for *Lost Highway*, a large selection of tracks was written by Barry Adamson, a British composer and producer who had been one of the bad seeds in Nick Cave and the Bad Seeds before he went solo with his EP *The Man with the Golden Arm* in 1988. His third album, *Soul Murder*, was short-listed for the prestigious Mercury Music Prize four years later.

STEPHAN EICKE: *How did you get involved in* Lost Highway?

BARRY ADAMSON: I was very fortunate that a relation of a music publisher that I worked with was working in the office of David when he was working on *Lost Highway*. [That person] was playing [my album] *Moss Side Story*. I think she even said, "I think you should hear this, David," and she put it on and David thought, "Oh my God, this is the sound of the film!" At the time, the cut was something like four hours long. The way I heard it was that Angelo was getting a little bit like, "Gee, how much more of this do I have to do?" He had done a lot of work already. David had a perverse idea because of the way the film is with the lead characters. There were two of everything, so you could have two composers. You can then use my music, Angelo's music, crossing them over, mixing them together in the abstract. He thought, "This could be really good, to have a B person around to pick up," while Angelo felt it was getting a bit much. He was almost finished with the project and then David went into this cut that was four hours long …

STEPHAN EICKE: *You did not get involved during pre-production, then?*

BARRY ADAMSON: The film was already in post-production. David was cutting scenes together. I don't think it was a problem, but he joked with me about Angelo and his mood. I likened it to a kind of 50's pulp way of speaking: Angelo had this hard-boiled approach to composing as opposed to a sweet revelation about things—which I am sure he does have [as well]. I have seen the clip where Angelo talks about composing "Laura Palmer's Theme," but there is also a gruff New York side to him. It had this sort of tone in the way David joked about it.

He was just editing a new cut. It was almost like saying, "I finished the film but I need to start again." So I got the job for adding atmospheres and themes. […] We talked about this idea of putting reggae in. I was messing around with that for [the piece] "Hollywood Sunset" which was quite bizarre. For some reason I felt compelled to put in this bass line that I had and work from there. It played out for ages across the scenes and linked them together.

That's how I got involved.

Then there was a very strange story in that he called me up. It is just odd to pick up your phone and hear David Lynch on the other end. At the time I was in a really bad situation. I just had a hip replaced so I was in a wheelchair, and on that day he called me up. I sort of had enough and I thought, being in this wheelchair like Ironside drives me crazy. So I thought, what do I do? I had computers brought from the studio and I started to write a theme. I do this brassy burlesque thing, "Mr. Eddy's Theme." And then I got the call from David saying, "I have been listening to your music for ten hours straight and I love it! I am going to send you a script and a piece of film. Show it to no one."

He sent me Mr. Eddy's scene in the car. The piece of music that I was working on that day I just put to the film. There's Mr. Eddy going, "Okay, kid … " It all seemed to be an organic thing. I sent it back and he said, "You got it. You know what's going on." He said, "How was the script for you?" I said, "Absolutely fantastic. I just got it." There are many ways you can "get" *Lost Highway* but I got it in a way that resonated to me and he said, "Yeah, it's right up your alley, eh?" That was it then. I was brought in to fill in or add things.

STEPHAN EICKE: *David is, as you know, a very spiritual person. He would have appreciated the story of how "Mr. Eddy's Theme" came about. Did you tell him?*

BARRY ADAMSON: I am not sure I did. I appreciate the synchronicity of it. I have been working myself in a way of laws of attraction. I remember I said to a friend, "I am getting involved in film music." He said, "Oh yeah? You have never done that before. Who are you gonna work for?" "I don't know. Quentin Tarantino, Oliver Stone, David Lynch … " Already I was trying to manifest a way to see myself involved in these positions. I didn't mention it to David because at that time I didn't think of David in terms of discussions about spirituality. I saw him as more from the art side of expressionism.

STEPHAN EICKE: *A short while later we hear a variation on "Mr. Eddy's Theme." What did David discuss with you in terms of structure and placement?*

BARRY ADAMSON: The variation was that he really liked the track "The Man with the Golden Arm" that I had made. There is a breakdown section in the piece which is a sample of an orchestra, [a sharp staccato]. He goes, "That is great! Can you get that in somewhere?" I thought after the confrontation where he drags the driver out, that is the place to do it. You hold this organ, so it's a moment of tension. Then I knew I could just go back to the theme without the theme but with the backing of the theme and let soloists play. I had some samples of brass guys playing long notes, starting quiet and then building. I knew they were atmospheric and could fit in. It was sculpting. You have your elements, then you sculpt and it becomes a remix based on the new information about this idea from "The Man with the Golden Arm," the second half. That explosion of Mr. Eddy's fury that he holds all the time, it seems. That was really the only direction with that.

STEPHAN EICKE: *Had you seen the scene before you sat down and wrote your music for it?*

BARRY ADAMSON: I wrote to picture afterwards, but I didn't have to change a lot for the first part. Then every time Mr. Eddy appeared it was like a link motif. Maybe [it appears] three times. Then there is the moment when the cops say, "It's Dick Laurent." There is just a hint of the theme. Then there is a lot of atmospheres, spinning orchestras. It becomes this dream, playing around with time. It became a link motif. [David] was very aware of it. He said, "Don't overdo it," because we know that language in film now. It's not the 50s anymore. You don't have to introduce characters musically all the time.[5]

The sharp staccato bursts in the variation of "Mr. Eddy's Theme" are a harbinger of darker, more violent things to come. As Pete returns home, he stands in a dimly lit corner of his bedroom—a scene that mirrors Fred's disappearance in his own home during the film's first section. Accordingly, Pete's disturbed look as he touches his head is accompanied by low, dense writing for clarinets. The same subdued music has played during Fred's earlier disappearance, so Lynch creates a visual and acoustic link to that scene.

The cracks in Fred's aka Pete's dream start to widen. He flees from this threatening reality by seeking pleasure—much like Sailor and Lula did in the course of *Wild at Heart*. Moments of pleasure are accompanied by easy jazz, laid back and cool. Lynch uses such a piece as Pete drives up to his girlfriend Sheila's house. She gets in the car with him, offering herself to him by pulling up her sweater. Sex is pleasure, and Fred as Pete can have it wherever and whenever he wants it. Women are available to him. He is the sexually aggressive, always potent lady's man who never fails to satisfy his partner, the opposite of Fred Madison.

Naturally, Fred as Pete wants nothing to do with his earlier persona, and it comes as no surprise that he swiftly turns the radio in the garage off as, in the next scene, "Red Bats With Teeth" starts playing. The cue is replaced

---

[5] Author interview with Barry Adamson, March 23, 2021.

by a tonal, rhythmic, jazzy piece for solo piano. Only a short while later Pete meets the woman of his dreams: Alice, Mr. Eddy's mistress. She is, of course, Renee, but seen as a dream image on Fred's part: beautifully made-up, with gorgeous blond hair, wearing a seductive, expensive dress. "This Magic Moment" as sung by Lou Reed starts playing on the soundtrack. It is hardly a subtle choice. Fred is convinced his dream can only get better from here: he has been introduced to one of the most gorgeous women he has ever laid eyes on, and they are about to embark on a steamy affair without any consequences.

Things turn out differently. Initially, Pete has reasons to hold on to his high hopes. As he talks to Alice later in the evening, Barry Adamson underscores their lascivious conversation with "Hollywood Sunset," a laid-back electronic New Age instrumental composition so dreamy it could be used during a yoga class. It continues playing as Pete and Alice have sex for the first time—which follows swiftly after their initial conversation. Pete is, after all, irresistible.

It is a fitting piece for lovemaking, and Pete and Alice experience an outpouring of sensuality. Both are excited to go to bed together. What follows mirrors in crucial ways an earlier lovemaking scene between Fred Madison and Renee. In both scenes, the duration of the foreplay is the same, as is their position. But there are also noticeable differences: Fred used to stare desperately into Renee's eyes, trying to see an absent flame of passion as she lay there passively. If anything, she appeared impatient to get the sex over with. The opposite is the case in Fred as Pete's dream: both he and Alice are excited by their sex, enjoy the experience, and are satisfied by it. Barry Adamson's approach underlines this, his music being sensual yet laid back. Sex is, after all, not meant to be hard work accomplished under crippling pressure. The piece that had underscored Fred's and Renee's sex is "Song to the Siren" by This Mortal Coil—one of Lynch's favorite pieces, and one he had wanted to use in *Blue Velvet*. As pensive as "Song to the Siren" is, it is neither sensual nor serene. Instead, its haunting quality and lyrics about a lover in despair give it an edge that makes the earlier sex scene even more uncomfortable than it already is, with its close-ups of Fred's face drenched in sweat, teeth clenched.

For Pete, his encounter with Alice is the high point of his life. His life will soon continue to disintegrate: as Pete looks in Alice's eyes during their lovemaking, already a distant, low rumble is audible on the soundtrack. He is afraid he will see in her eyes what he saw as Fred in Renee's eyes: boredom. It gets worse. Shortly after, Alice tells him she can't see him anymore. Preceding her announcement, Lynch used heavy thunder and lightning for an establishing shot of Pete's house. Underneath Alice and Pete's conversation is the low rumble of "firewood" that could both be sound design and music. Following Alice's call, Pete experiences blurred vision, and sees a spider crawling up his walls. He suffers from a headache.

Underneath it all is a dark swooshing. More rumbling. Acoustically, the audience is now back in Fred's world. The rumble bleeds into the most violent song in *Lost Highway* yet: "Apple of Sodom" by Marilyn Manson plays as Pete has loveless, dispassionate, and angry sex with his girlfriend, Sheila. She has to suffice as an ersatz Alice.

A pivotal scene follows a short while later, as Pete arrives back at his parents' house and they ask him to talk to them. They sit in the near-dark. They "know," they tell him, though they keep to themselves what it is they claim to know. Still, Pete realizes they know enough—too much. He can't control his dream any longer. It is slipping away from him. Quietly in the background a synthesizer loop is playing, an electric buzz. As the conversation between Pete and his parents grows more uncomfortable still, the music grows louder. It becomes distinguishable from the sound design, a minimalist ambient piece in the style of Brian Eno and contemporaries. Like "Mr. Eddy's Theme" and "Hollywood Sunset," it was written by Barry Adamson.

> STEPHAN EICKE: *How did David discuss with you what he wanted for a specific scene?*
>
> BARRY ADAMSON: I would take cues from him about how things should be. He would screen the film and come back to me and say how it went in terms of where the music was. I wrote music for the scene in which the parents talk to Pete. David said, "That scene, you could hear a pin drop because the audience were suddenly drawn in by the sound." I had this synthesizer loop and I gently put it in. He gave me one of the best directions I have ever heard: "When you are writing, Barry, look at their eyes."
> It wasn't about all the stuff that was going on. It was about the stuff that was going on in their eyes. That stayed with me for a long time. It's something I have done. I have actually moved a chord when someone shifts a look. It's so small you don't see it. There are also the scary beds which I brought back in when I went back to London [from LA]. I had an idea of just giving him beds of sound which I call scary beds which he quite liked. He could use these pieces like a library. Sonic strangeness. He would say, "Give me a bit more of that one," or, "No, that's not it." We worked them in.
>
> He came to London for a day. He was picking up an award for something and he stopped by my studio. It was strange to have this factory space in West London and David is walking down the corridor trying to find a space to stay in the light because of his jet lag. It was a surreal experience because I was just walking again. By the time I got to LA I was on crutches and one day he said to me, "Barry, your shoelace is undone. You don't want to fall over."

He came over, got on his knees and started tying my shoelaces. The irony is not lost on him. Everybody in the office stared. Yes, this is David Lynch tying Barry's shoelaces. It was very sweet.

STEPHAN EICKE: *The scene with the parents is an interesting one because at first you take the music for sound design. That fine, imaginary line between music and sound design is where it gets interesting.*

BARRY ADAMSON: It's a synthesized loop that I worked in and then added some layers of sound to it. I guess the loop is the sound design, the atmosphere. The other textures from the chord are the emotion. I agree with you regarding sound design. Of course they are very specific things and film people should be aware of what each of these things are.

STEPHAN EICKE: *Did David discuss the sound design in the film with you at any point?*

BARRY ADAMSON: I don't know if there is a start and end thing. Things get added. He told me to get the atmosphere in the room he would take a microphone and just record the room and then slow it down. Everything feels like it's slowed down. Like the cops go, "Did you … " when they are talking to Renee and Fred. You feel this awkward stagnation of naturalness, of what is natural. This is designed. It's anti-sound design because you can hear the room. It becomes something different. He was sculpting and molding things as he went along.

There was a very interesting session where we sat outside and David got a huge ghetto blaster and put it on. He played me some Krzysztof Penderecki, the Polish composer, dissonant, very loud. The track that was written for the victims of Hiroshima. We were listening to it so loud. [David] was saying, "You can hear the planes coming over, you can hear the bombs dropping." What that allowed me to do was to take that influence onboard. I went and researched Penderecki and how he put things together. I learned the notation. Instead of dots on staff maybe I would put a triangle which means you can slide down for an octave at your own pace. I gave it to some violinists. To other violins I would say, "Strike with the bow when you feel like it." That whole language of dissonance really helped in nailing the atmosphere he was hearing and wanting to put in the movie. I was quite pleased with the way that worked. I allowed for things to happen.

STEPHAN EICKE: *Would you say you had a lot of freedom as a composer then?*

BARRY ADAMSON: I think it was a little bit of give and take with that. "Hollywood Sunset" was supposed to be a very small scene where [Alice] appears in the garage. The guys are there and I let it play and play. I could be wrong but I thought this works as a piece. Then it stayed that way. Other areas are quite specific. I'll say it again: the scary beds just came in where they come in. I do remember writing for some scenes maybe only a little bit when Fred goes to the house and that guy hits his head on the table. There's a lot of stuff around there.

STEPHAN EICKE: *The scary beds that you mentioned—are they in the first half of the film as well?*

BARRY ADAMSON: I think there was a few little bits there in the house, in the corridor, some murmuring, some more of the scary beds. The scary beds are more apparent there.

STEPHAN EICKE: *Were they mostly electronic recordings?*

BARRY ADAMSON: Sometimes, yes. Other times I would take some of the orchestral stuff and put that in the sampler and slow that down myself and mess around with using a bed of sound to mix in with the electronics. Mainly they were generated from an electronic source, though.

STEPHAN EICKE: *When you watched the finished film, were you surprised how David used some of your pieces, or which pieces didn't get used?*

BARRY ADAMSON: No. [...] He was incredibly intelligent about the music and where he needed to put it. Also, there was a fluidity because of the scary beds that could be put in, when the camera is coming down the corridor for example. He could put that in. He became the composer with the pieces of music he did. When you feel someone is doing that, you don't think, "Wait, this is not what I wanted to do." I have not had this with a lot of filmmakers where you do feel that the work you do is honored in such a way that you are adding to what the director wants to do. It is very pure. There is a sort of connection. You feel all things are meant and connected. I feel it was very easy to trust him as a manipulator in the best sense. If people are going to the cinema, sitting in the dark and being manipulated, it is a very strange thing to give yourself over to. In the hands of David Lynch that's being taken care of very well.

STEPHAN EICKE: *How much music did you write for* Lost Highway?

BARRY ADAMSON: I wrote about forty-five minutes. I think it ended up being thirty-five in the film which is quite a bit.[6]

While the first act of the film mostly features music by Angelo Badalamenti and a large part of the second act relies on Barry Adamson's pieces, the final act of *Lost Highway*—Pete's eventual, inevitable collapse—belongs to rock

---

[6] Ibid.

musicians, namely Trent Reznor, Marilyn Manson, and the German band Rammstein. When Rammstein's music starts playing, Pete's life can't get any worse: following a tense meeting with Mr. Eddy—Pete is now convinced that the gangster boss *knows*—Lynch's hero meets Alice to discuss their possible way out. Here again, Lynch mirrors a scene from the first half of the film: Alice confesses to Pete she was working in porn. A "guy" had given her the job. Fred's subconscious is drawing conclusions: his wife Renee had told him about a possible job she might take. However, Fred was too timid and afraid to ask for details. As Pete's scene with Alice makes clear, he is convinced it must be a degrading, disgusting, and exploitative job that would result in him sharing his wife with other men. Lynch illustrates Fred's vision of Mr. Eddy's porn business, and it is—unsurprisingly—not a pretty one. As Alice auditions for the gangster, Marilyn Manson screams "I Put a Spell on You" on the soundtrack. It's a dark song with distorted guitars, a rough voice, and relentless percussion, a very different piece from "This Magic Moment," the song used when Pete first laid eyes on Alice.

When Pete then reaches the porn producer Andy's house to steal money, Lynch skillfully combines orchestra, avant-garde effects, and a drum solo to heighten the tension. Now, all hell breaks loose—in Fred's mind and on the soundtrack. As he sees images from a porn film starring Alice, Rammstein's iconic "Heirate mich" starts playing, a somber and bleak piece from a heavy metal band that stirred up the German music scene in the 1990s (and caused great concern for parents) with their violent lyrics and provocative videos. "Heirate mich," describes a man's anguish over his dead partner: one night, senseless from grief, he creeps into the cemetery to lie down next to the gravestone of his beloved. He then starts digging, opens her coffin, and tries to tenderly kiss her. Shockingly, she has been dead for a year and her body is so decayed there is little left to kiss—only tatters of what used to be skin.

Rammstein returns only a short while later. After Andy's death and Alice's appearance—accompanied by Badalamenti's moody clarinets, orchestral avant-garde effects à la Penderecki, and electronic drones—Pete wanders upstairs, his vision blurred. He is barely able to keep himself upright. As he opens room 26 and encounters a couple having sex, the song "Rammstein" starts playing; it describes various violent images without an apparent story linking them, such as a mass grave, blood running on asphalt, mothers crying for their children. Rammstein put out their official music video for the song in 1998, a year after the film's release. In their video, they proudly include several clips from the film. There is no doubt how pleased they were about the inclusion of their music in *Lost Highway*.

> *This German band, Rammstein, kept sending me stuff and I didn't listen to it. And then—fate again—having just finished the script, I sat down and listened to it and, bang! I couldn't wait to have this in the picture. Rammstein sent us fifty cassettes, because the crew started freaking out,*

loving the music. And with these fifty CDs floating around, there wasn't one day on the shoot that Rammstein wasn't blasting from some truck. It became really, really big with the crew. And then I met Trent Ressner [sic] from Nine Inch Nails and started working on some things with him. Trent did two songs and some drone work for the picture—he's got a great mind for music and sound.[7]

DAVID LYNCH

Trent Reznor contributed a few synth patches for the third act of the film. It was the musician's first work on a motion picture. He would later receive two Academy Awards, one for his collaboration with Atticus Ross on *The Social Network* and one for his work with Ross and Jon Baptiste on Pixar's *Soul*. Reznor later remembered that his work with Lynch was unlike any of his other experiences working on movies: "That was several odd days spent looking for sounds. [...] He would scribble a thing on a pad: 'This is what I want it to sound like.' And it would literally be a spider-web scribble."[8]

Prior to shooting, Lynch had traveled from Los Angeles to New Orleans to work with Reznor on some musical ideas for *Lost Highway*. The filmmaker was impressed by the amount of synthesizers the musician had in his studio—and by the colorful sounds they could create.[9] In the Big Easy Lynch, through Reznor, also met Marilyn Manson. Manson has a cameo in the film—as a porn star. Lynch cast the *enfant terrible* of rock spontaneously. He lends the scenes he is in an additional amount of malice that a more ordinary-looking extra would have not been able to provide.

Reznor also contributed an elaborate instrumental, "Driver Down," for one of the last scenes in the film, after Lynch has revealed that it was Fred Madison himself who had left the mysterious message of Dick Laurent's passing. Now in constant flight, Fred runs away from the police. He jumps into his car and enters a never-ending highway. By then, the aural landscape of *Lost Highway* has started to become more calm. All has been revealed, Fred's dream has been destroyed. It was a painful process for the saxophonist, accompanied by a dissonant collage of pre-existing songs such as "Song to the Siren," Angelo Badalamenti's avant-garde orchestral textures, Barry Adamson's loops, and Trent Reznor's electronic sketches. As Pete's world collapses, Lynch uses "Song to the Siren," "Rammstein," and "Heirate mich" to mirror earlier scenes: This Mortal Coil chants their eerie ballad as Pete and Alice make love passionately one last time in the desert. Again, the

---

[7] Rodley, *Lynch on Lynch*, p. 241f.
[8] Gilbey, Ryan, "David Fincher and Trent Reznor on Mank: 'People Were Like: Huh. This Is Very Niche'," *The Guardian*, March 25, 2021, https://www.theguardian.com/film/2021/mar/25/david-fincher-and-trent-reznor-on-mank-people-were-like-huh-this-is-very-niche (accessed June 19, 2024).
[9] Lynch & McKenna, *Room to Dream*, p. 357.

viewer is thrown back to the film's beginning when Fred and Renee rather dispassionately have sex—one of the key scenes in the movie since it makes plain both visually and acoustically how uncomfortable the couple are with each other, particularly when in bed. As "Song to the Siren" plays again toward the end of the film, Fred's dream is collapsing while he still tries to cling on to his delusions. "I want you," he whispers to Alice. "You will never have me," she replies coldly as "Song to the Siren" bleeds into an aggressively dissonant string piece with layered tremolos by Badalamenti. Fred should have known: as Alice and he arrived in the desert, Alice tried in vain to find a station on the car radio. There was only a static. The music has stopped. Unlike earlier when he was in the garage, he can no longer switch stations to find comforting tunes.

Badalamenti's aggressive string clusters and tremolos recur when Pete wakes up as Fred and, following the disappearance of Alice, meets the Mystery Man, who reveals himself to Fred in a shack in the desert. "What the fuck is your name," he asks the frightened Fred, trying to force the dreamer to face reality—while paradoxically the Mystery Man himself is only a figment of Fred's imagination, much like Mr. Eddy is. The Mystery Man now shouts angrily to keep Fred in check. Following their previous, initial meeting at a party, he now has to remind Fred of who he really is and warn him of dangerous feelings, such as jealousy and inappropriate thoughts. Fred does what he does best—he flees. In the Lost Highway Motel he kidnaps Mr. Eddy aka Dick Laurent and locks him in the trunk of his car. "Rammstein" starts playing again, linking the scene with an episode in Andy's mansion where Pete witnessed a couple having sex. Now, Fred imagines Mr. Eddy as the kind of man his wife Renee would have an affair with. In his mind, Renee is sleeping with Mr. Eddy, aka Dick Laurent. Fred does not have to be an eyewitness. He simply is convinced. In a brief flashback, Lynch then visualizes Fred's worst fears, having Mr. Eddy enjoy sex with Renee in the mansion where pornographic films are shot. They are surrounded by a small group of friends and businessmen who all watch couples copulate on screen. Through the recurrence of "Heirate mich," the scene is linked to Pete creeping into the villa and seeing Alice having sex in a porn film.

The real-life inspiration (within the film's story) for the mansion was shown earlier, in the film's first section, when Fred met both Andy and the Mystery Man for the first time. David Lynch turned to Barry Adamson to provide the background music.

> STEPHAN EICKE: *You didn't write "Something Wicked This Way Comes" for the film, did you? You had developed it for an album.*
> BARRY ADAMSON: I had just finished an album and I was sat there one day working away on something else. David said to me, "I will show you this scene. Do you think there is anything that

could go here?" It was people at the swimming pool and then going to the Mystery Man. I instinctively went, "Yes, I have this piece of music that I have just written for this new album that is coming out. It's called 'Something Wicked This Way Comes.'" He knew this title from an old movie. He said, "Let's hear it." I put it on the film and it happened. Another synchronistic little moment there. It had a slight party feel but then it also had a weirdness with these looping samples.

STEPHAN EICKE: *The title fits perfectly, of course ... it's the first "real" appearance of the Mystery Man.*

BARRY ADAMSON: It's so strange, yes.

STEPHAN EICKE: *Did you understand the meaning of the Mystery Man then?*

BARRY ADAMSON: I think I had an instinct about it. Isn't there an earlier scene when [Fred] is in bed with Renee and sees the Mystery Man? I understand this idea of extreme negative projection manifest as a person. I got that, yes. If I looked at that scene you would have thought the music needed to be stranger, but he fazed the party, so the atmosphere is the party. There is a great juxtaposition between mystery and what you would see as people having a good time. It gives it a good social distance from what's happening in the world. For me that magnifies the scene.[10]

The unreality of the scene is achieved primarily through "sound-freezing." Fred is not enjoying himself at the party. This is hardly surprising. By then, the viewer has had ample opportunity to observe that Fred does not enjoy anything except playing his saxophone on stage. What makes the evening at the party even worse for him is that it takes place in the mansion of Renee's friend Andy, of whom Fred is intensely jealous. Is his wife cheating on him with the slimy entrepreneur?

"Something Wicked This Way Comes" counterpoints Fred's mood and behavior. The instrumental gently and yet quickly fades out as Fred observes the Mystery Man entering and walking toward him. Fred is more convinced than ever that his wife sleeps with Andy. The saxophonist displays not only an arrogant disinterest in his surroundings, and therefore other guests, he is also harboring increasingly negative thoughts which weigh heavily on him. The Mystery Man appears as a figment of Fred's imagination and an evil he himself has invited by allowing negative projections to enter his mind and fester there. Lynch hints at the fact that the Mystery Man with his chalk-colored face, lack of eyebrows, and purple lipstick is only imaginary. Robert Blake's character looks grotesque. As he and Fred meet at the party and start

---

[10] Author interview with Barry Adamson, March 23, 2021.

talking, Lynch freezes all sound except for a subtle room tone. When Fred calls the Mystery Man at his house, dark sounds slowly creep in. Initially Fred does not appear to understand what the man is telling him, the man who at the same time is both opposite him and on the other end of the line. He only senses that this unusual-looking man poses a threat to him. Fred might not understand that the Mystery Man is a warning that he needs to better control his doubts and fears, but he does realize that something sinister is going on—his nagging, negative thoughts have already become pervasive. Fred wants to hold on to them. They are second nature to him. As the Mystery Man can't help but laugh at Fred's befuddlement and turns away, Barry Adamson's "Something Wicked This Way Comes" fades in again. The party is back on.

Fred escapes after the Mystery Man, as an especially persistent figment of his deranged mind, kills Mr. Eddy, another imaginary figure. Fred leaves his message at his own front door (as seen at the beginning of the film) and starts to drive onto the lost highway. After its appearance in the opening credits, David Bowie's "I'm Deranged" plays again here, as the end credits start rolling. "I'm Deranged" is, as has now become clear by the film's conclusion, an especially revealing choice. In three brief words, it gives away the film's plot.

> *This went to the beginning of* Lost Highway *and it dictated a certain speed. So, the scene was shot with the camera six inches off the pavement at six frames per second over twenty-five minutes of going down a highway several times to get that thing. A piece of music can add so much magic to a thing.*[11]
>
> David Lynch

As the song appeared for the first time, viewers were, of course, oblivious to its significance to the film's plot. Only gradually does Lynch reveal that his main character, Fred Madison, suffers from jealousy, delusions, and homicidal tendencies, all of which will eventually lead to his experiencing a psychogenic fugue. He can't uphold this new existence for long, though.

Surprisingly, Lynch even later admitted in an interview his character suffers from a psychogenic fugue. With that, he explains Fred's inner life and the actions that follow his imprisonment: "I love the term psychogenic fugue. In a way, the musical term fugue fits perfectly, because the film has one theme, and then another theme takes over. To me, jazz is the closest thing to insanity that there is in music."[12]

---

[11] *Le son de David Lynch*.
[12] Pizzello, Stephen, "Highway to Hell," *The American Society of Cinematographers*, March 1997, https://theasc.com/magazine/march97/hiway/pg2.htm (accessed December 18, 2024).

It is no coincidence then that Lynch made Fred Madison a saxophonist specializing in avant-garde jazz. "Red Bats With Teeth," Fred's performance in his club, gives a taste of the wild performances Fred specializes in. His playing is the only way he can express himself. The complete breakdown of communication between himself and his wife is what eventually leads to his downfall and her death. This breakdown becomes apparent early on, as Lynch shows them making love. After they finish and Renee pats her husband on the back, Lynch uses an excerpt of an aggressively dissonant Badalamenti piece with crashing cymbals and string clusters, different yet similar in tone and style to the music used toward the end of the film as Pete has sex with Alice one last time. As Renee lies with Fred, it becomes clear that, despite the air being thick with unspoken conflict, they are not going to talk about the alienation they are experiencing in their marriage, or the fact that Fred can no longer please his wife in bed. Performing jazz, though, is a different matter, as writer Keith Phipps accurately observes: "On stage, Fred expresses himself through atonal jazz played at maximum volume, wielding his instrument like a weapon, his stage manner closer to Jimi Hendrix than Coleman Hawkins."[13]

The instrumental score, though, is not jazzy. Nevertheless, Badalamenti's music, with its avant-garde writing, the clusters, glissandos, and dissonant layering, precisely captures Fred's state of mind. The composer even uses a fugue-like piece for a brief scene toward the end of the film: the same policemen who investigated Fred and Renee's house now examine Andy's mansion following his brutal death. Although "Police!," as the piece is called on the album, is not a pure fugue, Badalamenti chooses a fugue-like approach in his layering of the strings. One section joins after the other, each mimicking the other's part. A pure fugue is, in comparison, much more complex. Here, a theme is introduced before it is repeated as a variation by a different voice. Badalamenti conveys the idea of a fugue, rather than actually developing one.

STEPHAN EICKE: *Did David tell you the film's main character was experiencing a psychogenic fugue?*

ANGELO BADALAMENTI: Yes, I remember David telling me that that's what *Lost Highway* is about. What I did on the music, based on what he was saying and what works so great for him and his movie is I didn't write a typical straight fugue. A fugue establishes one theme, that theme continues, another theme comes in five steps lower, goes along, a third one comes up an octave higher and then a fourth and then they work beautifully together.

---

[13]Phipps, Keith, "Industrial Soundscapes," in *Beyond the Beyond*, eds. J. C. Gabel & Jessica Hundley (Hat & Beard Press, 2016), p. 92.

For *A Late Quartet* I wrote my own fugue, a film about a string quartet that performs Beethoven's famous string quartet opus 131, the one that everybody loves and that has a fugue in it.

For *Lost Highway* I didn't use the musical fugue but I did my own thing which David picks up on and absolutely loves. He has tried to explain to people what it is about Angelo's music. "Is it the melody? Is it the harmony? How does he do what he does to get what he gets?" There is one little thing that I learned in my last year of high school. I was totally in love with Johann Sebastian Bach. I just loved his music. The more I played Bach, the more I realized his use of suspension. In other words, he would have a chord, a C and a G, he would put a note that is slightly dissonant against a middle voice, not a melody or a bass harmony but in the middle, a suspension that rubs a little wrong and resolves and so forth. I was so in love with this that I used my own harmonic structures and used these kinds of suspensions—but different suspensions. Then of course I would create my kind of melody. It's the use of this middle voice. David says, "It's this middle voice that you are not even aware that you hear that's affecting you." I guess there's a lot to that. Thank you, Johann Sebastian Bach!

STEPHAN EICKE: *Did David then explain the meaning of* Lost Highway *to you?*

ANGELO BADALAMENTI: David never tells you too much. David never gives you an analysis or breaks anything down. The question that everybody asks is, "David, what do you mean with that? What are you trying to say?" There is never a straight answer. We were in Cannes for *Mulholland Drive* with Naomi Watts, Laura Elena Harring, Justin Theroux on that panel. David was there too, of course. David said to us before we went out on the stage, "If they ask you what it means, please answer them, 'What do you think it means?' How do you perceive it? What do you think?'" He will never give you a straight answer.

STEPHAN EICKE: *How come you did not end up writing "Mr. Eddy's Theme"?*

ANGELO BADALAMENTI: You are working on a movie, and someone comes in. Barry had played David a bunch of themes. David heard this one theme and said, "This could be great as Mr. Eddy's theme." That's great. Barry had a theme that David liked and he used it. Mazeltov. It's a good thing.

STEPHAN EICKE: *There are a few clips available showing of David during the shoot of* Lost Highway. *He is shooting to music ...*

ANGELO BADALAMENTI: Yes, I can confirm that. We went into a studio and we would always have a synthesizer up. I would just play. David would talk to me in poetry and we would record and record. Then he would realize that a lot of that stuff is really going to work in the mood and timing for *Lost Highway*. He would take those tapes—because actors have told me this—and he would play it on the set sometimes while they are getting ready to get on. It would set a mood and a tempo for the actors. He would play that music as they are moving around. I have heard this from a bunch of people that that's what he has done. He plays it on the set for the actors.[14]

In an interview to promote the film, Patricia Arquette revealed that David Lynch would direct her the same way he directed Angelo Badalamenti when sitting by his side at the keyboard: "He'd say, 'Dreamier, dreamier, slower.' As an actor you're usually rushed. But David gives you more time than even feels comfortable. You're given so much rope that at first it's scary, and then it's so soothing that you sort of get giddy in between takes, even though the movie is so dark."[15]

Despite David Lynch mentioning to Badalamenti that Fred Madison suffers from a psychogenic fugue, the composer experienced problems with the film. Whereas he had had no issues placing himself in the shoes of characters in *Blue Velvet*, *Twin Peaks*, and *Wild at Heart*, *Lost Highway* stumped him, as the composer later confessed: "The only time I couldn't understand [David's ideas] was when I was reading *Lost Highway*. There's a great storyline that's going on, and all of a sudden this guy in jail transforms into another person. I started scratching my head and saying, 'Oh boy, here we go again!'"[16]

By the time Badalamenti saw any footage of Lynch's then-recent film, he had already composed the main bulk of the score. His confusion concerning the meaning of the film did not lead to a writer's block as could otherwise have been the case. As usual, the composer had sat down with the director to develop musical ideas based on the latter's ideas and dream imagery.

Fred's insanity is expressed in the wild orchestral collages that Badalamenti developed and which were born out of Lynch's notion that the film demanded a more jagged, atonal approach than *Blue Velvet* or *Wild at Heart*. The director was also inspired by his then-partner Mary Sweeney, mother of Lynch's son Riley, and editor on *Lost Highway*. It was Sweeney who encouraged him to use live strings as opposed to synthesizers in the original score. Live strings could push the envelope in a way electronic instruments could not—certainly not for what Lynch and Badalamenti

---

[14]Eicke, "Mein Bruder David," p. 23f.
[15]LaSalle, Mick, "Patricia Arquette Bares Her Soul," *The San Francisco Examiner* [San Francisco], February 23, 1997.
[16]Schweiger, "The Madman and His Muse," p. 44.

aspired to do, which was to create a homage to Penderecki. Lynch adored avant-garde concert music and pushed his composer in that direction.[17]

David Lynch had loved the experience of recording Badalamenti's music for *Blue Velvet* in Prague. His composer, though satisfied with the quality of the recording, had been less impressed by the austerity and bleakness of the city in the mid-1980s. Still, ten years later both traveled to the Czech Republic to record the music for *Lost Highway*. While Lynch would add certain effects such as a reverb, and apply several filters to the recordings later during post-production, he and Badalamenti also used special analog recording techniques in Prague.

> *We thought it would be great to go back to Prague and do some modern orchestration—abstractions and stuff like that. Certain parts of the film are dark and noir-like, and when I started talking to Angelo about what feel is needed, this certain set of instruments just jumped into our minds. Angelo just started writing and we came up with a modern use of an orchestra. It took a long time—just Angelo playing certain sounds and different kinds of things—but we locked into something finally. And then, once you catch it, it just flows. Angelo felt very pressured on this movie because it was all very last-minute—the last three weeks before we were going to Prague he was scrambling.*[18]
>
> DAVID LYNCH

For a few days the recording stage in Prague became David Lynch's mixing studio. Across the street from the studio, construction workers were working at the pavement when Lynch approached them and asked to borrow some plastic tubes. Back in the recording studio, the director placed microphones at the end of these tubes. That way, the various noises captured by these microphones—room tone, music, the pushing of chairs—were naturally distorted. Similarly, Lynch and his recording team placed a microphone in a large Czech wine bottle. The sounds recorded in the bottle—a technique also used by Lynch and Alan Splet for *Eraserhead*—were as eerie and strange as the director had anticipated. The tubes not only added a natural reverb to Badalamenti's music but also changed its pitch: low bass rumblings now sounded as if they were played an octave or so higher than they actually had been. David Lynch loved these distortions.

Recording music through tubes was not a spur-of-the-moment decision. Lynch had toyed with that technique already in his studio in Los Angeles prior to his trip to Prague. For the recording of sound effects and their distortions, Lynch had used three Kems—long, tubular microphones that

---

[17] Rodley, *Lynch on Lynch*, p. 240.
[18] Ibid.

have two audio tracks each. With his Kems, Lynch wanted to record music and other, more abstract sounds coming out of a boombox. However, while experimenting, Lynch found that the noises from the Kems themselves were too loud. The sounds he had set out to capture were therefore not clean enough. Remembering his experiments with Alan Splet in the early days of his career, Lynch diverted a four-inch vacuum tube from its intended use. One end of the tube was put up directly against the speaker, with a Kem microphone being put into the other end:

> I started at the boom-box, got it, and then I'd move over to one Kem and get a sound going there. I could move closer and increase the volume and move into the other Kem, then swing back and at the very end I came over to my Kem, which had the music on it. They were all cued: they had to start and stop and blend.[19]

The tube had altered the sound to Lynch's liking.

Lynch was so in love with that process that he endeavored to follow a similar approach when recording Angelo Badalamenti's music in Prague. The orchestra was conducted by the composer Štěpán Koníček, who had a long-standing relationship with the Czech Film Symphony Orchestra and conducted—amongst many others—the music for films including the Oscar-winning *The Shop on Main Street*, the French fantasy *The City of Lost Children* (with music by Badalamenti), and who would later record Wojciech Kilar's music for Roman Polanski's *The Ninth Gate,* and *Mulholland Drive* for Badalamenti and Lynch. Koníček passed away in 2006.

> *The orchestra we used is called the Film Symphony Orchestra of Prague [sic], and they have this one studio that they have had there for years, but they have updated their equipment. This is a very dark score. It's kind of a dark movie, but even in its uneasiness and disturbing nature there is a beauty, and that is what we are looking for. There is just a mood about this place. We loved walking from the hotel and you come on to a very quiet street. You go into this place with these gigantic doors. They must weigh a thousand pounds each. Everything was muted tones. Sepia colors. The musicians just had all their little place in life. The bass players each had a little hole on the floor where they would just every day put their basses in.*[20]
>
> ANGELO BADALAMENTI

---

[19]Ibid.
[20]*Pretty as a Picture: The Art of David Lynch*, Dir. Toby Keeler, USA: Image Entertainment, 1997 [Film].

Some of Badalamenti's music, particularly in the film's first act, is mixed so low, it is barely audible, and often it is indistinguishable from Lynch's elaborate sound design. Nevertheless, the first notes of Badalamenti's score draw the viewer into Fred Madison's world through a collage of moody rumblings, faint screeches, and dissonant clusters, all mixed in with Lynch's dark sound patches. Fred's world is as tense as the streets of Prague were before the fall of the Iron Curtain. Even the first appearance of Fred's wife Renee—beautiful despite her unflattering make-up—is underscored by dissonant and therefore slightly threatening notes for jazz piano.

Fittingly, before "Song to the Siren" is heard for the first time—as Fred and Renee make love—Lynch uses a string composition by Badalamenti ("Fred & Renee Make Love" on the album) to raise the temperature on screen. The piece is tense, terse, and dense, performed initially only by cellos and basses, before violas and violins join in. Long, sustained chords double what can already be seen on screen. It is purely descriptive music, in that it enhances Fred's desperate struggle to please his wife and himself. What is he trying to find in Renee's eyes as he stares into her face like a mob boss might stare into the face of an accountant? Fred wants his doubts about his wife's faithfulness destroyed. He is though so convinced of her infidelity that in her long, emotionless return stare he only sees confirmation. Here, "Song to the Siren" begins. "I'd been waiting and waiting, and there it was, and it's definitely high on my list as one of the all-time most beautiful songs," David Lynch recalled.[21] While the song is used in the film multiple times, it does not appear on the soundtrack issued at the time of the film's theatrical release. Producer and 4AD label co-founder Ivo Watts-Russell did not grant Lynch the rights to exploit the piece outside the picture.

Only a fraction of the music Badalamenti wrote for the project was used in the film. As the director assembled more and more musical material—preexisting songs, new compositions by Adamson and Reznor, his own sound design work—some of Badalamenti's recordings had to be sacrificed. With Lynch, the production process has always been a fluid one. As previously described, the director often finds recordings during editing that he decides to use if they fit and are affordable. *Lost Highway* was no exception. The songs eventually used came to Lynch through various channels. "This Magic Moment," for example, would not be in the film without the input of the story's co-writer. It was, after all, Gifford, who turned Lynch on to Doc Pomus's *Greatest Hits*. As soon as the director heard Lou Reed singing "This Magic Moment," he was hooked.[22]

David Lynch worked diligently on the film's sound effects and soundscapes as his own sound designer. It was only a natural next step. The director had

---

[21]Douridas, "Interview."
[22]Rodley, *Lynch on Lynch*, p. 242.

expressed clear ideas about sound and proven to be hands-on when working with Splet on *Blue Velvet, The Elephant Man,* and with Randy Thom on *Wild at Heart*. On *Twin Peaks: Fire Walk with Me*, he had felt confident enough to develop, refine, and finish his own sound design tapestry. By the time *Lost Highway* went into post-production, Lynch had built his own sound stage and recording studio.

In 1994, one of Lynch's neighbors had passed away, enabling the director to purchase his house. He now owned three houses next to each other. In his newly acquired property, right next to his painting studio and living quarters, he carefully built an extensive space that allowed him to record music and sound effects, mix and master them, and more generally experiment with sound. Alan Splet would always be with him: some of his ashes were buried beneath David Lynch's mixing console.

Splet had died in 1994 following a long battle with cancer. Shortly before his death, he had started work on Anthony Minghella's adaptation of *The English Patient*. Splet was survived by his wife Ann Kroeber and their twins, a son and a daughter. Since Splet always enjoyed hiking in the hills of the Bay Area, a memorial service was held on Mount Tamalpais, his favorite place to walk and let his mind wander.

> STEPHAN EICKE: *I remember you mentioning that David asked you to record "dreamy winds" that he could use in* Lost Highway.
>
> ANN KROEBER: He wanted dreamy winds, and dreamy winds for me meant high tones, angels singing. That kind of stuff. I put together those kinds of winds for him to hear. He listened to them and said, "No, no, dreamy." Dreamy was dark and darker for him. It was a nightmare dream, and eventually I went, "Oh yes, right." I went back to my sound library and chose other stuff. Then he said, "Yes, here we go."
>
> STEPHAN EICKE: *Is it true that some of Alan's ashes are in David's studio?*
>
> ANN KROEBER: Yes. When Alan was cremated, there was a Brahma priest who came. David suggested it, he wanted it. I said okay. The guy came. He was a big guy, the head of his organization. He was a really important person. He came and we went into this room outside of where the crematorium was. I said to him when he came in, "It would be nice to know what you are doing and for me to tell you a bit about Alan." He said, "Yes, please." We sat down and talked and he was such a nice man. He was so kind, and he really got it. I told him that Alan wasn't religious but that he had a spiritual side. When we went into the ceremony, he ad-libbed and sang. We were like close friends. We would hum and chant. It was really profoundly beautiful. There was this point when we were doing it—we did it over Alan's body before he was cremated—and

all of a sudden this incredible white light came out of Alan, like a spirit roaring out of the body and up into the sky. The priest and I both saw it, smiled and nodded. It was spectacular. It was one of the most incredible things I have ever experienced in my life. It was like a spirit was coming and taking Alan's soul up into the next realm. Alan wasn't there anymore in that body. His spirit was gone, and so I said, "I think we can go into the crematorium now." It was okay to go because Alan wasn't in there anymore. It was so incredible.

STEPHAN EICKE: *David is very spiritual. Did he see it?*

ANN KROEBER: David didn't know about it. I told him about it later. He didn't see the spirit coming out of Alan. He missed it completely. He was doing something so he couldn't come to the ceremony. We had these ashes and we spread some around town, around Alan's favorite places, in the mountains around San Francisco. I kept a little bit in a special container.[23]

For Lynch it was always essential to be actively involved in the sound design process. He had worked intensely with Alan Splet, and Randy Thom had even given him his own fader when working on *Wild at Heart*. By the time *Twin Peaks: Fire Walk with Me* went in production, Lynch could no longer imagine entrusting somebody else with crafting the sound design for his films. For him it is an integral part of the movie-making process. Just as some composers would never dream of handing their sketches to an orchestrator because the orchestration for them is what makes the piece, Lynch cannot rely on somebody else to capture and model the sounds he hears in his head. They are already too closely intertwined with the images he has shot long before post-production commences.

> *You always work with other people. And we had some great people, you know, working on sounds. But every single thing you as a director are involved in, it has to be a certain way in your mind to work with the whole. It's critical, and it's based on a feel. And so it's working with people to get all these different sounds to be correct, and also taking advantage of serendipity and accidents. So it's a group effort but passing through one filter. [...] I'm sitting at the board. I'm actually on the board mixing music, but I think, as in the case of everyone on the crew, after a while everyone tuned into that one original doorway that Barry and I experienced, and pretty soon things start going right in tune with those original ideas and so you move as one.*[24]
>
> DAVID LYNCH

---

[23]Author interview with Ann Kroeber, September 11, 2020.
[24]Douridas, "Interview."

Following the harsh reviews for *Twin Peaks'* second season and its subsequent cancellation, as well as the mixed reviews for *Wild at Heart* and the abysmal box office failure of *Twin Peaks: Fire Walk with Me*, David Lynch's new opus was eyed with skepticism from the moment it was announced. Though it did fare better in all respects than the *Twin Peaks* prequel, the tide had not turned yet: while Lynch's work was regarded highly in Europe, especially France, American critics still were at best perplexed, if not repulsed by his work.

The reviews were far from kind, and American critics largely didn't seem to believe in the director as an influential filmmaker able to bring his unique vision successfully to the screen. Little did they know that this often maligned artist was to surprise everybody with his next project, after which he would then craft his grandest work of all.

8

Meditation

The Straight Story

Alvin Straight's road trip really was Alvin Straight's road trip. The elderly man who drove from Iowa to Wisconsin did so in real life. He was not an imaginary figure invented for the screen.

In the early summer of 1994, Alvin Straight heard that his brother Henry had recently suffered a stroke. Yearning to be at his side, Alvin decided to travel from Laurens, Iowa, where he lived, to Blue River, Wisconsin, his brother's place of residence (Mount Zion in the film). The problem was that Alvin's eyesight was so poor he could not obtain a driver's license. He was also, despite their repeated offers, even pleas, apparently too proud to let family members drive him. However, there was a simple reason behind his refusal that has nothing to do with pride: Alvin wanted to repent. He wished to show his estranged brother how much he still meant to him. Taking a bus or being escorted by friends in their car would be too simple. Being driven through the early summer landscape of the American Mid-West is no atonement.

Alvin had never let anything stop him, so on July 5, 1994, at the age of seventy-three, the Second World War veteran started his journey on a lawnmower that he had recently bought, a 1966 model from John Deere. In a ten-foot trailer, he hauled gasoline, clothes, food, and camping equipment.

Of course, David Lynch loved this story. It's a story about determination, something the director has always had himself, and a quality he has always admired in others. Without determination, Lynch would not have spent five years shooting his debut feature, *Eraserhead*. Alvin Straight's journey is a meditation on aging and life in general. It stands for the journey that is life. In the film, based on Alvin's adventures, the senior selflessly imparts his wisdom on—and shares his experiences with—the people he meets: the young runaway, the middle-aged couple who offer him shelter, the fellow veteran. The dialogue in the film is invented, written by Mary Sweeney and John Roach, but Alvin's journey was reproduced faithfully, hardly diverging from the real odyssey the war veteran had undertaken.

In several interviews, David Lynch proclaimed *The Straight Story* to be his most experimental film, which means it was the most unusual for him, being his most linear. In important respects, though, it was not an unusual film for the filmmaker at all, as several writers and critics acknowledged when the film came out. When *The Straight Story* was shown at the Telluride film festival in 1999, a reporter for the *Los Angeles Times* noted correctly: "Viewers were amused to see that *The Straight Story* is also a G-rated Disney picture, that's sentimental, full of expressions of conventional family values and modest. But Lynch has always showed a puritan strain. That's why he's so interested in sin."[1]

It would be misleading to claim Lynch's attitude toward family life has been Puritan: Jeffrey Beaumont's parents are mostly absent in *Blue Velvet*, replaced by an abusive gangster and an exploited night club singer as surrogates. Leland Palmer rapes his own daughter over the course of several years in *Twin Peaks*. Marietta is partly responsible for her husband's death in *Wild at Heart,* and plots to have her daughter's boyfriend killed. In *Lost Highway*, parents are absent for the most part, and its vision of domestic life is a bleak one. As the audience finds out in the course of *The Straight Story*, the Straights are dysfunctional in a more mundane way, but like in Lynch's other films, this rupture brings with it great suffering. Implied in this and other films by the director is that the happy, beaming all-American family hugging in front of a white picket fence is the ideal everybody should strive for. It's an image that displays Lynch's conservatism. Lynch as a storyteller wants his characters to achieve redemption, a state of bliss that sometimes is so pure and naive it verges on kitsch in all its sentimentality: the robin at the end of *Blue Velvet*; Laura Palmer's release in the arms of the angel in *Twin Peaks: Fire Walk with Me*; Sailor and Lula's passionate, fiery kiss in *Wild at Heart* that says they have grown up while their flame of love burns as brightly as it had on its first day. In *Lost Highway*, Fred Madison experiences an awakening of sorts—he goes through an inner hell, but at least he has left the dream he held onto for so long.

Moreover, Lynch has always loved the outsider, and his films have always been, as discussed previously, about the outsider's journey to their redemption. In *The Straight Story*, Alvin not only leads the people he meets on his journey to their moment of awakening (the runaway is the most obvious example) but also observes a transformation in himself when, for

---

[1] Movshovitz, Howie, "Telluride: An Eclectic and Rewarding Schedule," *The Los Angeles Times* [Los Angeles], September 8, 1999, p. 75.

the first time, he shares his secret with a fellow veteran. It is not altogether surprising that Lynch was quoted as saying, "I just fell in love with this thing and wanted to do it. [...] I felt this story. There was so much emotion in the script."[2] Then there are the typical Lynchian touches, scenes verging on the absurd, such as the woman who, much to her consternation, on her way to work kills a deer every single morning.

> *I didn't write* The Straight Story. *It was something of a departure for me, because it's completely linear. But then, I fell in love with the emotion of the script. So you can fall in love with something that already exists, too, and it's similar to falling in love with an idea. You get that feeling of what it could be on film, and that guides you.*[3]
>
> DAVID LYNCH

In the end it didn't matter that *The Straight Story* was not written by David Lynch, that it is the only feature film he has made that he did not devise himself (even the *Dune* script had been co-developed by Lynch). Mary Sweeney was his partner at the time, had given birth to their son Riley in 1992, and would marry the director in 2006. Certainly, Sweeney (who had first worked with Lynch on *Blue Velvet*) knew him better than most other people, and had a hunch that he would take to the story.

Lynch could feel at home in such company. He also assembled a cast and crew consisting mostly of people he knew well or had worked with before: Sissy Spacek, who plays Alvin Straight's daughter Rose, has been married to Jack Fisk, Lynch's set designer and one of his oldest friends. Harry Dean Stanton plays Alvin's brother. Everett McGill from *Twin Peaks* makes an appearance as a John Deere dealer. The film was edited by Mary Sweeney, and Freddie Francis let himself be coaxed out of semi-retirement. The British cinematographer and director had worked with Lynch on *The Elephant Man* and *Dune*. When the cameras started rolling, he was eighty-one years old and *The Straight Story* was to be his last film. Looking back on his experience, Francis considered the film fondly as a fitting conclusion to his oeuvre: "[David] rang me and said, 'Freddie, I'm doing this picture, I'd love for you to do it.' And I said, 'David, listen, I'm getting too old to mess around working twenty hours a day. I don't want to do it.' But he said, 'Well, how many hours would you work?'"[4] Francis made an exception for Lynch. He was willing to work ten hours a day. Lynch agreed and proved a man of his word, as the cinematographer remembered: "We never did work as

---

[2]Beckerman, Jim, "Lynch Makes a Family Picture," *The News and Observer* [Raleigh], November 22, 1999, p. 46.
[3]Lynch, David, *Catching the Big Fish* [10th Anniversary Edition] (Tarcher Preigee, 2016), p. 69.
[4]Francis, Freddie, *Freddie Francis, BSC, Cinematographer* (Camerimage, Tumult Foundation, 2002), Pages unnumbered.

many as ten hours and we finished three days ahead of schedule. I mention this because I'm sort of horrified with the way movies go these days, so far over budget. When David and I get on a film we discuss it as we go along. We never make copious plans."

Another familiar member of cast and crew was Angelo Badalamenti.

> *He approached me and I read the script. It was in the Americana style. And it wasn't eerie at all! But, ironically, I had been working on country music at the time. So David came over and we were in my house. I had a synth and he had some footage he had shot. I really didn't relate to it at first; I wasn't feeling inspired. But then we started talking about Sissy Spacek's character, Rose, who stutters. So anyhow, David and I talked at length about Sissy's character. And the more we got into the minds of the characters, the more I began to understand them.*[5]
>
> ANGELO BADALAMENTI

David Lynch and Angelo Badalamenti had—similarly as on *Lost Highway*, the script for which had puzzled the composer—a difficult start together making *The Straight Story*. Devising country and folk-inflected music did not present a challenge to Badalamenti, though this time the duo only started work on the score in post-production. Ever since *Blue Velvet*, Badalamenti had not watched any of the footage shot by Lynch when he sat down to develop the music. The change of approach on *The Straight Story* quickly threw him off. As he revealed, it was not the footage that would inspire the composer, but the characters themselves. In this case, it was Alvin's daughter who helped unlock the film to Badalamenti: Rose is a tragic character, a sweet and soft-spoken woman who takes great care of her father even though he resents being catered to and being treated like the old man he now is. Alvin and Rose never speak about the tragedy that befell her several years earlier, when her four children were taken away from her following an accident for which she still unjustly blames herself.

As Alvin recounts the story of his daughter's tragedy to the runaway, Angelo Badalamenti's "Rose's Theme" is heard quietly, one of several themes and motifs he developed for *The Straight Story*. Badalamenti and Lynch did not attempt to catch Rose's stutter in her theme—an approach that would have cheapened both the music and the film. Rather, they put her longing into music, her theme becoming a universal expression of yearning and the strength of family. Shortly after Alvin has shared his daughter's story with the runaway—accompanied by the soulful theme performed on guitar—the teenager leaves him, presumably to return to her parents. As Alvin gets up the next morning and discovers a bunch of sticks by the campfire—a symbol

---

[5]Badalamenti, "An Interview with Angelo Badalamenti."

for the strength of family in the film—the theme returns. There is no question that Alvin's session with the pregnant girl had made a lasting impression on her, that it was above all Rose and her story that made the teenager turn back.

> RUNAWAY: My family hates me. They'll really hate me when they find out.
> ALVIN: You didn't tell them?
> RUNAWAY: No. No one knows. Not even my boyfriend.
> ALVIN: Well, they may be mad, but I don't think they are mad enough to want to lose you or your little problem.
> RUNAWAY: I don't know about that.
> ALVIN: Of course neither do I, but a warm bed and a roof sounds a might better than eating a hot dog on a stick with an old geezer who is traveling on a lawnmower. My daughter Rose is ... some people call her a little bit slow, but she is not. She's got a mind like a bear trap for facts. She keeps everything organized around the house. She was a real good mom. She had four kids. One night somebody else was watching the kids and there was a fire. Her second baby got burned real bad. Rose had nothing to do with it but on account of the way Rose is the state figured she wasn't competent to take care of them kids and they took them all away from her. There isn't a day that goes by that she don't pine for them kids. When my kids were real little I used to play a game with them. I would give each of them a stick and one for each one of them and I would say, "You break them." Of course they could real easy. Then I would say, "Tie them sticks in a bundle and try to break that." Of course they couldn't. Then I would say, "That bundle, that's family."

FIGURE 25 *Rose's Theme (from* The Straight Story, *1999).* *Transcribed by Andrew Morley.*

The scene of Alvin's retelling of Rose's tragedy both visually and acoustically connects to an earlier scene in the film. Shortly before Alvin announces he is going to visit his stricken brother in Wisconsin, Lynch shows Rose gazing forlornly out the window at night, looking at the garden hose and a ball rolling into the frame. Shortly afterwards, a young boy appears, chasing after his toy. The audience is not yet familiar with Rose's history, and therefore, the images she sees outside the window, in front of her garden, have no particular meaning ascribed to them. However, they are accompanied by Badalamenti's "Rose's Theme"—the connective tissue that will later accompany Alvin's telling of Rose's story.

"Rose's Theme" returns later in one of the film's funniest and at the same time most touching scenes: after Alvin has had his lawnmower repaired by local brothers Harald and Thorvald, he not so much negotiates with them about the price but righteously declares that he will not pay the amount they dare to charge him. Furthermore, Alvin continues, they should stop fighting all the time. After all, they are brothers. Brothers should support each other. Together, they are like a bundle of sticks; and the use of "Rose's Theme" evokes that particular image. The music continues playing as Alvin bids his host Danny goodbye. Both men are barely able to hold back their tears. While Rose is not in these scenes, they are about Rose as a character and a symbol. She stands for the strength of family. Correspondingly, the theme also plays as Alvin comes close to his brother's home, just as his lawnmower is about to break down. It is also heard as he and Lyle sit on the terrace and gaze up to the stars. In this way, "Rose's Theme" is like "Audrey's Theme" in *Twin Peaks*: it changes its meaning over the course of the story. While "Audrey's Theme" had originally been ascribed to Bobby, "Rose's Theme" had been composed for Alvin's daughter. It is a description of her character who survived a tragedy but was forever marked by it. Over the course of the film, it becomes a hymn in gentle celebration of family values.

> STEPHAN EICKE: The Straight Story *certainly sounds different from your other scores for David Lynch. The arrangement for strings and guitars, the folksy approach, was new. How did you develop it?*
>
> ANGELO BADALAMENTI: I composed this music the same way as anything else. David came to my home. I have a home and I had my studio in my basement. The home next to mine is now used as a recording studio. I do all my work there. It's right across the driveway and it's fantastic. There are four bedrooms in there as well, a kitchen and everything you want. I composed *The Straight Story* with David sitting next to me and describing things. He did have a video at that time and was showing me things. But as I was looking at the video, there was one scene that I couldn't get into. David stopped the tape and said, "Let me just talk." Sure enough, he talked and it worked. It's a film I love very much. There are so many beautiful scenes in it. It's a touching film, totally different from the other films David has done, and it's a score that I've not totally been associated with. The performance of the composition, especially the acoustic guitar work, is stellar. There is something about it that hits people right in the heart. It was very well accepted at Cannes. They really loved it.

STEPHAN EICKE: *The film was backed by Disney. Did that have any effect on your work? Did they send notes?*
ANGELO BADALAMENTI: No, not at all. Of course not. The deal is a deal, whether it's Paramount for whom I did *Cousins* or Warner Bros. for whom I did *Christmas Vacation*. It doesn't matter. Disney actually makes life easier because everything is very much above board. Everything is recorded under the union and you don't have to worry about going to Prague to record the music. You can record right here in America. It was the first session that David had in his room. My contract was equal if not better than any other.[6]

Badalamenti drew inspiration from Puccini. He sought to channel the composer's gift for memorable melodies and tie it to music arranged for a small ensemble in a folk style. It quickly became clear to Badalamenti and Lynch that *The Straight Story* called for pieces that left blanks, empty spaces. The film needed to breathe and let the sounds of nature speak. *The Straight Story* was not a film that called for the dense string writing Badalamenti would later employ for *Mulholland Drive*, or for the atonal Penderecki homages of *Lost Highway*, or the electronic and jazz-oriented abstract montages of *Twin Peaks* and *Fire Walk with Me*.

After Badalamenti had found a way into *The Straight Story* with "Rose's Theme," he developed a theme for Alvin. It is a gentle, tender, and yet upbeat composition featuring elaborate violin solos with guitar accompaniment. It plays as Alvin sits on his lawnmower, admiring the falling dusk. Shortly thereafter, he experiences a near-fatal accident when he unsuccessfully tries to apply the brakes on his lawnmower.

One of Alvin's fellow travelers—and, in fact, his only constant companion—is "Laurens Walking," a piece of music which appears in various iterations. It plays whenever Alvin is on the move, riding through the landscapes of the Midwest. Its most prominent feature is the underlying rhythm provided by violins, a steady, repetitive pattern that propels Alvin forward. Consequentially, it appears, for example, as Alvin Straight leaves

FIGURE 26 *Alvin's Theme (from* The Straight Story, *1999)*. Transcribed by Andrew Morley.

---

[6]Eicke, "Mein Bruder David," p. 24.

Laurens for the first time; as he leaves it a second time following his purchase of a new lawnmower; after he resumes his journey following a torrential rain storm; and as he bids Danny Riordan goodbye and heads again toward Wisconsin.

Angelo Badalamenti did not plan to use his compositions in the specific scenes as just described. Typically, he wrote the music away from the film, and it was similarly recorded—by fourteen musicians—not to picture. It was up to David Lynch to use the cues wherever he saw fit. And, as always, Lynch was guided by his intuition in the music editing and mixing process. What felt right ended up in the movie.

Since *The Straight Story* had been shot on location, Lynch had not played pre-existing music to the actors to guide them or to provide an atmosphere he sought to capture. Playing music over headphones was easy in a studio, but back then it proved a logistical and technical nightmare when shooting outside, and the crew was on a tight schedule. As a result, Lynch did not use "temp music" on location.

The fact that Lynch did not play music on set also meant that scriptwriter and editor Mary Sweeney was not provided with music to which to cut the film. She had to request it. It was up to David Lynch's studio manager John Neff, who worked as score engineer and re-recording mixer, to provide music for the editing. Badalamenti's score had not been recorded yet. Neff was an experienced musician, producer, and music recordist in his own right, and gleefully set about providing Sweeney with music for the picture—temp music that would later be replaced by Angelo Badalamenti's original pieces. These were recorded late during the editing, when Sweeney had nearly completed the process. Meanwhile Neff assembled temp tracks from old records of his, as he explains: "I used some old tracks from an album I did in Maui with a fellow named Littlejohn. The bar room veteran story scene is 'The Most Requested Song' from an album called *Strange Tales of the Late West*. I took strings and an acoustic guitar and sometimes some other instruments from that album without vocals."[7]

Angelo Badalamenti listened to the temp music, but was not guided by it when it came to his own composition. Such becomes clear when listening closely to *The Straight Story*. Two of John Neff's pieces remain in the film, and they are vastly different in style and approach to Angelo Badalamenti's sparse, country-infused chamber music for fourteen players. One of Neff's

FIGURE 27 *Laurens Walking (from* The Straight Story, *1999)*. Transcribed by Andrew Morley.

---

[7]Author interview with John Neff, June 18, 2021.

tracks can be heard as Alvin enters the doctor's office early in the film. The slightly distorted electric guitar loops capture Alvin's underlying fear of the doctor's diagnosis, although he tries his best not to show it. The other piece by Neff—"The Most Requested Song"—fades in during one of the film's pivotal scenes, as Alvin tells his war-time secret to Verlyn Heller, a fellow veteran who is deeply touched by his new friend's honesty. Alvin's story brings him to tears and makes his own memories come flooding back. Neff compiled more temp tracks than the two aforementioned pieces. However, they were all replaced, as intended, by Angelo Badalamenti's compositions, which were recorded in January of 1999.

> *When I work with Angelo [Badalamenti], it's generally the image that shapes the sound. But the opposite can happen, or the two can emerge at the same time. In this film, we sometimes reworked the sequence of images because we needed more footage here or there in order to let the sound breathe. Each scene has its appropriate tone. And the sound can either amplify or destroy that ambience. Once you get the right sound, it's all about the right level. Finding the rights formula was not so simple for* The Straight Story. *No grand events take place. It's a story so simple, so pure, that introducing a new element risks making it distracting and out of place.*[8]
>
> DAVID LYNCH

What is true for the music also applies to the sound design: it unmistakably belongs to a Lynch film, but is stripped down, more restrained and introspective than in his previous works. The sound design in *The Straight Story* is light-footed, floating. Gone are the dense hums and dark drones of *Blue Velvet* and *Lost Highway*. *The Straight Story* is a movie that breathes visually and acoustically, that is not suffocated by the dense soundscape that Fred Madison or Laura Palmer—or even Henry from *Eraserhead*—had to navigate like a thick river of molasses. The obvious difference is that *The Straight Story* is largely set outdoors in mostly natural landscapes, which is different to the earlier films.

As in his other films, though, Lynch uses the sound design and effects for their raw emotional power: as Alvin falls down in his kitchen, the camera stays outside. Just a heavy hump can be heard—a noise that could mean any of several things. It is, however, accompanied by a low, barely audible hum, not dissimilar to the intrusive room tone in Fred Madison's house. It is this low buzzing that signals to the viewer that something bad has just occurred. The audience cannot see it immediately, but feel an unease triggered by the thud in conjunction with the dark ambience.

---

[8] Henry, Michael, "David Lynch: A 180-Degree Turnaround," *Positif*, November 1999. Reprinted in *David Lynch Interviews*, ed. Richard Barney (University Press of Mississippi, 2009), p. 219.

Lynch only gets one brief opportunity to insert his beloved industrial sounds, as the grain elevator in Laurens is shown at night. But even the sounds these elevators emit are light and high, far removed from the wasteland in *Eraserhead*. Here, the sound design is reassuring, not threatening. A journalist once remarked that even the sound design in *The Straight Story* is "euphoric," suggesting the "forces of life."[9]

Indeed, the lightness of touch of *The Straight Story* is remarkable. Moments such as the aforementioned scene in the bar, and shots such as that of the bundle left behind at the burned-out campfire, pack an emotional punch: as restrained as they are, they stand out amid the light, airy tone of the film. Certain scenes appear like a dream. The woman who keeps hitting deer appears completely out of place, almost otherworldly.

Another moment deserves to be highlighted for its sound design alone: as the runaway appears for the second time, as she emerges from the dark while Alvin is roasting a sausage over the open fire, she is accompanied by a barely audible bell sound. She is like a mystical figure out of a fairy tale making her entrance. Like in many other scenes in Lynch's film, the sound effect here is not diegetic, since it does not seem to come from a visible source on screen. The director announces the runaway as an eerie but benevolent apparition; a symbol, someone who doesn't exist in real life. As it turns out, she really does exist, as the bundle of sticks she leaves behind makes clear. At the same time, she is a way for Lynch to go deeper inside Alvin's mind. It is she who makes him share the story of his dead wife and his daughter Rose. The runaway is like a mirror for the soulful traveler with the sad eyes. What he sees in her eyes is himself, the regrets and pains he has had to live with. He wants to spare her the suffering he fears life has in store for her.

> It's one of the elements that's the most critical to the whole. You don't know everything going in but you act and react as you go in. It's always an experiment. Mary [Sweeney] will tell you I sit sometimes in the editing room and she turns around and I'm crying. Emotion is a thing that cinema can do. But it's tricky. It really shows you how this balance point is critical. A little bit too much and the emotion goes away. A little bit too little and it doesn't happen. On The Straight Story it was another experimental film to try and find that tender balancing point. It's not that you start out setting about to do a certain type of film. The ideas tell you what kind of film it is and a lot of times you don't realize what it is until it's nearly over. It's strange how they unfold as they go.[10]
>
> David Lynch

---

[9] Ibid.
[10] Festival Cannes, "*Mulholland Drive* Press Conference."

In another pivotal scene, Lynch again uses sound design not just to evoke the necessary mood but to place the audience into the characters' heads. In the bar scene with Alvin and Verlyn Heller, the 1940s are playing out: as Alvin confesses to be an alcoholic because of his time in France as a soldier, the jukebox plays "Happy Times," a standard recorded by Jo Stafford in 1949. As Verlyn starts to recount one of his wartime memories, the song ends and a sustained, quiet synthesizer note holds the tension before sounds of the war—explosions and airplanes—commence as illustration for Verlyn's tale. These sounds let the audience know which images are playing in the former soldier's mind. Lynch puts his viewers straight into the veteran's memories. He employs the same tactic with Alvin as he finally confesses— for the first time—the crime he committed fifty years before. The sounds of war are still haunting both men. Later, fragments of John Neff's "The Most Requested Song" appear, soothing and gentle music, seemingly at odds to the experience that Alvin has just relived and which has brought him and Verlyn to tears. But for Lynch, the act of confession, of coming to terms with one's own past by no longer suppressing the pain, is something to cherish and value. Unburdening oneself is an act of cleansing.

The Straight Story was John Neff's first experience of recording and mixing a film score, but nothing in the film reveals that innocence. The guitarist had joined his first band in 1963 and released his debut record two years later, *So Good* by The Ascots. After having released several more albums, Neff started work as a session player at United Sound in Detroit, where he played on more than 125 records without receiving credit. His work was for hire. After joining Steppenwolf in 1977 as a bass player for their then current tour, Neff played with Hoyd Axton before settling in Maui—where he founded a record label, hosted a morning show on the radio, and established his own recording studio. Later, he built a commercial recording studio with Walter Becker of Steely Dan fame in Ulupalakua. After fourteen years in Maui, he moved to Phoenix and built another studio. Then in 1995 he moved to Los Angeles and started tech:ton engineering, a division of studio bau:ton with Peter Maurer and Peter Grueneisen at its head. The duo designed the wiring loom and made the equipment selection for recording studios. One of their clients was David Lynch.

STEPHAN EICKE: *How did you come to work for David Lynch?*
JOHN NEFF: I started working with David on the design of his studio
and specified the cinema sound because he had a 22 by 11-foot
screen in a theater. It was a fourteen-seat mixing theater, and so
we specified all the gear that was going to go in. He already had
a Euphonics console in storage, and we had to design the studio
around that console. In August of 1997 David asked me if I would
mix a commercial. We were still installing the studio. He had shot
a Honda Passport ad. It had no voice-over in it, it was all images,

music and sound effects. It was a great commercial, it ran the whole year. The next week we were finishing the installation and David said, "You are the only one that knows how this studio works, you have to run it." I said, "Oh my God." I couldn't afford the pay cut. I was making really good money at tech:ton. He upped his offer and I came down 25 percent and we made a deal. I went to work for him running his studio.

STEPHAN EICKE: *Did David have specific requirements for his new studio?*

JOHN NEFF: Yes, he was very involved in the finishing of the studio. He has a beautiful wood shop next door to the studio and he made all of the solid maple diffusers for the studio in his wood shop to very stringent specifications by the architect. It turned out beautifully. He also designed the furniture for the 14 theater seats, including his command seat right in the middle with a telephone and an intercom. He wanted to be able to record music. He wanted to be able to have some orchestral players in the studio, so there was a big distance between the screen and the console. He wanted isolation rooms for voice-over work and ADR and amplifiers and things like that. We had three isolation rooms, a big space between the console and the screen. That's where the string players for *The Straight Story* sat. I recorded them into ProTools and three guitars players on the session were in the three isolation booths so I had no string bleed onto the guitar tracks and no guitar bleed onto the string tracks. The guitars were the lead instruments anyway in the songs they were featured in, so the isolation was good. That was the first orchestral recording in the studio. January 30, 1999. It came out terrific.

STEPHAN EICKE: *What did a typical day in David's studio look like for you?*

JOHN NEFF: I was in charge of maintaining the studio. I had done a technical design on it, so I knew it intimately. David and I, first thing in the morning, would have a big coffee and decide what we wanted to do that day. Some days he would say, "Fire up the amplifiers," and that meant we were going to record. It was always at David's whim. Now, sometimes he would go up to the painting studio and paint. There would be no work in the studio so I would edit things and do rough mixes of things independent of Dave and then get his approval or his notes.

A normal day was from ten to seven. Five days a week. But when we were involved in a project I would work six days a week and sometimes longer hours into the evening. It was all salary except I had a tiered salary. If I was just working with David and there wasn't a commercial or a movie or anything like that in the house I got a certain salary. When we were working on commercials, it was more. When we were working on films, it was double. I was able to make some fair money but it was all salary so there wasn't any overtime for the long days or extra days. It was a fair deal.

STEPHAN EICKE: *The Straight Story was your first feature film project. How terrified were you?*

JOHN NEFF: The first few days I was very nervous. But a week before we started the mix—the score was already recorded—I asked David who was going to mix the picture, who I was going to work with. He looked at me real funny, like, "What planet are you on?" He said, "You are going to mix the picture. That's what you are here for." "Oh my God."

I had just built a new home in Santa Clarita, California, and I put in a 50-inch projection TV—the flat screens weren't in yet—and a 5.1 surround system. I rented two DVDs a night for a week before the start of the mix to listen to what people put in sub-woofers and in surround. It was all over the map. There is no guideline. So, the first few days it was very difficult to hold it together.

I was working with [sound mixer] Ron Eng and Patrick Giraudi, who was a dialogue editor, and Walter Spencer, who was the dialogue editor. He treated the dialogue, took out prompts, comments and so on, so all we had left were the actual lines. These guys were all experienced movie guys. Patrick had worked with Lynch on *Lost Highway*. So, all of a sudden I realized on the third or fourth day, this is no different than a record mix. Voice is king. The dialogue must be king, and I became comfortable. David gave me guidance on the surrounds. He said, "No more than ten percent ambiences on the surrounds," but I put a fair amount of sound into the sub-woofer for impact, like when the big truck blows by Alvin and he loses his hat, and when he is surrounded by trucks just before he reaches the bridge. I went to a truck stop with a portable DAT recorder and recorded all these trucks idling and starting off. I just made a cacophony of truck noises for the scene and put it all in the sub-woofer.

There is a scene where a car comes right through a scene from the left, and I got to drive that off into the back right surround. So the car drives right through the theater, and David thought that was a pretty trick but he didn't let me do much more than that. I got to put the tractor into the surrounds a few times, but I became very comfortable and just forged ahead and followed the direction of David. Ron Eng had some good input on the mix structure because he had mixed fifty films already, so he helped me out. He was the sound effects editor and sound supervisor. I was the lead mixer although in the mixing credits I think we did it alphabetically. It was Ron, Dave and myself, but I was the one running the console and ProTools. In the end I was really comfortable with it and I'm happy with the way it turned out.

STEPHAN EICKE: *Did you have to get used to David's abstract descriptions?*

JOHN NEFF: It was difficult in the beginning because he would say, "I want a reverb on this to sound like it's in a canyon." That's easy enough. Then he says, " … a black marble canyon." Well, what does that mean? There is no black marble canyon preset on any of the reverbs, so I had to start building a reverb. A shiny canyon would have a lot of echo, so I put an echo device in line before the reverb. When the signal hit it, it would get an echo splash and then the reverb. David loved it. It worked. But he is very abstract in his descriptions.

STEPHAN EICKE: *You mentioned Ron Eng and Patrick Giraudi. David himself developed the sound design for* The Straight Story …

JOHN NEFF: I was extremely close to that process. David reserves the sound design credit for himself. That's an agreement when you start. But I was heavily involved in it. It was a team effort, the sound design on *The Straight Story*.

STEPHAN EICKE: *What were your tasks regarding the sound mix on* The Straight Story?

JOHN NEFF: Building all the special reverbs, EQing and mixing in elements, because a lot of sound design was multiple elements. I would build the cue with David's guidance. Things like the ratios of elements to each other and all that sort of thing was my contribution to the design.

STEPHAN EICKE: *David likes organic sounds. Did he record many new sounds for this film?*

JOHN NEFF: David took a stereo portable DAT recorder with him to the set, so he was recording elements the whole time they were shooting. In one scene he wanted crickets, when Alvin is talking to the girl with the twigs, the runaway. I dubbed in some crickets. He walked into the studio and said, "What's that noise?" I said, "That's your crickets." He said, "Those are day crickets. I got to have night crickets!" I had to go and find the DAT that said night crickets and import that. He could tell the difference between the day crickets and the night crickets and I couldn't.[11]

---

[11] Author interview with John Neff, June 18, 2021.

Lynch had recorded sounds that caught his attention on set, put them on tape, and labeled the tapes accordingly. That made it easy for John Neff to find the required night crickets and place them in the scene. It made for a smooth working-process.

Among the other sounds Lynch had recorded on set was a lawnmower. The director (and sound recordist in one) had let the mower idle, climb a hill, and speed up and slow down. These sounds as recorded in the field were then later enhanced and transformed by John Neff and Ron Eng in collaboration with Lynch in his studio. Their approach was not unlike the one David Slusser described for *Wild at Heart*.

In *The Straight Story*, the scene in which Alvin seeks shelter from a raging rainstorm serves as the perfect illustration for how Lynch liked to transform his field recordings. The director had shot the scene in question without recorded sound, so all the sounds, the whirring of the lawnmower and the torrential rain storm, were created in the studio, in post-production. Although Lynch had recorded several lawnmower noises, none of them proved appropriate for the scene in question. Therefore, Eng and Neff took a recording of a lawnmower running and put it into a sampler. Eng used his portable keyboard with a pitch wheel to increase the pitch of the lawnmower engine as Alvin climbs the small hill. It worked perfectly: thanks to the pitch wheel on Eng's keyboard, the lawnmower ended up sounding exactly as it would in real life when driving up a hill as steep as the one seen in the film.

Throughout the process, Lynch was hands-on, as actively involved in the mix as he had been on his previous movies. Lynch ran eight faders to adjust various picture elements, including the sound effects, whenever he saw fit. It was work he focused on with a keen ear for detail. As the director explained multiple times, the balance is key, and Lynch kept adjusting the volume of the dialogue once Angelo Badalamenti's music had been recorded and mixed into the film. During the final mix, Lynch kept making fine adjustments until he was satisfied with the balance. Frequently, he would ask his studio manager and scoring engineer John Neff to build new endings for Angelo Badalamenti's cues when they ran too long for a scene. (One disadvantage of writing and recording music away from picture is that sometimes the lengths of various cues need to be adjusted during the mix to fit the corresponding scenes.)

STEPHAN EICKE: *Were you present when David and Angelo had one of their famous sessions at the synthesizer?*

JOHN NEFF: Yes, Angelo had a synthesizer session with David in early December of 1998. David and I put the synthesizer up into the cinema sound so it sounded huge. David would sit over Angelo's shoulder and Angelo would play ideas and David would go, "No. Slower. Darker." He would talk to Angelo while Angelo was playing. I was recording it all into DAT as well so Angelo took those ideas home to him.

STEPHAN EICKE: *Angelo lives in New Jersey. How often would he come over to David's studio?*

JOHN NEFF: He would always stop by when he was in town scoring other movies. In fact, in December of 1998, when we had the idea session for *The Straight Story*, he had just finished a movie in LA and took a few extra days to work with David before going back home.

STEPHAN EICKE: *Did Angelo leave room for the musicians to improvise in* The Straight Story?

JOHN NEFF: Angelo wrote everything out. We had a copyist in the dining room of the studio with a printer set up. If a cue didn't work Angelo would write with pencil the changes on the score and then the copyist would print out copies for all the players.

STEPHAN EICKE: *Did David give Angelo detailed feedback or require changes during the recording?*

JOHN NEFF: He and Angelo had one talk on a break and Angelo made some score adjustments and the copyist printed out new sheets for the players. But other than that David sat at the console listening to it as it went down and had no interaction with Angelo. It was totally Angelo driving the boat.

STEPHAN EICKE: *The score was not recorded to picture. How did you know where to put the various pieces?*

JOHN NEFF: I did it with David's guidance. He said, "I want that 'Laurens, Iowa' to open the film," and then "Rose's Theme" had been cut for the sprinkler scene where we learn that Rose had lost her child. Those were specific, and the others we would be mixing and David would say, "Let's try this one here," so I would get it, bring it in and edit it to the scene. Then we would mix it into the scene.

STEPHAN EICKE: *How many changes were made from the first few days of mixing to the last day of the final mix? Were a lot of pieces moved around?*

JOHN NEFF: No, very little. David had a very good idea what he wanted and where he wanted it. My job was to edit the music to the scene that he wanted it in so that it sounded seamless. Sometimes we would start partway into a cue or start at the head of the cue but take out the end. I would have to build an ending for the scene that sounded like the score was ending there. There was a lot of editing that went on to cut to the specific scenes, but David knew pretty much where everything was going to go.[12]

---

[12]Ibid.

It was the second time John Neff collaborated with Angelo Badalamenti. They had met while working on the Honda Passport commercial David Lynch directed a year before the shoot of *The Straight Story*, which had also been the first time Neff worked with Lynch on a creative project. The commercial sees a young man leaving a subway station and discovering the new Honda Passport in a shop window. Entranced by the vehicle that promises to transport him to the steepest mountain region, in seconds he transforms into a mountain man. All this is accompanied by Angelo Badalamenti improvising on a synthesizer. The one discordant cluster in the music was added later by David Lynch himself by pressing several high keys on a keyboard simultaneously. Though working on the Honda Passport commercial proved a fertile playground for Lynch, Badalamenti, and Neff, not everything went smoothly. Initially, they did not have appropriate sound effects for the man's ascent from the subway station. Lynch had ordered multiple foley files from the company Digital Sound and Picture, but none fitted the action. The steps the man was climbing were made of concrete. The foley files, though, sounded as if every step was recorded on wood. Lynch immediately noticed the discrepancy. Fortunately, his studio was already up and running, and one of its features was a fairly large cement pad behind the mixing console. John Neff plugged in the microphones and recorded himself walking on the concrete pad in his Italian leather shoes. The sounds were perfect and ended up in the commercial. Post-production took Lynch, Badalamenti, and Neff only one evening.

The box office numbers for *The Straight Story* were a disappointment. With a budget of approximately $10 million, it grossed under $100,000 on its US opening weekend, and its total box office worldwide was only $6 million.[13] It was especially ironic considering *The Straight Story* was Lynch's most approachable film, a mainstream vehicle and among his critically most praised work to date. The harshest reviews still appreciated the gentle warmth of Lynch's drama. Indeed, reviewers heaped praise on Lynch and *The Straight Story*. Even Roger Ebert, who had taken part in an infamous, heated debate with fellow critic Gene Siskel over what he perceived was a humiliating treatment of Isabella Rossellini's character in *Blue Velvet*, awarded *The Straight Story* four stars, his highest possible rating.[14] It was surprising, considering Ebert had not even appreciated *The Elephant Man*.

Ebert dedicated a paragraph to the film's sound design and its raw emotional power and impact, writing:

---

[13]https://www.imdb.com/title/tt0166896/?ref_=ttsnd_snd_tt.
[14]Ebert, Roger, "The Straight Story," *Chicago Sun-Times*, October 15, 1999, https://www.rogerebert.com/reviews/the-straight-story-1999 (accessed June 19, 2024).

There are fields of waving corn and grain here, and rivers and woods and little bed barns, but on the soundtrack the wind whispering in the trees plays a sad and lonely song, and we are reminded not of the fields we drive past on our way to picnics, but on our way to funerals, [...] when the roads are empty.

The images and sounds in *The Straight Story* are vastly different to those in *Wild at Heart*, David Lynch's other road movie. His new film was about an old man's journey into his past, while the earlier title charted a young couple's escape into what they hope will be a better future. Their journey is doomed, and Lynch made that clear visually with red-hot images, filters, and appearances of the Wicked Witch of the West. He underlined it acoustically with punchy, intrusive sound effects and a dark, brooding sound design, added to which was Angelo Badalamenti's "Dark Spanish Symphony," a dense and passionate love theme that is as tragic as Rose's and Alvin's themes in *The Straight Story* are melancholic. The themes in Lynch's later road movie explore an introspection that Sailor and Lula as characters lack. The pieces are skeletal in their transparent orchestration, while "Dark Spanish Symphony" is an extroverted love letter to abundance, a homage to Richard Strauss. It captures the flame of youth, whereas Badalamenti's compositions for *The Straight Story* are, as Roger Ebert wrote about the screenplay, like dialogue by Hemingway, raw and to the point. The story of Alvin Straight as portrayed by Richard Farnsworth would always remain one of Badalamenti's favorite films, a work especially close to his heart.

> *The Straight Story is a beautiful film that truly showed David Lynch's versatility. He can do anything. Of course, I started out as a songwriter and so I had experience in so many genres including a bit of country (Can you imagine; a kid from Brooklyn?). So, this wasn't much of a stretch for me. But of course, it probably helped people recognize my versatility in film scoring. I am grateful for the opportunity and I am really proud of that score.*[15]
>
> ANGELO BADALAMENTI

The Straight Story put David Lynch back in the reviewers' good books, and the film's sensitivity and its technical mastery prepared them for what was to come—the filmmaker's best work yet, a groundbreaking and seemingly impenetrable picture that with its alluring atmosphere of mystery would grab even those who were left puzzled by the story's meaning.

---

[15] Schweiger, Daniel, "Interview with Angelo Badalamenti," *Film Music Magazine*, February 3, 2014, http://web.archive.org/web/20140409072727/http://www.filmmusicmag.com/?p=12490 (accessed June 19, 2024).

9

Questions in a World of Blue

Mulholland Drive

Doppelgängers, dreams, jealousy, crime, and guilt—all of David Lynch's favorite subjects are present in what to this day is widely considered his cinematic masterpiece, *Mulholland Drive*. All these elements inform a story of the poisonous side of show business. *Mulholland Drive* is Lynch's *Sunset Boulevard* and can be named with *All About Eve*, *Opening Night*, and *All About My Mother* when discussions turn to unflinching studies of aspiration and toxic rivalry on stage and screen.

Here, as in *Eraserhead*, *Blue Velvet*, and *Lost Highway*, evil cannot win. A person who commits a sinful act will not be able to live with that act. You may try to escape, flee into your dream world, but in the end you will have to wake up. The burden on your conscience is simply too overwhelming. This awakening is an act of cleansing. This view is evidence of Lynch's puritan streak, and the director does not pretend that the world is not an evil, dangerous place, as *Twin Peaks* clearly shows. Lynch is not a cynic like Woody Allen, who has his hero shrug off killing in *Crimes and Misdemeanors*, Allen's most Dostojevskian film. For Lynch, penance is required, if not inevitable.

Two versions of Lynch's *Mulholland Drive* exist: a TV pilot and a theatrical film. The former does not feature most of the film's second half, since the pilot was supposed to continue as a series. Only the feature affords its viewer a conclusion. Through careful, focused examination, the audience learns that Diane Selwyn is a young, aspiring actor in Hollywood. Having just arrived in La-La Land, she quickly lands an audition and falls in love with Camilla, a fellow actor and thus a competitor. As it happens, the role Diane fought so hard for eventually goes to Camilla, who—so Diane believes—must have slept with the director, Adam Kesher, in order to get the job. (The parallels with *Lost Highway* and specifically Fred Madison's insecurity and paranoia are obvious.) Boiling with jealousy, Diane hires a contract killer and has Camilla murdered.

Tormented by her act, Diane creates a parallel, alternative dream world in which the film's first half takes place: Camilla (now calling herself Rita) has taken the place of Diane, here called Betty. Rita is involved in a car crash and, as a consequence, loses her memory. Seeking shelter, she finds refuge in the empty apartment of Betty's aunt, Ruth. Only a short while later, Betty arrives to attend some auditions in Hollywood with the dream of becoming a celebrated movie star. She discovers Rita and makes it her mission to help recover the brunette's memory. Her detective work, though, will lead Betty ever closer to the truth that she has tried so hard to suppress. In the film's climax (and toward the end of the TV pilot), Betty and Rita stumble across what appears to be Betty's/Diane's corpse. In this pivotal scene, Lynch indicates that Diane is already dead, though she is still clearly dreaming and therefore conscious. Paradoxically, she will kill herself later, after she herself has stumbled across her own corpse in her dream.

The realization that Lynch's introduced diegesis is therefore not "absolute," as Pascal Couté puts it, adds to the confusion the film evokes.[1] The reality is not the reality, and even the dream cannot be trusted, since its timeline is discordant with what the audience believes to be reality.

Mulholland Drive was David Lynch's most intricate, oblique work to date. Like *Twin Peaks*, it could have developed into a series, had executives at ABC, which had commissioned the pilot, not rejected the ninety-minute TV pilot and shelved it.

> Mulholland Drive *was originally going to be a continuing story on television. We shot it as a pilot: open-ended, to make you want to see more and more. I heard that the man at ABC who was making the decision whether to accept the pilot or not saw it at six a.m. He was watching television across the room while having some coffee and making some phone calls. And he hated what he saw; it bored him. So he turned it down.*[2]
>
> DAVID LYNCH

Lynch's relationship with ABC had been fraught for some time before his pilot was rejected. Though clearly enthusiastic about the project, which Lynch shot in early 1999 for the channel, he soon found himself diametrically opposed to the constraints that network television presented.

---

[1] Couté, Pascal, "A peine eut-elle franchi la routem," *David Lynch, l'écran omnivore: Éclipses* 34, no. 1 (2002): p. 46.
[2] Lynch, *Catching the Big Fish*, p. 60.

John Neff remembers Lynch's dismay while on post-production on the pilot: "We were working seven days a week in the end to hit the satellite deadline to upload it to the ABC affiliates. They put us up at a hotel in Century City, myself and Ron Eng, the sound supervisor. We worked from 9 in the morning until 1 in the morning, seven days a week to get the pilot done."[3] The pilot was two hours long. This proved a point of contention, as Neff continues: "David found out it could only be eighty-eight minutes and ABC said, 'We sell advertising, sixteen minutes an hour.' He had to cut the pilot, and he was very angry about it. He butchered it. When we screened it for the affiliates, nobody picked it up. Nobody liked it."

Lynch was furious and upset about how his work had been treated. He vowed to never work in television again. But this would not be the end of *Mulholland Drive*. Fifteen months after it had been dismissed by the executives, David Lynch received a call from producers at the French company Ciby2000 that asked him to expand his *Mulholland Drive* ideas for a feature film. The problem was manifold: since the pilot was supposed to develop into a series and was therefore open-ended, the director had never conceived an ending for the story. Further plot developments would have been devised by him and associates later. The pilot was just that: a pilot. And even if he could think of a conclusion, he would have to rehire the crew and shoot additional scenes—a logistical nightmare considering the sets had already been taken down by ABC, which, to complicate matters, also owned the rights.

Meditation saved Lynch, *Mulholland Drive*, and boosted Naomi Watts' career (which had not yet taken off prior to the Cannes screening of the feature). Neff continues: "All of a sudden one Friday night David after meditation got me on the intercom and said, 'I've got an idea! Call Gay!' That was his assistant, Gay Pope. 'Tell her she has to work this weekend.'"[4] Pope came in and typed the dialogue and scene instructions Lynch dictated. Everything went seamlessly, as Neff recalls: "Monday morning he called the French and said, 'I have got an ending.' So we put *Mulholland Drive* back into production, fifteen months after it had died."

> *Now, you don't use meditation to catch ideas. You're expanding the container, and you come out very refreshed, filled with energy, and raring to go out and catch ideas afterward. But in this particular case, almost the day I got the go-ahead to turn it into a feature, I went into meditation, and somewhere about ten minutes in, ssssst! There it was. Like a string of pearls, the ideas came. And they affected the middle, the beginning, and*

---

[3] Author interview with John Neff, June 18, 2021.
[4] Ibid.

the end. I felt very blessed. But that's the only time it's happened during meditation.[5]

DAVID LYNCH

The director's long-time friend and producer on *Mulholland Drive*, John Wentworth, was skeptical, as he admits. The film would be, after all, a patchwork: "It was one of those adventures that David went on that I was like, 'Man, I have no idea how you want to make this work. When you build a TV pilot you are setting up characters and narrative lines. You are a genius, so I'll trust you'll figure this out, but I can't see it.'"[6] Wentworth was astonished when he then saw the final cut, which he deemed a compelling piece of cinema: "He has that artist mind. His roots are in painting and abstraction and association so he can make associations that you can put on a piece of paper and that make sense but it's an intuitive cinematic sense that you simply have to trust. It worked."

One of the many new scenes Lynch shot to turn the pilot into a film features a dinner party. It is an integral part of the plot. Here, toward the end of the film, Diane sees her hopes of a long-term love affair with Camilla dashed: invited by the latter, Diane agrees to join her and Adam Kesher for an elegant reception at the director's house, and it is immediately clear that Camilla has been in a relationship with Adam, who is preparing to make an announcement—possibly of a romantic nature—perhaps in regards to an engagement or a pregnancy. The announcement itself is blocked out by Diane. At the party, she sees various guests she will imagine in her dream in various roles. A man dressed in a cowboy outfit will later become "the cowboy" who threatens Adam. A heavy-set, middle-aged man becomes a mafioso who forces Adam to cast Camilla (as opposed to Diane) in his film. In the actress's mind, a lack of her talent cannot possibly be the reason for her failure to secure the role in Adam Kesher's film. Rather, there must have been a plot to prevent the artist from hiring her. The role of the heavy-set man at the dinner party—who transforms into the mafioso character Luigi Castigliane—was played by Angelo Badalamenti in his second on-screen credit for a David Lynch film, the first having been *Blue Velvet*.

> STEPHAN EICKE: *How did you get cast in* Mulholland Drive?
> ANGELO BADALAMENTI: It was great fun to do. David called me on the phone and told me that he wanted me to be in the movie. I said, "Thanks for inviting me to do the music again, David." "Of course you are going to do the music, but I want you to be an actor." "You have to be out of your mind, David. I am not an

---

[5]Lynch, *Catching the Big Fish*, p. 60.
[6]Author interview with John Wentworth, January 30, 2021.

actor!" "No, you are going to be perfect for it. It's a cameo role but you are perfect because do you remember you told me this story about this man you met in Northern New Jersey when you went to this dancer's house, the girl you did some arrangements for? You met her husband and you described what it was like?" "Yeah." "I want you to be that guy. The way you told me that story, the way you looked, was perfect."

I went to have dinner [with said dancer]. I met her husband and I went to this unbelievable palatial place with Lamborghinis out there and Rolls Royces and butlers and maids and money up the kazoo. She introduces me to her husband. I call him Frankie. We had dinner and we sat around the table, me and my wife, this singer and her husband. He had the sternest look. We were sitting at the table and he doesn't say a word to me. Not a single word. I don't have to tell you the tension that caused. As he is eating, I said, "Hey Frankie, you got some house! What kind of work do you do?" He doesn't answer me, he just looks at me with his cold eyes. I said, "Are you in construction? Are you a builder?" And he says, "Sort of." Half an hour later he still says nothing. I said, "Frankie, my man, where is your basement? You got waterfalls, a Hawaiian room, the brickwork, you must be in some kind of masonry work. Are you a mason?" "Kind of." That's all he ever said. I was telling the story and David was looking at me and staring at me. He was close to my face. A year and a half later he calls me and he says, "I want you to be an actor and I want you to be that guy. Act and look like the way you looked at me." That's the story of the espresso and *Mulholland Drive*.[7]

The other mafioso—Luigi's brother—is played by Dan Hedaya. As mentioned earlier, Badalamenti had attended Seth Low Junior High School at the same time as Hedaya. The director mused that Badalamenti and Hedaya looked like brothers and were, therefore, perfect for their respective role. Lynch joked that following the film's premiere the acting bug bit his composer, and Badalamenti wouldn't stop begging him for a role in a new film.[8]

Badalamenti cherished playing a mafioso as much as he had enjoyed accompanying Isabella Rossellini in *Blue Velvet*, and nearly as much as belting out "A Real Indication" for *Twin Peaks: Fire Walk with Me*, the performance that gave David Lynch a hernia. The composer leaped into his new responsibility with passion and great self-confidence. Had he not

---

[7]Eicke, "Mein Bruder David," p. 25.
[8]Barney, Richard A., "Mulholland Drive, Dreams, and Wrangling with the Hollywood Corral," in *David Lynch Interviews*, ed. Richard Barney (University Press of Mississippi, 2009), p. 234.

possessed these two qualities, he would never have worked with Nina Simone and met Lynch in the first place. He might have retired as a teacher.

Shooting the dinner party scene was decidedly less fun than shooting the espresso scene though; it became increasingly hectic and stressful. Badalamenti had only one evening to shoot the scene before he was due to fly back to New Jersey. Unfortunately for everyone involved, it was during that evening that the crew had to leave the premises prematurely and wrap up filming. Without hesitation, the director instructed his cinematographer Peter Deming to focus the camera on Badalamenti while everybody else packed up their equipment and left the room. Thanks to Deming's close-up, the commotion is not visible in the final film, and Lynch could keep his composer in the frame as an integral part of the scene.[9]

One year following the premiere of *Mulholland Drive*, in May 2002, Badalamenti was back at Cannes, helping to promote a film he had recently scored called *L'adversaire*. In one of the festival tents, he spent a few hours in the company of David Lynch and Martin Scorsese, passing time before attending the gala dinner. Badalamenti later remembered jokingly: "Marty said to me 'I saw you in *Mulholland Drive* and I must say that you and I have a lot in common, not least because we are both Sicilian. One of these days I'm going to write a script and you and I are going to play brothers.' I'm still waiting for that call."[10]

By the time Badalamenti appeared in front of the cameras as Luigi Castigliane (both in the TV pilot and the feature film), he had already developed the main theme for *Mulholland Drive*. Several years before David Lynch shot his intricate LA noir mystery, the director had conceived some basic ideas for what would become *Mulholland Drive*. While sitting in his composer's studio on the East Coast, he asked Badalamenti to play something dark and Russian on his Fender Rhodes. The musician did as he was told and came up with the theme for *Mulholland Drive*, a subdued, slow, and dark melody in minor key that satisfied Lynch's needs. As always, Badalamenti had recorded his improvisation on a tape, a copy of which he gave to his friend. The director would later use it during the shoot of the TV pilot. As with most other pieces that Badalamenti devised for Lynch, the main theme for *Mulholland Drive* was not written to picture.

The music for the TV pilot is remarkably different to the score written specifically for the feature film. Though the cues written for various scenes in the two versions of the story are often similar in mood and atmosphere, they have little else in common. While Badalamenti and Lynch retained the main theme for *Mulholland Drive* and used it in the movie, the other cues

---

[9] Lynch & McKenna, *Room to Dream*, p. 390f.
[10] Joy, Nick, "A Very Engaging Score," *Film Score Monthly* 9, no. 10 (November/December 2004): p. 19.

featured in the theatrical version were newly written by Badalamenti, as John Neff explains: "We approached the film as a completely new project. We used nothing from the pilot mix. We started all over again."[11]

> *Basically, the music went from a synth score to something that was mostly orchestral. When David got the okay to turn* Mulholland Drive *into a feature, I also ended up writing another ninety minutes of score. But I did a tremendous amount of music for* Mulholland Drive *because there was a tremendous amount of musical options for it. [...] David asked for [the main title] to be used at different places and in different ways in the film, to come back like a good old friend. He wanted the audience to relate to the main theme, whether they'd realize it or not.*[12]
>
> ANGELO BADALAMENTI

The most obvious difference between the music for the TV pilot and the feature film is that the cues for the former were performed entirely on a synthesizer, for the simple reason that Lynch and Badalamenti did not have the budget to hire an orchestra. The composer wrote the score for the TV pilot at breakneck speed: "on the fly," as John Neff remembers.[13] He then sent the tapes to David Lynch's still relatively new studio in Los Angeles.

A direct comparison between the music used in the TV pilot and in the feature film makes clear how little Lynch retained of Badalamenti's earlier work. The following table compares the scenes in the pilot with those in the feature. If no cue title is available, the music in each individual scene is described in italic. If there is no music in a scene, a blank space is left. The titles for cues used in the feature film that are also on the film's official soundtrack release are in bold and italics.

TABLE 2 *Music Cues in the TV Pilot and the Feature Film*

TV Pilot	Feature
	Jitterbug Contest *Jitterbug*
	Diane lying in bed
	Opening Credits as "Rita" is being driven around Mulholland Drive
Mulholland Drive theme	***Mulholland Drive****, interrupted by aggressive interlude with brass and percussion*

---

[11]Author interview with John Neff, June 25, 2021.
[12]Schweiger, "The Madman and His Muse," p. 27.
[13]Author interview with John Neff, June 25, 2021.

TV Pilot	**Feature**

                    "Rita" crosses Sunset Boulevard

excerpt from "Sunset Boulevard"   **Rita Walks**
  title music by Franz Waxman

               Two detectives examine scene of accident

Mulholland Drive theme   **Sunset Boulevard**

       "Rita" hides in front of Aunt Ruth's apartment, walks in

spheric, tense music   **Aunt Ruth** as "Rita" hides under the table

                  Dan and Herb sit in Winkies. The former confides to the latter about his dream
                  Diner

                  Mr. Roque makes a few calls
                  Mr. Roque

        Betty walks out of the airport, arrives in Los Angeles

dreamy, tinkly music   **Betty's Theme**

                  Irene and her companion drive off, Betty arrives at her aunt's apartment
                  Mulholland Drive (edit)

                Coco shows Betty around

              Betty explores her aunt's apartment

repeat: dreamy, tinkly music

 Betty discovers "Rita" in the shower and they introduce themselves to each other

Mulholland Drive theme

Woman is shot and attacked in an office building
steady, rhythmic percussive music

Adam Kesher enters the production office
brief, tense music

 The Castigliane Brothers arrive at the production office and make their demands

sustained, tense music

TV Pilot	Feature
	Adam Kesher rejects Camilla Rhodes as lead actress
tense, slow music	
	Adam Kesher wrecks the Castigliane brothers' car, then flees the scene
orchestral avant-garde, Penderecki-like piece	*jazzy, percussive, instrumental piece*
	Ray enters Mr. Roque's place, asks for his demands
	Woman is shot and attacked in an office building
Betty speaks with Aunt Ruth and confronts "Rita" about her identity	
Mulholland Drive theme	*spheric, electronic music as "Rita" discovers the money and the blue key in her purse*
Ray enters Mr. Roque's place	
*spheric, tense music, similar to **Mr. Roque** cue on album*	
The Castigliane brothers discover their wrecked car	
aggressive, avant-garde music with clusters	
Betty tries to trigger "Rita's" memory; Mr. Roque makes a few calls	
spheric, sustained suspense	
	The contract killer meets his friends at Pink's
	Adam Kesher drives home, about to discover his wife cheating on him
	instrumental, percussive jazz
Betty and "Rita" are in Aunt Ruth's apartment. "Rita" remembers the name of Mulholland Drive	
Mulholland Drive theme	*firewood, drones*
Adam Kesher drives home, about to discover his wife cheating on him	Adam Kesher drives home, about to discover his wife cheating on him (continued.)
"Take Five" by Dave Brubeck	*instrumental, percussive jazz (continued), segues into **The Beast***

TV Pilot	Feature

Adam Kesher gets into a fight with the pool cleaner and his wife, drives off

The Beast ctd.

Betty and "Rita" hide the latter's purse in aunt Ruth's apartment before they call the police from a phone booth

elegiac, slow adagio with a shade of what will later become the **Diane** *&* **Camilla Theme**

Betty and "Rita" sit down in Winkies

elegiac, slow adagio sets in again   *brief, tense string-interlude*

Betty and "Rita" are back in Aunt Ruth's apartment, calling Diane Selwyn

elegiac, slow adagio followed by dissonant clusters   *sustained, low bass chords*

Big guy comes looking for Adam Kesher, gets into confrontation with Kesher's wife and the pool cleaner

brooding sound design accentuated by metal clangs and suspense music   **Bring It On Home**

Cookie informs Adam Kesher of his banking problems. Kesher calls his assistant

Betty and Rita decide to pay a visit to Diane

low suspense music   *low suspense music*

Louise knocks on Betty's door and engages in a brief conversation
rumbling sound effect and music collage

Adam calls his scriptwriter friend

Adam drives up to meet the cowboy

"Take Five" by Dave Brubeck   *dark sound design collage*

Adam speaks with the cowboy

TV Pilot	Feature

Adam is left standing in the field by the cowboy.
Cut to Betty rehearsing her script with "Rita"

spheric, sustained drone   *bass tremolo*

The two detectives discover recent findings about the accident on Mulholland Drive

     Coco discovers "Rita" and speaks to Betty about the mysterious guest

     As Betty prepares to leave, two men in suits and glasses drive by Aunt Ruth's apartment
     low, ominous drone

     Betty leaves, drives up to film studio
     excerpt of **Mulholland Drive/Love Theme**

Establishing shot of film studio

excerpt from "Sunset Boulevard"   *excerpt of* **Mulholland Drive/Love Theme**
title music by Franz Waxman   *ctd.*

Betty delivers her audition

slow, elegiac music with discordant climax

Casting agents walk up to the elevator with Betty

Adam Kesher holds his audition

"Sixteen Reasons"   *"Sixteen Reasons"*

Adam Kesher speaks with auditioning actress, before Camilla Rhodes walks in

     low, droning firewood

Camilla Rhodes auditions

I've Told Every Little Star   *I've Told Every Little Star*

Adam Kesher announces "This is the girl"

humming, electronic drone   *I've Told Every Little Star ctd.*

Betty flees Camilla's audition

TV Pilot	Feature
I've Told Every Little Star (fading back in)	first notes of ***Dwarfland***
	Betty and "Rita" drive up to Diane Selwyn's place and investigate the premises, discover the corpse, head back home
discordant suspense	elements of ***Dwarfland*** as sound collage
	Betty transforms "Rita"
slow, elegiac piece	*low, brooding electronic music followed by ringing and humming sounds*
	Betty and "Rita" lie down to sleep and start making love ***Mulholland Drive/Love Theme***
	"Rita" wakes up in the middle of the night, asks Betty to go out with her *beginning of **Silencio***
	"Rita" and Betty walk into Club Silencio, listen to the magician's speech *sound design, segues into **Silencio***
	Rebekah del Rio sings ***Llorando**, followed by edited variation of **Mulholland Drive***
	"Rita" and Betty are back at the apartment. The latter takes out the blue key and puts it in the lock of the blue box *droning, ominous sound design*
	Aunt Ruth looks around her own apartment
	The cowboy appears in Diane Selwyn's bedroom, telling her to wake up *dark, brooding, crescending sound design collage*
	Diane wakes up, engages in a brief conversation with her neighbor
	Diane briefly sees Camilla *spheric, floating drone*
	Diane and Camilla make out ***Go Get Some***

TV Pilot	Feature
	Adam directs Camilla for a scene *Pretty 50s*
	Diane and Camilla have a confrontation *aggressive sound design collage of crescending clusters*
	Diane masturbates *Pretty 50s*
	Camilla calls Diane, urging her to come to the party
	Diane drives up to Mulholland Drive **Mulholland Drive**
	Diane and Camilla walk up to the party **Mulholland Drive/Love Theme**
	Diane and Camilla arrive at the party **Dinner Party Pool Music**
	Diane converses with Adam's mother *One Dog Bark (Thought Gang)*
	Diane watches Camilla kiss a blond girl before Adam prepares his announcement **Mountains Falling**
	Diane hires a contract killer at Winkie's *low firewood leading into:*
Camera slowly moves toward the man behind Winkies **Mr. Roque** *variation*	Camera slowly moves toward the man behind Winkies (different shot than in pilot) *dense, electronic sound design*
	Diane's dream collapses *sound design segways into* **Mulholland Drive/Love Theme**

What becomes immediately apparent is that pivotal scenes in the film feature brooding, foreboding suspense music, while the same scenes in the pilot were scored with more elegiac, or sometimes even upbeat compositions. Betty and Rita at Winkie's, and Adam Kesher's driving up to meet the cowboy at his ranch serve as examples. In the pilot, the significance of these scenes is left unexplored since no ending had been developed. In the film, Lynch hints at the inherent danger and importance of these encounters through the use of his music. The compositions here serve as signifiers or symbols, since by then Lynch knew the plot's outcome and meaning for its characters.

Lynch uses "Take Five" by Dave Brubeck twice in the pilot, one of his favorite pieces of music that he will later also insert into *Twin Peaks: The Return* to great effect. Here, "Take Five" accompanies Adam while driving, as he is about to discover something that will leave him dumbfounded. Lynch uses it before Justin Theroux's character finds his wife in bed with the pool cleaner, and before he engages in a cryptic conversation with the cowboy. The highly rhythmic, catchy, and light-footed composition underlines the obvious absurdity of Kesher's situation. His life seems about to be destroyed, but in comical, surreal fashion.

FIGURE 28 *Take Five (1959).*
Transcribed by Stephan Eicke.

In the film, the sounds that accompany him on his way to a meeting with the cowboy are dark, discordant notes, part of a sound collage, foreboding and threatening. It sets an entirely different mood than the famous drum solo of "Take Five." Brubeck's piece is, though, an appropriate soundtrack for Kesher's cool arrogance, which was on full display during the meeting with the mob. Adam Kesher doesn't suffer fools gladly (as Lynch made clear when he has the director smash the car of the Castigliane brothers).

Musically, the *Mulholland Drive* TV pilot is not unlike the *Twin Peaks* pilot in that hardly a scene is left unscored, the whole eighty-eight minutes drenched in music. The main theme recurs nearly as often as "Laura Palmer's Theme" does in *Twin Peaks*—like a trusted old friend. But while Laura Palmer's theme stands for the sadness that engulfs her friends and neighbors, the *Mulholland Drive* theme does not stand for any person or situation in particular. It evokes a mood that Lynch felt necessary for the scenes in which he used it. It so perfectly captures a feeling of mystery and unease that it transforms the seemingly most trivial scenes into tense, enigmatic signposts on the road to the riddle's solution. Accordingly, it is used as Camilla is driven toward Mulholland Drive; as the two detectives examine the scene of the accident; as Betty discovers Camilla as Rita in Aunt Ruth's shower, and as Betty sits down with her houseguest and new friend to solve the mystery of her identity.

> BETTY: I wonder where you were going.
> RITA: Mulholland Drive.
> BETTY: Mulholland Drive?
> RITA: That's where I was going. Mulholland Drive.
> BETTY: Maybe that's where the accident was. There must be a police report. We could call.
> RITA: No.
> BETTY: We could call anonymously from a pay phone, just to see if there was an accident. Come on, it'll be just like in the movies. We'll pretend to be someone else. I want to walk around anyway. I'm in Hollywood, and I haven't even seen any of it. Come on, Rita. Do you feel up to it?
> RITA: Okay, but just ... just to see.
> BETTY: Just to see if there was an accident on Mulholland Drive.

FIGURE 29 *Mulholland Drive Theme (from* Mulholland Drive, *2001). Transcribed by Stephan Eicke.*

Another cue that appears more than once in the *Mulholland Drive* TV pilot is a reference to one of David Lynch's own favorite movies: *Sunset Boulevard*. As Camilla/Rita flees from the scene of the accident and crosses Sunset Boulevard, a few notes of Franz Waxman's main theme for Billy Wilder's film can be heard—and again as Lynch uses an establishing shot of a movie studio. Movie studios were, of course, the obsession of Norma Desmond, the former film star at the heart of *Sunset Boulevard*. Like Diane Selwyn, Norma cannot accept that her star has faded. While Diane never has been a star on the international screen, Norma is convinced she can make a comeback that will put her in the headlines again. Like Diane, she considers it unjust that she has not received a movie offer lately. She is delusional. (Narratively, Wilder's *Sunset Boulevard* is as absurd as David Lynch's *Mulholland Drive*. The former is told in voice-over by a corpse, the latter in an unreliable dream flashback in which the audience sees the corpse of the dreamer.) In the feature film, Lynch dispenses with any musical reference to *Sunset Boulevard*. Again, the significance of the scenes in question differs from what the audience could gather from them in the pilot.

But while Lynch used different pieces for the same scenes in the TV pilot and the feature film, these pieces more often than not evoke a similar mood, which indicates that Lynch from the beginning envisioned *Mulholland Drive* as an exploration of Hollywood's darker side. The "spheric" music that appears as Camilla/Rita hides in front of Aunt Ruth's apartment is as similarly tense as the cue "Aunt Ruth" used in the feature. As Diane/Betty arrives in Los Angeles, the TV pilot features tinkling, floating music that is as dreamy as "Betty's Theme" is soaring. They are both pure and innocent, full of hopes that will soon be dashed. When Betty speaks with Rita in Aunt Ruth's apartment about her identity, the "Mulholland Drive Theme" is as similarly threatening as the ominous electronic drones used in the feature film as Rita discovers the money and the signature blue key in her purse. The same goes for a moment that occurs just a few scenes later, as Rita remembers the name of Mulholland Drive. Both "Dwarfland" and the suspense music that appears as Betty and Rita investigate Diane Selwyn's neighborhood and flat are droning, threatening, and discordant. Both cues are layered, though the feature film version more elaborately so due to the budget, time, and the fact that it features orchestral elements.

> *I have a feeling underneath it all he knows what the music should be. Where he gets it from I don't know. I put these little notes down that seem to be what I think he's thinking about and hearing in his soul. Sound design in these days especially in movies is a very important thing. Layers of sound and music together these days are becoming more and more important but you still need the important melody from time to time to be able to reach the heart of people. It's that combination. David is an expert on sound design and it's one of his great loves.*[14]
>
> ANGELO BADALAMENTI

By the time *Mulholland Drive* went into production as a pilot, David Lynch had already perfected mixing music and sound design in order to create a mélange that was impossible to label but which evoked exactly the atmosphere he desired. As in, particularly, *Twin Peaks: Fire Walk with Me* and *Lost Highway*, music and sound design/effects often are indistinguishable. A noteworthy example is the scene in Club Silencio, the theater Betty and Rita walk into after the latter has woken up in the middle of the night and muttered the word "Silencio."

Accompanying the mysterious magician's speech is a thick, heavy collage of ominous organ drones played by Badalamenti, solos by a clarinet and

---

[14]Festival Cannes, "*Mulholland Drive* Press Conference."

a trombone, before a trumpet sets in. Underneath it all is a vibrating, dark, and heavy carpet of slowed-down electronic chords and orchestral "firewood." In the film, Lynch adds various sounds such as thunder and a heartbeat to create a rich tapestry that is as disorienting acoustically as the images are visually. The moment is an integral, essential part of the story, one that has a function similar to the appearance of the Mystery Man in *Lost Highway*. Here, Betty/Diane is reminded (after stumbling across her corpse earlier) that her illusion, her dream, is about to crack. "It is all recorded, it is all a tape," cries the magician after he has presented the trumpet player who didn't actually play the trumpet. Nothing is real. "It is an illusion." The scene makes Betty/Diane aware that she can no longer continue to flee from her feeling of guilt—she has to face up to what she has done. The magician reminds her that the comparatively comfortable life she has led in the past few days was not reality. Like the Mystery Man, the magician is an intruder. The scene alerts the audience that nothing they have seen can be trusted. What Lynch has presented so far was not real. It was an illusion, a dream. Here, in this scene of *Mulholland Drive*, images and music in conjunction drive home that point much more effectively and elaborately than visuals alone could have done. It is a stunning example for the emotional and intellectual power of David Lynch and Angelo Badalamenti's collaboration.

The singer Rebekah del Rio is then announced. She enters the stage to give a Spanish language rendition of Roy Orbison's classic "Crying" ("Llorando"). It is the perfect summation of the magician's speech and the scene in Club Silencio as a whole. Thematically, it fits like a glove. After all, Roy Orbison begins his crooner hit by stating that he was happy for a while and able to smile as long as he suppressed thoughts about his romantic break-up. As soon as he sees his former lover again, he breaks down, unable to contain himself from crying violently. Betty/Diane was alright for a while, as long as she suppressed the memories of her object of desire.

Considering how perfectly the song captures the essence of the scene and of the film as a whole, it is tempting to suggest Lynch specifically chose that song for its inclusion in *Mulholland Drive*. And yet, the use of "Llorando" is another example of Lynch's instinctual decision-making. The director, naturally curious and always open to what may present itself, only decided to include the song after he had met Rebekah del Rio. "Llorando" only became part of *Mulholland Drive* after Rebekah del Rio had, on the spur of the moment, decided to sing that particular version of "Crying" for the director. Lynch liked to make spontaneous decisions, as long as they felt natural to him. Always working from the subconscious, he was open to using chance and coincidence to further his art.

STEPHAN EICKE: *Were you there when David met Rebekah del Rio?*
JOHN NEFF: Yes. She was brought to meet David by Brian Loucks of CAA [Creative Arts Agency] and to see if they clicked and if

maybe they could work on some music together. She and Brian get to the studio. David orders coffee all around and the office boys come over with coffees. We are not even partway into an open discussion. We haven't known each other ten minutes yet and David goes, "I hear you are a singer." "Why, yes." It was just to meet him and see if there was any connection. But she stood up and started singing, "Llorando," and David said, "No, hold it, wait." I had a really nice microphone set up in one of the vocal booths with a nice pre-amp and a nice reverb on it. He said, "Go down there and sing." She goes, "Into the microphone?" He goes, "Yes." She goes down, I start ProTools and she sings what you hear in the movie, uninterrupted. It went down just like you hear it in then film, and he wrote her into the movie because of that.

STEPHAN EICKE: *Can you talk a bit about the recording of the* Mulholland Drive *score?*

JOHN NEFF: We went into post-production on *Mulholland Drive* in 2000. Then in December of 2000 David, Angelo Badalamenti and I went to Prague, Czech Republic, to record the score for the feature. It was wonderful. They flew us business class, put us up in a five star hotel within walking distance of the scoring studio in Prague, and we walked past the old state opera house. This was of course where they had filmed *Amadeus*. That was a beautiful thing to see. We had a ninety-piece orchestra in Prague and we split it up into three days of recording. We recorded the strings on one day, for the whole movie. Then the next day we overdubbed brass and woodwinds because Dave wanted the option to use just string cues or full orchestra cues. I learned how to overdub the orchestra. It came out beautiful. So, on the third day we recorded the jitterbug elements which I arranged from elements and with David's help. We basically rewrote the jitterbug and made it from pieces.

We went fourteen weeks mixing the film, starting in January 2001, and we finished in March and submitted it to the Cannes Film Festival. They accepted it. We weren't quite done with the soundtrack yet, so we had to finish it before May 1, which we did. Then the film premiered at the Cannes Film Festival in May of 2001. We got a 10-minute standing ovation at the end of it. It was a brilliant evening.

STEPHAN EICKE: *You mentioned you arranged the jitterbug elements. What did you mean by that?*

JOHN NEFF: The jitterbug opening for *Mulholland Drive* was all "found music." That basic trio was recorded in Prague and horn parts were recorded but not to the track, just wild. Then David wanted me to pitch them down an octave, so I did, and then I constructed a jitterbug melody based on these odds and ends that

we had from the Prague sessions. It was all an octave lower. [...]
It's Angelo's music, but I arranged it. We only had two weeks
to put all the music together and basically mix it. The mix for
Mulholland Drive started on January 2, 2001. I had these pieces,
these horn pieces and trumpet pieces and the basic jitterbug
rhythm track. David and I just went fishing and found little hooks
that we liked. Then I put them into the track and edited them in.

STEPHAN EICKE: *These weird, surprising blasts from the brass in "Jitterbug" certainly are ear-catching.*

JOHN NEFF: That was done during the mix. David wanted these emphasis points and he wanted to mess with it. We built these blasts from sound effects in the library. Actually, one of them is a synthesizer discordant chord, and the other one was found sound effects. I don't remember which sound effects we used for it.

STEPHAN EICKE: *How did Angelo react to you adapting his jitterbug like that?*

JOHN NEFF: I don't know. He would have had that talk with David, not me. He certainly never complained about it, and it opens the film.[15]

For David Lynch, Angelo Badalamenti's compositions are as much a blueprint as his own scripts. They are to be modeled, transformed, and edited in service of the film and its story. "Jitterbug" is only one example, countless others have already been described (the use of "firewood," the layering of music and sound design, the encouragement of David Slusser to develop new material based stylistically on Badalamenti's recorded work). Badalamenti and Lynch's creative relationship would not have endured, had the composer not agreed with the director's sentiment that his music is like a piece of clay. The composer is a craftsman, hired to fulfill a service. It is up to the director to take the recording and do with it as they please.

Over the course of the decades, Badalamenti proved himself as a supportive, magnanimous collaborator who—although frequently openly proud of his work—put his ego in his pocket. While others may have complained about the transformation of one of their pieces, Badalamenti did not once speak out against it, or made public the decisions and action taken behind the scenes. Badalamenti understood that in film it is essential for a composer to put trust in the director, as he explained: "The most important thing is the respect that we have for each other, and the trust. I trust him and of course his instincts with music. He trusts me when I say, 'Hey, David, I really want to use it this way.' 'Well Angelo, I don't know.' 'David, I really do.'"[16] Sometimes Lynch would relent and let his friend give it a try, as the

---

[15] Author interview with John Neff, June 18, 2021.
[16] Marcone & Philp, "Interview with Angelo Badalamenti."

latter continued: "He can't tell you the notes to write, but he comes up with these strange things. He is a genius with his concepts visually and he is able to inject ideas that are strange. 'Why don't we just honk some horns?' 'But this is a beautiful ballad!' 'No, lets do it!'"

Badalamenti went on to cite the jitterbug from *Mulholland Drive* as an example: the unexpected honking horns are a result of Lynch's instincts, which Badalamenti trusted completely. The jitterbug is not the only element of the *Mulholland Drive* score that was heavily altered by Lynch and his team in post-production. In fact, the whole composition is a patchwork. The composer had written approximately ninety minutes of music for the movie, which was orchestrated by his long-term-collaborator Phil Marshall and Hollywood arranger Patrick Russ (who worked on Elmer Bernstein's *Ghostbusters* among others) for a full orchestra—including strings, woodwinds, brass, and percussion. For the film, Lynch dispensed of all elements but the strings (with the exception of the cues "Silencio" and "Diner," which feature low bassoons and brass low in the mix). As John Neff explained, the woodwind and brass sections were overdubbed, recorded separately from the strings as per Lynch's request, since he wanted to have the freedom to use woodwind and brass only occasionally, if at all. Thus, the score as heard in the film and on the album is just a part of what Badalamenti, Lynch, and Neff recorded in Prague. Still, the composer never complained.

He also didn't complain that Lynch decided not to use one of his most yearning melodies, the theme for Diane and Camille.

FIGURE 30 *Diane and Camilla (from* Mulholland Drive, *2001)*. *Transcribed by Andrew Morley.*

Although it is featured on the album, the music cannot be heard in the film. Lynch had asked Badalamenti to develop themes for the characters, but in the end decided that this particular piece did not fit. For Lynch, it was a common practice to dispense with recorded cues. The music was not recorded to picture and therefore had not been written with a specific scene in mind. Whenever Lynch felt the emotional balance on screen tipped to one side or the other, it needed to be adjusted. Elements needed to be lost. It was all a feeling thing.

> STEPHAN EICKE: *Can you talk a bit about the recording of* Mulholland Drive? *You went back to Prague after having recorded* Blue Velvet *and* Lost Highway *there.*

Angelo Badalamenti: We recorded a lot more material with the orchestra. *Mulholland Drive* is more of a hybrid score. We used synthesizers and orchestra. The story that goes with that is that David loves music that sounds Russian. As a matter of fact, for the main title theme of *Blue Velvet*, David asked me to write something Russian. There is a Russian sound to the strange melodic line. He loves music that sounds Russian and the whole Eastern European melodic thing. He wanted me to do that for the opening title of *Mulholland Drive*. He wanted it to be Russian but "Your kind of beautiful, Angelo."

We were in the studio and once again David asked for something that I could write and that could be used in different places and in different ways in the film to come back, a repetition that goes around in your head but done with different kinds of orchestration. He wants the audience to relate to the main theme, whether they realize it or not. I sat down at my keyboard and recorded the theme immediately. That recording that I did—from top to bottom—was used in the film. Of course I did other variations on it and then I would add an orchestra, but what I did on synths was exactly what it was—no click track, nothing. Just off the top of my head what David was asking me. That was for the TV pilot.

The whole opening of the movie with the big band was different. David asked me to write a song like Glenn Miller's "In the Mood" from the 1940s. We did that in Prague but it was recorded in an abstract way. You can never do anything straight with David. There is no such thing. There is always something there that makes it a little different. Julee Cruise could be singing, for example. That's David's thing. At first you think, "What the hell," and then you get hooked and think, "That's actually pretty cool."

I had to write something original in the '40s-style, but he wanted me to insert the brass playing all those lines like Glenn Miller, almost using dissonant notes in the background and speeding it up a bit. That's what made it unique. It's recorded in an abstract way so you don't know what the heck is going on. David asked me for a strange off-center blues piece for the magician's scene when the girls are in the theater. He needed a piece, very off-center with the trumpet. Even before that there is a piece of music that was possibly written for something else, an off-center blues. I was always writing music that was very close to me. It's a little jazzy. *Mulholland Drive* is just about a wall-to-wall combination of music and sound design. There is hardly a moment when there is not something going on underneath it all.

I recorded six or seven scores in Prague and Štěpán Koníček has always conducted. He became my best buddy. After every session, every night, he would take me in his little car and say, "Come on Angelo, come with me. We will get some good beer now." I like good beer. I have to tell you, the beer in America is like pisswater. I like real beer. "I am going to take you to some place, Angelo, where there is good beer." Stepán would take me in his car, we would travel for about forty minutes and get into a little town, to a little square—a dark little place and on the tables would be paper cloths. The waiter would come on and bring a big jug with the Pils from the barrel. I got to tell you something: I don't think there is any better beer in the world. You get that Czech beer from the barrel. I see *Mulholland Drive*—it's on TV every week—and in the credits it always says recorded by Štěpán Koníček. He was my man. We lost him a couple of years ago. I don't think I ever want to go back to Prague again.

STEPHAN EICKE: *You mentioned you wrote about ninety minutes of score for* Mulholland Drive. *How much music do you usually write per film?*

ANGELO BADALAMENTI: Every film, not only our films together, that was ever made, requires a different duration of underscore. The bottom line is whatever the duration is, the impact of whatever music you are writing is a heck of a lot more important than the duration. On average I would guess I write about forty-five to sixty minutes of music per film. But that doesn't even include the songs we write together. They are included either as songs or on camera. On some of these projects we would get the orchestra with low strings and make them record dissonant tones working against each other very slowly. David would take this stuff and slow it down, twist it and turn it. Then you get great sound design. I would call that more sound design than music. I don't consider that a score-score. It's a tough decision these days: what's sound design and what's score? Is it sound design or is that part of a music score? It's very tough for composers, and publishers have a hard time sometimes how to put that down on the cue sheet.

STEPHAN EICKE: *Presumably you also recorded "firewood" for* Mulholland Drive … ?

ANGELO BADALAMENTI: We recorded celli and basses playing long, sustained, dissonant notes. It can be fifteen to twenty minutes. We did that in Prague. We were adding dissonances and then getting them resolved. That sounds strange enough there. David would say, "Make me 'firewood,' Angelo." David would then take these recordings with all those strings, slow them down and create these sound effects. They have no harmony or melody. He is creating sound design. I am not present when David does this. Once again, he has been doing it for a long time, and sound design is sound design. David loves doing this and he is the best at it. He knows what he needs for his movie.

David is the director and sometimes he would listen to what I have to say, sometimes he didn't. If he didn't I would come back, repeat myself and once in a blue moon he might back off, but just a little. His instincts are infallible, even regarding music. He is very gifted. When he hears something and he knows that it's right, he also sees pictures. Then he is able to turn that into music and marry that picture. When he listens to music that is right for him, I know he sees pictures because I see him looking out into space, mesmerized in a way. I know he is keying in to certain scenes that he will shoot, not that he has even shot, and the music sometimes gives him ideas in shooting a film.[17]

Like all of David Lynch's pictures, *Mulholland Drive* is notable for its songs, some of which were written and recorded by the director himself, without any involvement from Badalamenti. "Go Get Some" and "Mountains Falling" are two of them, originally composed for Lynch's album *BlueBOB*, which he worked on with John Neff and which was released in 2001. "Go Get Some" is used in the film's third act, as Diane imagines Camilla lying naked on her couch and as they begin to have sex. Notably, this last part of the film is more colorful musically than anything that precedes it. Whereas the action that took place before the duo's arrival in Club Silencio was underscored mostly by Badalamenti's string laments and brooding sound design (as well as few standards such as "Sixteen Reasons"), nearly every individual scene afterwards follows a different musical approach, adding to the state of confusion and chaos that Diane experiences before the audience's eyes. As Diane's life is collapsing, the soundtrack, approximately twenty-five minutes before the end credits start rolling, begins to oscillate wildly between Lynch's own post-industrial minimalist, instrumental rock; Badalamenti's orchestral elements; the abstraction of Thought Gang (at the dinner table); raucous, audacious sound design and innocuous, and tender homages to the 1950s ("Pretty 50s").

Both Lynch's own recordings and the source music showcase a detached coolness. "Go Get Some" serves as an example: the laid-back, sexy attitude of the instrumental track fits Camilla's behavior, her ice-cold smile and threatening remark, "We shouldn't do this anymore." Similarly, "Pretty 50s," a nostalgic, simple piece that sounds like the backing track for one of the countless crooner ballads popular after the end of the Second World War,

---

[17]Eicke, "Mein Bruder David," pp. 23ff.

plays as Adam Kesher kisses Camilla Rhodes in the car. Kesher instructs his actor how to properly treat Camilla's character in the scene they are preparing. Meanwhile, Diane looks on haplessly, her make-up garish, her outfit frumpy. Clearly, she is distraught at the kiss between Kesher and Camilla, especially as both seem to enjoy it tremendously. This is not the sort of music that one would normally expect to underscore a scorned lover's feelings. The piece is a surprising choice for the scene in which Diane is masturbating violently, finishing off by hitting her genitals with great force, illustrating a state of mind diametrically opposed to what "Pretty 50s" would seem to be suggesting. Lynch's songs and instrumental pieces do not represent Diane's feelings, do not capture her emotional turmoil. By now, they seem to mock her. Nothing fits. Everything is in turmoil. Diane is no longer in control.

The same applies to "Mountains Falling," a piece originally written for Lynch and Neff's *BlueBOB* album but not included on it. This music plays as Diane watches Camilla and Kesher at the dinner table. The former is slowly losing her composure, her eyes reddening, her hands shaking. It is music wildly inappropriate for a dinner such as the one depicted (particularly because it is remarkably different to the diegetic piece used earlier for Diane's arrival). Is "Mountains Falling" indeed a diegetic piece as source music? The cool, suave off-handedness of the repetitive percussion and the crashing guitars accurately capture Adam Kesher and Camilla Rhodes' carelessness that Diane objects to. It serves as descriptive music, a quality rarely afforded to source pieces other than in the films of Federico Fellini (see *Amarcord*)—and David Lynch.

In that respect, the choice of music represents a remarkable divergence from the film's first two acts—the dream that is shown as Diane's reality. In the scenes in which Diane as Betty is present, Lynch makes the audience see the world through her ears. For example, as she arrives in Los Angeles, the soaring, even saccharine and sentimental "Betty's Theme" is introduced, which could be taken as a parody of the extreme sweetness of Hallmark TV movies. Whenever Betty and Rita (aka Diane and Camilla) discuss the latter's possible past and, with great excitement, uncover more clues, the soundtrack emits tense, often discordant and suspenseful notes emanating from Badalamenti's "firewood" and Lynch's sound design. As Louise knocks on Betty's door, the latter is rightfully scared, and the brief clip of sound design and music captures her feeling accordingly. As Betty and Rita kiss for the first time, Lynch does not use the cool and detached "Go Get Some," but the infinitely more romantic love theme by Badalamenti.

This is what can be heard. And then there is what can not be heard. Composer Guy Farley was intrigued when he watched *Mulholland Drive* for the first time. He couldn't explain why even the early scenes of Betty's stay in LA unsettled him because nothing in the images warranted his dread. A young woman going about her daily chores is hardly remarkable, after all. Being a musician, he analyzed the scenes in question. What he found astonished him. Farley shares:

> I found that [Lynch] had used a drone, a sonic drone, a synth drone, but low down in the mix. I also found the drone had parts to it. It wasn't a single tone. It moved, it evolved, like it had life to it. You don't notice it when watching, not at all. But take it out and there you have it! All the tension is gone. I remember working out the drone was at something like -20db. It was such a clever use of musical or rather non musical ambience to create tensions, constant tension.[18]

In Diane's dream world, everything is seen and heard through her eyes and ears—it is, after all, her dream, her conception. As that dreams start to crack, there is a clear dissonance between her emotions and the soundtrack that accompanies her. It captures the inner turmoil and chaos of the aspiring actress who is bitter, frustrated and lonely—as in reality she suspects that nobody cares about her.

> *I had always wanted a studio to experiment with sound, so in the '90s I got this house and built that studio as a place to experiment and mix films. I use electric guitar to make sound effects but they're musical. They don't have to be musical but they got more musical as I went along and one thing led to another and I went into that, but like I say, I play the guitar upside down and backwards. I'm not a musician. It's more about sound effects for me. I just love the sound of it.*[19]
>
> DAVID LYNCH

David Lynch played guitar on "Pretty 50s," "Go Get Some," and "Mountains Falling." The latter two pieces were, as mentioned previously, part of Lynch's album *BlueBOB* which came out after *Mulholland Drive* had made its debut at the film festival in Cannes. By then, it appeared that the director had finally been rehabilitated after the colossal commercial and critical flop that was *Twin Peaks: Fire Walk with Me*.

After *BlueBOB* and *Mulholland Drive*, John Neff and David Lynch kept working together. When not busy recording music with the director, the studio engineer was mixing Lynch's films in 5.1 sound for planned DVD releases. Around two years after *Mulholland Drive* came out, Lynch and Neff started work on what would later become *Inland Empire*, though Neff left Lynch's employ in late 2004 to build his own studio in Marine County.

---

[18]Author interview with Guy Farley, July 10, 2024.
[19]Gabel & Hundley, "Interview with David Lynch," p. 27.

Mulholland Drive was the last theatrical feature that David Lynch and Angelo Badalamenti worked on together. Later they would collaborate on *Twin Peaks: The Return*, for which Badalamenti supplied a few themes which the director used.

Mulholland Drive stands as the pinnacle of his work with Lynch, a perfect summation of their creative work that seamlessly blends music and sound design and that is unlike any other work between a director and a composer. While the composer is always in service of the film and the director's vision, no director (with the possible exception of Jean-Luc Godard) has regularly gone as far as Lynch when it comes to taking apart his composer's recordings and using them in his own, specific way—layering with other elements, mixing with his own music, using only small portions, leaving out whole sections of the orchestra, and slowing it down. In *Mulholland Drive*, Lynch did all of these things to benefit the film.

Accolades went to both Badalamenti and Lynch. Though his compositions had been severely altered (unbeknownst to the public), in 2002 Angelo Badalamenti was nominated for a BAFTA Award, a Saturn Award, an AFI Award, a Chicago Film Critics Association Award, a Golden Globe Award, the OFTA Film Award (Online Film & Television Association), and took home the Online Film Critics Society Award. Badalamenti had never been showered with more praise and recognition for any feature film work than for *Mulholland Drive*. Even the most negative reviews of the film were positive.

In the film world, Lynch and Badalamenti went out with a bang.

PART THREE

Angelo. David

10

The Most Wonderful Collaborator

Whereas *Law and Disorder* and *Gordon's War* had not led to an influx of work in film, the international success of *Blue Velvet* turned Angelo Badalamenti into one of the busiest composers working in the industry. From 1987 to 1989 alone he worked on seven motion pictures—six of which would retain his score, while his lounge jazz contribution to Bob Balaban's little-seen black comedy, *Parents*, was rejected.[1]

The New Jersey-based composer was riding high, grateful to finally be invited to join the community he had admired for many years. One of the first scripts that landed on his agent's desk following the premiere of *Blue Velvet* was *A Nightmare on Elm Street 3: Dream Warriors*, arguably the best sequel to the popular horror classic. Directed in 1987 by Chuck Russell, the film follows a group of teenagers in a mental hospital terrorized by Freddy Krueger. The final cut features a hodgepodge of Badalamenti's (purely electronic) music, cues from Charles Bernstein's score for the original film in the series, and additional music by Ken Harrison. The movie had a troubled post-production in terms of the score, which explains its idiosyncratic mélange of different musical sources. Director Russell remembers: "I was a huge fan of […] *Blue Velvet*, and pushed hard for [Angelo]. Unfortunately I was a first-time director on a low budget film, and Angelo was in Italy. We allowed him to score the film in Italy within his own schedule. I never got to collaborate with him in the manner I've done with other composers since."[2]

Badalamenti—staying in Italy—was not available during the film's post-production and final mix. It was an unusual situation on a film since the composer normally only starts work in post-production. As a result of Badalamenti's unavailability, Russell needed additional music and turned to composer Ken Harrison, who recalls his stressful, manic schedule during

---

[1] Aenensen, Jon, "Jonathan Elias," *My Blog of Interviews*, February 2, 2010, https://my-blog-of-interviews.webnode.page/jonathan-elias/ (accessed June 19, 2024).
[2] Author interview with Chuck Russell, January 5, 2021.

those few days: "I was sent tapes and then I ended up spotting [the film] myself ... where they wanted music to come in and go out. [...] They were on the dubbing stage when I got the call. I had to write it, record it and mix it. They were there every day for four or five days, collecting music every morning."³

Harrison provided music for the scene featuring the character Phillip Anderson (played by Bradley Gregg) sleepwalking in the film's first act and, most notably, a dream involving Kristen Parker (Patricia Arquette, a decade before *Lost Highway*) being consumed by a monster that appears from under the rug in a haunted, dilapidated house. Dr. Gordon's apparition of the nun in white, on the other hand, features pre-existing music by Charles Bernstein, as do several other scenes.

Despite the film's problematic post-production, Russell appreciated Badalamenti's contribution: "His score was brilliant, evocative and moody. It's one of the things that elevated [*A Nightmare on Elm Street 3*] and distinguished it from previous *Elm Street* films." While Badalamenti does not regret having worked on the film, in early 1995 he admitted that violent mainstream horror had never been to his liking.⁴

Other projects Badalamenti was more enthusiastic about—Norman Mailer's last feature film as director, *Tough Guys Don't Dance*, for example. Starring Isabella Rossellini and released in 1987, it tells the story of an ex-con, played by Ryan O'Neal, who can't remember if he killed the woman whose severed head he finds in his marijuana stash. Badalamenti particularly enjoyed his experience on the (critically maligned) work since Mailer encouraged him to write music prior to the film's shoot. Only a short while later, Badalamenti would commence doing the same in his collaboration with David Lynch to get the actors in the required mood and develop a rhythm for the individual scenes long before editing started.

That same year, Badalamenti developed a working-relationship with director John D. Hancock, whose previous work included *Let's Scare Jessica to Death*, and *Bang the Drum Slowly*, the latter film providing an early starring role for Robert De Niro. Badalamenti and Hancock's first of three film projects together was *Weeds*, a critically acclaimed low-budget film starring Nick Nolte as a convict who is serving a sentence in San Quentin. In prison, he writes and stages a play that makes headlines nationwide. As he soon experiences, his success has a downside.

Hancock uses Badalamenti and Lynch's "Mysteries of Love" in its instrumental incarnation during the staging of the play that gives the scene an uplifting feeling. It marks the film's visual and acoustic highlight. With Gustav Mahler, Richard Wagner and Jimi Hendrix used as part of the temp

---

³Author interview with Ken Harrison, August 3, 2020.
⁴Müthing, "Ich schreibe in vielen unterschiedlichen Stilen."

track and with its songs by Melissa Etheridge, *Weeds* presented itself as an opportunity for Badalamenti to show his versatility as both composer and arranger. He was also a magnanimous, encouraging collaborator who was not precious with his own work: on their three projects together, Hancock altered his composer's work noticeably in post-production.

STEPHAN EICKE: *You used "Mysteries of Love" in* Weeds.

JOHN HANCOCK: I've used it in four or five of my films. I used it in *Prancer*, I used it in a film I made seven years ago, *The Looking Glass*. To me that instrumental does something to your heart and soul as if it's running its way toward some realization. It's working toward something. I found it useful over and over. Angelo had to ask David Lynch if it was alright and David said okay. Angelo received some award in Belgium in 2008 [World Soundtrack Award in Ghent], and the orchestra there recorded a version of it. It's wonderful. He was able to provide it for *The Looking Glass*. That way it wasn't Angelo on his synthesizer anymore.

STEPHAN EICKE: *How did Angelo present his original composition for* Weeds *to you?*

JOHN HANCOCK: He would present cues that he intended to orchestrate that were just played on his synthesizer. Then we would sign off on them and he went to Australia to record it. I was not happy with the Australian Philharmonic's version of the Wagner [piece]. The Wagner has 120 players or so, so he didn't have the instruments to render the *Rheingold*. I had hoped for more from the Australian session. I then did something else which was to kind of fuse it into an artistic whole. I got Garth Hudson, a musician, to do several accordion tracks over some of the more symphonic cues from Australia to make it a little tackier, to place it more into a convict world. I was happy that I did that. I thought it thickened it and made it both aspirational on the part of these criminals. I did not discuss it with Angelo. I just did it and said, "I hope you don't mind." He said it was fine.

STEPHAN EICKE: *Your next projects with Angelo,* A Piece of Eden *and* Suspended Animation, *were shot on a shoe-string budget. What attracted Angelo to them?*

JOHN HANCOCK: Angelo was willing to do it without a lot of money. That was one thing. But we had had a very happy working relationship on *Weeds*. He was also attracted by the Italian subject matter of *A Piece of Eden*. I sent him the script and he sent me back a theme. I loved it and used it a lot in the picture. He really caught what I wanted. Then once I had a cut and had it temped, I took it to New York to Angelo. When he is doing things without a lot of money, he sits at his keyboard. We watch the film together and he improvises to it. I don't know if he works out ideas before in his head. I don't think so. Often it was very good, and you would then orchestrate or enhance what he played with other instruments. In that case I added a violin, cello, flute, and mandolin to what he had improvised on the keyboard. I think we spent an afternoon in his studio in New York and his score resulted from that, in addition to the main theme he had composed before we started to shoot. I sat next to him while he was improvising and gave immediate feedback. Mostly my feedback was, "This is wonderful."

STEPHAN EICKE: *You heavily altered his recordings?*

JOHN HANCOCK: In both cases I added live musicians to what he had done. I have a guy here called Chris who has an orchestral sampler. Those have become very good, so we would take Angelo's track and Chris would redo it with his orchestral sampler. We got around the synth sound by using a good orchestral sampler and sweetening it with live instruments. We got a violinist in to play and record over himself several times, so it sounds like several violins. Angelo wasn't involved in recording the live instruments. He had sent MIDI files, improvised cues. Chris has something that will print out sheet music from a MIDI file, so the violinist had sheet music that they could look at.[5]

Angelo Badalamenti's humility, his quickness, and openness to collaborate won him many gigs over the course of his career. When, in 1989, Dominique Deruddere needed a score within just a few days for his American feature film debut, *Wait Until Spring, Bandini*, he called on Badalamenti to provide the appropriate music. Based on the novel by John Fante, the drama tells of the plight of an Italian family in the United States of the 1920s. "Sant' America," the most prominent piece of music in the film, was not written by Badalamenti but by Paolo Conte. The latter had originally been signed as composer for the film. However, the singer was unable to write for an orchestra and was thus replaced by Badalamenti. "He saw the cut of the film without music and loved it," says Deruddere. "He was my savior."[6]

Seeing Badalamenti's enthusiastic reaction, the director didn't lose any time and flew straight from Belgium, his home country, to New York. By that point, a mere few days after the composer had screened the film, Badalamenti had already prepared several themes to present to the filmmaker. The duo discussed the drama while the musician played the piano and the director

---

[5] Author interview with John Hancock, July 3, 2020.
[6] Author interview with Dominique Deruddere, June 2, 2020.

gave feedback. Afterwards, Deruddere flew back to Belgium and left Badalamenti to his own devices. Just one week later, the director returned to the United States to attend the recording session for the film's score. In the span of one week, Badalamenti had written approximately forty minutes of music for a small ensemble.

And so, project by project, Angelo Badalamenti made a name for himself in the industry as a quick, empathetic, reliable pair of hands. His biggest commercial success in the world of feature films was yet to come, though: *National Lampoon's Christmas Vacation*, the third installment in a series of comedies revolving around the Griswold family. It was Jeremiah Chechick's first feature film, and Angelo Badalamenti guided him through the process eloquently and with great warmth and kindness.

> STEPHAN EICKE: *Why did you choose Angelo Badalamenti as your composer?*
>
> JEREMIAH CHECHICK: [Angelo's] work with David Lynch, his embrace of the absurdist neo-dramatic tonality of David's work, so fitted my own kind of a fan base. It came from such an original thinker in terms of score. I don't think I had ever heard a score like *Blue Velvet*. [...] I never considered anyone else to do the score. I had in mind from when I was shooting that he was somebody that I wanted to work with. [...] I did not want to apply normal comedic tropes to an already funny movie, in other words putting a hat on a hat. The layering of these things is important because I knew that the intention of the movie, while being funny, would not make any long-term sense since I obviously wanted to make a movie that lasted, to show a more classical Currier-and-Ives/Rockwell view of America that we have now left far behind. It was always a myth but now the myth has come to the surface. One had to be on the main character's emotional level, which sounds funny in retrospect because it is such a silly comedy. [Clark Griswold's] passion to do something right for his family created a condition in which he would almost destroy them. You had to be with the things that were all the Sturm und Drang in his heart. They had to be identified somehow, not with a heavy hand but it had to be present in the score. That's why I felt the choice and his score was so successful and so fun.[7]

Though it received mixed reviews upon its release, *National Lampoon's Christmas Vacation* has become a modern classic of American cinema.

---

[7] Author interview with Jeremiah Chechick, July 23, 2020.

Apart from his work with David Lynch, no other singular relationship with a director creatively challenged the composer as much as the one he enjoyed with Paul Schrader. Over the course of five projects and fifteen years, Schrader encouraged Badalamenti to flex his muscles as a composer and come up with vastly different approaches to a wide range of films, starting with *The Comfort of Strangers* in 1990, Harold Pinter's adaptation of Ian McEwan's celebrated novel. The American director found much joy in the power play between the various characters: Rupert Everett and Natasha Richardson are a young couple whose relationship is on the rocks as they visit Venice. However, an apparent chance encounter with a sinister local, played by Christopher Walken, and his reclusive wife, Helen Mirren, reinvigorates their sex life and changes the dynamic in their romance. Angelo Badalamenti's music, a favorite among his own works, was largely inspired by architecture, and is infused with a Middle Eastern flavor. Schrader recalled he went to Istanbul for several days to study the local architecture and design: "I was at a dinner party and Lina Wertmüller was there and she was asking me about the film. I told her this idea that I thought I was going to play Venice as Turkey. She said, 'That's impossible, how are you going to do that?' I said, 'Well, just shoot Moorish architecture and play Turkish music.'"[8] They did exactly that. Schrader continued: "Virtually every bit of architecture chosen for the film has a Moorish/Arabic flavor and coloring. Then between the very Puccini-like score that Angelo did it would be counterpointed by Middle Eastern melodies."

> STEPHAN EICKE: *Why do you think you have been so successful in your job?*
>
> ANGELO BADALAMENTI: To be a long-term music film composer, one must have the ability to write in any style and any genre. A director might say, "I want you to write a turco-arabesque score for this scene because we are in Venice and the architecture is turco-arabesque." This is exactly what happened to me. Paul Schrader called me to do *The Comfort of Strangers*, which is a film I absolutely adore. He writes me this letter from Venice and says, "I would like you to be the composer and I am thinking of doing a turco-arabesque score because of the architecture and all these homes that all have these wall rugs, and I like turco-arabesque music." I didn't have a clue. If a film calls for you to write a turco-arabesque score and you have no idea what it means, you just have to listen. Listen a lot to recordings in that style. If you have it in you and if you are a sensitive musician you are going to capture

---

[8] *Audio Commentary by Paul Schrader in* The Comfort of Strangers, Prod. Vic Pratt, UK: BFI, 2018 [Blu-ray Special Features].

the soul of it and understand why the music written in that style affects you emotionally. When you first hear it, it can sound like a bunch of noise, but if you are sensitive musically you are going to find the soul of the music—it can be rap, it can be Shostakovich. You just have to listen and keep an open mind and let that music get inside you. If you have that ability, you can really get into it and write something that sounds pretty darn authentic. It's a beautiful thing if you get inside another world.[9]

Auto Focus by Schrader was shot on a slim budget. It is a biopic of the actor Bob Crane (*Hogan's Heroes*), played by Greg Kinnear, who befriends an oily video camera salesman and subsequently finds himself in a seedy underworld full of sex and debauchery. The story enabled Badalamenti to write both smooth jazz and disturbing, dissonant electronic soundscapes to accompany Crane's deepening crisis, as the audience is drawn into the seemingly sunny, carefree world of 1960s show business, beginning with an appropriately catchy jazz number as sung by David Johansen. "Snap!" was written by Badalamenti and Schrader together. The latter remembered: "David Johansen sang it and we assembled a big band and we did it. Angelo did reject some of my couplets. The one I like best that he didn't put in is, 'A little back door lovin' gets all the priests shoving.'"[10]

Badalamenti's music accompanies Bob Crane's fall. While at the top of his career, Crane's adventures are underscored with subtle, light-hearted instrumental jazz, but then his life become consequently darker. As Crane loses his prestige job on *Hogan's Heroes*, as his marriage ends and he becomes an alcoholic, the visuals and the music change. Schrader begins to rely on Dutch angles, and everything is drenched in a sickly green light. The last third of the movie is underscored by an uninterrupted electronic music cue with chords nervously rubbing against each other, creating dissonances that are far removed from the sunny '60s jazz heard at the beginning. Moreover, Schrader added distorted sound effects such as animal squealing and metal twisting to Badalamenti's music, giving it an additional flavor of abstract horror.

In late 1997, Badalamenti started work on Mark Pellington's *Arlington Road*, a paranoia thriller starring Jeff Bridges as a university professor in Virginia who befriends his new neighbors, played by Tim Robbins and Joan Cusack. Slowly, Bridges' character starts harboring doubts that the people next door really are as charming and peaceful as they seem.

Badalamenti's music for Pellington's film is not unlike his work for *Lost Highway* in tone, which had been written shortly before. His orchestral

---

[9]Unpublished quote for Eicke, "Mein Bruder David," pp. 20–5.
[10]*Audio Commentary with Director Paul Schrader in* Auto Focus, Prod. Nick Redman, USA: Twilight Time, 2018 [Blu-ray Special Features].

score is brooding and dark, revolving around a powerful lament ("Lament for Leah") as the emotional focal point of both the score and the film. As with his works for David Lynch, Badalamenti was not the sole musician involved, since Pellington had also contracted the services of tomandandy—duo Tom Hajdu und Andy Milburn—with whom he had worked previously. While Badalamenti would be responsible for the score's orchestral elements, tomandandy were to provide the electronic, textural elements. As always, Badalamenti was an enthusiastic collaborator, though he did not work directly with tomandandy.

With the encouragement of Pellington, Badalamenti recorded his orchestral cues with several variations—an octave higher or lower, leaving out some instruments and adding others. It was then up to tomandandy to take these recordings and add electronic textures. For the film's climax, the duo took Badalamenti's recording ("The Escape" on the soundtrack album), separated strings and horns from everything else and added an electronic rhythm track.[11]

> STEPHAN EICKE: *How did you experience Angelo as a collaborator?*
> MARK PELLINGTON: We were nearing locking the picture when he came out to Los Angeles. He walked into the room where I was working with the music editor. We had been temping stuff, working on the temp score. I had a little keyboard there, a little Yamaha pad. I'm not a musician at all, but I'm musical. I would mess around with my Angelo Badalamenti imitations but I would only play the white keys because I didn't know how to play music. I would only play super simple minor chord melodies. Then Angelo comes in. I think I had seen a picture of him, but I had no idea he was going to be this short, fat Italian guy who looked like he owned a restaurant in New Jersey with this friendly face. I had this image of Angelo Badalamenti like he was going to wear a cape or something. He walks in, gives me a big handshake and a hug. He is like, "Nice to meet you," and he looks at the keyboard. "What's that?" I was so afraid, I was mortified. "Oh, it's a little keyboard." "What do you do?" "I imitate you." "What?" "I imitate you." "Play something!" "No, no." "Play something." So I do some little, three-note loop over and over again. He sits down next to me and starts playing on top of it. He told the music editor to record it, so he recorded it. I still have the tape somewhere, the DAT tape. It went on for twelve minutes or so. From that moment on, he proved to be the most wonderful collaborator.[12]

---

[11]Author interview with Mark Pellington, June 23, 2020.
[12]Ibid.

One of Angelo Badalamenti's next projects was Danny Boyle's ill-fated adaptation of Alex Garland's acclaimed novel, *The Beach*. Released in 2000, Boyle's film had everything going for it: a successful director, a beloved source novel, a stellar cast including Leonardo DiCaprio and Tilda Swinton, exotic locations, and a script by Boyle's long-time collaborator John Hodge (*Trainspotting, Shallow Grave*). Yet, the film sank quickly, grossing only $40 million domestically on a budget of $50 million.[13] The reviews were hostile. *The Washington Post*, for example, called it "wholly annoying."[14]

Again, Badalamenti did not have the field for himself as composer, and post-production was troubled. Badalamenti had provided an orchestral, sometimes sweeping score with which he aimed to depict the limitless freedom the young people experience when they first discover the secret island—the titular beach. Music producer William Orbit took Badalamenti's memorable theme and created a techno version (entitled "Beached") in hopes of having the music and therefore the film appeal to a younger audience. The studio feared their target audience might not feel sufficiently swept up by the lush strings as recorded by Badalamenti. Yet another composer and arranger was brought on board late in post-production to jazz up the soundtrack (which also featured several contemporary songs and instrumental tracks by Moby, All Saints and others): Barry Adamson who had also worked with David Lynch on *Lost Highway* and provided *Mr. Eddy's Theme*.

> STEPHAN EICKE: *How did you get involved in* The Beach?
> BARRY ADAMSON: I felt so bad. I didn't think I needed to be brought in. I was given the tapes of what Angelo did and I loved it. I thought it was some of the most beautiful music I had ever heard. So what the fuck was I doing, adding stuff to it? I was asked to do something to different cues. A lot of the time this stuff wasn't used anyway. I thought, "This is not really doing my friendship with Angelo Badalamenti any good." He doesn't even know me, he hasn't met me, and there is this guy again stomping on his music, adding drums and all sorts of modern stuff to his orchestration. I don't think it needed it, but I think Danny Boyle was in a place where he had this great composer, had these great compositions, but also pressure from the younger people to have something

---

[13] https://www.the-numbers.com/movie/Beach-The#tab=summary.
[14] Hunter, Stephen, "'The Beach': Trouble in Paradise," *The Washington Post*, February 11, 2000, https://www.washingtonpost.com/wp-srv/entertainment/movies/reviews/beachhunter.htm (accessed June 19, 2024).

modern rather than a Hollywood kind of score, which was what Angelo did. It was unbelievable music with children's choir. I was brought in with my assistant Will, who is very good at putting beats together. We had to make the music more modern. I didn't feel that good about it, to be honest.[15]

In the film, a torso of Angelo Badalamenti's work remains. Other directors and studios rejected whole scores by the composer. Originally signed to provide music for Wolfgang Petersen's *Shattered* in 1991, he was later replaced by Alan Silvestri. Three demos by Badalamenti were later included on a promotional CD release by his orchestrator, Andy Barrett. For several months, Badalamenti worked closely with director James Mangold on his film *Identity*, released in 2003.[16] Again, he was later replaced by Alan Silvestri. Brief excerpts of Badalamenti's original score for the comedy *Other People's Money* starring Danny DeVito remain in the finished film, which was re-scored by David Newman late in post-production.[17]

Between these bigger Hollywood studio productions, Badalamenti always enjoyed working on small-scale independent films of which there are many, including the aforementioned *A Piece of Eden*, and *Suspended Animation* as well as *Lathe of Heaven* and *The Blood Oranges* by Philip Haas (and starring Sheryl Lee) and *Julie Johnson* by Bob Gosse, a 2001 production that was conceived as a theatrical feature before the production company collapsed and the film was released on DVD only.

One of Angelo Badalamenti's favorite projects was realized in 2004: for *A Very Long Engagement*, a French production starring Audrey Tautou, he was reunited with director Jean-Pierre Jeunet, with whom he had worked on *The City of Lost Children* in 1995, and on which he had collaborated with Marianne Faithfull as singer.

Again, it was *Blue Velvet* that had led to Badalamenti's fruitful collaboration with Jeunet, since the director had temp-tracked *The City of Lost Children*, a dark fantasy, with Badalamenti's music for Lynch's violent fever dream.[18] When it came to *A Very Long Engagement*, Jeunet again used various cues from several of Badalamenti's scores as temp tracks. He then sent the composer the storyboard and a rough cut of the film. Badalamenti agreed to work on it immediately.

Having been brought onboard comparatively early, the composer and director worked together closely for the next few months, developing a

---

[15] Author interview with Barry Adamson, March 23, 2021.
[16] Koppl, Rudy, "When Dreams Become Reality," *Music from the Movies*, Double Issue 35/36 (2002): p. 47.
[17] Library of Congress, *Other People's Money*, https://www.loc.gov/item/jots.200018273/ (accessed June 19, 2024).
[18] Schweiger, "The Madman and His Muse," p. 44.

string-heavy score with noteworthy French horn solos. By the time *A Very Long Engagement* premiered to international acclaim, Badalamenti had already enjoyed considerable success in French film. His regular attendance at the Cannes Film Festival and the success of *The City of Lost Children* in particular had led to him receiving several offers from Europe, which he accepted enthusiastically. Among them were Josée Dayans *Cet amour-là* in 2001, Nicole Garcia's *L'adversaire* in 2002, and later, *Un baiser papillon* by Karine Silla in 2011.

Another European production came his way in 2004, when David Grieco asked Badalamenti to provide the music for his feature film debut, *Evilenko,* starring Malcolm McDowell. Based on a true story, the film depicts the hunt for a serial rapist and killer in Ukraine in the 80s. Produced by an Italian company and shot in English, it was filmed in Ukraine. Grieco and Badalamenti had already met in 1999, when as a journalist the former interviewed the latter for Sky TV. Following the interview, Grieco explained his passion project to the composer over dinner. The journalist confidently explained that if he ever managed to make his film, he would want Badalamenti to provide the music. The composer agreed. Four years later, he received a rough cut.

The music for *Evilenko* is particularly noteworthy for Badalamenti's collaboration with Dolores O'Riordan of The Cranberries. "Angels Go To Heaven" and "No Way Out" appear in the film. Two other songs, "The Butterfly" and "Secrets of Love," were later conceived and recorded for another motion picture idea which Grieco had. Unfortunately, the director could not attain financing and the project was ultimately shelved.

> STEPHAN EICKE: *How did the collaboration with Dolores O'Riordan come about for* Evilenko?
> DAVID GRIECO: When we were working together on the score for *Evilenko* when one day [Angelo] told me something. Angelo uses the answering machine. He never answers his phone straight. He said, "There is a woman calling me all the time, every day. She has a strange name. I don't know what she wants from me. Her name is Dolores O'Riordan." Of course I knew Dolores O'Riordan from The Cranberries. I was a great fan. I said, "You have to call her back, she is a great talent. She is like all the female talents you have been working with!" So he made the call in front of me and said, "Thanks to my friend David I'm calling you because otherwise I wouldn't have called you." In the course of the conversation, she said, "Can we start working together for this film that David has made?" This is why I have two songs by Dolores O'Riordan in the film. This is how the relationship between Dolores and Angelo started. When he called me, Angelo was with me in Rome working on the score. I was over the moon.

Then I met Dolores. Then I developed a friendship with Dolores after that. They prepared two songs for me for a film called *Secrets of Love*. They produced both "The Butterfly" and "Secrets of Love" for my film.

STEPHAN EICKE: *You told me earlier that Angelo and Dolores recorded an album together which was shelved after her death ...*

DAVID GRIECO: The album was nearly finished. I think they had ten tracks. [...] I knew that Dolores was losing herself. Angelo and I knew. When she died we were shocked but we knew that would have happened. She and I met many times in Italy, in England, in the US, but not in the last two or three years. In the last few years when she left both her husband and her children she was kind of going ballistic.[19]

Always curious to explore new approaches and collaborations, over the years Angelo Badalamenti worked on record productions for various artists. After the worldwide success of *Twin Peaks* especially, he received many opportunities to arrange and produce songs and albums for renowned singers and bands, and although he enjoyed writing film scores, it was by no means the only outlet he sought for his creative talent: "I like doing maybe three film scores a year and some television and Broadway. I try to pick my properties very carefully."[20]

Particularly noteworthy is Badalamenti's 1998 collaboration with David Bowie on a new arrangement of "A Foggy Day in London Town": as part of *Red Hot Rhapsody*, an AIDS benefit album that year, record label Mercury hired the composer to arrange the song by George Gershwin. The label would then contract a contemporary singer to record the piece. Badalamenti's version of "A Foggy Day in London Town" is typical for the composer's work on David Lynch's films—slow, dark, somber, with subtle abstract effects, it retains nothing of the original's suave charm and swag. Mercury was enthusiastic about the demo which the composer had provided. He had sung the vocal himself. Eager to sign a big name, the label sent the demo to David Bowie who considered the track "fantastic" and agreed to sing it.[21]

After Bowie had been signed, Angelo Badalamenti received a call from Bono, driving in a car through the Irish countryside. Burning to record "A Foggy Day in London Town" with the composer, Bono could not contain his

---

[19]Author interview with David Grieco, August 4, 2020.
[20]Murray, "Twin Peaks," p. 30.
[21]Marcone & Philp, "Interview with Angelo Badalamenti."

excitement for the demo he had just been listening to. However, Badalamenti had to break the news to him that he had just promised David Bowie the gig. Bono's terse reply was: "He sings pretty good, too." The collaboration between David Bowie and Angelo Badalamenti came off smoothly, and their version of Gershwin's beloved classic is a highlight on *Red Hot Rhapsody*. Years later, Bowie recalled: "Angelo is a perfect producer to work with, as he knows exactly what he wants but knows how to leave room for the artist's contribution."[22]

Around the time they worked on Jean-Pierre Jeunet's film *The City of Lost Children*, Marianne Faithfull and Angelo Badalamenti also collaborated on the album *A Secret Life*, which was released in 1995. The composer arranged the songs after Faithfull had fallen in love with Badalamenti's work on *Twin Peaks*. And indeed, many well-known names from the *Twin Peaks* universe appear as musicians on the record: Vinnie Bell played guitar and mandolin, Kinny Landrum performed at the keyboard, and Art Polhemus recorded the vocal and rhythm track in New York. Angelo's son André played the clarinet.

In 2017, another collaboration came Badalamenti's way via a European film production he was working on, *The Gold Coast*. Composer Lasse Martinussen had worked with singer Sahar Pour as the duo Pinki Rings and they had tirelessly tried to create a suitable arrangement for their song "Gone," when Magnussen started working with Badalamenti on the music for *The Gold Coast*, a Danish film. After they had become acquainted with each other, Magnussen played the demo for "Gone" to the composer who loved it and agreed to write a string arrangement. The ballad was released in 2017.[23]

Though it is one of Badalamenti's high-profile collaborations, his work with Paul McCartney on "Is It Raining in London?" remains officially unreleased. The former Beatle had asked the composer to arrange and conduct the piece for him in London. Recorded at Abbey Road Studios in 1992, it was co-written by Paul McCartney and Hamish Stuart, who was also supposed to be the lead vocalist. Unfortunately, the latter never recorded his part. As a result, the song was only featured in the documentary *Moving On* from 1993 but has never appeared on a record. Badalamenti enjoyed the collaboration with McCartney though, and never tired of telling an episode particularly amusing to him. McCartney said to Badalamenti: "I was invited by the Queen's office to perform forty minutes of my music at Buckingham

---

[22]de la Vina, "A Composer Hitting His 'Peak'," p. 56.
[23]Dom, Pieter, "Listen to Angelo Badalamenti's Haunting Pop Ballad with Pinkie Rings," *Welcome to Twin Peaks*, March 22, 2019, https://welcometotwinpeaks.com/music/angelo-badalamenti-haunting-pop-ballad-pinki-rings/ (accessed June 19, 2024).

Palace to celebrate her birthday. I was very excited. So the night of her birthday, my band is on stage, I'm about to go on and the Queen comes by and says 'Mr. McCartney, it was so lovely to see you today.'"[24] McCartney announced he would be performing for Her Majesty. She had other plans: "'Oh, Mr. McCartney, I'm so sorry, I can't stay. It's five minutes of eight—I must go upstairs and watch *Twin Peaks*.'"

Whether the anecdote is true remains doubtful.

A personal tragedy befell Angelo Badalamenti and his family when his son André unexpectedly passed away in 2012 at the age of forty, leaving behind his wife and two daughters. A self-employed musician and music instructor, André had been involved with the Delbarton School clarinet and saxophone ensembles. He had also played in several Broadway orchestras.[25] Badalamenti's life was upended.

"When his son died he was out of reach for everybody," recalls Badalamenti's friend, director David Grieco. "At one point I was looking for him desperately, like all his friends. [...] He then called me just to say what he was feeling. His son had been his best friend. That was something that marked his life very deeply." André had been a hemophiliac. Grieco shares: "That was disaster for him, a tragedy. The very first thing he said to me was, 'If I had had a gun I would have shot myself.'"[26]

In his later years, Badalamenti mostly provided themes for film and television productions. For the documentary *Koi*, produced by David Grieco's son Manuel, the composer wrote the theme, an electronic arrangement of his cue "Fire to the Stars," originally written for and used in the British feature film *The Edge of Love* in 2008. For the short, *Nowhen*, starring his nephew Stephen, Badalamenti provided several moody, electronic pieces and a jazz track in the mold of his *Twin Peaks* compositions such as "Freshly Squeezed" and "Audrey's Dance." For the 2018 picture *Between Worlds*, starring Nicolas Cage and Franka Potente, Badalamenti wrote the dissonant and somber main title evoking memories of his "Dark Introduction" from *Twin Peaks*.

Angelo Badalamenti's last big-budget production was Fedor Bondarchuk's Russian 3D IMAX war epic *Stalingrad* in 2013, telling the story of heroic Russian soldiers defending Stalingrad against the German army during the Second World War. It was one of the biggest projects the composer had ever taken on: involved early by the director, Badalamenti wrote nearly two hours of orchestral music, which was recorded in Moscow. Following the orchestral sessions, the composer recorded famed Opera singer Anna

---

[24]Deyneko, "Angelo Badalamenti."
[25]Staff, "Andre Badalamenti," *Suburban Trends* [West Milford], February 29, 2012, p. B6. 26 Author interview with David Grieco, August 4, 2020.
[26]Author interview with David Grieco, August 4, 2020.

Netrebko in New York for her solo in the score.²⁷ The song "Legenda" was performed by Russian pop star Zemfira.

Despite his greatly reduced workload—Badalamenti celebrated his eighty-fifth birthday in 2022—the composer remained popular, and his albums continued to sell well, especially on vinyl. In 2017, Death Waltz Recording Company released *Twin Peaks: Fire Walk with Me* as a double vinyl LP. Several limited editions of *Twin Peaks* on vinyl followed in 2020 (customers could choose between translucent blue vinyl [Laura Palmer Ice Blue] and brown marble [Damn Fine Coffee]). In 2017, *Blue Velvet* was re-issued on vinyl by Varèse Sarabande, and four years later, the same company released the score in an expanded edition featuring previously unreleased music, including the "firewood" recorded by Badalamenti. In 2019, Rhino Records released *Twin Peaks: Season Two Music and More* as a four LP set. The composer's work was featured heavily in *The Music of David Lynch*, a concert the director organized in 2016 to raise money for The David Lynch Foundation.

As Lynch's films were being remastered and re-released on Blu-ray, Badalamenti was frequently invited to share anecdotes and insights about his work with David Lynch in the bonus features. Angelo Badalamenti's influence on Lynch and his work is undeniable. The ethereal music of modern artists such as Chrysta Bell, Cat's Eyes, Anna Calvi, and others is oftentimes heavily inspired by Badalamenti's collaboration with Julee Cruise. The smooth jazz of *Twin Peaks* has often been parodied in film and television. Being instantly recognizable, it is uniquely suited for satire. Julee Cruise died on June 11, 2022, aged sixty-five. Suffering from depression and lupus, which caused her great pain, she chose to end her life.²⁸

Plagued by ill health for some time, Angelo Badalamenti passed away on December 11, 2022, at the age of eighty-five. Immediately following the announcement of his death, tributes poured in from filmmakers, celebrities, critics, and fans alike. Actor Natasha Lyonne, for example, tweeted a video of Badalamenti explaining the origin of "Laura Palmer's Theme," adding: "Internet only exists for this video to be spread to all corners. Sleep well #AngeloBadalamenti."²⁹ One day following his passing, David Lynch—who had begun to regularly mention pieces of music dear to him—announced in

---

[27] Schweiger, "Interview with Angelo Badalamenti."
[28] Genzlinger, Neil, "Julee Cruise, Vocalist of 'Twin Peaks' Fame, Dies at 65," *The New York Times*, June 10, 2022, https://www.nytimes.com/2022/06/10/arts/music/julee-cruise-dead.html (accessed June 19, 2024).
[29] https://twitter.com/nlyonne/status/1602530853950836736 (accessed June 19, 2024).

his daily weather report: "Today, no music."[30] One day later, on December 13, preceded and followed by a long silence, he said Angelo Badalamenti's name.[31] On December 14, he mentioned: "Today, I'm thinking about Angelo Badalamenti, and listening to his music."[32] David Lynch ended his daily weather update for good on December 16, 2022.

---

[30]David Lynch Theater, "David Lynch's Weather Report 12/12/22," *YouTube*, December 12, 2022, https://www.youtube.com/watch?v=J2FiFAuQOK8 (accessed June 19, 2024).

[31]David Lynch Theater, "David Lynch's Weather Report 12/13/22," *YouTube*, December 13, 2022, https://www.youtube.com/watch?v=gxwLO434EkA (accessed June 19, 2024).

[32]David Lynch Theater, "David Lynch's Weather Report 12/14/22," *YouTube*, December 14, 2022, https://www.youtube.com/watch?v=0R38gIgjkOU (accessed June 19, 2024).

11

The Logical Continuation of a Trajectory

As shown over the course of this book, David Lynch had always been heavily involved in the scoring and sound design process for his movies. It was only the next logical step for Lynch to write and record music himself, sometimes with Badalamenti, sometimes by himself—as he would eventually do—sometimes with John Neff or Dean Hurley, his studio engineers.

Shortly before Lynch started work on *The Straight Story*, he had already used his own studio to record an album called *Lux Vivens* in collaboration with British singer Jocelyn Montgomery, who at the time was married to Lynch's friend Monty Montgomery (co-producer of *Wild at Heart*, associate producer of the *Twin Peaks* pilot and *Hotel Room*). In 2001, he would portray the mysterious cowboy in *Mulholland Drive*. Before *Lux Vivens* was recorded, Jocelyn Montgomery had already worked with David Lynch and Angelo Badalamenti on a track called "And Still."

The song was based on verses by Hildegard von Bingen, a twelveth-century nun, and arranged and produced by Lynch in collaboration with his studio-engineer cum manager John Neff in late 1997 and early 1998.

For Lynch and Neff, it was like being in a playground. Sound effects are an important part of *Lux Vivens*, and oftentimes music and sound effects are indistinguishable. Transforming sound effects into music and vice versa was handled in the same way as in Lynch's films, and as previously described by David Slusser and John Neff respectively. For Jocelyn Montgomery's album, Lynch and Neff recorded various effects, such as a finger running around a crystal ball. These sounds would then be pitched lower or higher, transformed into individual notes the duo could "play" on faders on Lynch's brand-new mixing console as an accompaniment to Montgomery's singing.

Lux Vivens is noteworthy for David Lynch's participation as a musician. The director not only produced the record but also played guitar on it. His style was anything but conventional: carefully listening to Jocelyn

Montgomery's singing, Lynch would slap the neck of his guitar—tuned down to C-sharp—and achieve a mean, bubbling, distorted sound, "going after it with his whammy-bar," as John Neff remembered.[1] "He got this guitar down in the mud," Neff continued, "just bubbling. Then he would bring it up to where it would just be riding pitch with her voice and she would change the note and he would find a new one."

As a child, Lynch had played trumpet, and had learnt to read musical notation, even if he rarely needed to, his music recordings coming about as a series of carefully rehearsed improvisations. Frequently, John Neff would notate chord changes before he and Lynch commenced to prepare percussion tracks out of found sound—pre-existing elements that they distorted. Sometimes, Neff and Lynch made use of the latter's drum set in the studio. After they had recorded four songs as a duo in the late 1990s, the director looked at his studio manager and announced matter-of-factly: "It looks like we have to have an album."[2]

Lynch and Neff continued experimenting together. Although both were serious about their work as musicians, the collaboration that would eventually become the *BlueBOB* album was always a sideshow that had to be put on hiatus several times. It was eventually released on CD in December of 2001 on David Lynch's own label, Absurda.

Working on *BlueBOB* was unlike any other experience John Neff had enjoyed. The collaboration was elaborate and inventive, not unlike Lynch's approach to painting and film-making. His first idea was to build rhythm tracks with machine noises, as Neff explains: "We had samples of these big electric racks and generators from the Berklee lab that he and Alan Splet had recorded years before, so we made a rhythmic pattern out of sparks and zaps and cracks, and then a metal stamping machine, like an 80-ton metal press as the kick drum, and a printing press as the hi-hat."[3]

They repeated their experiment, this time with sound effects made from mining equipment that Lynch had stored in his sound effects library. Out of various sound effects tracks, Lynch and Neff built a percussion track as the foundation for some of their pieces. They continued to improvise and build chord changes on their guitars while the percussion played in the background.

Some of their songs featured vocals. In the case of "Pink Western Range," it was John Neff's voice that was recorded. The lyrics were written by Lynch, and Neff had the same immediate reaction to his collaborator's poems as Angelo Badalamenti had had when presented with "Mysteries

---

[1] Waves Audio, "Interview with John Neff (Blue Velvet, Wild at Heart, The Elephant Man)," *YouTube*, June 10, 2013, https://www.youtube.com/watch?v=BB_5WS0zqAs (accessed June 19, 2024).
[2] Author interview with John Neff, June 18, 2021.
[3] Waves Audio, "Interview with John Neff (Blue Velvet, Wild at Heart, The Elephant Man)."

of Love." The director had pulled two different poems out of a box and handed them to Neff, instructing him to choose lines from each one and sing them in the recording booth. The musician was dumbfounded—the poems were disjunctive, featuring different lengths of meter and sentence. Even so, without being able to study or memorize the lyrics, Neff was shoved into the recording box, where yet another surprise lay in store: although Lynch at first directed Neff, the poet quickly cut the sound of Neff's own voice, so he couldn't hear himself as he sang. The playback in his headphones was delayed, which led him to lose his rhythm and fall out of time. Of course, Lynch loved it. And so, "Pink Western Range" was born.

> STEPHAN EICKE: *You worked on* BlueBOB *with David for a few years in total. Two of the pieces on the album ended up in* Mulholland Drive. *How?*
> JOHN NEFF: BlueBOB was finished before the [*Mulholland Drive*] film, after the pilot. [...] David asked me to pull [the songs] up and put them in the scene and see how they fit. We were working on another song that wasn't on the album, called "Pretty 50s." That's in the scene when Adam Kesher kisses Laura Harring in the old car. "Kill the lights!" There was a fourth piece: We've got "Mountains Falling," "Pretty 50s," "Go Get Some," and I play guitar on the pool party dinner scene music. Angelo cut that track and I added a jazz guitar on it. It's when Betty and Rita are walking up to the party. There's this jazz trio playing in the background. I played guitar on that. It's bookended by two of Angelo's pieces.
> STEPHAN EICKE: *Part of the release launch [for* BlueBOB] *was a concert in Paris. I heard David didn't enjoy playing on stage.*
> JOHN NEFF: He was terrified. We rehearsed the set for a week in the south of Paris in a rehearsal studio with really good players, and the show came off well although we were not supposed to be the headliners. We were supposed to open for Beth Gibbons of Portishead. The day of the concert they switched it and we weren't prepared for it. That was a little glitch. It went well but our set was short and part of the audience was upset with us for playing only thirty minutes. That's all we had. We were supposed to be an opening set. I played guitar in the concert. On the record I play guitar, bass, and sometimes drums.
> STEPHAN EICKE: *Were there any other songs that you and David had planned to include in* BlueBOB?
> JOHN NEFF: I wrote "No Stars" as a *BlueBOB* song back in 2000. David had the English lyrics and decided he wanted Rebekah [del Rio] to sing it. So he called her in and asked her to write Spanish lyrics and to sing a mixture of both. She wrote the Spanish lyrics and wrote the melody and sang the song all in one

afternoon. That was back in 2000 and it's been sitting on the shelf ever since, except we put "No Stars" on her *Love Hurts Love Heals* album that came out in 2011. That version you hear in *Twin Peaks: The Return* was my mix. David used what we had.[4]

David Lynch continued to grow into himself as a musician, and one project led to another: a planned web series, a feature film, collaborations with other musicians, and then his own singles and albums. The 2000s was a musically rich and rewarding decade for Lynch, the logical continuation of the trajectory he had been on since he had learned to play the trumpet as a young boy. Discussing his album *Crazy Clown Time* (released in 2011) is impossible without acknowledging the previous singles "Good Day Today" and "I Know," which in turn are difficult to assess without examining Lynch's previous work with singer Chrysta Bell—which can be heard in *Inland Empire*. It was this work that started life as a web-series. Therefore, *Inland Empire* is impossible to approach without mentioning the director's enthusiastic foray into the depths of the internet first.

In late 2001, David Lynch's website went live. For him, davidlynch.com was—like most things—a potentially rewarding playground. He shot *Rabbits*, a series featuring Naomi Watts and Laura Elena Harring as two of three humanoid rabbits whose lives have become a surrealist, nightmarish sitcom. *Rabbits* would later make its way into *Inland Empire*. Each episode of *Rabbits* is accompanied by eerie sound design such as dark winds, as well as low, moody suspense music for synthesizer recorded by Lynch himself. The germ for *Inland Empire* was a different idea, though.

> STEPHAN EICKE: Inland Empire *was the last project you worked on for Lynch.*
>
> JOHN NEFF: It started out as a website series called *A Meeting Upstairs*. It was Laura [Dern] climbing the stairs of the painting studio, the scene which seems to take forever. Then you have her talking to God. It's a 56-minute monologue. We were going to cut that up into 5-minute segments and put it on the web. When she was done, everybody was in tears, she was so marvelous. David goes, "I'm fucked." We all looked at him like he is crazy. "What do you mean? That was tremendous!" "I can't put it on the web, I have to make something else with it."
>
> He had this idea for a series for the website axxon.n. That was a woman, sort of a shut-in, who saw this shop across the street from her dingy apartment where people went inside and never came out. One day her curiosity got the best of her and she went

---

[4] Author interview with John Neff, June 25, 2021.

across the street and went in the door, turned left and was in a new life. That was the concept. Those two ideas came together and became *Inland Empire*.

We started shooting in July of 2003, the monologue. Then David would write little vignettes and scenes, and we would assemble a crew. The office boys were the cameramen. I was the location sound guy. We would go to locations and shoot individual scenes. Nobody heard the words *Inland Empire* until after a year of working on it. He didn't have a title, it was just an ongoing project. We were just shooting scenes and everybody got a $100 bill as payment. It was non-union, no overtime except the $100 payment. He was paying for it out of his pocket. The grand experiment.

STEPHAN EICKE: *What exactly did you do on the project that would eventually become* Inland Empire?

JOHN NEFF: I only did location sound, and I co-wrote "Polish Poem," Chrysta Bell's song that is in the movie. We wrote "Right Down to You" in 2002 and recorded it. We wrote "Real Love" in 2003 and recorded it. "This Train" was also in 2003. "Polish Poem" was in 2004. So we worked for a couple of years on and off together and then "Polish Poem" showed up in *Inland Empire*. *This Train*, [Chrysta Bell's] album, didn't come out until just a few years ago. She was wonderful to work with. Excellent singer. [...] I also recorded room tone [for *Inland Empire*]. Either at the beginning or the end of a shoot, David would holler for quiet on the set and I would record one minute of room tone. If we had traffic or birds in it, it didn't matter. It was the sound of the location. Then I mixed some scenes from it before I left, like the barbecue scene. That was the hardest scene to record because we had crows, and I had eight channels of wireless on the Polish circus performers and on Laura [Dern] and Peter [J. Lucas]. I was recording to a mobile ProTools rig with a laptop and a hard drive. Ten channels wide, two booms, and eight channels of wireless. The poor video editor had to import all that crap.[5]

Inland Empire premiered two years later and is Lynch's last motion picture. Like *Mulholland Drive* it is a movie that came together accidentally, assembled out of parts. While the LA noir morphed from a TV pilot into a feature, *Inland Empire* uses *Rabbits* and *A Meeting Upstairs* and strings them together with a story the director developed subsequently. Laura Dern plays Nikki, an actress who wins the sought-after main role in *On High in*

---

[5]Ibid.

Blue Tomorrows, a love story shot and set in Los Angeles. Little, at first, does she know that the film is a remake of sorts. It is based on a Polish folk tale which was used as a blueprint for a European movie that was never finished because both the main actors were murdered. Nikki and her co-star Devon (played by Justin Theroux) are unsettled as their director (Jeremy Irons) reveals to them why the project was abandoned. Shortly after rehearsals commence, Nikki starts to confuse reality with fiction as she starts an affair with Devon which threatens her marriage. As she discovers a door in the sound stage that serves as a rehearsal space for *On High in Blue Tomorrows*, she enters a portal in which she is confronted with her worst fears. The portal also allows her to investigate the circumstances of the actors' deaths that occurred during the filming of the original version of the film she is now making.

"Polish Poem" opens the film, as Lynch cuts from a brief scene in a run-down Polish hotel to a young woman. Deeply moved, she is sitting on a bed, nude, holding a red velvet gown close to her chest, staring transfixed at a television screen. The screen is filled with static, until *Rabbits* comes on, Lynch's warped parody of an American sitcom. "Polish Poem" serves as a bookend since it also closes the film. The piece draws a connection between the first and last scene in which the young woman from the film's opening is now on a television screen herself, as she receives a visit from Nikki. Typically for Lynch, there is the hint of redemption, or at least solace in that Nikki warmly embraces and kisses the young woman. Her tears are slowly being wiped away while in the background the same scene is transpiring on the young woman's television screen. It is being replayed endlessly, into eternity on screen, on screen, on screen.

The lyrics—written by Lynch and Chrysta Bell—again are typical for the director. They pick up images, descriptions, and themes close to his heart and that had often appeared in his films, songs and paintings. Following a break-up, a woman in torment is crying out, longing for salvation from her angst and depression, seeing "shining waves" and hearing "the wind blow outside" before something starts to happen, a mystery unfolding "as a wing floating." The dense synthesizer chords and Bell's breathless, dreamy incantation evoke Julee Cruise's work for Lynch and Badalamenti, which was influenced by "Song to the Siren" by This Mortal Coil. A homage to Lynch's favorite song is also present in the lyrics of "Polish Poem" with its ocean imagery and longing for a partner who has abandoned their formerly loved one. As a result, the latter is now on a quest, crying out without giving up hope.

"Polish Poem" is part of a fruitful collaboration between David Lynch and Chrysta Bell which started in the late 1990s. Bell, born in Texas, had been part of the swing band 8½ Souvenirs before she tried her luck as a solo singer. Through her manager she met with Brian Loucks, Lynch's friend and an agent at CAA, who in turn suggested Bell have a meeting with the director. After all, the two seemed to share a musical sensibility. Thus, "Polish Poem" came to be, one of the first tracks the two would work on together.

David Lynch relishes collaborating with other musicians. With Angelo Badalamenti he had sat at his side and dictated his ideas for music, while now he often joined musicians such as John Neff and Chrysta Bell on the guitar, an active player himself. One of the musicians he discovered was Marek Zebrowski, a Polish pianist and composer. In the fall of 2004, the director invited the musician to his studio in Los Angeles to record some improvisations. Though Lynch accompanied Zebrowski on a synthesizer, their approach was similar to his collaborations with Badalamenti: the director would describe a short scene to Zembrowski before they sat down and played on two keyboards whatever they deemed appropriate music for the images they saw in their minds. When they felt an ending approaching for the music, they nodded at each other and gently stopped.[6] The stories would differ, but the imagery and mood were always uniquely Lynchian: dark streets, blowing wind, factories, and machines.

In 2011 Lynch released *Crazy Clown Time*, his first record as a solo artist. The album had been preceded in 2010 by the release of "Good Day Today" and "I Know" as singles. His two solo records—*Crazy Clown Time* and *The Big Dream* released two years later in 2013—feature all the trademarks of Lynch as a musician, characteristics he had developed before, bit by bit, through his work with Splet, Badalamenti, Cruise, and others. They feature the same sort of relentless steady rhythms ("So Glad," "Noah's Ark") that Grady Tate had supplied for *Twin Peaks*. Sound design effects such as gunshots and rain were altered, slowed down and played backwards, just as Badalamenti's "firewood" had been, or had the language spoken in the Red Room in *Twin Peaks*. Lynch's guitar-playing was heavily influenced by his love for industrial sounds and Badalamenti's deployment of guitars in scores such as *Lost Highway*. The low organ points on the synthesizer were unmistakably inspired by Badalamenti—Lynch's teacher. The simplistic lyrics are similar to the poems Lynch has forwarded to his composer, to Chrysta Bell, John Neff, and others. Now, Lynch sang them himself, having observed and learned from his close collaborators and friends, soaked up their expertise and tricks like a sponge.

Reviews for *Crazy Clown Time*, Lynch's foray into music as a solo artist, were mixed. Professional, long-time music reviewers appeared to have trouble taking the director seriously as a musician, and advised him indirectly to stick to his guns and focus on making films as opposed to

---

[6] Lynch & McKenna, *Room to Dream*, p. 419.

dabble in areas he has no business in—that, at least, was the view of the *Rolling Stone*, which called the record "numbing."[7]

Dean Hurley was pivotal in getting both *Crazy Clown Time* and *The Big Dream* recorded and released. Following the departure of John Neff, David Lynch needed an expert to run the studio and thus enable the director to record and mix music and sound design. In January 2005 Hurley, a self-taught engineer from Virginia, became Lynch's new musical collaborator. "Ghost of Love," used in *Inland Empire*, was one of the first projects they worked on together, and Hurley quickly understood his new boss's idiosyncratic approach to music-making. When about to record a song, Lynch would often cite favorite pieces of his and listen to them with Hurley at his side. More often than not, it was the atmosphere, the mood of a piece that the director aspired to emulate in a new recording. Together with Hurley, he would then try to figure out what specifically gave the song its unique quality. Before recording "Ghost of Love," Lynch mentioned Janis Joplin's "Balls and Chain," with its distinct three-chord blues. Hurley would write down a set of chords that pleased Lynch and provided a drumbeat which the director then looped and deformed. After Lynch and Hurley had laid the foundation for the recording, the former wrote down lyrics and performed them. Thus, "Ghost of Love" was born.[8]

Fox Bat Strategy he released in 2009 as a download. In 1994, buoyed by the recording of "The Pink Room" for *Twin Peaks: Fire Walk with Me*, Lynch had assembled some of his favorite musicians in a recording studio to continue their work. Drummer Steve Hodges and guitarist Dave Jaurequi had been part of the "Pink Room" ensemble and were excited to record again with the director in the same way they had two years earlier. Lynch would describe images to them and then afford them room for improvisation. Rarely did they record more than two takes. Lynch even gave Jaurequi—who passed away in 2006 and to whom the album is dedicated—some poems to sing, similar to the ones he had provided to Julee Cruise and to those he would later furnish Chrysta Bell with.[9]

Although Lynch's planned documentary about Maharishi Mahesh Yogi, the founder of the Transcendental Meditation movement, was never finished, the filmmaker had by no means lost interest in making films. Still, nearly a decade would go by before *Twin Peaks: The Return* was announced. In the meantime, Lynch had written a feature film script he hoped to get off the ground, but for which he could find no financial backers, especially after

---

[7]Catucci, Nick, "Crazy Clown Time," *Rolling Stone*, December 7, 2011, https://www.rollingstone.com/music/music-album-reviews/crazy-clown-time-255449/ (accessed June 19, 2024).
[8]Lynch & McKenna, *Room to Dream*, p. 420.
[9]Hodges, MonosonicJukeJoint, "Daivd [sic] Lynch Fox Bat Strategy behind The Music."

Inland Empire had proved a financial disappointment. *Antelope Don't Run No More*—written in 2010—features space aliens, talking animals, as well as a musician named Pinky, and would have cost around $20 million to make. Although, allegedly, the script found great acclaim, nobody was willing to finance it, since paradoxically it was neither cheap nor expensive enough. A $20 million film would fall between the cracks, Lynch was informed.[10] Similarly, a script for an animated movie called *Snootworld* he co-wrote, failed to find financial backing.[11]

David Lynch left one last gift to the medium of television. In 2014, a return of *Twin Peaks* on television was announced. It was to become Lynch's largest-scale project, the last film or television endeavor he undertook. It would also be the last collaboration between him and Angelo Badalamenti.

There are clear differences between the limited series and the two seasons that aired in 1989 and 1990. Apart from some continuing characters and various crew members, they have little in common. The original series presented multiple stories at once and frequently afforded its characters to go off on tangents. It depicted developments that were either unrelated to, or only indirectly concerned with, Laura Palmer's murder—the plot against Jocelyn Packard, for example, or Leo's drug-running business that was, after all, little more than a red herring. Conversely, in *Twin Peaks: The Return* every scene is crucial to the mystery that lies at the heart of the story. Even minor characters like Freddy and his magic glove prove essential to the show's resolution. People who had hoped for a rehash of the original series were sorely disappointed.

Twin Peaks: The Return tells the story of how Agent Cooper leaves the Black Lodge, an extra-dimensional location as a place of pure evil, twenty-five years after he entered it at the end of season 2. While the Good Cooper has been kept in the Lodge for all this time, Evil Cooper has been left roaming freely. The latter has used the intervening time to build an empire. Evil Cooper knows that after twenty-five years his counterpart, the Agent Cooper who never tires of fighting crime, will be allowed to leave the Lodge. When that happens, Evil Cooper will have to go back in, and thus abandon the lifestyle he enjoys—assaulting women, stealing, and trafficking drugs. Since he isn't willing to disappear into an alternate reality, Evil Cooper manufactures Dougie Jones, an insurance salesman from Las Vegas who closely resembles Good Cooper.

---

[10] Lynch & McKenna, *Room to Dream*, p. 475.
[11] Wiseman, Andreas, "David Lynch Is Still Hoping to Make Animated Movie 'Snootworld' Which He Scripted with 'The Addams Family' & 'Edward Scissorhands' Writer Caroline Thompson: 'It's a Story That Children and Adults Can Appreciate'", *Deadline*, April 8, 2024, https://deadline.com/2024/04/david-lynch-animated-movie-snootworld-netflix-addams-family-edward-scissorhands-writer-caroline-thompson-1235877710/ (accessed June 19, 2024).

Lynch and Frost carefully designed parallel dimensions—a mauve house among the stars, a dilapidated villa in which the Fireman lives—and let the camera slowly fly through an exploding atomic bomb underscored by Penderecki's celebrated *Threnody for the Victims of Hiroshima*. Therewith, they combine past with present, reality with allegory. *Twin Peaks: The Return* is slow, gory, at times unashamedly abstract (FBI Special Agent Phillip Jeffries—introduced in *Twin Peaks: Fire Walking with Me* as played by David Bowie—is represented by a tea kettle). As such, it is the only logical sequel to what was a visionary, genre-bending television show in the late 1980s and early 1990s.

In many ways, *Twin Peaks: The Return* is the culmination of Lynch's work. By the time he started writing the script with Mark Frost, the director had fully established his creative world, his themes of dreams, doppelgangers and enlightenment. All these subjects are elaborated on in the latest reiteration of *Twin Peaks*. Everything shows the trademark of David Lynch the conceptual artist.

This extends to the show's music and sound design. When he started work on *Twin Peaks: The Return*, the director had for many years created his own sound design. Some of his work with Dean Hurley was used in *Twin Peaks: The Return*. In episode 8, for example, Lynch's and Hurley's "Slow 30's Room" can be heard as Senorita Dido sways to the music coming from the gramophone. The track was originally conceived for an art exhibition of Lynch's work and featured on his album *The Air Is on Fire* in 2007.

Lynch and Hurley's "Sub Dream" is used in episode 17 as Mister C walks to Jack Rabbit's Palace. Hurley's own music is similar to his work with Lynch—and starkly different to Angelo Badalamenti's contributions to *Twin Peaks*. Often, Hurley's ambient pieces are indistinguishable from the show's sound design and effects, closer to Brian Eno and his contemporaries than to Badalamenti's cool jazz, bittersweet melodies and even his slowed down "firewood."

Lynch uses Hurley's compositions frequently in *Twin Peaks: The Return*, most notably "Intro Cymbal Wind" in the opening of the first episode prior to the credits; "Tube Wind Dream" as Agent Cooper is floating through the glass box; "Electricity I" as Cooper encounters the girl without eyes in the purple zone; "Tone/Slow Speed Prison/Low Mood" as Balthazar Getty's character intimidates Audrey's son.

Lynch also employed several pieces by musician Johnny Jewel, who at that time was still a member of the electronic music band Chromatics before the Portland-based group split up in 2021. The song "Shadow," inspired by the dreamy, electronic approach of Julee Cruise and Angelo Badalamenti, was part of their oeuvre and caught the attention of Dean Hurley, while he and Lynch were brainstorming which acts could perform at the Roadhouse after each episode of *Twin Peaks: The Return*.

As a big fan of the director, Jewel decided to record instrumental pieces for *Twin Peaks: The Return* on spec. Initially, Jewel submitted five to seven hours of compositions and improvisations to Lynch's team. By the time the director had finished editing, the music Jewel sent to him had grown to twenty hours.[12] Aware of the fact that Lynch wanted his most recent artistic endeavor to be more sparse musically than the first two seasons of the show, the composer developed subdued ambience pieces not dissimilar to Dean Hurley's own work and pieces by Brian Eno.

Jewel had provided David Lynch with material to play with. It was entirely up to the director to use what he deemed suitable. Jewel made clear that he would not impose any restrictions on what Lynch could do with his music. Indeed, the filmmaker selected several instrumental pieces by Jewel of which "Windswept" is featured most prominently in the show as a signature theme for Dougie Jones. It can be heard, for example, as the Good Cooper stands in front of Lucky 7 Insurance in Nevada, staring at a statue as if hypnotized and seemingly unable to move. Several pieces, including "Windswept," Jewel later released on "Bandcamp," describing his contributions to *Twin Peaks: The Return* as a project that "began as a sonic exploration of the sounds I was hearing in my nightmares. [...] I wanted to find my way out of the maze by focusing on beauty over fear—like the way the fractured sunrise looks in a dream."[13]

Only a few pieces from the original show and its cinema prequel, *Twin Peaks: Fire Walk with Me*, were used. Most of them are firewood, sustained drones to evoke dread, despair, and danger. For example, as Hawk walks through the woods in the first episode, "Dark Mood Woods/The Red Room" is playing; "Windom Earle's Motif" can be heard in Norma's diner at the end of episode 7; "Abstract Mood" is used for a shot of the Sheriff's station in episode 9. Badalamenti's catchy cool jazz pieces only make brief appearances. To Dean Hurley, it was clear from the beginning that *Twin Peaks: The Return* would be radically different from the first two seasons and the feature film.

There is little room for Badalamenti's quirky cool jazz in *Twin Peaks: The Return*. In the twenty-five years since the original series premiered, the world had changed, and with it the universe Lynch had created. The world portrayed in *Twin Peaks: The Return* is even more violent than in the show's original two seasons. Over everything hangs a thick miasma of despair.

---

[12]Roffman, Michael, "The World Spins: Johnny Jewel Talks Twin Peaks, David Lynch, and What's Next for Chromatics," *Consequence*, September 4, 2017, https://consequence.net/2017/09/the-world-spins-johnny-jewel-talks-twin-peaks-david-lynch-and-whats-next-for-chromatics/ (accessed June 19, 2024).

[13]https://johnnyjewel.bandcamp.com/album/themes-for-television (accessed June 19, 2024).

Lynch uses few snippets of pieces written for the original show, particularly Grady Tate's percussion solos. Here, they are associated with the glamor of Las Vegas. "Solo Percussion 1" plays briefly as the camera flies over the city's skyscrapers in episode 1. "Grady Groove" accompanies Dougie Jones as he enters the elevator in his Las Vegas insurance company in episode 5, and "Deer Meadow Shuffle" from *Twin Peaks: Fire Walk with Me* is heard in episode 9 as Detective Fusco prepare to arrest Ike the Spike.

Similarly, "Laura Palmer's Theme" is used sparsely and carefully. While in the *Twin Peaks* pilot alone it was used eight times, in the whole series of *Twin Peaks: The Return* it only makes its appearance on three occasions. This limited series is not nostalgia. Lynch uses the theme for the first time in episode 4, as Bobby—now on the side of the law as part of Sheriff Truman's team—walks into the investigation room and sees Laura's photo on the table. Unable to control his emotions, he bursts into tears. It is a catharsis. As an old investigation is being re-opened, so are old wounds. The audience is back in Twin Peaks.

"Dark Introduction" is used in episode 12, when Hawk arrives at the Palmer house and briefly speaks with Sarah. Here, several things are happening at the same time: Lynch cuts to the whirring fan on the first floor twice. In the first instance, the audience shares Hawk's point of view as he glances up to the building. He is reminded of the earlier case involving Laura Palmer, seeing the fan as a symbol of death and misery, a harbinger of evil. Badalamenti's "Dark Introduction" underlines his emotion of dread. A few seconds later, Hawk indicates to Sarah that he and his colleagues are re-opening the case. The disheveled, alcohol-addicted mother takes the information in but betrays little surprise. She has long come to accept her inability to escape the ghosts of the past. Hence, a re-opened investigation means little to her emotionally. In the same scene, Lynch shows how grief and trauma follow us around and affect not only those closest to us but—as we had seen previously in the same episode—passing acquaintances in our life, such as the cashier in the supermarket who is unsettled by Sarah's odd, inquisitive behavior. As Hawk speaks to Sarah and offers her his help, he hears a noise from inside the house. Is somebody else in or does he simply imagine an ever-present evil lurking there? Lynch leaves it open to interpretation while underscoring the doom and anxiety that lingers in the home with the musical motif that foreshadowed and indicated negative events and emotions.

The love theme, as a variation on "Laura Palmer's Theme," makes its last appearance in episode 17, as Cooper and Laura meet in the woods. It is preceded by a flashback of the last meeting of Laura and James prior to her death. In stark black-and-white images, Lynch reveals it had been the Good Cooper from the future who Laura had seen while shaken with anxiety and revealing her feelings to her boyfriend. Now, Cooper is freed and therefore able to save Laura. This is exactly what he does in one of the most emotionally resonant scenes in the whole show: after Laura has run off, she encounters Cooper. Serenely, he offers her his hand while Badalamenti's signature tune plays on the soundtrack. They will be going home, he says. With that, the images of the homecoming queen wrapped in plastic disappear. Laura is saved thanks to Coopers ability to travel back in time. The music is her absolution as it suggests her nightmare will end in bliss. It does not find its finale in her violent passing. Badalamenti's music ties the earlier scenes—the flashbacks—together with the present while also supplying the appropriate emotional message with its notes of love and hope.

Lynch also uses excerpts from "Frank 2000," a near-twenty-minute avant-garde/ambient collage that he and Badalamenti had devised and recorded in the early 1990s under the pseudonym Thought Gang. Inspired by their work on *Twin Peaks*, the duo had invited musicians such as Grady Tate and Buster Williams—a revered bassist—into a New Yorker studio to develop music based on Lynch's descriptions. One result of these experiments they called "Frank 2000," a moody, dark, rumbling soundscape that proved ideal to accompany brief scenes of anxiety and turmoil, such as Becky stealing her mother's car in episode 11, in *Twin Peaks: The Return*. "Frank 2000" was prompted by a comparatively literal, clear description by Lynch, as he later remembered: "There's a bar or club downtown at night. It's very late, like two or three in the morning and people are coming out, and there's a shootout. There's guns going off and cars careening around and girls and guys piling in the backs of pickup trucks and heading out of LA into the desert."[14]

Although *Twin Peaks: The Return* had a different mood and atmosphere to the original series from the outset, the director nevertheless wanted to work with his regular composer again. The new show needed additional music, some compositions in Badalamenti's unique style, though there aren't many original pieces in *Twin Peaks: The Return*.

Whereas Badalamenti had written hours of music for the first season alone, he contributed only a couple of cues to the eighteen-hour sequel. These new compositions may be few in number but are given space to breathe as they accompany some of the pivotal scenes in the show.

However, it takes five episodes for the first new piece by Badalamenti to appear—and it is only a few seconds long: as Dougie Jones leaves the house with Janey in the morning and steals a loving glance at his son, the "Farewell Theme" slowly fades in, bringing a warmth and tenderness to the relationship between father and son that previously was lacking. It marks the start of a strong bond that will form between the two. Fittingly, the theme is used again to mark the end of their (physical) bond. Dale Cooper eventually wakes up from his trance and realizes he does not belong

---

[14]Grow, "David Lynch and Angelo Badalamenti on Their Wild Jazz Experiment."

to the family in Rancho Rosa. Instead, he is on a mission. As a special agent, he must protect Laura Palmer, to catch his dangerous doppelganger and put an end to the evil that was inflicted upon the earth. His spiritual awakening forces him to say goodbye to Janey and her son. It is a difficult, painful farewell that is linked musically to Cooper's earlier tender glance at "his" son and the blossoming of his paternal feelings. Beginning and end are part of a circle.

On the soundtrack album that was released to coincide with the series' premiere on Showtime, the "Farewell Theme" is preceded by a piece accompanying arguably the most haunting moment in all three seasons of *Twin Peaks*: "Accident." Written prior to shooting, "Accident" is used after a young boy is killed by Audrey's son speeding through the city. While the mother, screaming in anguish, runs toward her bleeding, lifeless child, cradling him desperately as his soul is leaving its body, Badalamenti's high octave chords on his Fender Rhodes barely change. It is music of shock as it captures the inability to speak and move following a traumatic event. Nothing will ever be the same again.

"Heartbreaking," another new composition by Badalamenti, is equally tender and gentle, although more romantic in nature than both "Accident" and "Farewell Theme." The piece was not written in pre-production, but after the shoot had wrapped. In the show, it can be heard at the end of episode 11, as Dougie Jones sits down with the Mitchum Brothers in a fancy restaurant to enjoy a delicious piece of cherry pie. It is employed similarly to the music playing as Audrey dances in her father's office and James and Donna meet in the school's hallway in the original show, in that it defies categorization as either diegetic or non-diegetic music. It is clearly emanating from the piano in the restaurant as played by Robert Miles. And yet, underneath the piano notes there is a subtle overlay provided by a Fender Rhodes. No other instrument than the piano is visible on screen. Therefore, "Heartbreaking" does not qualify as a diegetic piece. Its effect, though, is stark: the tender melody starts as Jones observes an elderly lady from the casino he had previously encountered. It is the same woman who had previously been dirty, lonely, homeless. Thanks to Cooper's guidance, she had subsequently won the jackpot, is now elegantly dressed, accompanied by her son, and grateful for the house she has been able to buy. She showers Cooper with gratitude—the person who is guided by a light, who improves the lives of people he meets and bestows bliss on everybody around him.

> LADY: Mr. Jackpots!
> [*To* SON:] This is the man I have told you about. I wanted to see you again. I have thought of you every day, what you did for me. You changed my life. This is my dear son, Denver. He is back in my life again. I have a little dog. I have a house! I have my life back again. How can I ever thank you?

[*To* MITCHUM BROTHERS:] I hope you realize what a special person you have dining here. He saved my life.
BRADLEY MITCHUM: Sure saved us a lot too.
LADY: Thank you Mr. Jackpots. I am so thankful I got a chance to say thank you again.
DOUGIE JONES: Thank you again.

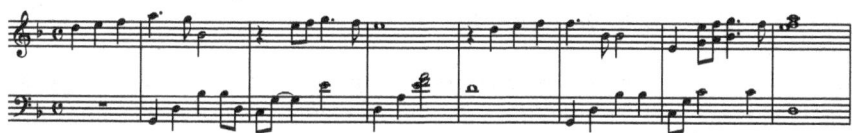

FIGURE 31 *Heartbreaking (from* Twin Peaks: The Return, *2017). Transcribed by Stephan Eicke.*

During shooting, pianist Robert Miles had to mimic playing since the music hadn't been written yet. As he recalled: "[David Lynch] created mental pictures for me to play soft, romantic Italian music with my eyes closed. I did it in a couple of takes and he said he was happy with it."[15] Later, Lynch called up Angelo Badalamenti to request different instrumental songs for the restaurant scene—one of them peppy, another one slow. The compositions were then edited in during post-production. David Lynch, initially busy with various pre-production tasks and then later with shooting, did not travel to New Jersey to sit by Angelo's side as he had done previously. This time in their collaboration, phone calls and Skype conversations had to suffice.

The physical distance between Los Angeles and New Jersey was not ideal, but didn't prevent Lynch and Badalamenti from communicating and the composer from developing new material based on their conversations via Skype. On a technological level, it was up to Dean Hurley and Angelo Badalamenti's assistant Jim Bruening to make it happen. Hurley explained: "There was this Source-Connect plug-in that you could insert in a Protools session on a track and it was like a full hi-resolution mp3 broadcast of whatever another studio was playing anywhere around the world, with minimal latency. Essentially it was like a portal where David could hear Angelo in full resolution as if he was playing in David's studio."[16]

---

[15]Dom, Pieter, "The Story behind Angelo Badalamenti's 'Heartbreaking' and the Pianist Playing It in Twin Peaks Part 11," *Welcome to Twin Peaks*, July 26, 2017, https://welcometotwinpeaks.com/music/angelo-badalamenti-heartbreaking-the-pianist/ (accessed June 19, 2024).
[16]Stone, "We Talk to the Man behind the Twin Peaks Soundtracks."

Songs are an essential part of this collage. Some are used as non-diegetic music, as an alternative to an instrumental underscore. When, in episode 5, a woman is having a tense conversation over the phone, "I Am Old (Old School Hip Hop Beat)" by BluntedBeatz can be heard—possibly as source music, though it is difficult to be certain. A few episodes later, when Ike the Spike goes out to kill the woman, enters her room and drives a spike into her chest until he is splattered with her blood, the song plays again, as non-diegetic music. It was a piece David Lynch had found on YouTube one day and decided to use in his series simply because he liked it.[17] It became Ike the Spike's leitmotif.

At the end of almost every episode songs are being performed live as the credits roll. At the roadhouse, little had changed since it was first seen in the original series. The music by artists standing on this stage is difficult to square with the traditional musical environment in a small, rural town in America's northwest. Lynch assembled some old friends for a reunion: Rebekah Del Rio, for example, sings "No Stars." In 2001, she had been part of *Mulholland Drive* where she sings in one of the movie's pivotal scenes. Here, she is accompanied by Moby, a friend of Lynch. Julee Cruise performs "The World Spins." Nine Inch Nails rock the stage with "She's Gone Away," having collaborated with Lynch on *Lost Highway* two decades prior. A band called Trouble (appearing in episode 5) consists of Alex Zhang Hungtai as well as the director's son Riley Lynch and his long-time studio manager and musical collaborator Dean Hurley.

Audrey spontaneously decides to start swaying her hips at the roadhouse as "her" dance, "Audrey's Dance," is announced—a surprising meta-moment in the show: for Audrey, the piece never had a name in her world, the character's reality. Now it has officially become "Audrey's Dance." Finally, it is given a title in the universe of *Twin Peaks*. Another character enjoys the spotlight at the roadhouse: James Hurley. In episode 13, actor James Marshall enters the stage to perform "Just You," the ballad he had sung with Donna and Madeleine two decades prior. Ever since Lynch had devised initial plans for a third season of the show, he had been eager to see Marshall go on stage and give a rendition of that particular song.

James' singing of the lyrics in the second season of *Twin Peaks* had quickly become infamous because his voice is artificially high-pitched. And why does he have professional recording equipment on the floor? How come the audience suddenly hears other instruments playing in the background when there clearly is no band in the room ("no hay banda!")? Donna and Madeleine look convincingly uncomfortable. The simplistic lyrics are

---

[17] Mejia, Paula, "Charting the Vast Musical Universe of Twin Peaks," *Vulture*, July 27, 2017, https://www.vulture.com/2017/07/the-vast-and-unsettling-musical-universe-of-twin-peaks.html (accessed June 19, 2024).

unmistakably Lynchian; minimalist, pure, naive even, not dissimilar to "Mysteries of Love."

The scene had come about spontaneously: James Marshall occasionally brought his guitar to the set and one day was asked by the ever-curious Lynch if he was comfortable singing and playing his instrument on the show. Angelo Badalamenti happened to be in Los Angeles as parts of the second season were being filmed and the trio went to the set of the Hayward house to develop a song for James and the girls to perform. Marshall imagined a ballad in homage to the 1950s. Promptly, Badalamenti put his fingers on the piano and started improvising a piece based on standards of that period. Lynch started singing, joined by his composer, and "Just You" was born. Two weeks later, the instrumental was recorded, though not in Marshall's key. As a result, he found himself forced to perform in "ultra-high falsetto" on set.[18]

In *Twin Peaks: The Return*, Lynch uses the original recording with Sheryl Lee's and Lara Flynn Boyle's vocals. "Just You" is a song that aptly portrays and underlines James' sweetness to the point of caricaturing him (Lori Eschler calls him "essentially a teddy bear"). But David Lynch has always been unashamed to revel in extremes, and here it is James' utmost purity that is reflected in his song.

The performances at the roadhouse serve as an example of Lynch's efficiency. Perhaps because *Twin Peaks: The Return* took four and half years to get off the ground, not a minute was wasted during production. All performances at the venue—nearly two dozen—were shot in a single day in Pasadena.[19]

The show premiered in May 2017. Eighteen hours of David Lynch's universe were unleashed. Reactions were at first mixed. The network had decided not to furnish reviewers with copies. Showtime had even placed an embargo on those who had attended the Los Angeles premiere of the first two episodes. It led many critics to judge the whole show from a small part of the whole alone. Little did they know what an odyssey the show would become (although *The Washington Post*, for example, reviewed the first four episodes as opposed to only the first two, as the *New York Times* did when they were eventually allowed to).

By the time all eighteen episodes had aired, it was clear that—unsurprisingly—*Twin Peaks: The Return* was not to everybody's liking. While the first two episodes had attracted half a million viewers each, by the last episodes the viewership was down to half of that. However, Lynch aficionados were stunned and satisfied indeed. *Cahiers du cinéma* announced that *Twin Peaks: The Return* was the best film of that year,

---

[18]Dukes, *Reflections: An Oral History of Twin Peaks*, p. 181.
[19]Lynch & McKenna, *Room to Dream*, p. 487.

based on the fact that the script had been written as one long, uninterrupted work of fiction.[20]

Sight & Sound placed *Twin Peaks: The Return* behind *Get Out* as Film of the Year.[21] One year following its premiere, *Esquire* proclaimed: "After sixteen hours and twenty-five minutes of some of the most ambitious, soul-searching, spiritual storytelling that I have ever seen, I still can't believe what David Lynch with his return to the 1990 ABC series achieved, and I simply cannot get it off my mind."[22]

Lynch and Frost had enhanced the *Twin Peaks* world and turned it on its head. It was a spiritual, gory journey, a nearly eighteen-hour film filled with mysticism, violence, and child-like, silly humor, with a plot that was so complex and intricate students would spend many weeks and months analyzing what they had witnessed on their screens. Some would shoot YouTube videos about it, sometimes many hours in length.

STEPHAN EICKE: *Aren't you tired of constantly being asked about your work with David Lynch? You have, after all, done so much more than that.*

ANGELO BADALAMENTI: It's one hell of a beautiful way to collaborate. What's better than that? How do you beat that? David and I have had an unbelievable relationship. How many composers have been that lucky? There have been a few. Henry Mancini, for example, and Danny Elfman with Tim Burton. We are very lucky people. Both parties are very lucky, not just composers but directors as well. All you have to do is look at each other, and without opening your mouth you know each other's feelings. You get along and you have respect for each other. It's a very fortunate thing.

STEPHAN EICKE: *He called you his brother.*

ANGELO BADALAMENTI: I received the Henry Mancini Lifetime Achievement Award, which was given by ASCAP. David was my presenter. In front of this whole audience of rather sophisticated people he said, "Now I'd like to present the award to my brother

---

[20]Raup, Jordan, "Cahiers du cinéma's Top 10 Films of 2017 Includes 'Twin Peaks: The Return', 'Split', and 'Good Time'," *The Film Stage*, December 5, 2017, https://thefilmstage.com/cahiers-du-cinemas-top-10-films-of-2017-includes-twin-peaks-the-return-split-and-good-time/ (accessed June 19, 2024).

[21]Tartaglione, Nancy, "'Get Out' Tops BFI's *Sight & Sound* Poll as Film of the Year; 'Mother!' Enters Top 25," *Deadline*, December 5, 2017, https://deadline.com/2017/12/sight-and-sound-2017-poll-get-out-film-of-the-year-twin-peaks-list-1202219362/ (accessed June 19, 2025).

[22]Nero, Dom, "One Year Later, I Can't Stop Thinking about Twin Peaks: The Return," *Esquire*, May 21, 2018, https://www.esquire.com/entertainment/tv/a20716164/twin-peaks-the-return-one-year-later/ (accessed June 19, 2024).

Angelo." (*Laughs.*) We are brothers because we are the best of friends. I am the godfather of his son. In all these years there has never been a serious argument, only every now and then creative, mild conflicts—but always mild![23]

In 2020, it became public that Lynch had written a thirteen-part limited series initially titled *Wysteria,* which was then changed to *Unrecorded Night.* It was rumored to be a *Twin Peaks* spin-off to be financed by Netflix. However, the series was never officially announced by Lynch and the global pandemic that started in 2020 made it more difficult than ever to prepare and shoot a thirteen-hour series. The show was never produced. Instead, Lynch became an international YouTube sensation, an influencer who, sheltered at his home while Covid-19 was raging, once again devoted a substantial chunk of his time to recording videos for his fans. And so, Lynch returned to the *Weather Report* he had started with the launch of his website. He also produced regular videos about what he was building as a carpenter in his studio (*What Is David Working on Today?*), as well as featuring him drawing a number out of a glass bowl (*Today's Number Is ...*).

David Lynch's last feature film was *Inland Empire*. His admirers have had a chance to revisit his work, both at home and sometimes theatrically. Due to the advance of digital technology, *The Elephant Man* and *Mulholland Drive* were carefully restored and presented in 4K by StudioCanal. The company issued the restored films in pristine quality on discs and streaming platforms, and also re-released them in theaters, which aided the re-assessment of Lynch as a screenwriter and director by, mainly American, critics who had always been suspicious of his work. It helped that prestigious labels such as The Criterion Collection issued (nearly) all of Lynch's films—*Blue Velvet, Eraserhead, Twin Peaks: Fire Walk with Me, Lost Highway, Inland Empire, The Elephant Man, Mulholland Drive*—with a plethora of archival and newly shot special features. Following the Blu-ray release of *Twin Peaks: Fire Walk with Me*, Lynch's feature, universally loathed when it premiered, was seen through different eyes, as an important part of his filmography and essential to understanding the director as a filmmaker: "*Fire Walk with Me* has [...] garnered a greater appreciation and is seen as a key work in Lynch's canon, marking as it does the end of a period in which, as an independent filmmaker, he had worked, albeit with varying success, within the commercial, mainstream areas of cinema and television."[24]

As the years went by, Lynch grew increasingly popular as a filmmaker. His fan base expanded as the artist who had unsettled moviegoers for

---

[23]Eicke, "Mein Bruder David," p. 21.
[24]Collins, Frank, "Twin Peaks: Fire Walk with Me (1992) • Blu-ray [Criterion Collection]," *Medium*, September 8, 2021, https://medium.com/framerated/twin-peaks-fire-walk-with-me-1992-blu-ray-criterion-collection-89b91f1966ac (accessed June 19, 2024).

decades was discovered by a new generation, not least because of his strong internet presence on YouTube and in the form of memes. The American artist has become an idol, a guide—inventive, practical, highly disciplined, curious, experimental and uncaring about what others might think of him, somebody comfortable in his own skin with decades of life experience to share. He appeared to fulfill a desire and need for authenticity.

The fact that Lynch has become a pop culture phenomenon (not unlike his friend Werner Herzog) is mirrored in the number of guest appearances on celebrated shows (such as *Family Guy* and *Louie*) that Lynch has made, and can be measured by how often he is referenced and by the films he has inspired (such as *Donnie Darko* by Richard Kelly, *Under the Silver Lake* by David Robert Mitchell, the German Netflix series *Dark*, and the feature film production *Schlaf* by Michael Venus, as well as Jane Schoenbrun's *I Saw the TV Glow*, to name just a few).

The years following Angelo Badalamenti's passing were difficult for David Lynch. More and more collaborators and friends died. His wife, Emily Stofle, filed for divorce in 2023, demanding sole custody of their daughter. In early 2024, Lynch made public that he was suffering from an emphysema and had quit smoking. In irregular interviews the artist made clear he hadn't withdrawn, though. Although he could no longer leave the house due to the risk of catching Covid, he wasn't retired.[25] And in August of 2024, he released a new album, *Cellophane Memories*, which he recorded with his longtime collaborator Crysta Bell. Angelo Badalamenti was never truly gone for Lynch: several of the composer's firewood recordings found their way into the new record as a continuation of Lynch's work with Julee Cruise, John Neff, and Dean Hurley. For Bell, he had jotted down brief lyrics, which she subsequently recorded without rehearsals. Her voice was then cut up and reversed, with Lynch adding synths and drones to the archival sound collages.[26]

In this way, Badalamenti never left Lynch. The director shared:

> We were like brothers, I just love Angelo, I just love him. And when he passed over, went to the other side, it struck me harder than—so many people have died that I've worked with, I miss every one of them, and I just don't see why people have to die. But Angelo, it really hit me. I'm

---

[25]Stolworthy, Jacob, "David Lynch Says He Can No Longer 'Go Out' due to Covid Fears after Health Diagnosis," *The Independent*, August 5, 2024, https://www.independent.co.uk/arts-entertainment/films/news/david-lynch-age-movies-emphysema-smoking-b2591296.html (accessed August 13, 2024).

[26]Shuttleworth, Alastair, "Sublime Eternal Love Exists within Each One of Us: David Lynch on Music, Friendship and Life's Biggest Mystery," *The Guardian*, July 26, 2024, https://www.theguardian.com/music/article/2024/jul/26/sublime-eternal-love-exists-within-each-one-of-us-david-lynch-on-music-friendship-and-lifes-biggest-mystery (accessed July 27, 2024).

not going to be able to call Angelo on the phone, I'm not going to be able to hear his voice anymore, I'm not going to be able to work with him. All this music that's in him, it's not going to come out. It's just horrible.[27]

David Lynch's creative flame continued to burn brightly throughout Covid, his diagnosis with emphysema and Angelo Badalamenti's passing. Yet his health took a turn for the worse in the course of the wildfires in Los Angeles, which in January of 2025 resembled a Lynchian hellscape.
"Fire Walk with Me."
Forced to evacuate from his home in the Hollywood Hills, Lynch sought refuge at his daughter's house. There he died a few days later, on January 15, five days before he would have celebrated his seventy-ninth birthday. The announcement of his death sent shockwaves through the film community. Directors, actors, producers, fans, and friends poured out their love for Lynch. In countless tributes one was reminded of his vast influence on film and television; of his unique standing in what is commonly referred to as "the industry"; and of his singular, original, uncompromising vision.

Like no other filmmaker, Lynch combined challenging, oblique avant-garde with an American shucksiness. The latter was expressed in references to 1950s pop culture and in images of kitsch and sentimentality. The robin singing at the end of a menacing nightmare in *Blue Velvet*, and Laura Palmer ascending to dance with the angels in *Fire Walk with Me* after she was repeatedly abused, show his unique devotion to the weird and wholesome in equal measure.

Although his work in film, television, painting, and music was dark and violent, he remained an optimist until he took his last breath. He treated his characters with humanism, warmth, and compassion. His preoccupation with the human struggle and our collective yearning for inner peace, freedom, and happiness is evident in all of his creations. He understood our dreams. This is what his work makes clear—he reached deep to touch on fundamental anxieties, which he then expressed in a series of sensory experiences. To him, it was the only way to reach the subconscious and thus pave the way to enlightenment. Feel it, don't say it.

His family in their announcement of his passing, used a fitting quote of his: "Keep your eye on the donut and not on the hole."

---

[27]Sweet, Matthew, "David Lynch Interview: 'Even in the So-Called Dark Things, There's Beauty'," *BBC*, May 26, 2023, https://www.bbc.com/culture/article/20230525-david-lynch-interview-how-the-mulholland-drive-director-worked-with-composer-angelo-badalamenti (accessed June 19, 2024).

Conclusion

Over the course of more than thirty years, David Lynch and Angelo Badalamenti developed a symbiotic relationship, drawing out each other's strengths and amplifying them. This happened gradually, as their first collaboration, on *Blue Velvet*, was more traditional than their subsequent working methods. David Lynch started to describe images to his composer, often long before the editing process had started, sometimes even before shooting had commenced. For Lynch, it was natural to have some music recorded for the shoot in order to influence the actors' movements and performances on set. After all, he had ideas about music while writing his scripts, as *Ronnie Rocket* makes clear, the film that never went into production but for which music demos were still recorded.

The images in Lynch's mind influenced the music, and the music would further influence his images. It was action and reaction, guided by emotions and gut feelings. This process didn't end when shooting had wrapped, as the editing process presented further ideas to Lynch. Occasionally, Badalamenti would be called back to record more music. When he wasn't available, additional musicians were brought in by Lynch, who grew into his role as a musician himself. During editing he often changed his composer's material—the library music approach to the *Twin Peaks* score and the jitterbug for *Mulholland Drive* serve as examples here.

Some directors worked similarly, notably Jean-Luc Godard, and Francis Ford Coppola on *The Conversation*. But these are exceptions to the rule, particularly, for budgetary and scheduling reasons, in Hollywood. Throughout, Badalamenti proved a magnanimous collaborator, who didn't mind having his works altered. After all, he saw himself as the humble servant of the film. Moreover, he respected David Lynch's vision and approach, as nebulous as these were to him at times. Badalamenti could not explain to himself why his collaborator suddenly wanted him to start growling "The black dog runs at night." He also did not understand the meaning of *Lost Highway*. It didn't appear to matter, as each time Lynch steered him in the right direction. Had Badalamenti not been as versatile a composer, this might not have worked. But both artists were true renaissance men, adept at working in different styles and disciplines. They also shared some of the same philosophy and taste in that, for example, both enjoyed developing a musical contrast to the images on screen.

This contrast can sometimes be disorienting. It can also give valuable clues to a story's interpretation. The sound design in David Lynch's films fulfills the same function; not just providing mood and emotion, but drawing the viewers' attention to objects and gestures that prove important for unlocking the story—the ever-increasing volume of the fan in the Palmer's house, for example. The uneasiness that some of the scenes elicit stems not solely from the images, but from Badalamenti's brooding score and Lynch's own sound design that sits sometimes barely noticeably underneath them—be it room tone that was pitched down, or carefully crafted "sound spheres" and drones. The latter especially only reveal themselves by close examination of the sound design and its elements, hardly perceptible for casual—or even passionate—moviegoers on a first viewing.

There were other methods Lynch employed to disorient the audience. Badalamenti was his partner in crime when—disregarding traditional approaches to source music—Lynch blurred the lines between diegetic and non-diegetic pieces. The dinner scene in *Wild at Heart* is one example, "Audrey's Dance" in *Twin Peaks*, and the student in the hallway snapping his fingers to the rhythm of Badalamenti's non-diegetic music in the same show are others.

As the director repeatedly said, he was not an academic filmmaker. He found it difficult to verbalize his ideas. It is impossible—and beside the point—to contemplate whether they amount to conscious plans to disorient and unsettle.

If this book has managed to do one thing, I hope it is to showcase how David Lynch reacted from his gut and feelings, how he was directed by spontaneous ideas and even dreams. These ideas built via action and reaction throughout the entire filmmaking process.

The artist who made films about the inability to communicate and his difficulties with language found it easy to evoke music from Badalamenti, not by showing him images, but by describing ideas and dreams. Music and sound design freed him. In turn, they enabled him to venture further into music-making on his own.

Music gave Lynch a voice, and the influence of Angelo Badalamenti is palpable in his solo song albums and in his collaborations with other musicians. The electronic layers of "Mysteries of Love," and the suspensions in orchestral music found their way into his own work. The same is true for the sound design, which Lynch treated as of equal importance to the music. His working-relationship with Alan Splet was similar to that which he enjoyed with Angelo Badalamenti. From the beginning, the director had clear ideas and emotions about what he wanted to hear. He worked in close collaboration with his composer and sound designer. In the course of these processes, he found the confidence to devote more time and effort to develop music and sound design on his own.

The results in both music and sound design, though, wouldn't have been as successful had Lynch and Badalamenti not given each other and the musicians they collaborated with room to introduce their own ideas and suggestions—an authoritarian approach is stifling, the death knell to any creative endeavor. The lead sheets for *Twin Peaks* allowed for the musicians' input. They gave it freely, and to Badalamenti and Lynch's gratitude. The openness of the creative duo to collaborate and listen to other people's expertise and ideas created an atmosphere that made everybody feel appreciated and, in turn, appreciative, even when working under great pressure. The accounts of Lori Eschler, David Slusser, Randy Thom, and others give testament to a fulfilling work environment as a playground for creatives. This has been helped by the fact that Lynch and Badalamenti always openly either named their collaborators or rewarded them financially (see Lynch paying David Slusser for *Twin Peaks: The Missing Pieces*).

The conclusion of this book reads like a manual for creatives and aspiring directors and composers about how to work together to achieve satisfying results. Think of music as well as sound design and their placement even before shooting starts in order to leave room for each element and to let everything influence everything else. Bring in strong ideas but encourage others to bring their own. Appreciate their efforts and reward them. At the same time, be meticulous and always persevere until you are as close to the result you were aiming for as possible. Always be open to developments that might spark new ideas, even late in the process. Never stop learning. It will help you grow and lead you to new creative ventures—be it solo music, your own sound design, or anything else that you are passionate about. Don't limit yourself.

At the same time, Lynch's work was particularly successful creatively because he did not adhere to preconceived rules or traditions laid down by the industry. And had he not met a kindred spirit in Angelo Badalamenti, the manual described above would undoubtedly look starkly different.

But as it turned out, meeting each other was a dream come true.

BIBLIOGRAPHY

Barney, Richard, ed. *David Lynch Interviews*. University Press of Mississippi, 2009.
Chion, Michel. *David Lynch* [2nd edition]. BFI Publishing, 2006.
Gabel, J. C. & Hundley, Jessica, eds. *Beyond the Beyond*. Hat & Beard Press, 2016.
Lynch, David. *Catching the Big Fish* [10th Anniversary Edition]. Tarcher Preigee, 2016.
Lynch, David & McKenna, Kristine. *Room to Dream*. Canongate, 2018.
Norelli, Clare Nina. *Soundtrack from Twin Peaks*. Bloomsbury, 2017.
Rodley, Chris, ed. *Lynch on Lynch* [Revised edition]. Faber and Faber, 2005.
Stone, Oliver. *Chasing the Light*. Monoray, 2020.
Xalabarder, Conrado. *The Music Script in Film*. Self-published, 2013.

INDEX

4AD 37
8 1/2 Souvenirs 240

A Meeting Upstairs (show) 238–9
A&R Studios 22
Abbey Road Studios 231
ABC 53–4, 61, 77, 90–1, 117, 121, 143, 191–2, 252
"Abstract Mood" 245
Absurda records 236
"Adagio for Strings" 16–17, 95
Adamson, Barry 148, 150–7, 159–62, 168, 227–8
AFI Award 215
AIDS 230
Air Is on Fire, The 244
Alexandria 6
All About Eve (film) 190
All about My Mother (film) 190
All Saints 227
"All the Way" 132
Allen, Woody 105
Alphabet, The (short) 8
Alvin, Dave 139
Amadeus (film) 207
Amarcord (film) 213
American Film Institute 8–9
"And Still" 235
Anderson, Michael J. 117
Anderson, Phillip 220
Angelo Badalamenti's Soundtrack from Twin Peaks (book) 68
"Angels Go to Heaven" 229
animation 8, 25, 243
"Annalisa's Dance" 27
Antelope Don't Run No More (unrealized film) 243
Apocalypse Now (film) 113
"Apple of Sodom" 155

Arlington Road (film) 225–6
Armer, Andy 139
Armstrong, Louis 21
Arquette, Patricia 147, 165, 220
Ascots, The 182
Astraf, David 20
"Audrey's Dance"
  diegetic use 64, 68–9, 250
  in TV pilot 80, 83–5
  in *Twin Peaks: The Return* 232
  leitmotif 66, 68–9
  style 65, 67, 127, 232
  versions 75, 86
Aunt Ruth 191, 197–205
Australia 221
Austria 6
Auto Focus (film) 225
Axton, Hoyd 182

"Baby Please Don't Go" 100
Bach, Johann Sebastian 164
Badalamenti, André 117–18, 231–2
Badalamenti, Angelo
  awards 90, 215
  childhood 19–20
  country compositions 27–8, 72
  death 233–4
  fatherhood 27, 117–18, 232
  French acclaim 229
  influences 20, 65
  marriage 27
  musicals 21–2, 25, 40, 119–20
  pop compositions 23–4, 27, 229–32
  rejected film scores 219, 228
  replacement gigs 222
  soul compositions 22–5
  teaching 21–2
  versatility 27, 72, 189, 221, 224–5, 257

INDEX

Badalamenti, Gaetano 19
Badalamenti, Lonny 27
Badalamenti, Stephen 232
Badalamenti, Steve 20
Badale, Andy – *see* Badalamenti, Angelo
Badale, Vince 19, 21
BAFTA Award 215
Bailey, Donald 135, 137–8
Balaban, Bob 219
"Balls and Chain" 242
Bancroft, Anne 13
Bang the Drum Slowly (film) 220
Banks, Teresa 121–3, 126, 128, 136, 140
Barber, Samuel 16–17, 37, 95
Barcelona 97
Barrett, Andy 228
Beach, The (film) 227–8
Beaumont, Jeffrey
  as love interest 36–7, 41, 44
  as private detective 44–5, 47, 49–50
  parents 32, 173
  perspective of 43–5, 50, 116
  transformation of 9, 31–2, 147
bebop 20, 132
Becker, Walter 182
Beckett, Larry 36
Beethoven, Ludwig van 164
Belgium 105, 221–3
Bell, Chrysta 233, 238–42
Bell, John 118
Bensonhurst 19–20, 35
Bergren, Eric 13, 17
Berklee 76, 238
Bernstein, Charles 219–20
Bernstein, Elmer 150, 209
"Best Friends" 134
"Betty's Theme" 197, 205, 213
Between Worlds (film) 232
Beymer, Richard 66
Big Dream, The (album) 241
Billboard charts 90, 105
Bingen, Hildegard von 235
"Black Dog Runs at Night, The" 123, 126–7, 144
Blake, Robert 161
Blood Oranges, The (film) 228
"Blue Frank" 139
"Blue River" 172

Blue Velvet (film) 55, 106, 133, 169, 190, 223, 228, 236
  Badalamenti cameo 36, 193
  budget 18
  composition of "Mysteries of Love" 36–40
  crew 1, 77, 174
  firewood 48–9, 70, 125
  home video release 253
  incest 32, 173
  inspiration for 5
  music recording 47–8, 166, 209
  musical perspective 43
  reception 52, 89, 188, 219
  Rossellini's vocal performance 33–6
  score release 233
  scoring process 41–3, 58, 123, 165–6, 175, 210, 256
  songs as storytelling device 12, 44–7, 73, 154
  sound design 48–52, 180
  storyline 9, 31–2, 53, 116, 147, 173
  temp music 40
  Wizard of Oz references 32
BlueBOB (album) 212–14, 236–7
"Blues Cake Jazz Icing" 101
BluntedBeatz 250
"Bobby's Theme" 68, 75, 80, 83–5
Boise 5
Bondarchuk, Fedor 232
Bono 230–1
"Bookhouse Boys, The" 65–7, 75, 80–1, 84, 125
Booth, Frank 32, 43–6, 49–50
Boston 6–7
Bowie, David 135, 148, 162, 230–1, 244
Boy Who Made Magic, The (musical) 25
Boyle, Danny 227
Boyle, Lara Flynn 251
Boys in the Live Country Band, The (musical) 40
Brando, Marlon 92
Brecht, Bertold 26
Bridges, Jeff 225

Briggs, Bobby
  appearances in TV pilot 79–80, 83–5
  appearance in *Twin Peaks: Fire Walk with Me* 104, 122, 124–8
  appearance in *Twin Peaks: The Return* 246
  criminal activity 86
  leitmotif for 65–6, 68, 75, 177
  relationship with Laura Palmer 59, 62, 122, 124–7
  relationship with Shelly 72, 122, 124–5, 127–8, 177, 246
Broadway 14, 22, 25, 119–20, 230, 232
Brooklyn 5, 19, 21, 117, 189
Brooklyn Academy of Music 117
Brooks, Mel 13–14
Brooksfilms 13
Brown, Ray 65
Brubeck, Dave 198–9, 203
Bruegel, Pieter 145
Bruening, Jim 249
Buckley, Tim 36
Burton, Tim 252
"Butterfly, The" 230
Bye, Bye, Birdie (musical) 22

Cabin Fever (film) 119
Caesar, Sid 21
Cage, Nicholas 105, 114, 232
Cahiers du cinéma 251
Calvi, Anna 233
Calvin de Frenes 8–9
Camus, Albert 101
Canby, Vincent 142
Cannes Film Festival 13, 114–15, 123–4, 142, 164, 177, 192, 195, 207, 214, 229
Capitol Records 139, 149
Carnegie Hall 96
"Caroline" 75
Carter, Ron 67
Caruso, Fred 33–4, 38
Castigliane, Vincenzo 20, 193, 195, 197–8, 203
Cat's Eyes 233
Catskills 21
Cave, Nick 151
Cellophane Memories (album) 254
Central Park 44
Century City 192
Cet amour-la (film) 229
Charles DeWolf Middle School 22
Chechick, Jeremiah 223
Cherubini, Luigi 132, 140
Chicago Film Critics Association Award 215
Chicago Tribune 125
"Child of Tomorrow" 26
Chion, Michel 125
Christmas Carol, A (musical) 21
Chromatics 244–5
Churchill, Cheryl 101
Churchill, Sarah 25
Churchill, Winston 25
Ciby 2000 123, 147, 192
Cinisi 19
City of Lost Children, The (film) 167, 228–9, 231
Clifford, John 21–2
Club Silencio 201, 205–6, 212
Cocoon II (film) 74
Coleman's 111
Columbo 136
Column, Bob 9
Comfort of Strangers, The (film) 224
Conte, Paolo 222
contrasts between image and sound 8, 27, 46, 104, 126, 136, 148, 257
Conversation, The (film) 256
"Cool" 66
"Cool Cool Kyle" 80–1, 85
Cooper, Dale
  appearance in *Twin Peaks* (show) 54, 60, 62–3, 66–7, 72, 81–4
  appearance in *Twin Peaks: Fire Walk with Me* (film) 121–2, 125, 135–6
  appearance in *Twin Peaks: The Return* (show) 243–8
Coppola, Francis Ford 70, 256
Cornfeld, Stuart 13
Cousins (film) 42
Couté, Pascal 191

Covid-19 2, 253–5
Cranberries, The 229
Crane, Bob 225
Crazy Clown Time (album) 238, 241–2
Creston 40
Crime in the Streets (film) 150
Crimes and Misdemeanors (film) 190
Criterion Collection, The 253
Cruise, Julee
   appearance in *Twin Peaks* (show) 83–4, 104, 136, 210
   appearance in *Twin Peaks: The Return* (show) 250
   appearance in *Wild at Heart* (film) 117
   biography 39
   "Falling" 44, 57, 90
   Floating into the Night (album) 55, 72, 117–18, 120
   legacy 233, 240–2, 244, 254
   "The Nightingale" 69, 72
   recording of "Mysteries of Love" 37, 39–40, 44
   "The Voice of Love" 125–6
"Crying" 44, 206
Cusack, Joan 225
Czech Film Symphony Orchestra 167

"Dance of the Dream Man" 66–8, 81, 85, 129, 136
"Danielle of Amsterdam" 27
Dark (show) 254
"Dark Introduction"
   appearance in *Twin Peaks* (show) 59–60, 63, 72, 75, 78–86
   appearance in *Twin Peaks: Fire Walk with Me* (film) 124, 129, 131
   appearance in *Twin Peaks: The Return* (show) 246
"Dark Mood Woods" 125, 245
"Dark Mood Woods/The Red Room" 245
"Dark Spanish Symphony" 96–9, 106, 108–9
David Lynch Foundation, The 233
Davis, Miles 65
Davis, Ossie 26

Davis, Richard 86
Dayans, Josée 229
Days of Our Lives (show) 73
Dayton, Pete 147–9
De Laurentiis, Dino 17–18, 34, 52, 54
De Niro, Robert 220
De Vore, Christopher 13, 17
Death Waltz Recording Company 233
"Deer Meadow Shuffle" 129, 134–6, 138, 246
del Rio, Rebekah 201, 206, 237, 250
Delbarton School 232
Deming, Peter 149, 195
Dern, Laura 118, 238
Deruddere, Dominique 222–3
Des Moines 40
Des Moines Symphony 40
Desmond, Chester 105, 121, 135–6, 140
Desmond, Norma 204
Detroit 182
DeVito, Danny 228
Diamond Records 23
DiCaprio, Leonardo 227
Dickens, Charles 21
Digital Sound and Picture 188
Disney 173, 178
dissociative fugue 146–7, 162, 165
Dolby Stereo 110
Donnie Darko (film) 254
Dove, Ronnie 25
Drake University 40
Dream of the Bovine (unrealized film) 147
"Driver Down" 159
Dune (film) 17–18, 51–2, 144, 174
Dunham, Duwayne 77, 113
Durango, Perdita 99–100
Durham 5
"Dwarfland" 201, 205
Dyker Heights High School 21

Earle, Wyndham 63
"Earle's Theme" 63
Eastman School of Music 21, 40
Ebert, Roger 188–9
Edge of Love, The (film) 232
electricity 12–13, 141, 244

"Electricity I" 244
Elephant Man, The (film)
   cinematography 174
   film score 15–17
   pre-existing music 16–17, 37, 95
   pre-production 13–14
   reception 17, 52, 188, 253
   sound design 14, 169
Elfman, Danny 252
Elias, Al 25–6
Empire Strikes Back, The (film) 17
Eng, Ron 184–6, 192
Engels, Robert 121, 147
English Patient, The (film) 169
Eno, Brian 155, 244–5
Eraserhead (film)
   production 9, 52, 172
   reception 1, 13, 34, 113, 131, 253
   sound design 10–11, 14, 49, 89, 166, 180–1
   soundtrack 12–13, 37
   story 9–10, 31, 95, 116, 190
Eschler, Lori 64, 70–2, 76–8, 86–7, 133–4, 139, 142–3, 251, 258
Esquire 252
Etheridge, Melissa 221
Everett, Rupert 224
Evilenko (film) 229–30
Excalibur Studios 56, 108
"Eye" 149

"Face It Girl, It's Over" 23–4
Faithfull, Marianne 228, 231
"Falling" 2, 24–5, 55–7, 61, 63, 65, 78, 90, 123
Falzone, Don 139
Family Guy (show) 254
Fante, John 222
"Far Away Chant" 94
"Farewell Theme" 247–8
Farley, Guy 213–14
Farmer, Frances 17
Farnsworth, Richard 189
Farragut, Johnny 100, 107, 109
Fellini, Federico 15
Fender Rhodes 25, 40, 63, 75, 96, 195, 248

Fenn, Sherilyn 102
Ferguson, Allyn 18
"Fire to the Stars" 232
Fisk, Jack 13, 174
Fisk, Mary 13, 174
Floating into the Night (album) 55–7, 72, 85, 117, 125, 131
"Foggy Day in London Town, A" 230–1
Four Last Songs 95
Fox Bat Strategy (album) 242
Frances (film) 17
Francis, Freddie 174
"Frank 2000" 144, 247
Fraser, Elizabeth 36
"Fred & Renee Make Love" 168
"Freshly Squeezed" 66–7, 75, 129, 232
Frost, Mark 54, 143, 244, 252

G Kenny 90
Garcia, Nicole 229
Garland, Alex 227
Garland, Judy 32
Gershwin, George 230
Get Out (film) 252
Getty, Balthazar 244
"Ghost of Love" 242
Ghostbusters (film) 209
Gibbons, Beth 237
Gibbs, Terry 65–6
Gielgud, John 13
Gifford, Barry 93, 143, 148, 168
Giraudi, Patrick 184–5
"Go Get Some" 201, 213–14, 237
Godard, Jean-Luc 215, 256
Goddess (book) 54
Gold Coast, The (film) 231
Golden Globe Award 215
Gomm, Carr 15
"Good Day Today" 238
Goodman, Benny 19, 73
Gordon's War (film) 26, 33, 219
Gosse, Bob 228
"Grady Groove" 246
Grammy 90
Grandmother, The (short) 8–10
Greenwich Village 40
Gregg, Bradley 220

INDEX

Grieco, David 229–30, 232
Grieco, Manuel 232
Grueneisen, Peter 182
Guthrie, Robin 36

Haas, Philip 228
Hajdu, Tom 226
"Half-Speed Orchestra 1 (Stair Music/ Danger Theme)" 71
Hallmark 213
Hancock, John D. 220–2
"Hank's Theme" 63
"Happy Times" 182
Harlem 26
"Harold's Theme" 63
Harring, Laura Elena 164, 237–8
Harris, Robert 17
Harrison, Ken 219–20
Hawkins, Coleman 163
Haycroft Theater 25
Hayward, Eileen 59, 251
HBO 143
"He Ain't Coming Home No More" 22
"Heartbreaking" 248–9
Hedaya, Dan 20, 194
"Heirate mich" 158–60
Heller, Verlyn 180, 182
Hendrix, Jimi 163, 220
Herbert, Frank 17
Herzog, Werner 254
Hill, Anita 142
Hiller, Wendy 13
Hitchcock, Alfred 53
Hodge, John 227
Hodges, Steve 139, 242
Hogan's Heroes (show) 225
Holloway, Red 100–1
Hollywood Hills 255
"Hollywood Sunset" 151, 154–6
Homer 36
Honda Passport 182–3
Hopkins, Anthony 13
Horne, Audrey
  appearance in *Twin Peaks* (show) 59, 62–5, 67–9, 74–5, 79–80
  appearance in *Twin Peaks: The Return* (show) 244, 248, 250

Horne, Benjamin 59, 62, 64, 66, 86, 88
"Horne's Theme" 64, 86
Hotel Room (show) 143–4, 235
Howard the Duck (film) 74
Huck, Jon 70, 100, 105, 110, 118–19, 128, 132–3, 136–7
Hudson, Garth 221
"Hula Hoppin'" 72
Hungtai, Alex Zhang 250
Hurley, Dean 46, 235, 242, 244–5, 249–50, 254
Hurley, James 250
Hynes, Jim 128

"I Am Old (Old School Hip Hop Beat)" 250
"I Hold No Grudge" 22–3
"I Know" 238
"I Put a Spell on You" 158
I Saw the TV Glow (film) 254
"I Want to Love You For What You Are" 23
"I'm Deranged" 162
"I'm Hurt Bad" 72
Idaho 5
Identity (film) 228
"Im Abendrot" 94–6
"In Dreams" 45, 73
"In Heaven" 12
In Sound From Way Out, The (album) 23
"In the Mood" 94
Industrial Symphony No. 1 (show) 72, 79, 92, 116–20
Inland Empire (film) 99, 214, 238–41, 253
"Insensatez" 149
"Intro Cymbal Wind" 244
Invitation to Love 73
Iowa 40
Irons, Jeremy 240
"Is It Raining in London?" 231–2
Isaak, Chris 105, 110
Istanbul 224
It's a Brand New World (show) 25
"It's Your Father" 125, 140
Italy 19, 219, 230
Ivers, Peter 12

Jackson, Milt 65
James, Harry 19
"James's Theme" 64–5, 75, 80–1, 84
Jaurequi, Dave 139–40, 242
"Jean Renault's Theme" 63
Jeffries, Phillip 136, 244
Jeunet, Jean-Pierre 228, 231
Jewel, Johnny 244–6
"Jitterbug" 196, 208
Jobim, Antonio Carlos 148
Johansen, David 225
"John Merrick Theme" 16–17
Johnson, Julie (film) 228
Johnson, Samuel 126
Jones, Dougie 243, 245–7
Jones, Freddie 7, 143
Jones, Quincy 90
Joplin, Janis 242
"Just You" 250–1

Kahl, Phil 23
Kansas 32
Karloff, Boris 23
Keeler, Bushnell 6
Keeler, Toby 6–7
Kelly, Richard 254
Kern, Jerome 27
Kesher, Adam 190, 193, 197–200, 202–3, 213, 237
Kilar, Wojciech 167
King Cole, Nat 22
Kinnear, Greg 225
Koi (film) 232
Kokoschka, Oskar 7
Koníček, Štěpán 167, 211
"Kool Kat Walk" 125
"Kosmogonia" 94, 99

L'adversaire (film) 195, 229
Ladd, Diane 99
Lady in the Radiator 12
Lafayette High School 21
"Lament for Leah" 226
Landrum, Kinny 56–8, 61, 63, 66, 75, 88, 103, 231
Late Quartet, A (film) 164
Lathe of Heaven (film) 228

"Laura Palmer's Theme"
  appearance in *Twin Peaks* (show) 59–63, 73, 75, 78–80, 88, 203
  appearance in *Twin Peaks: Fire Walk with Me* (film) 123–4
  appearance in *Twin Peaks: The Return* (show) 246
Laurens 172, 179, 181
"Laurens Walking" 178–9
Laurent, Dick 146, 153, 159–60
Law and Disorder (film) 26–7, 33, 219
Lee, Sheryl 109, 228, 251
Lemurians, The (unrealized film) 54
"Leo's Theme" 63
Lester, Ketty 46
Let's Scare Jessica to Death (film) 220
"Letter from Harold #2" 75
"Llorando" 201, 206–7
"Look for the Silver Lining" 27
Looking Glass, The (film) 221
Los Angeles
  film festival 13
  filming location 146, 197, 205, 213, 240, 251
  home of David Lynch 9, 37, 159, 196, 249, 255
  music scene 101
  post-production in 133, 139, 166, 196, 226, 241
Los Angeles Times 173
Lost Highway (film)
  additional music 150–3, 155–7, 159, 164, 227
  cinematography 149
  depiction of mental illness 147, 163–4, 191, 206
  inception 147–8
  interpretation 42, 149–50, 153–4, 159–60
  music editing 158, 167
  reception 171, 253
  score recording 47, 149, 166–7, 178, 209, 241
  shooting 149, 165
  sound design 156, 161–2, 169–70, 180, 184, 205
  story 146–9, 173, 190

theme of redemption 95, 116, 147, 256
use of pre-existing songs 39, 148–9, 154–5, 157–62, 165, 250
Loucks, Brian 206, 240
Louie (show) 254
Love Hurts Love Heals (album) 238
"Love Letters" 46–7
"Love Me Tender" 94
"Love Theme from Twin Peaks" 59, 62, 79–80, 82, 84–5, 124, 246
"Lowest Circle in Hell, The" 70
Lucas, George 17, 70, 73
Lucas, Peter J. 239
Lucasfilm 70, 109
Lumberton 5, 31, 123
Lux Vivens (album) 235
Lynch, David
  advertisements 182, 188
  anxiety 6, 9
  awards 52
  childhood 5–6
  death 255
  fatherhood 7–8, 11
  inspiration 7–9
  lyricist 12, 37–41
  meditation 9, 242
  painting 6–7, 244
  relationships 7–8, 13, 33, 165, 174, 254
  shooting with music 42, 105, 110, 132, 136, 159, 164, 212, 256–8
  smoking 6, 254
  unrealized projects 13, 17, 54, 123, 131, 139, 147, 243, 253, 256
Lynch, Donald 7
Lynch, Jennifer 7–8
Lynch, John 5
Lynch, Martha 5
Lynch, Riley 165, 174, 250
Lyonne, Natasha 233

MacKay, Dave 100
MacLachlan, Kyle 44
"Madame Stella Theme" 27
Madison, Fred 116, 146–9, 153–4, 159, 162–5, 168, 173, 180, 191
Mahler, Gustav 16, 220

Mailer, Norman 43
Man with the Golden Arm, The (album) 151
Mancini, Henry 252
Mangold, James 228
Manhattan School of Music 21
Mann, Herbie 20
Manson, Marilyn 148, 155, 158–9
Marine County 214
Marshall, James 250–1
Marshall, Phil 209
Martell, Pete 59
Martin, Steve 54
Martinussen, Lasse 231
Matera 19
Maui 179, 182
Maurer, Peter 182
McAlpin 127
McCartney, Paul 231–2
McDowell, Malcolm 229
McEwan, Ian 224
McGill, Everett 174
Mercury Music Prize 151
Merrick, John 13–17
midnight movie 13
Milburn, Andy 226
Miles, Robert 249
Miller, Glenn 72, 210
Minghella, Anthony 169
Mingus, Charles 65
Minneapolis Chamber Orchestra 40
Mirren, Helen 224
Missoula 5, 52
Mitchell, David Robert 254
Moby 227
modernism 2
Mojave 111
Mondo Balordo (A Fool's World) (film) 23
Monroe, Marilyn 54
Montana 5, 52, 70
Montgomery, Jocelyn 235–6
Montgomery, Monty 93, 235
Morello, Joe 105
Morricone, Ennio 97
Morris, John 14–17, 34–5
Moscow 232
Moss Side Story (album) 151

Mount Tamalpais 169
Mount Zion 172
"Mountains Falling" 202, 212–14, 237
"Moving On" 231
Mr. Eddy 147, 150, 152–5, 158, 160, 162, 164, 227
"Mr. Eddy's Theme" 150, 152–3, 155, 164
"Mr. Eddy's Theme II" 150
Mulholland Drive (film)
   cameo by Angelo Badalamenti 20, 193–5
   crew 1, 235
   cue card 196–202
   differences between TV and feature score 195–6, 202–5
   idea for film 192–3, 239
   inception of main theme 42, 195
   instinctual decision-making 206–8
   interpretation 95, 116, 147, 205–6, 213–14
   mix of music and sound design 205–6
   music editing 208–9, 256
   reception 77, 145, 164, 215, 250
   score recording 47, 167, 209–11
   shooting 193, 195
   songs 206–8, 212–15
   sound design 213–14
   story 116, 190–1
   TV pilot 190–2
   use of pre-existing songs 44, 237, 250
"Mulholland Drive Theme" 196–8, 200–5
Music Script in Film, The (book) 16
"Mysteries of Love" 12, 37–41, 44, 55, 220–1, 251, 257
"Mysterioso" 136, 141

Nance, Jack 149
"Nashville Beer Garden" 27–8, 72
National Lampoon's Christmas Vacation (film) 27, 223
Neff, John 119–20, 179–80, 192, 196, 206–9, 212–14, 235–9, 241–2, 254

Netflix 253
Netrebko, Anna 232–3
New Jersey 22, 187, 194–5, 219, 226, 249
New Theater Works 40
New York Film Festival 13
New York Times, The 142, 251
Newman, David 228
"Night Bells" 125
Night People (book) 148
"Nightingale, The" 69, 72, 84
Nightmare on Elm Street 3, A: Dream Warriors (film) 219–20
Nina Simone Enterprises 22
Nine Inch Nails 159, 250
Ninth Gate, The (film) 167
"No Stars" 237–8, 250
"No Way Out" 229
Noah's Ark 241
Nolte, Nick 220
Norelli, Clare Nina 68
North Carolina 5, 34, 44
Northwest Passage – see *Twin Peaks*
Nowhen (short) 232

O'Neal, Ryan 220
O'Riordan, Dolores 229–30
Odyssey, The (book) 36
OFTA Film Award 215
Olympic Games 1992 97
On High in Blue Tomorrows 239–40
On the Air (show) 143–4
Ondioline 23
"One Eyed Jack's Country" 72
One Saliva Bubble (unrealized film) 54
Online Film Critics Society Award 215
Opening Night (film) 190
"Opryland in Paris" 27
Orbison, Roy 44–6, 132, 206
Orbit, William 227
Orff, Carl 16
Oscar 17, 52, 167
Other People's Money (film) 228
Otis, Clyde 23

Pacific Film Archive 113
Paich, David 18
Paich, Marty 18

Palme d'Or 115, 123
Palmer, Laura
   appearance in *Twin Peaks* (show) 53–4, 59–65, 71–3, 79–86, 90–1, 203
   appearance in *Twin Peaks: Fire Walk with Me* (film) 116–18, 121–6, 173, 180, 255, 257
   appearance in *Twin Peaks: The Return* (show) 233, 243, 246–8
Palmer, Leland
   appearance in *Twin Peaks* (show) 60, 63, 72–3, 79, 88, 91
   appearance in *Twin Peaks: Fire Walk with Me* (film) 124–6, 131–2, 140–1, 147, 173
Palmer, Sarah 59, 71, 79, 85, 246
Palomar Pictures 26
Parents (film) 219
Parker, Charlie 65
Parker, Kristen 220
Pasadena 251
Passer, Ivan 26
Pastor, Tony 20
Pellington, Mark 225–6
Penderecki, Krzysztof 99, 103, 148, 156, 158, 166, 178, 198, 244
"Pennsylvania 6–5000" 72
Pennsylvania Academy of Fine Arts 8
"Perdita" 108–9, 135
Perrey, Jean-Jacques 23
Petersen, Wolfgang 228
Peterson, Oscar 65
Peyton Place (show) 53
Philadelphia 7, 66, 111
Phipps, Keith 163
Piece of Eden, A (film) 221, 228
Pink Room 104, 127, 130, 136, 242
"Pink Room, The" (cue) 136–40
"Pink Western Range" 236
Pinki Rings 231
Pinter, Harold 224
Platoon (film) 52
Polanski, Roman 167
Polhemus, Artie 56, 76, 231
"Police!" 163
"Polish Poem" 239–41

Pomus, Doc 168
Pope, Gay 192
Porcaro, Joe 100
Portishead 237
Potente, Franka 232
Pour, Sahar 231
Powell, Bud 65
Powermad 93
Prague 47, 166–8, 178, 207–11
Prancer (film) 221
"Prelude in C-Sharp Minor" (Rachmaninoff) 62
Prince With Many Castles, The (book) 25
Producers, The (film) 14
ProTools 48, 183, 185, 207, 239, 249
psychogenic fugue – *see* dissociative fugue
Puccini, Giacomo 178, 224

"Questions in A World of Blue" 125

Rabbits (show) 238–9
Rachmaninoff, Sergei 61
Raiders of the Lost Ark (film) 113
Rancho Rosa 248
"Real Indication, A" 104, 123, 126–8, 144, 194
"Real Love" 239
Reavey, Peggy 7, 13
"Recapitulation" 16
"Red Bats With Teeth" 148–9, 153, 163
Red Dragon (novel) 17
Red Hot Rhapsody (album) 230–1
Red Room 89, 130–1, 241
Reed, Lou 154, 168
Regni, Al 56, 67, 75
Requiem in C minor (Cherubini) 132, 140
Return of the Jedi (film) 113
Reznor, Trent 148, 158–9
Rheingold (opera) 221
Rhino Records 233
Rhodes, Camilla 190–1, 193, 198–205, 209, 212–13
Richardson, Natasha 224
"Right Down to You" 239

Rite of Spring, The (ballet) 141
Roach, John 173
Robbins, Tim 225
Rochester 21
Rolling Stone 242
Ronnie Rocket (unrealized film) 13, 17, 123, 131, 139, 256
room tone 11–12, 48, 111, 162, 166, 180, 239, 257
"Rose's Theme" 175–8, 187
Ross, Atticus 159
Rossellini, Isabella 32–8, 55, 188, 194, 220
Roswell, Mark 101
Rota, Nino 15–16
Roth, Eli 119–20
"RR Swing" 134, 138
Rubber City 108
Runfolo, Peter 34
Russ, Patrick 209
Russell, Chuck 219–20

Sacred Bones Records 144
Salzburg 7
Sandpoint 5
"Sant' America" 222
Santa Clarita 184
Saturn Award 215
Schlaf (film) 254
Schoenbrun, Jane 254
School of the Museum of Fine Arts 6
Schrader, Paul 224–5
Schumacher, Joel 42
Scorsese, Martin 105, 195
Scott, Jimmy 131
Secret Life, A (album) 231
"Secrets of Love" 230
Selwyn, Diane 190–3, 196, 199, 201–6, 209, 212–14
Sennheiser 111
Seth Low Junior High School 20, 194
"Shadow" 244
Shaft (film) 26
Shallow Grave (film) 227
Shattered (film) 228
"She's Gone Away" 250
Sheppard, Bob 149
Shinbone Alley (musical) 14

Shop on Main Street, The (film) 167
Short, Martin 54
Shostakovich, Dmitri 41, 43, 225
Showtime 248, 251
Sicily 19
Sight & Sound 252
Silla, Karine 229
"Silver Sombrero" 27
Silvestri, Alan 228
Simone, Nina 22, 25–7
Siskel, Gene 188
Six Men Getting Sick (short) 7–8
"Sixteen Reasons" 200, 212
Skywalker Sound 70, 73, 76, 106, 110, 115
"Slaughterhouse" 93–4
"Slow 30's Room" 244
"Slow Speed Orchestra 1 (24 Hours)" 71
"Slow-Speed Orchestra 2" 125
"Slower Speed Orchestra" 71
Slusser, David 57–8, 70, 73–6, 99, 106–15, 129, 133–40, 186, 208, 235, 258
Smashing Pumpkins 149
Smith, Jimmy 137
"Snap!" 225
Snootworld (unrealized show) 243
"So Glad" 241
"So Good" 182
Social Network, The (film) 159
"Something Wicked This Way Comes" 160–2
"Song to the Siren" 36–40, 154, 159–60, 168, 240
Soul (film) 159
Soul Murder (album) 151
"South Sea Dreams" 72
Spaceballs (film) 74
Spacek, Sissy 174–5
Spencer, Walter 184
Splet, Alan
  early work with David Lynch 9–10
  friendship with David Lynch 167, 169
  illness and death 169–70
  influence 110, 140, 167, 236, 241, 257

sensitivity 52, 113
work on *Blue Velvet* 48–50, 52
work on *Dune* 18
work on *Eraserhead* 10–14, 166
work on *Twin Peaks* (show) 89
Spokane 5
"Springtime for Hitler" 14
Stafford, Jo 182
Stalingrad (film) 232
Stanley, Sam 136, 140
Stanton, Frank 22–3, 25–7
Steely Dan 182
Steppenwolf 182
Stevens Jr., George 9
Stofle, Emily 254
Stone, Carl 70
Stone, Oliver 52, 152
Straight, Alvin 172–86, 189
Straight Story, The (film) 95, 145, 235
   additional music 179–80
   comparison to *Wild at Heart* 189
   conservative world view 173
   editing 179
   film mix 184–5, 187
   inspiration 172–3
   music as storytelling device 176–7
   music recording 179, 186
   pre-production 174
   reception 173, 188–9
   score production 175, 177–8
   shooting 174–5, 179
   sound design 180–2, 185–6
   "temp music" 179
Strange Tales of the Late West (album) 179
Strauss, Richard 95, 189
Stravinsky, Igor 141
Stuart, Hamish 231
StudioCanal 253
"Sub Dream" 244
subconsciousness 1, 12, 32, 117, 158, 206, 255
Sunbird Records 27
Sunset Boulevard (film) 190, 197, 200, 204
Suspended Animation (film) 221, 228
Sweeney, Mary 165, 173–4, 179, 181

Swinton, Tilda 227
Switzerland 7
"Sycamore Trees" 131
Symphony No. 15 (Shostakovich) 41, 43
Synclavier 106–9

Tarantino, Quentin 152
Tate, Grady 75, 135, 138, 241, 246–7
Tautou, Audrey 228
Taylor, Koko 100
tech:ton 182–3
Telluride Film Festival 52, 173
Tesla, Nikola 119
Texas 240
"The Most Requested Song" 179–80, 182
Thelma and Louise (film) 142
Them 100
"Theme from Fire Walk with Me" 129
Theroux, Justin 164, 203, 240
"This Magic Moment" 154, 158, 168
This Mortal Coil 36–9, 41, 148, 154, 159, 240
This Train (album) 239
Thom, Randy 110–15, 140, 169–70, 258
Thought Gang 144–5, 202, 212, 247
"Threnody for the Victims of Hiroshima" 244
Time magazine 142, 144
Today's Number Is ... (YouTube show) 253
Tokyo 70
tomandandy 226
"Tone/Slow Speed Prison/Low Mood" 244
TOTO 18
Tough Guys Don't Dance (film) 43, 220
Trainspotting (film) 227
Transcendental Meditation 9, 32, 242
Treves, Frederick 13–15
Trona 111
"Trouble" 250
Truman, Harry 63, 67, 79, 80–5, 246
"Tube Wind Dream" 244
Turkey 224

Twin Peaks (show)
  collaboration with Mark Frost 54
  composing with David Lynch 58–9
  contrast between image and sound 64, 104, 148
  crew 1–2, 235
  cue card for pilot 78–85
  development of main theme 55–8
  firewood 70–1, 73
  improvisation 61–2, 67, 241, 247, 258
  inception 53–4
  influence 121, 243, 253
  influence of score 97
  influence on score 24, 43, 64–6
  interpretation 116, 142, 173, 190
  leitmotifs 59–60, 62–3, 68–9, 177
  library approach 73–6, 86–7, 127, 140, 256
  music editing 70–1, 74, 76–7, 86–7
  musical inconsistency 63–4
  reception 89–91, 115, 117, 144, 171, 230, 232
  sound design 89, 110, 141, 178
  source music 72–3
  writing to picture 74, 78, 88
Twin Peaks: Fire Walk with Me (film)
  additional music 133–6, 242, 246
  contrast between image and sound 104–5, 194
  crew 1, 244
  depiction of depression 122, 126–7
  difference to show 121, 123–5, 127
  editing 133
  firewood 136, 141
  foreshadowing 129–30
  inception 123
  influences on Angelo Badalamenti 132
  injury before shooting 128
  music editing 125–6, 140–1
  musical style 43
  plot 121–2, 173
  pre-existing music 132
  reception 121–2, 142, 147, 214, 233, 253
  re-scoring 136–40
  shooting 128, 136–7
  sound design 140–1, 169, 178, 205
Twin Peaks: Season Two Music and More (album) 233
Twin Peaks: The Missing Pieces (show) 144–5, 258
Twin Peaks: The Return (show) 99, 144–5, 203, 215, 238, 242–7, 249, 251–2
Twitter 99, 233
Two Chained Monkeys 145

Uher tape recorder 8
Ulupalakua 182
Un baiser papillon (film) 229
Under the Silver Lake (film) 254
"Unease" 125
United Artists 54
Unrecorded Night (unrealized show) 253
"Up in Flames" 12, 100, 117
US Department of Agriculture 5

Vallens, Dorothy 32, 44–7, 49
Van Dyke, Dick 22
Varèse Sarabande 233
Vaughn Williams, Ralph 16
Venice 224
Venus, Michael 254
Very Long Engagement, A (film) 228–9
Vinton, Bobby 33
Virginia 6, 225, 242
"Visa to the Stars" 23
"Voice of Love, The" 125, 129–31

Wagner, Richard 220–1
Wait Until Spring, Bandini (film) 222
Walk on the Wild Side (film) 150
Walken, Christopher 224
Waller, Fats 12, 37
Warner Bros. Records 55, 90, 131
Washington 5, 128

Washington, DC 25
Washington Post, The 227, 251
Waters, John 13
Watts, Naomi 147, 164, 192, 238
Watts-Russell, Ivo 37, 168
Waxman, Franz 150, 197, 200, 204
Weather Report (YouTube show) 234, 253
Weeds (film) 220–1
Weill, Kurt 16, 22, 26
Wentworth, John 1–2, 110–12, 120, 133, 141, 143, 193
Wertmüller, Lina 224
West Side Story (musical) 66
What Is David Working on Today? (YouTube show) 253
"Wheeler's Theme" 63
White, Barry 26
"Wicked Game" 105, 110
Wild, Kenny 100
Wild at Heart (film)
  absurdity 101–2, 257
  additional music 10–19, 135, 138
  ambient sounds 110–12, 169–70, 186
  classical music 95, 99–100
  crew 1, 7, 76, 123, 235
  "Dark Spanish Symphony" 96–9
  fire as symbol 93–4
  mixing 110, 112–15, 133, 140
  novel 93
  original source music 12, 100–1
  picture editing 112–14, 133
  reception 115–16, 171
  road accident 102–4
  shooting to music 106
  storyline 92–3, 147–8, 153, 173
  theme of redemption 116
  use of irony 92, 95
  use of rock music 95
Wild at Heart: The Story of Sailor and Lula (book) 93
Wilder, Billy 204
Williams, Big Joe 100
Williams, Buster 247
Williams, John 97
Wilmington 33–4, 44
Wilson, Nancy 23–5, 27
"Windswept" 245
Winters, Ruby 25
Wisconsin 172, 176, 179
Wise, Ray 73
Wizard of Oz, The (film) 32, 47, 93
World Soundtrack Award 221
Wysteria – see *Unrecorded Night*

Xalabarder, Conrado 16–17

Yogi, Maharishi Mahesh 242

Zane, Billy 63
Zebrowski, Marek 241
Zemfira 233
Zorn, John 113